Researching Translation and

This volume offers a comprehensive view of current research directions in Translation and Interpreting Studies, outlining the theoretical concepts underpinning that research and presenting detailed discussions of the various methods used.

Organized around three factors that are responsible for shaping the study of translation and interpreting today—post-structuralist theory, growth of the language industry, and technological innovations—this volume is divided into three parts:

- Part I introduces the basics for conducting translation and interpreting research, emphasizing the importance of grounding studies in contemporary theory and outlining the steps necessary to ensure methodological rigor and validity of results.
- Part II provides a theoretical mapping of current translation and interpreting research, from queer studies to cognitive science.
- Part III explores the key methodological approaches to research in Translation and Interpreting Studies, including corpus-based, longitudinal, observational, and ethnographic studies, as well as survey and focus group-based studies.

The international range of contributors are all leading research experts who use the methodologies in their work. They present the research aims of these methods, as well as their limits and discuss modes of data collection and analysis.

This is an essential reference for all advanced undergraduates, postgraduates, and researchers in Translation and Interpreting Studies.

Claudia V. Angelelli is Chair in Multilingualism and Communication at Heriot-Watt University, UK. Her publications include *Medical Interpreting and Cross-cultural Communication* (2004) and *Re-visiting the Interpreter's Role* (2004). She is the co-editor of *Testing and Assessment in Translation and Interpreting Studies* (2009).

Brian James Baer is Professor of Russian and Translation Studies at Kent State University, USA. He is founding editor of the scholarly journal *Translation and Interpreting Studies* and author of the monograph *Translation and the Making of Modern Russian Literature* (2015). He is also the co-editor of *Russian Writers on Translation: An Anthology* (2013).

Researching Translation and Interpreting

Edited by
Claudia V. Angelelli and
Brian James Baer

Routledge
Taylor & Francis Group
LONDON AND NEW YORK

First published 2016
by Routledge
2 Park Square, Milton Park, Abingdon, Oxon OX14 4RN

and by Routledge
711 Third Avenue, New York, NY 10017

Routledge is an imprint of the Taylor & Francis Group, an informa business

British Library Cataloguing-in-Publication Data
A catalogue record for this book is available from the British Library

Library of Congress Cataloging in Publication Data
Angelelli, Claudia (Claudia V.) author.
Researching translation and interpreting / by Claudia V. Angelelli and Brian James Baer.
pages cm
Includes bibliographical references and index.
1. Translating and interpreting–Research. 2. Sociolinguistics. I. Baer, Brian James. II. Title.
P302.6.A64 2015
418'.02072–dc23
2014044177

ISBN: 978-0-415-73253-6 (hbk)
ISBN: 978-0-415-73254-3 (pbk)
ISBN: 978-1-315-70728-0 (ebk)

Typeset in Times New Roman
by Taylor & Francis Books

Contents

Acknowledgements

We have many people to thank for this volume—first and foremost, the many contributors, who took time out of their busy research and teaching schedules not only to provide a detailed overview of the current state of T&I research but also to contemplate future directions. We would also like to thank the Office of Research and Sponsored Programs at Kent State University and the Office of Research and Knowledge Exchange in the School of Management and Languages at Heriot-Watt University for covering the cost of indexing, and Christopher Mellinger for his invaluable help in preparing the manuscript for submission, and Christian Degueldre for his meticulous reading of the proofs.

Every effort has been made to contact copyright holders. If any have been inadvertently overlooked, the publishers will be pleased to make the necessary arrangements at the first opportunity.

Notes on Contributors

Claudia V. Angelelli is Professor and Chair of Multilingualism and Communication in the Department of Languages and Intercultural Studies at Heriot-Watt University, Edinburgh, UK and Professor Emeritus of Spanish Linguistics at San Diego State University, US. Her research lies at the intersection of sociolinguistics, applied linguistics, and Translation and Interpreting Studies. She is the author of *Medical Interpreting and Cross-cultural Communication* (Cambridge University Press) and *Revisiting the Role of the Interpreter* (John Benjamins), and the co-editor of *Testing and Assessment in Translation and Interpreting Studies* (John Benjamins). She is the guest editor of special issues of *International Journal of the Sociology of Language* (Translators and Interpreters: Geographic Displacement and Linguistic Consequences), *Translation and Interpreting Studies* (The Sociological Turn in Translation and Interpreting), and *Cuadernos de ALDEEU* (Minding the Gaps: Translation and Interpreting Studies in Academia). Her work appears in the *Annual Review of Applied Linguistics*, *The Critical Link*, *Cuadernos de ALDEEU*, *Interpreting*, *META*, *MONTI* (Monografias de Traducción e Interpretación), *The Translator*, *Translation and Interpreting Studies* (TIS), the *International Journal of the Sociology of Language*, and numerous edited volumes. She designed the first empirically driven language proficiency and interpreter readiness tests for the California Endowment and Hablamos Juntos (Robert Wood Johnson Foundation). Prof. Angelelli is the president of the American Translation and Interpreting Studies Association and she has served as director of the Consortium of Distinguished Language Centers and the American Translators Association. Currently she is the world project leader for ISO Standards on Community Interpreting.

Erik Angelone is Associate Professor of Translation Studies at Kent State University. He received his Ph.D. in Translation Studies from the University of Heidelberg. His current research interests include process-oriented translator training, cognitive processes in translation, and intercultural communicative competence. He recently co-edited, with Gregory Shreve, the volume titled *Translation and Cognition* (2010).

Edmund Asare is an Assistant Professor of French and African American Studies at Western Illinois University. He holds a Ph.D. in Translation Studies (Informatics) from Kent State University. He currently teaches various language, literature, and culture courses in the departments of Foreign Languages and Literatures and African American Studies at Western Illinois University.

Brian James Baer is Professor of Russian and Translation Studies at Kent State University, where he teaches translation-related courses at the undergraduate, Master's, and doctoral levels. He is founding editor of the journal *Translation and Interpreting Studies* (TIS), general editor of the Kent State Scholarly Monograph Series in Translation Studies, and co-editor of the Bloomsbury series Literatures, Cultures, Translation. He co-edited Volume XII of the ATA Scholarly Monograph Series, *Beyond the Ivory Tower: Rethinking Translation Pedagogy* (2003). His most recent publications include the edited volumes *Contexts, Subtexts, Pretexts: Literary Translation in Eastern Europe and Russia* (2011), *No Good without Reward: The Selected Writings of Liubov Krichevskaya* (2011), *Russian Writers on Translation. An Anthology* (2013), and a translation of Juri Lotman's final book-length work, *The Unpredictable Workings of Culture* (2013). His monograph *Translation and the Making of Modern Russian Literature* is forthcoming.

Mona Baker is Professor of Translation Studies at the Centre for Translation and Intercultural Studies, University of Manchester, UK and is currently leading the Citizen Media at Manchester initiative (www.citizenmedia manchester.wordpress.com). She is author of *In Other Words: A Coursebook on Translation* (Routledge, 1992; second edition 2011) and *Translation and Conflict: A Narrative Account* (Routledge, 2006); editor of the *Routledge Encyclopedia of Translation Studies* (1998, 2001; second edition, co-edited with Gabriela Saldanha, 2009), *Critical Concepts: Translation Studies* (4 volumes, Routledge, 2009), and *Critical Readings in Translation Studies* (Routledge, 2010). Her articles have appeared in a wide range of international journals, including *Social Movement Studies*, *Critical Studies on Terrorism*, *The Translator*, and *Target*. She is founding editor of *The Translator* (St. Jerome Publishing, 1995–2013), former editorial director of St. Jerome Publishing (1995–2013), and founding vice-president of IATIS (International Association for Translation & Intercultural Studies).

Claudio Baraldi is Professor of Sociology of cultural and communicative processes (Department of Studies on Language and Culture, University of Modena and Reggio Emilia, Italy). His research concerns communication systems and their structural and cultural presuppositions, including intercultural and interlinguistic interactions, adult–children interactions, and organizational meetings. He is interested in the analysis of intervention processes and their results, in particular in the development of techniques for dialogic facilitation of participation and mediation. He has published several papers on dialogue interpreting, in books (John Benjamins, Peter Lang) and international journals. With Laura Gavioli, he has edited the book *Coordinating Participation in Dialogue Interpreting* (John Benjamins, 2012).

Ursula Böser holds a Ph.D. in Film Studies from Edinburgh University. She is Professor of Intercultural Studies at Heriot-Watt University and a member of the Centre of Translation and Interpreting Studies in Scotland (CTISS) and the Intercultural Research Centre (IRC) in the Department of Languages and Intercultural Research at Heriot-Watt University, Edinburgh. Her research in Interpreting Studies focuses on the practice and teaching of face-to-face interpreting in institutional and non-institutional settings. She has contributed extensively to the CTISS research program Provision of Equal Access to Justice in Multilingual Societies through her work on present practice in police interpreting and on interpreting for minors in pre-trial settings. This work also included close cooperation in the context of EU (DG Criminal Justice) funded projects with international researchers and practitioners in the field. Ursula Böser teaches Conference and Public Service Interpreting and Audiovisual Translation at Heriot-Watt University.

Leo Tak-hung Chan is Professor and Head of the Department of Translation, Lingnan University, Hong Kong. His research articles have appeared in *Harvard Journal of Asiatic Studies*, *Perspectives*, *Comparative Literature Studies*, *TTR*, *The Translator*, *Babel*, *META*, *Across Languages and Cultures*, *Quaderns*, *Journal of Oriental Studies*, *Linguistica Antverpiensia*, and *Asian Folklore Studies*. His major scholarly publications include: *Readers, Reading and Reception of Translated Prose Fiction in Chinese: Novel Encounters* (St. Jerome, 2010), *Twentieth-Century Chinese Translation Theory: Modes, Issues and Debates* (John Benjamins, 2004), *One into Many: Translation and the Dissemination of Classical Chinese Literature* (Rodopi Editions, 2003), and *The Discourse on Foxes and Ghosts* (University of Hawaii Press, 1998). He is president of the Hong Kong Translation Society and chief editor of *Translation Quarterly*, a leading academic journal on Chinese-English translation available worldwide through EBSCO Host. Areas of interest: reception issues in translation, adaptation, translation, and Global English, and Sino-Japanese translation traditions.

Sonia Colina is Professor of Hispanic Linguistics in the Department of Spanish and Portuguese at the University of Arizona. She is the author of *Teaching Translation: From Research to the Classroom* (2003), *Spanish Phonology* (2009), and *Fundamentals of Translation* (2015). In addition to her work in Hispanic Linguistics, she has published in Translation Studies journals such as *Target*, *The Translator*, and *Babel*. She is the vice-president of the American Translation and Interpreting Studies Association (ATISA) and serves on the editorial boards of *Translation and Interpreting Studies* and the *Translator and Interpreter Trainer*.

Maureen Ehrensberger-Dow has a B.A. (Hons) in Psychology from Queen's University as well as an M.Sc. in Psycholinguistics and a Ph.D. in Experimental Linguistics from the University of Alberta, Canada. She is Professor of Translation Studies at the Institute of Translation and Interpreting in the School of Applied Linguistics at the Zurich University of Applied Sciences (ZHAW), Switzerland. Her research interests include cognitive translatology, translation processes, cognitive ergonomics, human-computer interactions, workplace practice, translation didactics, translation in the news, and conceptual transfer. She has been principal investigator of the interdisciplinary research project *Cognitive and Physical Ergonomics of Translation*, a follow-up of the *Capturing Translation Processes* project, and co-investigator of the interdisciplinary project *Overcoming Language Barriers in Homecare Nursing*.

María Manuela Fernández Sánchez is a Senior Lecturer in the Department of Translation and Interpreting at the University of Granada, Spain. A teacher of Interpreting Techniques and Translation Theories at both undergraduate and graduate level, she has also taught abroad in Belgium and Mexico. She has published widely in the areas of translation theory and translation and interpreting history. She is currently researching the diplomatic and international situation which required high-level interpreting during the first two decades of the Cold War era.

Laura Gavioli is Professor of English Language and Translation Studies and teaches English Language and Oral Translation at the University of Modena and Reggio Emilia, Italy. Her research work includes the study of spoken language, mainly in institutional settings, studies of bilingual corpora for language learning and translation, and the pragmatics of English–Italian interaction in intercultural or multicultural settings. For the last fifteen years, she has been engaged in research exploring authentic data of interpreter-mediated conversations involving speakers (not necessarily native speakers) of English and Italian, mainly in healthcare settings. In collaboration with Claudio Baraldi, she has edited the volume *Coordinating Participation in Dialogue Interpreting* (John Benjamins, 2012)

Leonardo Giannossa earned a Ph.D. in Translation Studies from Kent State University with a dissertation on a corpus-based approach to the investigation of lexical cohesion in Italian and English. At Kent State, he worked on the building of an electronic bilingual glossary of legal terms and taught several Italian language classes. He also taught Terminology, CAT tools, and other translation-related courses for the Center for Translation Studies at the University of Illinois, Urbana-Champaign. His research interests include corpora, terminology, machine translation, paratexts, lexical cohesion, and critical discourse analysis. He authored an entry on "Text-based Approaches to Translation" for the Wiley-Blackwell *Encyclopedia of Applied Linguistics.*

Daniel Gile is a conference interpreter for The International Association of Conference Interpreters (AIIC) conference interpreter and a former technical and scientific translator. He was initially trained in mathematics and went on to also study sociology, Japanese, and conference interpreting. His first Ph.D. focused on translator and interpreter training, and the second on the challenges of conference interpreting. He is the founder of the CIRIN network (www.cirinandgile.com) and one of the founding members of the European Society for Translation Studies. He was CERA Chair Professor in 1993, and he has had a long-standing interest in the development of Translation Studies as a discipline, in research-methodological issues, and in training researchers. He has published widely on these topics.

Miguel A. Jiménez-Crespo is an Associate Professor in the Department of Spanish and Portuguese at Rutgers University, where he directs the M.A. program in Spanish Translation and Interpreting. He holds a Ph.D. in Translation and Interpreting Studies from the University of Granada, Spain. His research focuses on the intersection of translation theory, translation technology, digital technologies, corpus-based Translation Studies, and translation training. He is the author of *Translation and Web Localization* (Routledge, 2013) and has published extensively in Translation Studies journals such as *Target*, *Perspectives*, *META*, *TIS*, *Linguistica Antverpiensia*, *JoSTrans*, *Translation and Interpreting*, and *Tradumatica*.

Klaus Kaindl is Associate Professor of Translation Studies at the Center for Translation Studies at the University of Vienna. Following his Ph.D. on opera translation (*Die Oper als Textgestalt*, Tübingen, 1995) he devoted his post-doctoral research to general issues of Translation Studies as a discipline and to comics translation (*Übersetzungswissenschaft im interdisziplinären Dialog. Am Beispiel der Comicübersetzung*, Tübingen, 2004). Subsequent projects include studies of popular music under translation and of fictional translators and interpreters (*Transfiction. Research into the Realities of Translation Fiction*, ed. together with Karlheinz Spitzl, Amsterdam/Philadelphia 2014). He is general co-editor, with Franz Pöchhacker, of the book series *Translationswissenschaft* (Gunter Narr) and is a founding member of the European Society for Translation Studies.

Ian Mason is an emeritus professor at Heriot-Watt University, Edinburgh, and part-time Guest Professor at the University of Sichuan, Chengdu, China. During a long career at Heriot-Watt University, he co-authored two books with Basil Hatim (*Discourse and the Translator*, Longman, 1990; *The Translator as Communicator*, Routledge, 1997) and has published on various aspects of the linguistics and pragmatics of translating and interpreting. He was guest editor of a special issue of *The Translator* (vol. 5, no. 2), entitled *Dialogue Interpreting*, and editor of *Triadic Exchanges. Studies in Dialogue Interpreting* (St. Jerome, 2001). Recent work includes investigation of the role and positioning of participants in interpreter-mediated exchanges and a study of communities of practice in translation and interpreting (in Juliane House (ed.), *Translation: A Multidisciplinary Approach*, Palgrave, 2014).

Françoise Massardier-Kenney is Professor of French and director of the Institute for Applied Linguistics at Kent State University, where she teaches in the graduate program in translation. She is the editor of the American Translators Association Scholarly Series. Her publications include the monograph *Gender in the Fiction of George Sand* (2001); the edited volumes of *Translating Slavery: Gender and Race in French Abolitionist Writing 1780–1830* (1999, 2009), and *Ourika and Its Progeny* (2010) with Doris Kadish; a translation of Madame de Duras' *Ourika* (1999), Sand's *Valvèdre* (2007), Antoine Berman's *Toward a Translation Criticism* (2009); and numerous articles on Sand, nineteenth-century women's writers, and translation. She is the co-editor with Carol Maier of *Literature in Translation* (2010).

Gary Massey received a B.A. in Modern Languages and an M.A. in Comparative Literature from the University of Manchester, UK, and a Ph.D. in German Literature from University College London. He is currently deputy head of the Zurich University of Applied Sciences' Institute of Translation and Interpreting, director of its M.A. program in Applied Linguistics with its Specialization in Professional Translation, and past head of the same university's undergraduate degree programs in translation and applied languages. A co-investigator of two nationally funded research projects on translation workplace processes and on the cognitive and physical ergonomics of translation, his other research and teaching interests focus on translation and e-learning pedagogy, translators' information literacy skills, translation expertise, and translation quality.

Christopher D. Mellinger is Assistant Professor of Spanish at Walsh University, where he teaches medical translation and interpreting as well as courses on Spanish for healthcare. Mellinger holds a Ph.D. in Translation Studies and an M.A. in Translation (Spanish) from Kent State University. Mellinger is an ex-officio board member of the American Translation and Interpreting Studies Association, and the managing editor of *Translation and Interpreting Studies*. His research interests include translation and cognition, translation process research, and translation technology.

Bernd Meyer is a linguist by training and a specialist in the analysis of multilingual communication in institutional settings. He received his Ph.D. from Hamburg University, for his dissertation on interpreter-mediated briefings for informed consent in 2003. Since 2010, he is Professor for Intercultural Communication and Cultural Studies at the Johannes Gutenberg-Universität Mainz (Germany) in the Department for Translation, Linguistics, and Cultural Studies. Having been a full-time researcher and principal investigator at the Research Centre on Multilingualism in Hamburg, he is an expert in the analysis of interpreter-mediated interaction in institutional settings, as well as in the application of such findings to interpreter training. More specifically, he conducted research on ad hoc interpreting in doctor–patient communication, and, together with Kristin Bührig, developed a training module for ad hoc interpreters in clinical settings.

Brenda Nicodemus is Associate Professor in the Department of Interpretation at Gallaudet University and the director of the Interpretation and Translation Research Center. She has worked professionally as an interpreter since 1989 and holds a Ph.D. in Educational Linguistics from the University of New Mexico. Previously she was employed as a research scientist at the Laboratory for Language and Cognitive Neuroscience at San Diego State University, where she studied the cognitive processes of signed language interpreters. Her areas of research include translation asymmetry in bimodal bilinguals, healthcare interpreting, and the use of prosodic markers to indicate utterance boundaries. Her publications include *Prosodic Markers and Utterance Boundaries in American Sign Language Interpreting* (Gallaudet University Press, 2009); with co-editor Laurie Swabey, *Advances in Interpreting Research* (Benjamins, 2011); and with co-editor Melanie Metzger, *Investigations in Healthcare Interpreting* (Gallaudet University Press, 2014).

Rakefet Sela-Sheffy is Associate Professor of Semiotics and Culture Research and Chair of the Unit of Culture Research, Tel-Aviv University. Her research interests and publications include culture theory, professional identity and status, talk and self-representations, diffusion and translation. In recent years she has conducted interview-based research on the identity and status of translators in Israel in semi-professional groups, with Israeli translators as a case in point (Israel Science Foundation 2006–9, with Miriam Shlesinger). Among her publications is *Literarische Dynamik und Kulturbildung: Zur Konstruktion des Repertoires deutscher Literatur im ausgehenden 18. Jahrhundert* (1999); *Identity and Status in the Translational Profession* (co-edited with M. Shlesinger, 2011); and *Culture Contacts and the Making of Cultures: Papers in Homage to Itamar Even-Zohar* (co-edited with Gideon Toury, 2011).

Anna Strowe holds a lectureship in Translation and Interpreting Studies at the University of Manchester (UK). She received her Ph.D. in Comparative Literature from the University of Massachusetts Amherst with a specialization in translation and Translation Studies and a focus on early modern Italian and English literature. She also holds an M.A. in Translation Studies from the University of Warwick (UK).

Sanjun Sun received his Ph.D. in Translation Studies from Kent State University in 2012. He is an Assistant Professor of Translation Studies at Beijing Foreign Studies University, where he teaches translation technology, research methods, and commercial translation. He has co-authored two books in Chinese—*A Translator's Handbook* (2010) and *Research Methods in*

Language Studies (2011)—and has published articles in *Meta*, *Target*, and other journals. His major research interests include translation process research, translation technology, and empirical research methods. He has extensive experience as a translator.

Laurie Swabey is Professor of Interpreting at St. Catherine University and director of the CATIE Center, where she leads a federally funded national initiative on healthcare interpreting. She holds a Ph.D. from the University of Minnesota in Linguistics, and her research interests include healthcare interpreting, relevance theory and interpreting, language access in healthcare settings, and the organization of deaf physician/deaf patient discourse. She has served as a member of the advisory board for the National Council on Interpreting in Healthcare (NCIHC) and the CCHI (Certification Commission for Healthcare Interpreters). Recent publications include Referring Expressions in ASL Discourse (in *Discourse in Signed Languages*, 2011), *Advances in Interpreting Research* (Benjamins, 2011) with co-editor Brenda Nicodemus, and "An Examination of Medical Interview Questions Rendered in American Sign Language by Deaf Physicians and Interpreters" with co-author Brenda Nicodemus (in *Investigations in Healthcare Interpreting*, 2014).

Sergey Tyulenev is Director of the M.A. program in Translation Studies at Durham University, UK. His recent publications include *Applying Luhmann to Translation Studies* (Routledge, 2011), *Translation and the Westernization of Eighteenth-Century Russia* (Frank & Timme, 2012), and *Translation and Society: An Introduction* (Routledge, 2014). His website can be found at www.tyulenev.org.

Luc van Doorslaer is the director of CETRA, the Centre for Translation Studies at the University of Leuven (Belgium), where he works as an Associate Professor in Translation and Journalism Studies. He is also the vice-dean for Research (Antwerp campus). As a Research Fellow he is affiliated with Stellenbosch University (South Africa). Together with Yves Gambier, he is the editor of the online *Translation Studies Bibliography* (10th edition, 2013) and the four volumes of the new *Handbook of Translation Studies* (2010–13). Other recent books edited include *Eurocentrism in Translation Studies* (2013) and *The Known Unknowns of Translation Studies* (2014). His main research interests are journalism and translation, imagology and translation, institutionalization of Translation Studies, and bibliometrics.

Michaela Wolf is Associate Professor at the Department of Translation Studies, University of Graz. Before entering academia, she worked in several projects of development cooperation in Brazil and Central America. Areas of teaching and research interest include translation sociology, cultural studies and translation, translation history, and translation and visual anthropology. She is the author of *Die vielsprachige Seele Kakaniens. Übersetzen und Dolmetschen in der Habsburgermonarchie 1848 bis 1918* (published in 2012) and has extensively published in Translation Studies journals and essay collections. Her present research focus is on interpreting and translating in Nazi concentration camps.

Introduction

Claudia V. Angelelli and Brian James Baer

Although translation and interpreting have been described as the world's "second oldest profession", the scholarly study of translation and interpreting is a fairly recent phenomenon (Shreve 2000: 219). Only in the last 50 years or so have anecdotal and largely prescriptive writings on translation and interpreting given way to empirical research and descriptive studies. Despite its late start, the scholarly study of translation and interpreting has expanded at a rapid pace. Borrowing freely from related disciplines in the humanities and social sciences, such as cultural studies, sociology, anthropology, and applied linguistics, scholars in Translation and Interpreting Studies have also developed their own theoretical and methodological approaches, which should be of use not only for new researchers in departments of Translation and Interpreting Studies, but also for researchers in disciplines across the humanities and social sciences that have begun to focus on what David Damrosch has called the "problematics of translation" (2009: 8), not to mention those who have yet to take the translation turn.

Given the rapid growth of the scholarly field and the appearance of new doctoral and master's degree programs in Translation and Interpreting Studies throughout the world, the time for a book on researching translation and interpreting that explicitly links theoretical concepts with research methodology and includes research paradigms in both Translation and Interpreting Studies is now. There are several works dealing with research methods for translation and interpreting, such as the collections *Intercultural Faultlines: Research Models in Translation Studies II* (2000), edited by Maeve Olohan; *Crosscultural Transgressions: Research Methods in Translation Studies II* (2002), edited by Theo Hermans; *The Map: A Beginner's Guide to Doing Research in Translation Studies* (2002), co-authored by Jenny Williams and Andrew Chesterman; *Teaching and Researching Translation* (2001/2013), by Basil Hatim, designed to promote action research; *Research Methods in Interpreting* (2013), by Sandra Hale and Jemina Napier, a practical guide for doctoral students; and, most recently, Gabriela Saldanha and Sharon O'Brien's volume *Research Methodologies in Translation Studies* (2014). The most systematic and comprehensive of these works is undoubtedly Saldanha and O'Brien's, and, as such, shares one of the goals of this volume in promoting greater rigor in research in our field.

That being said, our volume differs from that of Saldanha and O'Brien in several significant ways. First, this volume includes both translation and interpreting, including interpreting of spoken and signed languages. Second, it traces the adoption and adaptation of theories and models developed outside of Translation and Interpreting Studies (TIS) for the study of translation- and interpreting-related phenomena, contributing in this way to the study of how theories travel. Third, it promotes a mutually interrogative relationship between theory, research, and practice. And finally, the volume takes a firm position in advocating a post-structuralist approach to conducting research on translation- and interpreting-related phenomena, as discussed in Part I.

Moreover, while offering a broad and systematic mapping of research in the field, as Williams and Chesterman, and Saldanha and O'Brien do, this volume is decidedly forward-looking. The contributors were asked to speculate, based on their expertise in the field, on future trends in T&I research, suggesting not only where they think research is currently heading but also where it *should* be heading, that is, what important areas are under-studied or what new areas are emerging that deserve the attention of researchers. For example, while issues of gender and sexuality have been broadly and consistently discussed in relation to translation, they remain under-studied in the field of interpreting, which is surprising given the significant body of literature on gender and sexuality in sociolinguistics. On the other hand, while issues of stress and working conditions have been widely discussed in relation to interpreting (e.g., interpreters in war zones or in emergency situations), they deserve more attention in Translation Studies. Our commitment to covering research in both Translation and Interpreting Studies brings such imbalances to light. Moreover, whereas Saldanha and O'Brien decided not to cover translation history as an object of study, we have included it, as recent historical studies of translation and interpreting are perhaps the greatest caution against the tendency to universalize findings across cultures and time periods.

Overall, this volume is meant to buck the increasing diversification of the field by offering a synthetic view, uniting those aspects of the discipline that are often separated: pure and applied research, Tanslation and Interpreting Studies, empirical and theoretical research, and qualitative and quantitative paradigms. This integrated view of the field is meant to remind us of our shared theoretical foundations, and to encourage collaboration across fields and the use of mixed methods. As a consequence, this book is meant to highlight and promote the interdisciplinarity that has always been a hallmark of TIS.

This volume is divided into three parts. Part I contains an introductory essay by the editors that discusses the general features of a post-structuralist or post-positivist approach to research of translation- and interpreting-related phenomena, and outlines the basic components of the research journey. Part II provides a conceptual mapping of current translation and interpreting research, discussing the theoretical models and concepts underlying it, often borrowed and adopted and/or adapted from other fields. Our mapping of translation and interpreting research in Part II, that is, our selection and naming of the various chapters, as well as our guidance to the contributors, was largely shaped by three factors: the spread of post-structuralist theoretical approaches, the pace of globalization, and rapid developments in technology.

Underlying most translation- and interpreting-related research today, post-structuralist approaches are characterized by a rejection of essentialist claims, traditional positivist concepts, such as equivalence and fidelity, and the stasis of earlier linguistic-based models. These new approaches assume translation and interpreting to be highly dynamic, socially constructed endeavors, and translators and interpreters to be agents and cultural mediators, co-creators of meaning instead of transparent vessels, thoroughly imbedded in a specific cultural context. These theoretical precepts call for a reflective research practice that acknowledges that language can never be an entirely neutral instrument for communication.

The increasing communication demands in a rapidly globalizing world and the growing consensus that access to translation and interpreting services in legal and medical settings is a human right have highlighted the need for high-quality translators and interpreters. At the same time, the rapid diversification of translation- and interpreting-related jobs poses new challenges for translation and interpreting education programs and has made the language industry itself into an object of research. That research explores a variety of issues concerning translator and interpreting education and professional development, the professionalization of translation and interpreting, and the status and self-image of translators and interpreters.

Advances in technology over the last 15 to 20 years have also greatly expanded the objects of translation and interpreting research, which now include such phenomena as crowdsourcing, the use of computer-assisted translation tools, the translation of context-less strings, the post-editing of machine-translation output, and remote interpreting. In addition to generating new objects of research, new technologies have expanded the range of methods and tools available for the study of both product-oriented and process-oriented research, from corpus-based studies to eye-tracking and keystroke logging.

Part III explores the major methodological approaches to research in Translation and Interpreting Studies, including naturalistic, quasi-experimental, and experimental designs, as well as product- and process-oriented methods. Some of the specific methods discussed are corpus-based, observational, and ethnographic studies, as well as survey- and focus group-based studies. Chapter authors range from well-established researchers in the field who have used, and in some cases pioneered, the methods discussed to junior scholars, who will define the research trends of the future.

This book is aimed at advanced undergraduates and graduate students, new scholars in the field of Translation Studies, as well as practitioners interested in contributing to the scholarly study of the field through research. It is also aimed at another readership—doctoral students and scholars in disciplines across the humanities and social sciences who recognize the importance of considering questions of language and translation/interpreting in the generation of knowledge but may not be familiar with the methods for studying those questions that have been developed in the field of Translation and Interpreting Studies.

Overall, the volume should be of interest not only to graduate students and new researchers but also to more seasoned researchers inside TIS, as well as outside it, who are interested in the current and future state of T&I research and in exploring the ways Translation and Interpreting Studies can revitalize, if not revolutionize, ontological, epistemological, and research paradigms across disciplinary boundaries.

References

Damrosch, David. 2009. Introduction. "All the Time in the World." In *Teaching World Literature*, David Damrosch (ed.), 1–11. New York: MLA.

Hale, Sandra, and Jemina Napier. 2013. *Research Methods in Interpreting*. London and New York: Bloomsbury.

Hatim, Basil. 2013. *Teaching and Researching Translation*. Second edition. Harlow, UK: Pearson.

Hermans, Theo (ed.). 2002. *Crosscultural Trangressions: Research Methods in Translation Studies II*. Manchester: St. Jerome.

Olohan, Maeve (ed.). 2000. *Intercultural Faultlines: Research Models in Translation Studies II*. Manchester: St. Jerome.

Saldanha, Gabriela, and Sharon O'Brien. 2014. *Research Methodologies in Translation Studies*. Manchester: St. Jerome.

Shreve, Gregory, M. 2000. "Translation at the Millennium: Prospects for the Evolution of a Profession." In *Paradigmenwechsel in der Translation. Festschrift für Albrecht Neubert zum 70. Gerburtstag, Peter A. Schmitt*. (ed.), 217–34. Tübingen: Stauffenburg Verlag.

Williams, Jenny, and Andrew Chesterman. 2002. *The Map: A Beginner's Guide to Doing Research in Translation Studies*. Manchester: St. Jerome.

Part I

Exploring translation and interpreting

Claudia V. Angelelli and Brian James Baer

What is T&I research?

Research has been defined in various ways according to different paradigms and traditions. The conceptualization of research also varies among different communities of practice and speech communities. Research in Translation and Interpreting Studies has enjoyed an eclectic tradition, in line with its interdisciplinary nature. Researchers in Translation and Interpreting Studies (TIS) come from different paths of life (ranging from cultural studies to computer science and from languages and linguistics to educational or social psychology) and bring their own traditions and methods to the study of phenomena that cut across all areas of society: the rendering of written and verbal/signed communication of values, traditions, and information across time and space. Through the years we have seen research in TIS grow into a body of knowledge in its own right. By borrowing theoretical/conceptual frameworks and research methods from fields in both the humanities and social sciences, as well as by creating their own, researchers in Translation and Interpreting Studies explore phenomena related to communication, culture, and languages through new lenses, posing different and richer questions than were asked before.

For junior scholars and doctoral students in TIS, as well as for researchers coming from other disciplines, it is precisely the interdisciplinarity of our field that presents the greatest challenges and opportunities. Researching TIS today means researching transgression and re-construction, the displacement of texts (oral, written, or signed), as well as of peoples and communities (authors, readers, speakers, audiences, providers and recipients of information, translators, interpreters, and interlocutors), through space and time. Our object of study can be fuzzy and/or neat. Our lenses can be single, multiple, and complex, our paths linear, circular, and everything in between. TIS by its very nature allows us opportunities to study phenomena in more comprehensive and ethically sound ways that until now have been investigated rather narrowly, from a mainstream perspective (e.g., focusing on inaccuracies in communication and overlooking fundamental questions regarding access to communication) and within a traditional, positivist framework.

Given its mixed origins—in Applied Linguistics, Comparative Literature, and Cognitive Psychology—Translation and Interpreting Studies is uniquely positioned to break down the traditional barriers separating the humanities, social sciences, and hard sciences, and to drive the kind of transformation in doctoral education described in the 2010 MLA Report on Doctoral Study in Modern Language and Literature, by promoting interdisciplinarity, digital humanities, and teamwork and collaboration. If, as the authors of the report claim, "All modern scholarship necessarily includes ongoing reflection on the fundamental constitution of the discipline" (2014: 9), then the study of translation and interpreting, which relativizes the language we use to "know" the world, must play a central role in that ongoing reflection in every department and field. Such a transformation can happen, however, only if the research methodologies and theoretical approaches of other fields are not borrowed blindly, but are adapted and infused with a deep sensitivity to language(s). When we acknowledge language as both an object of study as well as the medium for conducting studies and for presenting research results, we blur the boundary established by positivists between ontology (what is) and epistemology (what we know about what is), necessitating a deeply reflexive research practice.

Linking theory, research, and practice

While acknowledging the transformational potential of this interdisciplinarity, it is not without its challenges, as it requires the merging of research paradigms that have traditionally been seen as diametrically opposed—namely, those developed in the hard sciences and social sciences, and those developed in the humanities, specifically in the field of literary studies. Consider, for example, the very different use of theory within these two paradigms. Within the paradigm developed in the hard sciences and social sciences, theory represents a model that is based either on tested hypotheses or on a systematic exploration that requires the collection and analysis of data. In the humanities, literary theory refers to something closer to philosophy, specifically, the philosophy of language, grounded in structural linguistics (Saussure), sociolinguistic critiques of structural linguistic models, and extensions and adaptations of structural linguistic models (i.e., Lacanian psychoanalysis, deconstruction, and semiotics). Merging these paradigms forces us to recognize language both as an object of study and as a vehicle for the cultural and communicative construction of that object, that is, language as a set of observable behaviors and at the same time as a generator and communicator of ideologies.

While post-structuralist approaches compel us to acknowledge the constructedness of our categories of analysis, the provisional and relative nature of the knowledge generated, and the situatedness of the researcher as one who is simultaneously framer and framed, they do not negate the possibility of empirical research. Rather, they call for a reflexive research practice, which encourages researchers to interrogate not only their interpretation of data, but also the very categories they design or borrow to generate that data. This is especially important when dealing with "other" cultures. Indeed, by invoking broad categories for cross-cultural analysis, such as French or Chinese, or male and female, researchers participate, unwittingly or not, in the reification of these identities, often at the expense of sub-national, class, and alternative gender and sexual identifications (to name just a few). Moreover, the reflection promoted by post-structuralist theories and methodologies is especially important today as institutions and governments attempt to measure scholarly output with strictly quantitative tools, which lend an aura of "objectivity," but hide as much as they reveal.

Another key feature of post-structuralist approaches is the call to situate cultural practices within specific social contexts, countering the temptation to universalize findings across languages and cultures, often in tacit or implicit support of hegemonic agendas. In Translation Studies, for example, corpus-based studies increasingly turn away from large language corpora in favor of corpora based on text type. In Interpreting Studies, recent work has emphasized the necessity of studying interpreting within the specific institutions or social contexts in which it is practiced. As Angelelli notes

> The constraints that any institution (be it a hospital, a courthouse or a national/international public/private organization) may pose on the act of interpreting need to be accounted for in a theory of interpreting. Even when medical, community, conference, and court interpreting seem to have strong common grounds (based on a linguistic or information-processing perspective), there are probably more differences than similarities based on the settings where these interpreting events occur and on the participants.
> (Angelelli 2004b: 21)

But while these post-structuralist approaches are increasingly common among researchers, the positivist illusion of capturing the one true meaning of an utterance survives not only in the popular understanding of translation and interpreting, but also in a variety of professional and educational settings. The professional world of translation and interpreting remains dominated by positivist notions of representation, which promote an essentially mimetic model that posits the existence of a priori meaning expressed in one language, which is then transferred, with a greater or lesser degree of fidelity, from that language to another. This conceptualization of the relationship between language and meaning is reflected to some degree in almost every aspect of translation and interpreting practice, from the T&I classroom to the testing industry and professional associations, from the certification of translators and interpreters to the creation of codes of ethics and standards of practice.

The designation made by St. Jerome in the fifth century of two fundamentally different approaches to translation—sense for sense or word for word—remains firmly entrenched today in many institutions. This model is institutionalized, for example, in many legal systems, where the interpretation of sense, or meaning (designated as the purview of lawyers and judges), is separated from the interpretation of words, or language (designated as the purview of the translator or interpreter). As a result, translators and interpreters have frequently been portrayed as neutral conduits of information. We see this positivism reflected, too, in certification exams, which often separate linguistic competence in the source language from all the other competencies required of the professional translator/interpreter. The translator/interpreter's role as "mere" language conduit, in turn, enhances the professional status of the domain expert, be it the diplomat, the judge, or the doctor, while diminishing that of the translator/interpreter, as reflected most blatantly in the salary differential between language and other experts.

The secondary status of the translator/interpreter was reinforced in the Romantic Age, which constructed the translator as the defining other of the "original" writer—a mere imitator. Hence the enormous interest among researchers today in translators and translation in pre-modern Europe (see Kronitiris 1997; Goldberg 1997; White 2011; Uman 2012; and Goodrich 2013), and in cultures outside the West (see Pollard 1998; Hung and Wakabayashi 2005; Hermans 2006; Cheung 2006; Bandia 2008; Kothari and Wakabayashi 2009; Inggs and Meintjes 2009; and Batchelor 2009). And so, the marginal professional status of translators and interpreters today is a valuable object of study insofar as it reflects deep-seated cultural anxieties over who controls meaning. As Rakefet Sela-Sheffy argues in this volume: "It is the contradiction between the potential power of translators and interpreters as cultural mediators (Bandia and Milton 2009), on the one hand, and their obscure professional definition and alleged sense of submissiveness, on the other, that makes them such an intriguing occupational group."

While Roman Jakobson suggested the theoretical untenability of the positivist separation of word and sense in his 1959 article "On Some Linguistic Aspects of Translation," researchers in the field of translation and interpreting over the last 20 years have provided an empirical basis for Jakobson's theoretical claim. Angelelli (2004a), for example, showed that the various roles played by interpreters in medical settings far exceed the prescriptive descriptions of the interpreter's role in the reigning codes of ethics. This disjunction contributes to the interpreter's uncertain self-image, discussed by Rakefet Sela-Sheffy in this volume, by instilling a sense that she is unable to conform to the dictates of the professional codes of conduct (Angelelli 2007). Research holds the key to resolving this situation by providing the kind of empirical evidence that should form the basis of our codes and our assessments, as well as our classroom practice.

For too long the professional field of translation and interpreting has been shaped by anecdote and intuition on the part of experts, or at least professionals—for, as Shreve (2002: 154–55) notes, not all professionals are experts. Nevertheless, resistance to the post-structuralist understanding of the relationship of language to meaning, i.e., that meaning is constructed in the act of interpretation, remains strong. In fact, the tension between the prescription to act as a neutral conduit of stable and fixed meanings and the reality of the translator and interpreter's role as co-constructor of meaning is evident from the very earliest stages in the professionalization of translation and interpreting in the postwar period. For example, in a 1955 article published in the *New York Times Magazine,* titled "Interpreter: Linguist Plus Diplomat," a professional U.N. interpreter is quoted as saying: "You must be absolutely faithful to what the delegate is *trying* to convey" (White 1955: 12; italics added)—not to what the speaker is saying but to what the speaker is *trying* to say, which casts doubt on the ontological status of the source utterance. Moreover, the addition of diplomat to the interpreter's role as language expert as suggested in the article's headline is not a simple add-on insofar as it authorizes the interpreter to consider a host of factors beyond the denotative semantics of the source utterance—it makes her a cultural mediator. As the interpreter interviewed puts it, "Sometimes you interpret *exactly* what he says and then *add* a few words to explain what he means," and later, "You do an editing job as you go along" (White 1955: 12; italics added). The interpreter's words express a fundamental tension within our modern understanding of translation and interpreting, which was especially acute in the 1950s, when the Sapir-Whorf concept of linguistic relativity competed with the promotion of machine translation and a model of translation as linguistic matching. While the former posits the inseparability of words and their meaning, placing limits on translatability and constructing translation as "a complex decision making process," to use Jiří Levý's phrase, the latter posits the separability of words and meaning, promoting an ideal of universal translatability.

The persistence of positivist notions is perhaps more acute in Interpreting Studies, Angelelli (2004b: 21) argues, because unlike Translation Studies "interpreting did not develop into Interpreting Studies with an underlying theory. The theory and research on which interpreting rests has been produced mostly by the field with little influence from other [fields] (even though interpreting is per se an interdisciplinary endeavor)." Hence the importance of breaking the closed circle in which prescriptive codes and anecdotes continue to influence the training and professional identity of interpreters. This situation, Angelelli contends, "leads to a complex field of practice lacking the insights of interdisciplinary research and theory and losing the opportunity to contribute to theory development" (2004b: 24). Creating a mutually interrogative relationship between theory, research, and practice offers the greatest hope of breaking that self-perpetuating circle.

The research journey

While post-structuralist theory challenges many of the positivist pieties of traditional research paradigms, it should not lead us to abandon the traditional research journey. In fact, it calls upon us to show even greater rigor and systematicity in order to reduce bias as much as possible and to validate our findings through the application of mixed methods. Conceptualized as an art and a craft (Booth, Colomb, and Williams 2008), the research journey begins with curiosity, interest in a topic, a hypothesis, a hunch, or a question on the part of the researcher. That being said, the research journey is not undertaken by the researcher alone. Research on cross-cultural communication, on how texts and information travel across space and time, touches the lives of many. It involves not only the researcher but also the authors, the readers, the audiences, the speakers of minority languages, all of whom have a direct or indirect interest in the results of the research. Research in TIS also brings scientific communities closer together as it stands at the intersection of many disciplines. So, the journey is shared.

Also, like a journey, research requires a great deal of effort and rigor. While several studies in T&I have used the methods discussed in this volume, they have not always shown rigor in respecting the integrity of the methods. For example, in the last 15 years we have witnessed a growth of M.A. and doctoral theses in TIS using surveys to measure perceptions, beliefs, qualities, etc. Surveys have become a popular way of gathering data (especially with free software like SurveyMonkey). Very few of the studies using this method, however, discuss the reliability and validity of the survey administered (required for any measurement instrument), simply assuming that the survey measures what the author intended it to measure. Another important point of rigor involves the manipulation and analysis of the data. Many studies do not exhibit the necessary rigor in sampling but, nevertheless, claim to generalize results. In addition, many times authors do not conceptualize a survey as a way of correlating variables and limit their analysis to descriptive statistics. Unlike specialized software designed for technical studies, many beginner software programs do not run correlations. Therefore, authors using this basic free software are not able to take full advantage of the data they have collected. And what is even more problematic is when the software rather than the research question seems to dictate the extension of the analysis.

And so, only when we are equipped with a commitment to rigor and systematicity are we ready to embark on the research journey, which we will describe below in terms of stages. While these stages do not necessarily follow one another in a particular order, some definitely come before others. But this will depend on the approach and the nature of the research. One of the earliest stages is the *statement of the problem*. This should clearly state and define the issue to be studied, its scope and nature, the need for this research, the gaps it will fill, why it merits our attention. Most generally, the statement of the problem culminates with a research question that will address the problem. Depending on the approach or paradigm, the research question can be an exploratory one that will be addressed by the study, a hypothesis to be accepted or rejected, or a hunch (not formulated as a question) to be followed.

The *theoretical framework* refers to the theory/set of theories on which the study will be grounded, the available lenses through which we can examine the problem. A research problem is like any other kind of problem. We can look at it from different perspectives depending on what we can see or what we want to see. Thus, the same data can be discussed differently according to the lens used. When we look at the problem through the lens of history or sociology, literature, feminism or agency, interaction, displacement or hegemony, we are framing the study in a way that will impact the very essence of it. The theoretical framework, therefore, cannot be considered a posteriori or as an add-on.

The *literature review* or *review of the relevant literature* is key to situating our research project in a larger context. Through the literature review, we participate in an ongoing dialogue and become part of a community of discourse. Research contributes to knowledge, to the advancement of a field of study, shedding light on a problem, and sometimes resolving it. It is therefore essential to be familiar with what has been written about the problem we are exploring, or similar ones, for two basic reasons. First, it does not make sense to re-invent the wheel. Second, and more importantly, as researchers we always stand on the shoulders of those who came before us. Acknowledging and citing previous work done in the field, giving credit where credit is due, is, therefore, the proper and ethical thing to do.

The *methods* section is closely linked to the research question and the theoretical framework. The lens we decide to use to look at the issue and the question we ask about it will establish how we will go about answering/exploring the question. It is not the other way around. We will not decide on a method a priori simply because we are more familiar or comfortable with it. Otherwise we will have to find a research question that lends itself to investigation with the method we have chosen. This is a case of the tail wagging the dog. Once the method has been selected, we collect a certain type of data (perceptions, texts, behaviors) that will be analyzed in a specific way, that is, according to the method.

The *data analysis section* is also closely linked to the research question and the method used. We analyze the data we gathered (which depends on the question) based on the method used to gather it. Different types of data allow for different types of analysis. And various research questions can be answered using different types of data (e.g., data resulting from surveys, which are generally quantifiable, or from direct observations). In this section we analyze the data and explain to the reader how we did it. This section does not necessarily present an interpretation of the data, as data may be interpreted in different ways.

The *results section*, also sometimes merged with the discussion section, is where the researcher takes a stand with her/his own interpretation of her/his results. This is, however, not arbitrary as it is bound by the lens used and the data collected, which derived from the method used, which was dictated by the research question. It is, together with the discussion section, one of the most exciting parts of the journey, as we are able here to present our contribution to the field.

The *discussion section*—which may stand alone or be merged with the results section or the call for further research section—links the results of the study to the review of the literature, argues how the results reinforce or differ from findings from other studies, and posits additional questions. The *conclusion section* is the one where the researcher revisits the research question to discuss how it was systematically answered. In so doing, the researcher links all parts of the study, beginning with the lens used (the theoretical framework) to study the issue at hand to recapping the results and their meaning. The *implications section* is also a crucial part of the study. Results of a study can have implications at both the theoretical and practical levels, and the implications may affect different groups or entities. So, this section connects research to the outside, to a community, a group, or a system.

In the process of breaking a whole into its parts to make it more manageable, one may think of a study and its write-up (whether it is a dissertation, a grant report, or a publication) as a collection of pieces (statement of a problem, research question, theoretical framework, review of relevant literature, methods, results, analysis, etc.) that must be present (to meet requirements, for example) just because. The truth is that each piece contributes to the whole in a unique way. There is nothing capricious about the collection of parts and there is nothing arbitrary about the structure. Although some research designs may be more or less flexible than others, depending on the question and the approach, all the parts contribute something unique. For example, while an experimental design imposes something—a treatment—on the participants, and the research question is firm, a naturalistic design does not impose any pre-constructed frame on the participants, and the research question may change to a certain degree. In any case, a question, be it about an individual or a group, a single text or a corpus, asked synchronically or asynchronically, at a macro or micro level, can be answered with confidence when the process (the journey) used to answer it has been systematic and rigorous.

Conclusion

The possible directions research into translation- and interpreting-related phenomena will take are limitless. New research directions will emerge from within Translation and Interpreting Studies proper, as well as any number of other fields that choose to take the translation/interpreting turn. And so, the map of the field provided in Part II, while comprehensive, will continue to evolve, as will the methods and tools presented in Part III. What will remain constant, however, is the necessity of investigating that most fascinating and complex aspect of our lives as human beings—communication across languages and cultures.

References

Angelelli, Claudia V. 2004a. *Medical Interpreting and Cross-cultural Communication*. Cambridge: Cambridge University Press.

——2004b. *Re-visiting the Interpreter's Role*. Amsterdam: John Benjamins.

——2007. "Validating Professional Standards and Codes: Challenges and Opportunities." In *Interpreting: International Journal of Research and Practice in Interpreting* 8(2): 175–93.

Bandia, Paul. 2008. *Translation as Reparation. Writing and Translation in Postcolonial Africa.* Manchester: St. Jerome.

Batchelor, Kathryn. 2009. *Decolonizing Translation. Francophone African Novels in English Translation.* Manchester: St. Jerome.

Booth, Wayne C., Gregory G. Colomb, and Joseph M. Williams. 2008. *The Craft of Research.* Third edition. Chicago: University of Chicago Press.

Cheung, Martha. 2006. *An Anthology of Chinese Discourse on Translation.* Manchester: St. Jerome.

Goldberg, Jonathan. 1997. *Desiring Women Writing. English Renaissance Examples.* Stanford, CA: Stanford University Press.

Goodrich, Jaime. 2013. *Faithful Translators. Authorship, Gender and Religion in Early Modern England.* Evanston, IL: Northwestern University Press.

Hermans, Theo (ed.). 2006. *Translating Others*, Vols. 1 and 2. Manchester: St. Jerome.

Hung, Eva, and Judy Wakabayashi (eds.). 2005. *Asian Translation Traditions.* Manchester: St. Jerome.

Inggs, Judith, and Libby Meintjes (eds.). 2009. *Translation Studies in Africa.* Continuum Studies in Translation. London and New York: Continuum.

Kothari, Rita, and Judy Wakabayashi (eds.). 2009. *Decentering Translation Studies: India and Beyond.* Amsterdam and Philadelphia: John Benjamins.

Kronitiris, Tina. 1997. *Oppositional Voices: Women as Writers and Translators in the English Renaissance.* New York and London: Routledge.

Pollard, David E. 1998. *Translation and Creation. Readings of Western Literature in Early Modern China, 1840–1918.* Amsterdam and Philadelphia: John Benjamins.

Shreve, Gregory. 2002. "Knowing Translation. Cognitive and Experiential Aspects of Translation Expertise from the Perspective of Expertise Studies." In *Translation Studies: Perspectives on an Emerging Discipline*, Alessandra Riccardi (ed.), 150–71. Cambridge: Cambridge University Press.

Task Force on Doctoral Study in Modern Language and Literature. 2007. Report. New York: MLA.

Uman, Deborah. 2012. *Women as Translators in Early Modern Europe.* Newark: University of Delaware Press.

White, Micheline (ed.). 2011. *English Women, Religion, and Textual Production, 1500–1625.* Farnham: Ashgate.

White, Peter T. 1955. "Interpreter: Linguist Plus Diplomat." *New York Times Magazine*, November 6, 1955: 12, 30, 32–33.

Part II

Mapping the field

1 Agency and role

Sergey Tyulenev

Overview

The notion of agency is relevant to T&I Studies in two ways: it can refer to translation/interpreting as a social activity and to the translator/interpreter as a social actor. The former is primary while the latter is derivative insofar as the actor's "typical 'action' … alone marks [him/her] out as belonging to a particular category" (Weber 1978: 21). The translator's/interpreter's social role is predicated on the translation/interpreting agency. The first question to be asked, therefore, is what constitutes translation/interpreting as agency; based on that, the role of the translator/interpreter can be discussed. In what follows, the term 'agency' will be applied to translation/interpreting as a social function, and the term 'role' to the translator/interpreter as a social actor.

Theoretical foundations

The word 'agency' comes from the Latin verb *agere* ('to do'). Agency is "any human action, collective or structural as well as individual, which 'makes a difference' to a social outcome" (*Collins* 2006). Sociology attempts to account for human actions in terms of their motivations and social consequences. The term 'role' is applied to individual actors and denotes culturally determined behavioral patterns (Linton 1936; Goffman 1956). The terminological usage of the word 'role' grew out of Shakespeare's famous metaphor of human life: "All the world's a stage, / And all the men and women merely players."

The most profound study of social action is found in works of Talcott Parsons. Social action is described by Parsons as consisting of four components: (1) an agent; (2) an end, "a future state of affairs toward which the process of action is oriented"; (3) a situation in which the action occurs and whose "trends of development differ in one or more important respects from the state of affairs to which the action is oriented, the end"; and finally, (4) "a certain mode of relationship between these elements" (1937/1949: 44). Social action is the social actor's choice between available means toward desired ends in the context of the social system, whose influence takes the form of norms and values.

Other theories, such as Weber's social theory, symbolic interactionism (the Chicago School), social phenomenology, ethnomethodology, and action-network theory (ANT), emphasize the role played by the actor in social interactions. The primary concerns of these theories are the degree of rationality of social action, its rules, and the ways actors learn and negotiate them. For instance, Erving Goffman's theory focusing on social roles (1956) is known as a dramaturgical approach. Goffman analyzes the performance of social roles in terms of impression management: actors act differently in different settings. Also in the mid-twentieth century, Ralph Turner developed a theory with a similar focus on social acting. Turner's was "a conceptualization of roles that emphasized the process of interaction over the dictates of social structures and cultural scripts" (Turner 1998: 384). Turner considered the emergence and exercise of roles in actors' interactions with other actors in organizational and other societal settings.

In his book *Social Theory and Social Structure* (1968), Robert Merton developed his version of role theory—a 'role-set' theory. Coming from the macrosociological camp, Merton considered social roles as suggesting a particular type of behavior expected from the actor by the society (cf. the notion of norms above). Merton also studied the relationships between the various roles that one and the same individual might play. He found that roles are not always easily compatible, some are difficult or impossible to reconcile, producing role-strains or even role-conflicts, leading actors in some cases to distance themselves from certain roles. The degree of rationality of social action, on the one hand, and the degree to which it is determined by social structures, on the other, underlie one of the most protracted controversies in sociology—the structure vs. agency dilemma. Depending on how a theory resolves this dilemma, it is said to belong to either macro or microsociology, although there have been attempts to elaborate theories striking a balance between the two approaches (notably, Bourdieu and Giddens).

Evolution of the topic in TIS

Translation/interpreting can be treated as either an action or a contributor to an action. As an action, translation/interpreting is studied in terms of its structure and properties; as a contributor to an action, the focus of inquiry is translation/interpreting's social function. Translation/interpreting mediates across differences, commonly understood as linguistic and cultural, but also intralingual and intersemiotic (Jakobson 1959/2012: 127; Petrilli 2003: 19). Translation/interpreting's social function is unique and cannot be fulfilled by any other social phenomenon.

Translation/interpreting "makes a difference" socially in that it enables/facilitates and affects, to a greater or lesser degree, social interaction. Translation/interpreting enables social interaction when social phenomena and/or actors cannot interact directly. In the early nineteenth century, Friedrich Schleiermacher wrote that translation is needed not only between different languages but also between different dialects of the same people across time and space, between “contemporaries who share a dialect but belong to different classes” and compeers who are “of different opinions and sensibility”; moreover, we need to translate “our own utterances after a certain time has passed, would we make them truly our own again” (1813/2013: 43).

Translation/interpreting's ability to facilitate social interaction has long been recognized, whereas the effect that translation/interpreting may have on interactions remains underappreciated, even in organizations employing professional translators and interpreters (Angelelli 2004b: 78–81; Koskinen 2008: 1, 70–72). Yet translation/interpreting's mediation is intrinsically of a hyaline nature, that is, the interacting parties see each other not directly but *through* translation/interpreting (cf. Brighenti 2010). Translation/interpreting is not transparent because it mediates between different semiotic (including linguistic) codes and different sociocultural systems, all of which are unique, and so mediation between them inevitably requires selection, reduction, and augmentation, making shifts inevitable. Some translation/interpreting strategies may be found justifiable, some even beneficial, while others, inept or detrimental to the mediated communication. Translation/interpreting may provide (more or less open) commentaries on potentially unclear or otherwise problematic features of the source for the sake of the target audience. Translation/interpreting may also censor or expurgate the source text or utterance (Merkle et al. 2010), and the alleged neutrality of translation/interpreting is often ‘obscured’ in various institutional settings (Mossop 1988; Metzger 1999).

Translation/interpreting's structure and properties manifest themselves in its unit act, “the ‘smallest’ unit of an action system which still makes sense as a part of a concrete system of action” (Parsons 1937/1949: 731). The unit act of translation/interpreting is the translated/interpreted communication event (TCE/ICE). TCE/ICE, in fact, consists of two communication events connected by mediation and involving at least three parties: A>B>C>B>A, where ‘>’ is the direction of communication and A and C are parties (not necessarily individuals) that interact through mediator B. Strictly speaking, only B belongs to translation/interpreting qua social action because only in B can the operational nature of TCE/ICE—mediation—be observed; the mediated parties (A and C) provide materials for mediation. B is inextricably linked with A and C, and cannot function without them insofar as each translation/interpreting has a source/sources and there is always a target audience. This holds true with necessary qualifications even in the case of pseudotranslations (Tyulenev 2012a: 112–13).

From the sociological point of view, the agent of translation/interpreting is not to be confused with a human individual. Machine translation is as legitimate an agent of translation as a graduate from a university translation/interpreting program. The translation/interpreting agent is not only someone who is called ‘translator/interpreter’ but also anyone or anything performing translation/interpreting, that is, mediating in a TCE/ICE. Function determines agent, not the other way around. In fact, the translation agent today often consists of a combination of human and non-human agencies. Non-human agency is represented by the technology often used both in translation and interpreting: e.g., computer-assisted translation (CAT) tools or the equipment in interpreting booths. Both translation and interpreting, therefore, represent a complex form of interaction between human and non-human agents (Quah 2006).

Moreover, translation/interpreting can be performed not only at the level of the "entire" individual but also at the infra- or supra-individual levels, such as the "lightning translation" in the mind of an individual speaking in a language that is foreign to him/her (Kaluza quoted in Reiß and Vermeer 1984/2013: 41), an entire nation as translator (Halperin 1985: 2–7), or intergenerational translation (Habermas 1970/1988: 148). Translation/interpreting agency is also exercised as part of complex networks: the final version of a translation/interpreting act is often a result of contributions from many agents and factors—teams of translators/interpreters, their project managers, editors, proofreaders, censors, patrons, the translator's/interpreter's expertise or the status of the source text, CAT tools, etc.—and versions of texts may follow such tortuous trajectories that it can be difficult to define their status in terms of "source" or "target" attributions (Bassnett and Lefevere 1990: 14–15; Milton and Bandia 2009; Federici forthcoming).

An end of TCE/ICE is not an "anticipated future state of affairs but only the difference from what it would be if the actor should refrain from acting" (Parsons 1937/1949: 732). In the case of translational/interpreting action, an end is primarily the production of a version of the source text (in whatever semiotic medium). Parsons' formalistic definition allows theorizing translation/interpreting as an action found anywhere between or at the extremes of the rationality/intentionality axis. T&I research into translation/interpreting as a process has shown that the translator's/interpreter's behavior has both rational and irrational aspects, reflecting complex intrapersonal psychosomatic interactions. For instance, Douglas Robinson studied translation in terms of somatic theory trying to overcome the body–mind opposition (1991, 2011, 1997/2012). There have been attempts to apply psychoanalysis to the study of translation (Gentzler 2008; Venuti 2013). Translational/interpreting action is not infrequently unintentional: the translator/interpreter cannot (fully) predict all possible results of his/her action. Moreover, the notions of rationality and intentionality cannot be applied to the non-human translation/interpreting agent.

The TCE/ICE situation is the state of affairs preceding and coterminous with a translational/interpreting action. Conditions and means are to be distinguished: "The situation constitutes conditions of action as opposed to means *in so far as it is not subject to the control of the actor*" (Parsons 1937/1949: 44; italics in original). The TCE/ICE situation includes the source text—a verbal or non-verbal organized structure of data—which is to be transferred by means of a translational/interpreting action from the source to the target domain. The definition of the TCE/ICE situation also suggests a discussion of the social context, which makes the translational/interpreting action necessary or superfluous, possible or problematic, ordained or forbidden. A classic example of describing social contexts in which translation takes center stage in literary systems is found in Itamar Even-Zohar's polysystem theory (1990: 47): translation plays an important role in a young literary polysystem, in a "peripheral" or "weak" polysystem, or in a national literature experiencing a crisis. Social settings also feature prominently in Dell Hymes' sociolinguistic model of communication, which Angelelli (2000) applied to the study of interpreting.

The concept of conditions of translational/interpreting action makes it clear why the translator/interpreter cannot be considered the unit of T&I research: there is a risk of overemphasizing his/her freedom from social constraints. As both macrosociology, starting from Marx and Durkheim, and microsociology, such as Schutz's phenomenology, demonstrated, individual freedom in society is a matter of degrees; it is never absolute. In this respect, translating/interpreting agency is always socially conditioned/constructed. While translators/interpreters have a certain amount of control over the means of reaching an end of their translational/interpreting action, the degree of their control is constrained.

In his theory of action, Parsons stressed that the means the agent chooses are "subject to the influence of an independent, determinate selective factor, a normative orientation" (1937/1949: 44–45). This normative orientation is the manifestation of social constraints influencing human agents. (Can norms be seen as operational rules in the case of a non-human translation agent, such as translation memory software?) In T&I Studies, the influence of various norms and conventions on translator/interpreter behavior has been studied since the late 1970s (notably, Toury 1978; Chesterman 1993; Nord 1991, on the basis of skopos theory; Angelelli 2004b; Sapiro 2008a, drawing on Pierre Bourdieu's sociological theory). Some T&I scholars argue for more personalized configurations of constraints determining translational action (e.g., Baker 2006, employing the notion of narrative; Meylaerts 2008, borrowing Bourdieu's notion of habitus and Lahire's concept of sociobiography).

The repertoire of choices the translation/interpreting agent has before him/her includes the possibility of error, "the failure to attain ends or to make the 'right' choice of means" (Parsons 1937/1949: 46). T&I norm-based approaches give prominence to norms as a factor determining translational/interpreting action, yet this is not sufficient. It has been suggested that norm-based approaches be complemented with the notion of error as another explicative parameter (Wilss 1977/1982: 196–215; Kußmaul 1986; Malmkjær 2004).

In translational/interpreting action, the relationship between actors, ends, and the situation (conditions+means) can be described by showing how TCE/ICE functions. Communication events consist of three basic elements: utterance (the expression plane of what is communicated), information (the content plane), and understanding (what is deduced from the utterance by the receiver of the message) (Luhmann 1984/1995: 137–75). When one person says "It's raining" (*utterance*), the other may deduce the *information* 'take an umbrella' and demonstrate his/her *understanding* by taking an umbrella. In relation to the three parties, TCE/ICE can be interpreted as B understanding A's utterance by selecting one (or a few) of all possible pieces of the information implied by A's utterance. B's understanding becomes the utterance aimed at C. Finally, C also selects one (or a few) piece(s) of the information of B's utterance and that constitutes C's understanding. Thus, presented schematically, TCE/ICE functions as follows: A: $\text{Utterance}_1 > \text{Information}_1 \cong$ B: $(\text{Understanding}_1 = \text{Utterance}_2) > \text{Information}_2 \cong$ C: Understanding_2 (Tyulenev 2012a: 38–42).

Social action, therefore, can be described as unfolding in a situation of double contingency. Parsons explains: "There is a *double contingency* inherent in interaction. On the one hand, ego's gratifications are contingent on his selection among available alternatives. But in turn, alter's reaction will be contingent on ego's selection and will result from a complementary selection on alter's part" (cited in Luhmann 1984/1995: 522–23). An action, in which both ego and alter narrow down available alternatives, moves, step by step, toward a clarification of the interacting parties' positions: "At first, alter tentatively determines his behavior in a situation that is still unclear. He begins with a friendly glance, a gesture, a gift—and waits to see whether and how ego receives the proposed definition of the situation. In light of this beginning, every subsequent step is an action with a contingency-reducing, determining, effect—be it positive or negative" (Luhmann 1984/1995: 104–5). In this sense, all communication can be interpreted as translation (Steiner 1975). Translation/interpreting's social function of mediation is, intrinsically, contingency reducing: in the beginning, the interacting parties face the overwhelming complexity of the situation, which they cannot tackle without some type of translation/interpreting. Translation/interpreting turns the initially incomprehensible and unmanageable into something that ego and alter can comprehend and manage. This seems to be true at all levels of interaction—from infrapersonal through interpersonal to intercultural (Tyulenev 2012b).

The Luhmannian model of communication is helpful for theorizing translation/interpreting as a selection process. Another helpful resource is Hymes' sociolinguistic model of communication, mentioned earlier, which has been applied to the analysis of interpreting in Angelelli (2000) (arguably, it is also applicable to translation). Because it takes into consideration as many as 13 speech components, one of the advantages of this model is that it helps to discuss similarities and differences between various forms of interpreting/translation.

As has been shown in T&I Studies, especially in the "cultural" turn (Bassnett and Lefevere 1990: 4), interpersonal communication is inevitably a dialogue of enculturated individuals. Hence, it is important to understand how translation/interpreting contributes to intercultural interaction, which may follow different scenarios, from mutually beneficial to detrimental (for a repertoire of possible scenarios, see Tyulenev 2014: 36–40). Until recently, translation/

interpreting was studied mostly in mutually beneficial intercultural interactions. Recently, however, numerous case studies have examined translation/interpreting in situations of conflict or rivalry (Copeland 1991; Baker 2006; Inghilleri and Harding 2010; Inghilleri 2012; a special case of translation agency in postcolonial intercultural asymmetries, "thick translation," is exemplified in Appiah 2013).

Finally, the agency of T&I scholarship and the role of the T&I scholar has also been discussed. T&I scholarship contributes to the translation/interpreting professional project (Tyulenev 2014: 67–80). In the sociology of professions, each occupational group is seen as striving to secure for itself a socially recognized niche. Such recognition is reinforced if the occupational group develops its own theoretical apparatus and terminology.

As regards the translation/interpreting professional project, many scholars argue that the scholarly study of T&I is indispensable, generating knowledge about translation/interpreting as an occupation, on the one hand, and as a social phenomenon, on the other. The former is put primarily to vocational use: future translators and interpreters are trained based on T&I theories, allowing new generations to benefit from the accumulated knowledge and experience of their predecessors. Learning about translation/interpreting as a unique phenomenon ensures T&I Studies' place among the other social sciences as none of them studies translation/interpreting in all its manifestations and as profoundly. Moreover, academic programs that prepare students for a professional career as a translator/interpreter enhance the visibility and respectability of the profession.

To play their role, T&I scholars observe translation/interpreting praxis, whether past or present, and learn from the previous generations of scholars by familiarizing themselves with their works. In this way T&I scholars contextualize their research and enable themselves to contribute to the discipline in innovative ways.

At the same time, it is imperative that T&I scholars realize that they are as much products of their socialization as are the practitioners whom they study. Scholars, too, may have "split loyalties" and experience "a conflict of roles" (Koskinen 2008: 9). Therefore, T&I scholars need to exercise self-reflexivity in order to attenuate bias in relation to the studied phenomena. The importance of such reflexivity has been stressed in T&I literature (Pym 1998: 27; Tymoczko 2002: 16, 22–23).

Key studies

The earliest T&I theories, which drew on action theory, were the skopos theory and the theory of translatorial action (Holz-Mänttäri 1984; Reiß and Vermeer 1984/2013). These theories are referred to as functionalist because, unlike earlier theories, they conceptualized translation/interpreting not as an attempt to establish equivalence between the source and target texts, but rather as a goal-oriented action determined by the required/likely function of the end product. To achieve his/her goal (Reiß and Vermeer used the Greek word *skopos*, hence the name of their theory), the translator/interpreter acts (Holz-Mänttäri theorized translation as 'translator's action'; hence the German title of her theory, *Translatorisches Handeln*) based on his/her analysis of the original text and by selecting translation/interpreting strategies in accordance with a brief (cf. Parsons' notions of 'conditions,' 'means,' and 'end').

Arguably, T&I research has benefited directly from macrosociological theories providing valuable insights into translation/interpreting's social function. So far, Niklas Luhmann's social systems theory and Pierre Bourdieu's theory of social fields, which originated within the macrosociological paradigm, have been explored (Casanova 2002; Angelelli 2004b; Wolf 2006; Sapiro 2008b; Inghilleri 2012; Tyulenev 2012a). The world-systems theory has been adapted to show translation in an emerging cultural world system (Heilbron 1999).

In the 1990s and 2000s, seeing translation/interpreting's agency from the macrosociological perspective has allowed theorizing translation/interpreting's contribution to important social processes, such as the creation of national/cultural identities, both modern and ancient (Brisset 1990/1996; Gentzler 2008; McElduff and Sciarrino 2011; Tyulenev 2012b), or power negotiations between 'major' and 'minor' languages and cultures (Cronin 1995; Branchadell and West 2005; see also the specialized journal *mTm*). Translation/interpreting has been shown to be a powerful agent in social development and post-colonialism (Bandia 2008; Tyulenev and van Rooyen 2013; Marais 2014). Translation/interpreting has also been studied in its interaction with gender and sexuality (Larkosh 2011; Spurlin 2014). The strategies used to re-construct realities in interpreting have been discussed in Wadensjö 1998 and Angelelli 2004a.

Discussions of the translator/interpreter role arose as a reaction against the perceived overemphasis on the text of translation/interpreting (Pym 1998) and the conception of the translator/interpreter as a mere conduit of interaction, effectively a "bilingual ghost" (Collado Aís 2002: 336). Elements of Goffman's theory, such as the notion of *footing*, have proved productive in Interpreting Studies (Wadensjö 1998; Metzger 1999; Roy 2000; Marks 2013; White 2014). Although the role the translator/interpreter plays in the process of translation/interpreting never went completely unnoticed, until the late 1990s it was discussed only on occasion, and rather sketchily and essentialistically (presenting the translator/interpreter as a bundle of fixed characteristics independent of the sociocultural context of his/her practice). One of the early examples comes from a Renaissance European treatise on translation by Leonardo Bruni (1426), who wrote that in order to produce a "good" translation, a "good" translator is needed, one who knows both the source and target languages and has a "sound" ear "so that his translation does not disturb and destroy the fullness and rhythmical qualities of the original" (1426/2002: 59; see discussion in Botley 2004 and Morini 2006).

More recently, Hans J. Vermeer criticized earlier translation theories for, among other things, viewing the translator "as a 'language mediator', a mere relay station or interface," while in his theory translators "participate in the communicative interaction, they gather information and they pass it on" (Reiß and Vermeer 1984/2013: 40, 60). Justa Holz-Mänttäri saw the translator as an expert participating in a translatorial action, described systemically as a complex structure involving different actors (with whom the translator deals during the process of target text production) (1986: 352–54). Yet all these portrayals of the translator are purely functional and do little to relativize their intrinsic essentialism.

Starting in the 1990s, voices have been raised in favor of studying translators/interpreters as persons with biographies (Delisle and Woodsworth 1995/2012); as products of their unique socializations (Meylaerts 2008); as having their own political and ideological agendas (Brisset 1990/1996); and as gendered individuals (Godard 1990; Simon 1996; von Flotow 1997; Delisle 2002; Santaemilia and von Flotow 2011). The role of interpreters as co-participants, visible in the interaction, has been studied in Wadensjö 1998, Metzger 1999, Roy 2000, and Angelelli 2004b.

Discussions of the social role of translators/interpreters have gained fresh insights from several sociological theories. The most prominent are Pierre Bourdieu's theory with its notion of 'habitus' (Simeoni 1998; Gouanvic 1999; Angelelli 2004b; Wolf 2006; Inghilleri 2012) and microsociological theories, such as Actor-Network Theory (ANT), which allow for the observation of individual translators/interpreters in their social environments (Buzelin and Folaron 2007). Theorizing translator/interpreter agency has been, directly or indirectly, meant to socially empower translators/interpreters (Tymoczko 2007) and make them more visible (Venuti 1995). One may argue, however, that a clear line should be drawn between T&I research as a scholarly enterprise and activism meant to improve the social status of translators/interpreters.

New directions

TIS has already applied a number of sociological theories. Yet other theories also show promise, notably, as has been demonstrated above, Parsons' sophisticated theory of social action (1937/1949, 1951/1959; Parsons and Shils 1951). Translation and interpreting need to be investigated in terms of the ratio and properties of collective and individual translation/interpreting, as well as of translation/interpreting's infra- and supra-individual manifestations. For example, the functioning of translation at the infrapersonal level (within an individual) is one of the under-studied directions of T&I research. Yet "[s]emioticians emphasize the mediatedness of experience, arguing that we are always dealing with signs and codes, not with an unmediated objective reality" (Chandler and Munday 2011: 270). T&I Studies can definitely contribute to research into how the individual uses signs and codes in the process of making sense of reality.

Human translation's interworking with non-human agents also needs further study. The sociological theory that specifically discusses social reality taking non-human actors into consideration is Michel Callon and Bruno Latour's Actor-Network Theory. There have been attempts to apply several ideas of ANT to the study of translation (Buzelin 2005; Bogic 2010), although a full-scale application still awaits its researcher.

Translation/interpreting seems to have more than one social function (Tymoczko 2006: 16; Renn 2006). The question of the relationship (or a hierarchy?) of these functions calls for focused research. The plurality of translation/interpreting's functions is relevant when the ends of translational/interpreting action are discussed. Sociological-anthropological functionalist theories may provide a guiding light (Malinowski 1944; Merton 1967). Sociological theories bridging the gap between micro and macrosociological theories will help researchers to overcome the reductionist vision of translation/interpreting as a purposeful activity. For instance, in his structuration theory, Anthony Giddens argues that agency is not necessarily intentional or in accordance with the agent's volition. That is why Giddens' theory of action is referred to as "purposive," rather than "purposeful" (Baert 1998: 101).

Another important characteristic of translation/interpreting's social agency that is gaining momentum in T&I Studies is translation/interpreting ethics (Basalamah 2009; Pym 1997/2012; Inghilleri 2012). The application of the sociological theory of one of the most influential sociological theorists discussing issues of ethics today, Jürgen Habermas (1981/1984, 1962/1989a, 1981/1989b), to the study of translation/interpreting has just begun (Tyulenev 2012c and 2013). The potential of studying the translator's/interpreter's role is far from exhausted. So far, the translator's role has been discussed mainly in terms of translators'/interpreters' visibility, self-esteem, and the socially relevant results of their work. In sociology the concept of role is significantly broader and may provide new inspiration. Applications of sociological theories discussing social roles (Goffman, Turner, Merton) may shed more light on translators'/interpreters' experiences and the interaction of their different roles in different settings.

References

Angelelli, Claudia V. 2000. "Interpreting as a Communicative Event: A Look through Hymes' Lenses." *Meta* 45(4): 580–92.

——2004a. *Medical Interpreting and Cross-cultural Communication*. Cambridge: Cambridge University Press.

——2004b. *Revisiting the Interpreter's Role: A Study of Conference, Court, and Medical Interpreters in Canada, Mexico, and the United States*. Amsterdam and Philadelphia: John Benjamins.

Appiah, Kwame Anthony. 2013. "Thick Translation." In *The Translation Studies Reader*, third edition, Lawrence Venuti (ed.), 331–43. London and New York: Routledge.

Baert, Patrick. 1998. *Social Theory in the Twentieth Century*. Cambridge: Polity.

Baker, Mona. 2006. *Translation and Conflict: A Narrative Account*. New York and London: Routledge.

Bandia, Paul. 2008. *Translation as Reparation: Writing and Translation in Postcolonial Africa*. Manchester: St. Jerome.

Basalamah, Salah. 2009. *Le droit de traduire. Une politique culturelle pour mondialisation*. Ottawa/Arras: Presse de l'Université d'Ottawa/Artois Presse Université.

Bassnett, Susan, and André Lefevere (eds.). 1990. *Translation, History and Culture*. London: Cassell.

Bogic, Anna. 2010. "Uncovering the Hidden Actors with the Help of Latour: The 'Making' of *The Second Sex*." *MonTI. Monografías de Traducción e Interpretación* 2: 173–92.

Botley, Paul. 2004. *Latin Translation in the Renaissance: The Theory and Practice of Leonardo Bruni, Giannozzo Manetti, Erasmus*. Cambridge: Cambridge University Press.

Branchadell, Albert, and Lovell Margaret West (eds.). 2005. *Less Translated Languages*. Amsterdam and Philadelphia: John Benjamins.

Brighenti, Andrea Mubi. 2010. *Visibility in Social Theory and Social Research*. Basingstoke: Palgrave Macmillan.

Brisset, Annie. 1990/1996. *A Sociocritique of Translation: Theatre and Alterity in Quebec, 1968–1988*. Translated by Rosalind Gill and Roger Gannon. Toronto: University of Toronto Press.

Bruni, Leonardo. 1426/2002. "On the Correct Way to Translate," trans. by James Hankins. In Douglas Robinson (ed.), *Western Translation Theory from Herodotus to Nietzsche*, 57–60. Manchester and Northampton, MA: St. Jerome Publishing.

Buzelin, Hélène. 2005. "Unexpected Allies: How Latour's Network Theory Could Complement Bourdieusian Analyses in Traditional Studies." *The Translator* 11(2): 193–218.

Buzelin, Hélène, and Deborah Folaron (eds.). 2007. "La traduction et les études de réseaux / Translation and Network Studies." *Meta* 52(4): 603–858.

Casanova, Pascale. 2002. "Consécration et accumulation de capital littéraire: La traduction comme échange inégal." *Actes de la recherche en sciences sociales* 144: 7–20.

Chandler, Daniel, and Rod Munday. 2011. *Oxford Dictionary of Media and Communication*. Oxford: Oxford University Press.

Chesterman, Andrew. 1993. "From 'Is' to 'Ought': Laws, Norms and Strategies in Translation Studies." *Target* 5(1): 1–20.

Collado Aís, Ángela. 2002. "Quality Assessment in Simultaneous Interpreting: The Importance of Nonverbal Communication," translated by Pamela Faber. In *The Interpreting Studies Reader*, Franz Pöchhacker and Miriam Shlesinger (eds.), 326–36. London and New York: Routledge.

Collins. 2006. *Collins Dictionary of Sociology*. Available online at http://search.credoreference.com.ezphost.dur.ac.uk/content/entry/collinssoc/agency/0 (accessed March 18, 2014).

Copeland, Rita. 1991. *Rhetoric, Hermeneutics, and Translation in the Middle Ages: Academic Traditions and Vernacular Texts*. Cambridge: Cambridge University Press.

Cronin, Michael. 1995. "Altered States: Translation and Minority Languages." *TTR* 8(1): 85–103.

Delisle, Jean (ed.). 2002. *Portraits de traductrices*. Ottawa: Presses Université d'Ottawa.

Delisle, Jean, and Judith Woodsworth (eds.). 1995/2012. *Translators through History*, Revised edition. Amsterdam and Philadelphia: John Benjamins.

Even-Zohar, Itamar (ed.). 1990. "Polysystem Studies." Special issue. *Poetics Today* 11(1), 1–170.

Federici, Federico. Forthcoming. *Online Translated News in Italy. Response to the Foreign and the Social Role of Translators.*

Gentzler, Edwin. 2008. *Translation and Identity in the Americas: New Directions in Translation Theory.* London and New York: Routledge.

Godard, Barbara. 1990. "Theorizing Feminist Discourse/Translation." In *Translation, History and Culture*, Susan Bassnett and André Lefevere (eds.), 87–96. London: Cassell.

Goffman, Erving. 1956. *The Presentation of Self in Everyday Life.* Edinburgh: University of Edinburgh.

Gouanvic, Jean-Marc. 1999. *Sociologie de la traduction: La science-fiction américaine dans l'espace culturel français des années 1950.* Paris: Artois presses université.

Habermas, Jürgen. 1981/1984. *The Theory of Communicative Action.* Vol. 1. Trans. by Thomas McCarthy. Boston: Beacon Press.

——1970/1988. *On the Logic of the Social Sciences.* Trans. by Shierry Weber Nicholsen and Jerry A. Stark. Cambridge, MA: MIT Press.

——1962/1989a. *The Structural Transformation of the Public Sphere.* Trans. by Thomas Burger with the assistance of Frederick Lawrence. London: Polity.

——1981/1989b. *The Theory of Communicative Action.* Vol. 2. Trans. by Thomas McCarthy. Boston: Beacon Press.

Halperin, Charles J. 1985. *Russian and the Golden Horde.* Bloomington: Indiana University Press.

Heilbron, Johan. 1999. "Towards a Sociology of Translation: Book Translations as a Cultural World System." *European Journal of Social Theory* 2(4): 195–212.

Holz-Mänttäri, Justa. 1984. *Translatorisches Handeln: Theorie und Methode.* Helsinki: Suomalainen tiedeakatemia.

——1986. "Translatorisches Handeln – theoretisch fundierte Berufsprofile." In *Übersetzungswissenschaft – Eine Neuorientierung*, Mary Snell-Hornby (ed.), 348–74. Tübingen: Francke.

Inghilleri, Moira (ed.). 2005. "Bourdieu and the Sociology of Translation and Interpreting." Special issue. *The Translator* 11(2), 125–275.

——2012. *Interpreting Justice.* New York and London: Routledge.

Inghilleri, Moira, and Sue-Ann Harding (eds.). 2010. "Translating Violent Conflict." Special issue. *The Translator* 16(2), 165–336.

Jakobson, Roman. 1959/2012. "On Linguistic Aspects of Translation." In *The Translation Studies Reader*, third edition, Lawrence Venuti (ed.), 126–31. London and New York: Routledge.

Koskinen, Kaisa. 2008. *Translating Institutions: An Ethnographic Study of EU Translation.* Manchester, UK and Kinderhook, NY: St. Jerome.

Kußmaul, Paul. 1986. "Übersetzen als Entscheidungsprozeß. Die Rolle der Fehleranalyse in der Übersetzungsdidaktik." In *Übersetzungswissenschaft – Eine Neuorientierung*, Mary Snell-Hornby (ed.), 206–9. Tübingen: Francke.

Larkosh, Christopher (ed.). 2011. *Re-Engendering Translation: Transcultural Practice, Gender/Sexuality and the Politics of Alterity.* Manchester: St. Jerome.

Linton, Ralph. 1936. *The Study of Man: An Introduction.* New York: Appleton-Century-Crofts, Inc.

Luhmann, Niklas. 1984/1995. *Social Systems.* Trans. by John Bednarz, Jr., with Dirk Baecker. Stanford, CA: Stanford University Press.

Malinowski, Bronislaw. 1944. *A Scientific Theory of Culture and Other Essays.* Chapel Hill: The University of North Carolina Press.

Malmkjær, Kirsten. 2004. "Censorship or Error: Mary Howitt and a Problem in Descriptive TS." In *Translation Studies: Claims, Changes and Challenges. Selected Papers from the EST Congress, Copenhagen 2001*, Gyde Hansen, Kirsten Malmkjær, and Daniel Gile (eds.), 141–55. Amsterdam and Philadelphia: John Benjamins.

Marais, Kobus. 2014. *Translation Theory and Development Studies: A Complexity Theory Approach.* New York and London: Routledge.

Marks, Annie R. 2013. "Participation Framework and Footing Shifts in an Interpreted Academic Meeting." *Journal of Interpretation* 22(1). Available online at http://digitalcommons.unf.edu/cgi/viewcontent.cgi?article=1011&context = joi (accessed May 22, 2014).

McElduff, Siobhán, and Enrica Sciarrino (eds.). 2011. *Complicating the History of Western Translation: The Ancient Mediterranean in Perspective.* Manchester: St. Jerome.

Merkle, Denise, Carol O'Sullivan, Luc van Doorslaer, and Michaela Wolf (eds.). 2010. *The Power of the Pen: Translation & Censorship in Nineteenth-Century Europe.* Berlin: LIT Verlag.

Merton, Robert K. 1967. *On Theoretical Sociology: Five Essays, Old and New.* New York: Free Press; London: Collier-Macmillan Limited.

——1968. *Social Theory and Social Structure.* New York: Free Press.

Metzger, Melanie. 1999. *Sign Language Interpreting: Deconstructing the Myth of Neutrality.* Washington, DC: Gallaudet University Press.

Meylaerts, Reine. 2008. "Translators and (Their) Norms: Towards a Sociological Construction of the Individual." In *Beyond Descriptive Translation Studies. Investigations in Homage to Gideon Toury*, Miriam Shlesinger, Daniel Simeoni, and Anthony Pym (eds.), 91–102. Amsterdam and Philadelphia: John Benjamins.

Milton, John, and Paul Bandia (eds). 2009. *Agents of Translation.* Amsterdam/Philadelphia: John Benjamins.

Morini, Massimiliano. 2006. *Tudor Translation in Theory and Practice.* Aldershot: Ashgate.

Mossop, Brian. 1988. "Translating Institutions: A Missing Factor in Translation Theory." *TTR* 1(2): 65–71.

Nord, Christiane. 1991. "Skopos, Loyalty, and Translational Conventions." *Target* 3(1): 91–109.

——1997. *Translation as a Purposeful Activity: Functionalist Approaches Explained.* Manchester: St. Jerome.

Parsons, Talcott. 1937/1949. *The Structure of Social Action: A Study in Social Theory with Special Reference to a Group of Recent European Writers.* New York: The Free Press; London: Collier-Macmillan Limited.

——1951/1959. *The Social System.* Glencoe, IL: The Free Press.

Parsons, Talcott, and Edward A. Shils (eds.). 1951. *Toward a General Theory of Action.* Cambridge, MA: Harvard University Press.

Petrilli, Susan (ed.). 2003. *Translation Translation.* Amsterdam and New York: Rodopi.

Pym, Anthony. 1998. *Method in Translation History.* Manchester: St. Jerome.

——1997/2012. *On Translator Ethics: Principles for Mediation between Cultures.* Trans. by Heike Walker. Amsterdam and Philadelphia: John Benjamins.

Quah, Chiew Kin. 2006. *Translation and Technology.* Basingstoke: Palgrave Macmillan.

Reiß, Katharina, and Hans J. Vermeer. 1984/2013. *Towards a General Theory of Translational Action: Skopos Theory Explained.* Trans. by Christiane Nord. Manchester: St. Jerome.

Renn, Joachim. 2006. *Übersetzungsverhältnisse. Perspektiven einer pragmatistischen Gesellschaftstheorie.* Weilerswist: Velbrück Wissenschaft.

Robinson, Douglas. 1991. *The Translator's Turn.* Baltimore, MD and London: Johns Hopkins University Press.

——2011. *Translation and the Problem of Sway.* Amsterdam and Philadelphia: John Benjamins.

——1997/2012. *Becoming a Translator.* London and New York: Routledge.

Roy, Cynthia. 2000. *Interpreting as a Discourse Practice.* New York: Oxford University Press.

Santaemilia, José, and Luise von Flotow (eds.). 2011. "Woman and Translation: Geographies, Voices and Identities." Special issue. *MonTI*, 3, 9–470.

Sapiro, Gisèle. 2008a. "Normes de traduction et contraintes sociales." In *Beyond Descriptive Translation Studies: Investigations in Homage to Gideon Toury*, Anthony Pym, Miriam Shlesinger, and Daniel Simeoni (eds.), 199–208. Amsterdam and Philadelphia: John Benjamins.

——2008b. *Translatio. Le marchè de la traduction en France à l'heure de la mondialisation.* Paris: CNRS Editions.

Schleiermacher, Friedrich. 1813/2013. "On the Different Methods of Translating," trans. by Susan Bernofsky. In *The Translation Studies Reader*, 3rd edition, Lawrence Venuti (ed.), 43–63. London and New York: Routledge.

Simeoni, Daniel. 1998. "The Pivotal Status of the Translator's Habitus." *Target* 10(1): 1–39.

Simon, Sherry. 1996. *Gender in Translation: Cultural Identity and the Politics of Transmission.* London and New York: Routledge.

Spurlin, William J. (ed.). 2014. "The Gender and Queer Politics of Translation: Historical, Literary, and Cultural Approaches." Special issue. *Comparative Literature Studies* 51(2), 201–343.

Steiner, George. 1975. *After Babel: Aspects of Language and Translation.* London and New York: Oxford University Press.

Toury, Gideon. 1978. "The Nature and Role of Norms in Literary Translation." In *Literature and Translation: New Perspectives in Literary Studies*, James S. Holmes, José Lambert, and Raymond van den Broeck (eds.), 83–100. Leuven: Acco.

——2012. *Descriptive Translation Studies – and beyond.* Revised edition. Amsterdam and Philadelphia: John Benjamins.

Turner, Jonathan H. 1998. *The Structure of Sociological Theory.* Belmont, CA: Wadsworth.

Tymoczko, Maria. 2002. "Connecting the Two Infinite Orders: Research Methods in Translation Studies." In *Crosscultural Transgressions: Research Models in Translation Studies II. Historical and Ideological Issues*, Theo Hermans (ed.), 9–25. Manchester, UK and Northampton, MA: St. Jerome.

——2006. "Reconceptualizing Translation Theory. Integrating Non-Western Thought about Translation." In *Translating Others*, Theo Hermans (ed.), 13–32. Manchester: St. Jerome.

——2007. *Enlarging Translation, Empowering Translators.* Manchester: St. Jerome.

Tyulenev, Sergey. 2012a. *Applying Luhmann to Translation Studies: Translation in Society.* New York and London: Routledge.

——2012b. *Translation and the Westernization of Eighteenth-Century Russia: A Social-Systemic Perspective.* Berlin: Frank und Timme.

——2012c. "Systemics and Lifeworld of Translation." In *Translation and Philosophy*, Lisa Foran (ed.), 139–55. Bern: Peter Lang.

——2013. "Translating in the Public Sphere: Birth Pangs of a Developing Democracy in Today's Russia." *Southern African Linguistics and Applied Language Studies* 31(4): 469–79.

——2014. *Translation and Society: An Introduction.* London and New York: Routledge.

Tyulenev, Sergey, and van Rooyen, Marlie (eds.). 2013. "Translation in Developmental Contexts." Special issue. *Southern African Linguistics and Applied Language Studies* 31(4), iii–506.

Venuti, Lawrence. 1995. *The Translator's Invisibility: A History of Translation.* New York and London: Routledge.

——2013. *Translation Changes Everything: Theory and Practice.* London and New York: Routledge.

von Flotow, Luise. 1997. *Translation and Gender.* Ottawa: University of Ottawa Press; Manchester: St. Jerome.

Wadensjö, Cecilia. 1998. *Interpreting as Interaction.* London and New York: Longman.

Weber, Max. 1978. *Weber: Selections in Translation.* Ed. by W. G. Runciman. Trans. by Eric Matthews. Cambridge: Cambridge University Press.

White, Julie A. 2014. "Cognitive Spaces: Expanding Participation Framework by Looking at Signed Language Interpreters' Discourse and Conceptual Blending." *The International Journal for Translation & Interpreting Research* 6(1): 144–57.

Wilss, Wolfram. 1977/1982. *The Science of Translation: Problems and Methods.* Tübingen: Gunter Narr Verlag.

Wolf, Michaela. 2006. "The Female State of the Art: Women in the Translation Field." In *Sociocultural Aspects of Translating and Interpreting*, Anthony Pym, Miriam Shlesinger, and Zuzana Jettmarová (eds.), 129–41. Amsterdam and Philadelphia: John Benjamins.

Wolf, Michaela and Alexandra Fukari (eds.). 2007. *Constructing a Sociology of Translation.* Amsterdam and Philadelphia: John Benjamins.

2 Bilingualism and multilingualism

Claudia V. Angelelli

Overview

Bilingualism and multilingualism refer to the phenomenon of two or more languages in contact. Language contact can occur within a person, between persons, or within larger groups (Valdés and Angelelli 2003). Therefore, bi/multilingualism and TIS can be studied at both the individual and the societal level. As an example of the former, we may state that a bilingual person has some degree of proficiency in more than one language (e.g., French and English), and for the latter we can refer to Canada as a bilingual nation. South Africa is a multilingual country. And, in this day and age, if we look at the linguistic diversity evidenced by the co-existence of indigenous, immigrant, and refugee languages in our societies, multilingualism in the world is the norm rather than the exception.

Many researchers in the field today are advocating for a redefinition of bi/multilingualism, away from the traditional concept of bi/multilingualism as the mastery of more than one discrete, standardized language, or linguistic code, to a vision of bi/multilingualism as representing the varied linguistic resources deployed by individuals to negotiate their identity in various social contexts. These resources would include varieties within a "single" language (e.g., registers), as well as non-standard varieties of other languages. This redefinition of multilingualism has brought new attention to the role of non-professional interpreters and translators (Angelelli 2010; Meyer 2012; Baraldi and Gavioli 2012), the "linguistic biographies" of immigrants, migrants, and heritage speakers (Alexander and Busch 2007; Hoff 2013), and the phenomenon of multilingual texts (e.g., Grutman 2006; Hokenson and Munson 2007; Meylaerts 2010a).

Bilingualism and multilingualism are deeply related to translation and interpreting (T&I). One could argue that they are prerequisites. At the same time, the ways in which bilingualism and multilingualism are conceptualized within T&I and other fields of study vary significantly. The intersection between bi/multilingualism and T&I is multifaceted. It is found in the levels of language proficiency of bilinguals, as their bilingualism is used for communicative purposes (as is the case with translators and interpreters), as well as in the degree of languages in contact (e.g., whether neighboring areas/countries that share borders use the same or different languages and thus require more/less use of translation and interpreting). In multilingual societies there is a need to provide access to services for linguistic groups that do not speak the societal language. In such cases, organizations may resort to bilinguals to act as ad hoc translators and interpreters, or they may use the professional services of qualified translators and interpreters (who by definition are also bi/multilingual). While not all bilinguals are translators or interpreters, all professional translators and interpreters are bilinguals.

> The intersection of bi/multilingualism and T&I goes beyond constructs of language proficiency, professionalism or access to services. In both T&I, issues related to bilinguals acting as translators or interpreters have been problematized, especially in diglossic societies.
>
> (Meylaerts 2010a: 228)

In addition to individual bilingualism, societal bi/multilingualism may arise when populations speaking different languages come into contact. Over time, such contact may result in the creation of new languages, such as creoles and pidgins, or it may result in a diglossic situation in which two languages exist side-by-side but are used to accomplish different functions. The language used by monolingual members of the elite group is considered the dominant or societal language, while non-elite monolinguals use the minority language(s) (Niño-Murcia and Rothman 2009). Bilinguals may choose to use a language depending on the context or environment in which they find themselves, as well as on the social value ascribed to each language (Hamers and Blanc 1989/2000). This unique ability is generally considered a valuable asset and allows bilinguals to adapt to distinct situations and identify with diverse linguistic and ethnic groups (Fishman 1991; Niño-Murcia and Rothman 2009).

Within bi/multilingual societies, and especially in border areas, where we see such phenomena as language maintenance and shift (Fishman 1991; García 2011; García and Wei 2014), language policy and planning (Ager 2001) are especially salient. These phenomena may or may not be studied or discussed in conjunction with T&I. For example, educational policy determining the amount of resources allocated to language X or Y could be a discussion in itself, independent from T&I. However, in areas of societal bi/multilingualism, interpreting and translating become more relevant activities insofar as they put the speakers of minority languages in contact with speakers of the dominant language. Without interpreters and translators, monolingual speakers of non-societal languages may be excluded from public discourse and denied access to services (van Dijk 2000; Angelelli 2010), as well as to other cultures and heritages. Bilingualism generally benefits both individuals and societies as it represents a bridge between distinct linguistic groups in our increasingly multicultural world (Fishman 1991; van Dijk 2000).

Theoretical foundations

Current conceptualizations of language differ widely from those of the past. Consequently, so do the conceptualizations of bi/multilingualism. In the mid-1950s languages were discussed as discrete and separate codes, both in relation to individuals and/or societies. We see these earlier constructions of language in discussions of acquisition, measurement, evolution, and displacement (see, for example, Richards and Rogers 2001 for methods of language teaching or Fishman 1991 for discussions on language maintenance and language shift). Current conceptualizations of languages do not view them as discrete systems but as pieces of a whole, as ecological resources (Bialystok 2007). In addition, languages are no longer seen as "belonging" to a particular nation or area. In the era of the "global village," languages are in contact, and borders are fluid. Viewed as resources rather than systems, languages are seen as interconnected rather than separated, and this interconnectivity presents opportunities for creativity, scaffolding, and collaborating at the individual, group, and societal level. As we have moved from the ideology of one language one nation to a concept of bi/multilingualism as representing the diversity of the world in which we live today, there has been a revival of interest in the preservation of all languages of all peoples (indigenous languages, languages resulting from immigration or political refugees, to languages that emerge as a result of code-switching or as new varieties of languages resulting from language contact) accompanied by a rejection of the traditional hierarchy of standard to non-standard linguistic codes.

In addition to languages being viewed as the sum of one's linguistic resources, the notion of languages being interconnected, in movement and flux, has caused us to revisit the conceptualization of communication altogether (Blommaert 2010). Constructs such as linguistic rights (Phillipson 2000), sociolinguistic inequality (Blommaert 2010), development or underdevelopment of linguistic repertoires (Valdés and Geofrion-Vinci 1998), linguistic competence and heritage speakers have acquired new meaning in our multilingual global village.

In the area of individual bilingualism, the seminal work of Valdés and Figueroa (1994) outlines a typology of bilinguals that has helped researchers understand the variability of individual bilingualism. Perhaps one of the most important contributions of this typology (ibid: 11) is the notion that languages are not static but change throughout the life of an individual, allowing bilingualism to be discussed across a continuum (age, life circumstances, context, etc.) rather than as a monolithic construct. The differentiation between elective and circumstantial bilingualism has also been a major contribution. An elective bilingual is one who chooses to learn another language, typically through language instruction or by entering a minority language community. Unlike elective bilinguals, circumstantial bilinguals are not given a choice to learn a second language. Due to life circumstances (generally beyond their control), these individuals must learn the societal or dominant language in order to survive (Valdés and Figueroa 1994: 12).

Individual bilinguals can also be classified according to the age at which they acquired their second language and the degree of their proficiency in the second language. Early, late, simultaneous, and sequential are terms that denote the stage in life at which the second language was acquired. Incipient, receptive, and productive, as well as ambilingual or equilingual, are classifications indicating level of proficiency (Valdés and Figueroa 1994: 11). All bilinguals and multilinguals, regardless of classification, are able to select and utilize the linguistic resources of those language systems in which they are proficient for a variety of purposes, something that, as stated before, translators and interpreters cannot do as they are bound by their work to use only one linguistic system.

Possession of a high level of proficiency (native or native-like) in both languages is one prerequisite for candidates applying to interpreter programs (Valdés and Angelelli 2003). However, assessing language proficiency presents challenges as there is no exact definition of native speaker ability. Moreover, the concept of language proficiency is complex and multifaceted, encompassing not only vocabulary, grammar, and pronunciation (Hamers and Blanc 1989/2000; Edwards 2012) but also sociocultural ability, or an understanding of the pragmatics of the language, among other sub-components. Moreover, when determining a bilingual's proficiency level, rather than test the individual's two languages against each another, each language is measured in terms of monolingual standards. In order to paint an accurate representation of a bilingual's linguistic proficiency, however, multiple methods must be used (Hamers and Blanc 1989/2000). In addition, bilinguals come from a variety of backgrounds and experiences. These differences may have an effect on the educational learning process of the individuals and may result in different learning outcomes (Angelelli 2010). This is of particular relevance when discussing T&I pedagogies (see Chapter 8, "Translation and interpreting pedagogy") or when assessing bilingual individuals who apply to T&I programs or claim language expertise when applying for a job.

Evolution of the topic in TIS

Bi/multilingualism is central to TIS. There has been, however, limited interaction between researchers in bi/multilingualism and Translation and Interpreting Studies (c.f. Valdés and Angelelli 2003). The linguistic giftedness or ability of bilingual youths and their potential to develop T&I skills have, however, attracted the attention of a few T&I scholars (e.g., Harris 1977, 1980; Toury 1995; Angelelli 2010). Recent studies (Bialystok 2007) have focused on the cognitive advantages of bilingualism in children, which include greater metalinguistic awareness. Research on educational linguistics, language, race and ethnicity, migration, and child T&I has expanded this focus by studying bilingualism from a different perspective (Valdés et. al 2000), exploring different types of linguistic ability, such as that possessed by some bilingual youngsters who can broker communication between family/friends and speakers of societal languages. Researchers now study the performance of these bilinguals as translators/interpreters, as well as their perceptions of their own bilingualism (Angelelli in press; Borrero 2006; Edwards 2012).

Some of the other topics related to bi/multilingualism currently being studied include research on young immigrant children/adolescents who serve as de facto ad hoc interpreters for their family and community. These young people develop the ability to speak and interpret using more than one language system (Zentella 1997; Valdés et. al 2000; Orellana and Reynolds 2008; Angelelli 2010). The use of minority languages has been discouraged in different countries in different historical periods, encouraging cultural and linguistic assimilation, and the use of one national language (Grosjean 1982; Valdés 1995; Valdés et. al 2000; Di Tullio 2003). This, in turn, devalues the importance of multilingual skills, leading to neglect of the heritage language and loss of proficiency.

While discussing individual bilingualism and T&I ability, one controversial discussion derived from the notion of a "born translator/interpreter." In the late seventies, some scholars posited that bilinguals possess, to some degree, however limited it may be, an innate ability to interpret or translate from one language to another (Harris 1977, 1978, 1980, 1992; Harris and Sherwood, 1978; Isham and Lane 1994), referred to by Harris as "natural" translators or interpreters. This was evident in the work that looked at bilingual children as language and cultural ambassadors (Harris 1977, 1978, 1980). This work was partly anecdotal and partly limited to a few observations. Empirical research findings conducted several years later, however, were unequivocal in debunking the myth of the born, or natural, translator/interpreter. While studying bilingual Latinos in the US, for example, Valdés, Chavez, and Angelelli (2000) and Valdés et al. (2003) proved that translation and interpreting competence is not a byproduct of bilingualism and that translators and interpreters, or language brokers (Angelelli 2010; Antonini 2010; Baraldi and Gavioli 2012), differ from "ordinary" bilinguals in that they possess a unique set of skills. Bilinguals are able to choose which language system to utilize depending on the interlocutors with whom they are communicating, as well as the context of the communicative event. They can also code-switch with varying degrees of success and show alignment with different linguistic communities. Extraordinary bilinguals acting as language brokers do not choose one language over another or code-switch, rather they mediate communication between monolingual speakers (Valdés and Angelelli 2003). Monolingual speakers of minority languages, specifically immigrants who do not learn the dominant or societal language and remain monolingual, depend on interpreters and translators in order to function within their new society, gain access to public services, and participate in public discourse (Grosjean 1982; Valero Garcés and Gauthier Blasi 2010).

Traditionally, interpreters have been circumstantial bilinguals belonging to minority language speaking groups. There is, however, not much awareness about (or interest in) the type of bilingualism possessed by these translators/

interpreters. Because of the narrow definition of language proficiency generally used in T&I (as the mastery of at least two discrete standardized languages rather than as a fluid construct that may continue to evolve, improving or diminishing), proficiency is assumed rather than problematized. Interpreting Studies tends to focus on early elective bilinguals with high native-like proficiency and mastery of multiple registers as the most likely candidates for successful professional (conference) interpreters. These skills are acquired over long periods of time through experiences and interactions occurring in real-life situations. Nevertheless, it has been shown that, because bilingualism is not static, it is possible for late elective bilinguals to develop the skills necessary to obtain near-native-like proficiency and become successful professional interpreters through interpreter and language instructional programs (Fishman 1991; Valdés and Figueroa 1994; Valdés and Angelelli 2003; Swender, Conrad, and Vicars 2012)

Some researchers in TIS continue to adhere to a narrow definition of bilingualism as native speaker proficiency in two discrete standard languages (almost an ambilingual in the typology of Valdés and Figueroa 1994: 11) for the purpose of deciding who is or should become a translator/interpreter. The construct of native speaker, however, has been discussed and problematized within the field of applied linguistics, specifically in second language acquisition and research on heritage speakers (see Davies 2003 and Hulstijn 2011, among others). A broader conceptualization of bilingualism sees it as a continuum (Valdés and Figueroa 1994). This view of bilingualism takes into account the intersection of language development and social factors (such as age, years of exposure to second language), as well as the communicative context (shaped by the content of the exchange, the setting, the interlocutors, etc.). Researchers working with non-professional translators and interpreters (e.g., Angelelli 2010; Antonini 2010; Baraldi and Gavioli 2012; Meyer 2012) have looked at the potential of bilingual individuals to successfully broker communication even with non-standard language.

When circumstantial bilinguals enter a T&I classroom, they typically conceptualize their role as that of "helping" their linguistic minority. Many of them begin brokering communication informally as children (Malakoff and Hakuta 1991; Valdés, Chavez and Angelelli 2000; Borrero 2006; Antonini 2010). Alternatively, most of the students populating conference interpreting programs are elective bilinguals. Conference interpreters are exceptional bilinguals who possess the necessary multilingual skills to act as professional interpreters. They are typically highly educated either simultaneous sequential bilinguals (more often than not belonging to the privileged classes who have lived abroad) or simultaneous bilinguals who have become circumstantial bilinguals due to migration (Valdés and Angelelli 2003). They typically engage in both consecutive and simultaneous interpreting.

Because simultaneous interpreting involves the concurrent activation of several cognitive processes, it is considered one of the most difficult language tasks to execute. While performing an interpreting task, the interpreter must be able to activate one language system in production while inhibiting the other (de Groot and Christoffels 2006; Christoffels, de Groot, and Kroll 2006). Individuals who are able to switch seamlessly from one language to another possess a high level of cognitive control. Many bilinguals and multilinguals show cognitive advantages over monolinguals, and possess distinct neural function and structure (Christoffels, Kroll, and Bajo 2013).

Key studies

Alexander and Busch's *Literacy and Linguistic Diversity in a Global Perspective: An Intercultural Exchange with African Countries* (2007) is the result of a unique transcontinental project between Europe and Africa. The volume presents a collection of papers that explores the relationship of linguistic and cultural diversity, individual empowerment, and economic sustainability and social cohesion. Through the lens of a globalized world, the papers explore the preservation of Africa's multilingualism in the service of the sustainable development of the continent. Blackledge and Creese's *Multilingualism. A Critical Perspective* (2010) presents a compilation of critical studies on the use of multiple languages in complementary schools in Britain. Focusing on classroom linguistic practices in Gujarati, Bengali, Chinese, and Turkish complementary schools, the authors explore questions of multilingual youngsters' use of language, their perceptions and negotiations of identity, and their reactions to phenomena such as language maintenance and language shift.

Looking at the use of multiple languages in professional settings, Tribe and Raval's *Working with Interpreters in Mental Health* (2002) is the first attempt to explore multilingual interpreter-mediated clinical work in Great Britain, where many service users are primarily speakers of languages other than English. Focusing on heritage languages, Valdés, Fishman, Chavez, and Perez (2006) shed light on the attitudes toward Spanish on the part of professionals who are heritage speakers. In addition, this study investigates practices and ideologies surrounding the teaching and learning of Spanish as a heritage language in secondary and post-secondary institutions. The study makes theoretical, pedagogical, and practical contributions to the maintenance, teaching, and learning of heritage languages in order to preserve linguistic diversity.

Valdés and Angelelli's "Interpreters, Interpreting and the Study of Bilingualism" (2003) examines the intersection of bilingualism and Interpreting Studies, while Weber and Horner (2012) adopt a critical and social perspective to present discussions on the basic areas of multilingualism (e.g., language contact and variation, language as a social construct, language and identity).

New directions

Current trends in Translation and Interpreting Studies continue to focus on various aspects of these phenomena, including cognitive and social bi/multilingualism.

At present there is a growing interest in how the use of English as a foreign or second language impacts interpreters' performance (Albl-Mikasa 2013). Speakers who normally uttered speeches in their own language (and used interpreters in their language combination and then on relay) are increasingly using English, thus minimizing language combinations for interpreting. This means interpreters are increasingly asked to work with speakers who communicate through their second or third language. In addition, the last two decades have witnessed the emergence of such "controversial" issues as child language brokers, ad hoc interpreters/translators performing in critical situations (see In-Zone Project in the References), and crowdsourcing, which have called into question more traditional conceptualizations of translation and interpreting. While earlier studies of bi/multilingualism were characterized by a focus on imbalances, more current resources focus on the variety of linguistic resources employed by every individual to negotiate social identities through language. Perceptions of identity, as well as distinctions between quality of professional and non-professional interpreters (Valdés and Angelelli 2003; Green et al. 2005; Rosenberg, Seller, and Leanza 2008; Niño-Murcia and Rothman 2009; Angelelli 2010), are examples of those.

So far the study of bi/multilingualism and T&I has approached the topic through a single disciplinary lens (e.g., linguistic, psycholinguistic, or sociolinguistic). The challenge for the future would be to address complex questions using an interdisciplinary lens. In this way we can begin to merge theoretical areas of TIS that so far have been fragmented or discussed in isolation.

References

Ager, Dennis. 2001. *Motivation in Language Planning and Language Policy*. Clevedon: Multilingual Matters Ltd.

Albl-Mikasa, Michaela. 2013. "EFL Speakers' Restricted Power of Expression. Implications for Interpreters' Processing." *Translation and Interpreting Studies* 8(2): 191–210.

Alexander, Neville, and Brigitta Busch (eds.). 2007. *Literacy and Linguistic Diversity in a Global Perspective: An Intercultural Exchange with African Countries*. Strasbourg: Council of Europe Publishing.

Angelelli, Claudia V. 2010. "A Professional Ideology in the Making: Bilingual Youngsters Interpreting for Their Communities and the Notion of (No) Choice." *Translation and Interpreting Studies* 5(1): 94–108.

Angelelli, Claudia V. (in press). "Looking Back: A Study on (Non-professional) Family Interpreters' Perceptions about Their Role." *Non-professional Translators and Interpreters*, R. Antonini, I. Torresi, L. Cirillo, and L. Rossato Oggetto (eds.). Amsterdam/Philadelphia: John Benjamins.

Antonini, Rachele. 2010. "The Study of Child Language Brokers: Past, Current and Emerging Research." *MediAzioni* 10 (special issue): 1–23. Available online at http://mediazioni.sitlec.unibo.it (accessed October 8, 2014).

Baraldi, Claudio, and Laura Gavioli. 2012. *Coordinating Participation in Dialogue Interpreting*. Amsterdam and Philadelphia: John Benjamins.

Bialystok, Helen. 2007. "Cognitive Effects of Bilingualism. How Linguistic Experience Leads to Cognitive Change." *The International Journal of Bilingual Education and Bilingualism* 10(3): 201–23.

Blackledge, Adrian and Creese (2010), Angela *Multilingualism: A Critical Perspective*. London/New York: Continuum International Publishing Group.

Blommaert, Jan. 2010. *The Sociolinguistics of Globalization*. Cambridge: Cambridge University Press.

Borrero, Noah. 2006. "Nurturing Students' Strengths: The Impact of a School-Based Student Interpreter Program on Latino/a Students' Reading Comprehension and English Language Development." *Urban Education* 46(4): 663–88.

Christoffels, Ingrid K., Annette M. B. de Groot, and Judith F. Kroll. 2006. "Memory and Language Skills in Simultaneous Interpreters: The Role of Expertise and Language Proficiency." *The Journal of Memory and Language* 54(3): 324–45.

Christoffels, Ingrid K., Judith F. Kroll and María Teresa Bajo. 2013. "Introduction to Bilingualism and Cognitive Control." *Frontiers in Psychology* 4: 199–201.

Davies, Alan. 2003. *The Native Speaker: Myth and Reality*. Clevedon: Multilingual Matters.

de Groot, Annette M. B. and Ingrid K. Christoffels. 2006. "Language Control in Bilinguals: Monolingual Tasks and Simultaneous Interpreting." *Bilingualism: Language and Cognition* 9(2): 189–201.

Di Tullio, Angela L. 2003. *Políticas lingüísticas e inmigración: el caso de Argentina*. Buenos Aires: Eudeba.

Edwards, John. 2012. "Bilingualism and Multilingualism: Some Central Concepts." In *The Handbook of Bilingualism and Multilingualism*, Tej K. Bhatia and William C. Ritchie (eds.), 5–25. Chichester and Malden, MA: Wiley-Blackwell.

Fishman, Joshua A. 1991. *Reversing Language Shift: Theoretical and Empirical Foundations of Assistance to Threatened Languages*. Clevedon and Philadelphia: Multilingual Matters.

García, Ofelia. 2011. *Bilingual Education in the 21st Century: A Global Perspective*. Malden, MA: Wiley-Blackwell.

García, Ofelia, and Wei, Li. 2014. *Translanguaging: Language, Bilingualism and Education*. London and New York: Palgrave MacMillan.

Green, Judith, Caroline Free, Vanita Bhavnani, and Tony Newman. 2005. "Translators and Mediators: Bilingual Young People's Accounts of Their Interpreting Work." *Health Care, Social Science & Medicine* 60(9): 2097–110.

Grosjean, François. 1982. *Life with Two Languages: An Introduction to Bilingualism*. Cambridge, MA: Harvard University Press.

Grutman, Rainier. 2006. "Refraction and Recognition. Literary Multilingualism in Translation." *Target* 18(1): 17–47.

Hamers, Josiane F. and Michel Blanc. 1989/2000. *Bilinguality and Bilingualism*. Cambridge and New York: Cambridge University Press.

Harris, Brian. 1977. "The Importance of Natural Translation." *Working Papers on Bilingualism* 12: 96–116.

——1978. "The Difference between Natural and Professional Translation." *Canadian Modern Language Review* 34: 417–27.

——1980. "How a Three-year-old Translates." In *Patterns of Bilingualism*, Evangelos A. Afrendas (ed.), 370–93. Singapore: Regional English Language Centre (RELC).

——1992. "Natural Translation: A Reply to Hans P. Krings." *Target* 4(1): 97–103.

Harris, Brian, and Sheila Sherwood. 1978. "Translating as an Innate Skill." In *Language Interpretation and Communication*, David Gerver and H. Wallace Sinaiko (eds.), 155–70. New York: Plenum Press.
Hoff, Erika. 2013. "Interpreting the Early Language Trajectories of Children from Low-SES and Language Minority Homes: Implications for Closing Achievement Gaps." *Developmental Psychology* 49(1): 4–14
Hokenson, Jan Walsh, and Marcella Munson. 2007. *The Bilingual Text: History and Theory of Literary Self-translation*. Manchester: St. Jerome.
Hulstijn, Jan. 2011. "Language Proficiency in Native and Non-native Speakers: An Agenda for Research and Suggestions for Second-language Assessment." *Language Assessment Quarterly* 8(3): 229–49.
In-Zone Project: A Humanitarian Initiative of the Interpreting Department, University of Geneva. Available online at http://inzone.fti.unige.ch (accessed January 7, 2015).
Isham, William, and Harlan Lane. 1994. A Common Conceptual Code in Bilinguals: Evidence from Simultaneous Interpretation." *Sign Language Studies* 85(1): 291–317.
Malakoff, Marguerite and Kenji Hakuta. (1991). "Translation Skills and Metalinguistic Awareness in Bilinguals." In *Language and Processing in Bilingual Children*, Ellen Bialystok (ed.), 141–66. Cambridge: Cambridge University Press.
Meyer, Bernd. 2012. "Ad-hoc Interpreting for Partially Language-proficient Patients. Participation in Multilingual Constellations." In *Coordinating Participation in Dialogue Interpreting*, Claudio Baraldi and Laura Gavioli (eds.), 99–114. Amsterdam and Philadelphia: John Benjamins.
Meylaerts, Reine. 2010. "Multilingualism and Translation." In *Handbook of Translation Studies*, volume 1, Yves Gambier and Luc van Doorslaer (eds.), 227–30. Amsterdam and Philadelphia: John Benjamins.
Niño-Murcia, Mercedes, and Jason Rothman. 2009. *Bilingualism and Identity: Spanish at the Crossroads with Other Languages*. Amsterdam and Philadelphia: John Benjamins.
Orellana, Marjorie Faulstich and Jennifer F. Reynolds. 2008. "Cultural Modeling: Leveraging Bilingual Skills for School Paraphrasing Tasks." *Reading Research Quarterly* 43(1): 48–65.
Phillipson, Robert (ed.). 2000. *Rights to Language – Equity, Power and Education*. London and Mahwah, NJ: Lawrence Erlbaum Associates.
Richards, Jack, and Theodore Rogers. 2001. *Approaches and Methods in Language Teaching*. Cambridge: Cambridge University Press.
Rosenberg, Ellen, Robbyn Seller, and Yvan Leanza. 2008. "Through Interpreters' Eyes: Comparing Roles of Professional and Family Interpreters." *Patient Education and Counseling* 70(1): 87–93.
Swender, Elvira, Daniel J. Conrad, and Robert Vicars. 2012. *ACTFL Proficiency Guidelines*. Alexandria, VA: ACTFL, Inc.
Tribe, Rachel, and Hitesh Raval (eds.). 2002. *Working with Interpreters in Mental Health*. Hove and New York: Brunner-Routledge.
Toury, Gideon. 1995. "A Bilingual Speaker Becomes a Translator: A Tentative Developmental Model." In *Descriptive Translation Studies and Beyond*, Gideon Toury (ed.), 241–58. Amsterdam and Philadelphia: John Benjamins.
Valdés, Guadalupe. 1995. "Bilingües y bilingüismo en los Estados Unidos: la política lingüística en una época antiinmigrante." *Alteridades* 5(10): 25–42.
Valdés, Guadalupe, and Claudia Angelelli. 2003. "Interpreters, Interpreting, and the Study of Bilingualism." *The Annual Review of Applied Linguistics* 23: 58–78.

Valdés, Guadalupe, and Richard A. Figueroa. 1994. *Bilingualism and Testing: A Special Case of Bias*. Norwood, NJ: Ablex.

Valdés, Guadalupe, and Michelle Geofrion-Vinci. 1998. "Chicano Spanish: The Problem of the "Underdeveloped" Code in Bilingual Repertoires." *Modern Language Journal* 82.4: 473–501.

Valdés, Guadalupe, Christina Chavez, and Claudia V. Angelelli. 2000. "Bilingualism from Another Perspective: The Case of Young Interpreters from Immigrant Communities." In *Research on Spanish in the United States. Linguistic Issues and Challenges*, Ana Roca (ed.), Chapter 2 (42–81). Somerville, MA: Cascadilla Press.

Valdés, Guadalupe, Christina Chávez, Claudia Angelelli, Kerry Enright, Dania Garcia, and Marisela González. 2003. "The Study of Young Interpreters: Methods, Materials, and Analytic Challenges." In *Expanding Definitions of Giftedness. The Case of Young Interpreters from Immigrant Communities*, Guadalupe Valdés (ed.), 99–118. Mahwah, NJ: Lawrence Erlbaum Associates, Inc.

Valdés, Guadalupe, Joshua Fishman, Rebeca Chavez, and William Perez. 2006. *Developing Minority Language Resources. The Case of Spanish in California*. Clevendon: Multilingual Matters.

Valero Garcés, Carmen, and Laura Gauthier Blasi. 2010. "Bordieu y la traducción e interpretación en los servicios públicos: hacia una teoría social." *MonTI* 2: 97–117.

van Dijk, Teun A. 2000. "Discourse and Access." In *Rights to Language: Equity, Power and Education*, Robert Phillipson (ed.), 73–78. New York: Lawrence Earlbaum Associates.

Weber, Jean Jacques, and Kristine Horner. 2012. *Introducing Multilingualism. A Social Approach*. Abingdon: Routledge.

Zentella, Ana Celia. 1997. *Growing Up Bilingual: Puerto Rican Children in New York*. Malden, MA: Blackwell.

3 Cognitive processes

Erik Angelone, Maureen Ehrensberger-Dow, and Gary Massey

Overview

The shift in interest from the product as the primary object of study in T&I (i.e., a focus on target texts and their relation to source texts) to the producer (i.e., a focus on cognitive processes) can be dated to the early 1980s. Holmes (1972/ 2004: 185) anticipated this shift by including process-oriented research in his much-cited map, placing it within the descriptive branch of Translation Studies and suggesting that this area might come to be known as "translation psychology or psycho-translation studies." Since then, process research has become almost synonymous with cognitive approaches to T&I. Toury's distinction between translation acts (1995, 2012; see also Chesterman 2013), or cognitive processes, and events, or *socially situated* processes, however, underscores the fact that cognitive processes are always embedded in a context. Perhaps more apparent in interpreting, which has long been identified as a socially situated activity (e.g., Berk-Seligson 1990; Wadensjö 1998; Angelelli 2004), the interaction between processes and contexts has developed into a vibrant area of research in T&I.

Theoretical foundations

Attempts by certain psychologists in the 1950s to explain language acquisition and use in behaviorist terms ushered in a cognitive turn in linguistics with far-reaching consequences for various disciplines, including T&I. The notions of competence and performance, introduced to differentiate knowledge of one's native language from use of it (Chomsky 1965), were broadened to account for knowledge structures underlying all types of communication (e.g., Hymes 1972; Canale and Swain 1981), including translation. Competence models of varying degrees of complexity have been proposed in T&I to account for the differences between translators and bilinguals (e.g., Cao 1996; Kalina 2000; PACTE 2000, 2003; Colina 2003), and expertise studies have provided insights into how translators and interpreters become "experts" in their field (e.g., Smith and Ericsson 1991; Ericsson 1996, 2006; Ivanova 1999; Moser-Mercer et al. 2000; Shreve 2006).

Models of the mental lexicon, although initially monolingual, soon encompassed bilingual processing, and attempts were made to explain lexical decision-making (e.g., Levelt 1983; de Bot 1992; de Groot 1997; de Groot and Kroll 1997; Paradis 1997, 2004) along the lines suggested by Broadbent's analogy of cognitive processing as a sequence of information-processing operations (1958). These were developed further into psycholinguistic models of comprehension and production, with T&I represented as flows of bilingual information- processing and decision nodes (e.g., Gile 1995; Krings 1986; Bell 1991). Theorizing about human memory helped explain difficulties in processing linguistic information in terms of working memory constraints (e.g., Baddeley and Hitch 1974). In addition, the distinction between declarative memory, comprising semantic and episodic memory, and procedural memory, involving motor skills, has been very useful in explaining the complexities and routine aspects of T&I activities.

Theory building about the cognitive processes involved in translation and interpreting has drawn on research into bilingualism (e.g., Malakoff and Hakuta 1991; Bialystok 1992; Grosjean 1997), as well as language comprehension and production. The cognitive process of understanding spoken or written texts can be understood as the building of a mental model of the propositional content (e.g., van Dijk and Kintsch 1983). Relevance theory (Sperber and Wilson 1986, 1995; Gutt 1991) has been used to explain translation as interpretative language use, guided by human inferential processes. More recently, notions from cognitive linguistics have helped us to understand translation and interpreting as mediating processes between conceptual worlds (e.g., Rojo and Ibarretxe-Antuñano 2013) and have fed into the development of cognitive translatology, which, alongside its commitment to empirical enquiry, embraces embodied, situated, and/or distributed cognition (e.g., Muñoz Martín 2010a, 2010b, 2013; Risku 2010).

Evolution of the topic in TIS

Interest in cognitive processes arose early in the area of conference interpreting, probably because of the high memory demands it imposes. One of the first attempts to describe the black box, the *théorie du sens*, later known as the *Interpretive Approach* (Seleskovitch 1968; Seleskovitch and Lederer 1984), divided the interpreting process into three interrelated phases: understanding, deverbalization, and re-expression. The first phase was assumed to involve not merely linguistic decoding but also cognitive inputs of encyclopedic and contextual knowledge, generating a "sense" on which the second phase, deverbalization, was based. The third phase, re-expression, was considered to be a process similar to monolingual language production, deriving directly from a non-verbal level of cognition. The view of an interpreter as an information-processing system prompted research into memory capacity and cognitive sub-skills, such as anticipation and inferencing, and into cognitive processing models (e.g., Moser-Mercer 1997/2002, 2000). Cognitively oriented research into conference interpreting also focused on the strategies interpreters seem to employ to cope with memory and processing limitations, such as generalizing, chunking, and omission (e.g., Kohn and Kalina 1996). Parallel attempts to describe the translation process drew on models of artificial intelligence, with decision-making flows indicating which strategies were used when problems were encountered (Krings 1986; Lörscher 1991). Seen from this perspective, translation could be considered a decision-making activity involving declarative and procedural knowledge, which could be broken down into the following stages: identifying problems, clarifying problems, accessing relevant information, solving problems, choosing solutions, and evaluating solutions (Wilss 1996).

Since translation and interpreting are multitask activities involving two languages, researchers have tried to break down the process in order to examine each step in detail. Psycholinguistic models represented the receptive stages of the translation process as top-down decoding or source-text (ST) analysis through visual word recognition, loops of syntactic parsing, and lexical retrieval through semantic and pragmatic processing, and target text (TT) production as bottom-up encoding or synthesis through similar levels and loops (e.g., Bell 1991; Gile 1995). In order to understand better the differences between the two activities, parallels have been drawn with reading and listening research (e.g., Danks and Griffin 1997). For example, the first steps of the process have been assumed to involve a linguistic analysis of the ST/ spoken input in order to build up a mental model of the content, with domain knowledge and metacognitive considerations of text function and audience playing an important role in comprehending the ST.

To gain information about how translators and interpreters approach their tasks and how they deal with problems, post-task interviews and retrospective commentaries have been used. These techniques, however, are limited by the constraints of selective and working memory and, like all self-report methods, may result in recitations of ideal procedures rather than actual self-reflection. An alternative window onto the black box of the translator's mind is offered by concurrent verbalization (also known as think-aloud). This technique was first used over a century ago (cf. Camps 2003; Göpferich 2008) and experienced a revival with the cognitive turn. The oral mode of data elicitation makes it unsuitable for investigating simultaneous interpreting, but it was quickly taken up as a method of choice by many researchers interested in the cognitive processes involved in translation (e.g., Krings 1986; Jääskeläinen 1999; Englund Dimitrova 2005). Ericsson and Simon's review of psychological studies (1984/1993) suggests that concurrent verbalization can yield valid data about sequences of thoughts and problem-solving processes if participants are asked to verbalize the contents of their working memory during a task, making it a significant advance over examinations of text products or observations of the process. Thinking aloud while translating, however, is not without its limitations as a research technique insofar as it may affect components of the process under investigation, such as lexical decision-making (cf. Jääskeläinen

2000) or revision (cf. Krings 2001), and is generally believed to slow down the process (cf. Jakobsen 2003; Ehrensberger-Dow and Künzli 2010). Used on its own, it cannot be linked directly to a problem the translator is dealing with at any particular time unless the verbalization includes enough of the ST or TT to make the location in the process clear. Of more concern is that thinking aloud seems to interfere with the process itself (known as "reactivity"; cf. Leow and Morgan-Short 2004), especially with professional translators (Jakobsen 2002: 203). One reason for this could be that more aspects of a professional's processes are internalized and automatized, and so bringing them to the surface by verbalizing them requires cognitive resources that would otherwise be employed in problem solving.

As computers became more common in the translation workplace, logging keystrokes and mouse movements and/or recording all activities on the computer screen made it possible to monitor the translation process more accurately than by simply observing translators or interviewing them afterward. In combination with concurrent verbalization, keylogging programs and screen recording software provide more precise reconstructions of problem-solving processes as they make possible the examination of pauses, deletions, insertions, and other revisions around predicted problems or "rich" points (cf. PACTE 2005). Moreover, the interference effects produced by concurrent verbalization and the memory decay limitations of many retrospective techniques can be circumvented by using the replay feature of logging and screen recording software to obtain self-report information (cf. Hansen 2006). Recording in the background as the translator translates, computer logging is non-invasive; the recordings can then be immediately played back to the translator, who comments on the translation as it unfolds. The metacognitive data elicited by these stimulated-recall retrospective commentaries can provide insights into the translators' underlying cognitive processes.

By combining computer logging techniques with verbal elicitation, researchers have identified and examined in detail various phases of the translation process. Alternatively termed preliminary (Krings 1986), orientation (Jakobsen 2002), planning (Englund Dimitrova 2005), or pre-drafting (Mossop 2007), the first phase involves reading the ST or segments of it, analyzing it, and doing any research necessary to aid comprehension. Although students are often taught to read carefully and analyze an ST before attempting to translate it, professionals seem to vary the length of the orientation phase and the number of cognitive activities performed during it, depending on the domain, the genre, the tools used, and their personal working style (cf. Alves and Liparini Campos 2009; Carl et al. 2011; Ehrensberger-Dow and Massey 2013). The orientation phase of some professionals consists of little more than glancing over the text; the reading, analysis, and research activities are incorporated into the next phase.

Once the first character of the TT is typed, the second phase of the process begins. The production of the TT draft has been called the main (Krings 1986), drafting (Jakobsen 2002; Mossop 2007), or text generation (Englund Dimitrova

2005) phase of the translation process. Rather than simply writing what has been previously formulated in the mind of the translator, as suggested in some psycholinguistic models of the translation process, the activities during this phase indicate that it comprises a complex recursive process of reading, comprehension, analysis, research, text production, reformulation, revision, rereading, and checking the emerging TT.

Although it can be difficult to determine precisely when the second phase of the process ends and the third phase begins, one definition that has proven useful is the point at which the last punctuation mark of the last sentence is typed. The follow-up (Krings 1986), revision (Jakobsen 2002; Englund Dimitrova 2005), or post-drafting (Mossop 2007) phase of the translation process has also been termed "self-revision" to distinguish it from revision done by someone else (which has been termed "other" revision by Mossop 2007). In Englund Dimitrova's study (2005), self-revision in the third phase was shown to be important in moving away from literal solutions produced in the previous phase (confirmed in a study by Pavlović and Antunović 2013). Researchers have also explored the cognitive processes involved in revising other people's translations (e.g., Künzli 2007).

Many investigations of the cognitive processes involved in translation compare students to professionals, based on the assumption that students have not yet developed translation competence whereas professionals have. Translation competence has been defined in various ways, from Pym's minimalist definition (2003: 489)—the ability to select one viable TT from a series, quickly and with justified confidence—to Shreve's inclusion of it as "a specialized form of communicative competence" (1997: 120). In Kiraly's model of the translator's mental space (1995: 99–109), the boxes, decision nodes, and unidirectional arrows of the earlier psycholinguistic models are replaced by a more interactional view of internal and external resources in combination with relatively uncontrolled and controlled processes. Interaction, represented by bidirectional arrows, has also been included in the PACTE group's holistic model of translation competence (2003: 60), which comprises various sub-competences or components: the bilingual sub-competence, the extra-linguistic sub-competence, the translation-knowledge sub-competence, the instrumental sub-competence, the strategic sub-competence, and psycho-physiological components. The model has formed the basis for much recent research into the cognitive processes involved in translation and was adapted by Göpferich (2008, 2009, 2013) for her own longitudinal study investigating the development of translation competence.

Parallel developments in Interpreting Studies culminated in Kalina (2000), which described the competences required for professional interpreters in similar terms. In addition to excellent linguistic skills and specialized domain knowledge, procedural knowledge about interpreting and strategic processing are necessary. The real-time nature of most interpreting tasks requires TT production/output to occur almost simultaneously with comprehension of ST input. The unique demands that this places on cognitive processing have been captured in so-called effort models (cf. Gile 1995, 2009; Seeber 2011, 2013), based on the assumption that there is a limit to an individual's cognitive resources at any particular point in time. With the increasing demands and time pressure involved with professional translation, such models are being re-examined by translation process researchers as well. The concept of "mental load" proposed by Muñoz Martín (2012) is an example of how translation and interpreting process research might be reconverging.

Key studies

One of the most widely cited and influential studies on cognitive processes dates back to the infancy of translation process research, when Krings conducted a think-aloud study of student problem solving (1986). Using color-coding of text to reflect different processes in conjunction with protocols of articulated thoughts, Krings' research was the first of its kind to link the process with the product in defining and empirically describing problems and subsequent problem-solving behavior. His research ushered in a decade of empirical studies on cognitive processes in translation using think-aloud protocols (TAPs, cf. Jääskeläinen 2002). In the mid-1990s, keystroke logging was introduced to the research arena as a tool for capturing process data. Along with multiple options for documenting cognitive processes came a series of studies dedicated to exploring potential impacts of the research tools and techniques themselves. Jakobsen (2003) discovered that having translators think aloud concurrently with task completion results in a reduction in translation speed and requires translators to process texts in smaller segments. In other words, translators were exhibiting tendencies that they would not otherwise exhibit while translating texts. This study was by no means intended as a call to move away from TAPs but rather to draw attention to the fact that different cognitive aspects of translation call for different analytic mechanisms.

Alves' 2003 volume, *Triangulating Translation*, introduced what is now widely regarded as a best practice in translation process research, namely exploring phenomena and eliciting data through multiple, combined methods, including (but not limited to) TAPs, keystroke logging, concurrent or retrospective summaries, eye-tracking, and screen recording. It is in this current era of triangulation that we have seen a series of breakthrough discoveries in such domains as attention, time and resource allocation, segmenting, variation among students, novices, professionals, and experts, and human-computer interaction.

In recent years, research on the allocation of cognitive resources has often overlapped with comparative research on the behaviors and tendencies of various populations, including students, novices, professionals, and experts. For example, in a study on allocation of effort across the three fundamental phases of translation—orientation, drafting, and revision—Jakobsen (2002) found that experts tend to demonstrate balanced cognitive rhythms, whereas the transition rhythms of novices are much more erratic. As a possible explanation, several studies have found empirical evidence that experts exhibit higher levels of metacognition, implying greater efficacy when critically reflecting on and monitoring their own performance (Alves and Gonçalves 2003; Hansen 2003: 26; Jääskeläinen 2010). In a follow-up study, Alves and Gonçalves (2007) arrived at another possible explanation for this, namely the tendency for professionals to have greater confidence in their decision-making processes and for novices to be more insecure in this regard, a pattern also observed by Künzli (2004).

Studies using eye-tracking technology have shed greater light on aspects of allocation exhibited by various types of translators through visual attention data, or information about where translators look on the screen, in which sequences, and for how long. Combined with the pause and temporal data provided by keystroke loggers, visual attention data adds a level of granularity that provides researchers with a more nuanced understanding of what might actually be going on in the translator's mind during task completion. Interestingly, the advent of eye-tracking challenged previous assumptions made about translation processes using keystroke logging alone. For example, using keystroke logging to capture pausing tendencies, Dragsted (2004) initially proposed the idea that cognitive segmenting is relatively linear, demarcated by start and end pauses. At the time, this was a very important discovery in that cognitive segments were shown not to correspond with the default sentential segments with which translators work when using translation memories. In a follow-up exploration of segmenting patterns using eye-tracking (Dragsted and Hansen 2008), however, the boundaries of cognitive segments were shown to be more fuzzy, with gaze evidence suggesting that processing is both inter-segmental and intra-segmental – in other words, far from linear. Comprehension and production were shown to transpire not so much in a fashion distinct from each other, but rather in a coordinated fashion, almost to the point of occurring simultaneously. In light of their findings, Dragsted and Hansen (2008: 27) introduced the concept of eye-key span (EKS), or the temporal duration between the first fixation on an ST component and the production of its equivalent in the TT, as a more accurate metric for empirical research on cognitive segmenting.

Eye-tracking has also provided more detailed information on cognitive process variations between novices and professionals at various stages or loci of translation, including planning, comprehension, transfer, production (drafting), and revision. For example, multiple studies have documented visual attention patterns, suggesting the tendency for students to allocate more attention to the ST and for professionals to allocate more attention to the TT (Jakobsen 2005; Sharmin et al. 2008; Jensen 2011). If time spent on task is a reflection of the cognitive effort allocated to problem solving, this variation may in part explain why students tend to struggle primarily with comprehension, whereas professionals deliberately focus more on the TT for purposes of evaluation and revision. Interestingly, Sharmin et al. (2008), which also examined the impact of time pressure on ST–TT attention allocation patterns, found that the number of fixations on the ST decreases under time pressure while the number of fixations on the TT remains the same. Perhaps the tendency of professionals to dedicate more attention to the TT is also a result of conditioning and experience in working under time pressure.

New directions

Research on cognitive processes in T&I will likely continue to be driven by two current trends, namely a dedication to methods involving triangulation and the embracing of interdisciplinarity (cf. O'Brien 2013). One current research trend that will continue to gain momentum in the coming years involves the empirical exploration of post-editing processes (O'Brien et al. 2014), with a particular focus on how human processing compares and interacts with machine processing. The past few years have witnessed increasing collaboration between machine translation researchers and translation process researchers, with the common goal of enhancing productivity by pinpointing how humans and machine applications can ultimately complement each other from a text (and information)-processing standpoint.

Building on findings regarding CAT (computer-aided translation) tool usability, a current wave of cognitive process research involves aspects of human-computer interaction (e.g., O'Brien 2012). Here we are seeing a fundamental paradigm shift involving a deliberate movement away from design driven by programmers to design driven by translators and interpreters, based on empirically documented cognitive patterns. Much of the current research in this area is taking one of two interrelated directions. One direction involves longitudinal projects, such as CASMACAT (Elming et al. 2014) at the Copenhagen Business School, which are focused on using triangulated process data (eye-tracking, keystroke logging, and screen recording, for example) to optimize user interface design and assistive technology. A second direction involves cognitive ergonomics (Massey and Ehrensberger-Dow 2011a; Ehrensberger-Dow and Massey 2014), which examines, in part, indicators of efficacious and inefficacious desktop management, awareness of automated translation resource features, and interface interaction.

In some regards, research on human-computer interaction and cognitive ergonomics is entering an ethnographic turn, expanding on some of the central tenets outlined by Risku (2010) in her discussion of situated cognition. Based on the fact that translation is inherently interactive and dynamic, situated cognition examines cognitive dimensions from a social-contextual perspective. Rather than attempting to pinpoint what is in the black box per se, studies based on situated cognition examine how translators' interaction with the actors and factors of their working environment shapes their thought and behavior. In the coming years, we will likely see scholars continue to take up Risku's call to engage in ethnographic research of cognitive processes on location, for example, in translation agencies or in the natural working environments of freelancers.

Situated cognition also holds potential for advancing research on aspects of expertise in translation and interpreting (Shreve 2006). While we still know relatively little about what distinguishes the expert translator from the professional (Jääskeläinen 2010), it would seem that a natural setting, such as an in-house agency in which highly successful language industry professionals engage in authentic tasks not constrained by variables associated with an experimentally controlled lab, could serve as fertile ground for discoveries. Such on-location research, grounded initially in participant observation, could yield concrete indicators of the behaviors and strategies that embody expertise (cf. Albl-Mikasa 2013). Establishing more concrete empirical and ethnographic profiles of highly efficacious translators and interpreters could, in turn, go a long way toward optimizing process-oriented T&I training. Given the steadily increasing interest in process-oriented training, thanks in large part to user-friendly technology, such as web-based keystroke loggers, screen recorders, and speech recognition software, we are likely to see the continuation of research dedicated to increasing process awareness through reflection on one's own and others' processes (Massey and Ehrensberger-Dow 2011b; Angelone 2013). The time seems ripe for more extensive research on how process efficacy can be formally assessed and quality assured.

In closing, it is important to emphasize that many of these new directions align with the central tenets of the cognitive translatology paradigm proposed by Muñoz Martín (2010a, 2010b, 2013). Cognitive translatology is first and foremost an interdisciplinary applied science (Muñoz Martín 2010b); it benefits from exploration of core concepts, such as the various manifestations of bilingual proficiency used in conveying ideas across language and cultures, through a variety of scientific methods. The analytic lenses and methods of process research can and should vary. However, if its ultimate aim is to establish generalizable knowledge of translation and interpreting, cognitive translatology must achieve a certain level of operational compatibility across research projects. Muñoz Martín proposes a three-tier model that can serve as an ideal framework in this regard (2014: 13). First, translation task models need to be delineated. Second, the component sub-tasks need to be defined. Finally, the cognitive processes of interest need to be described in detail. Transparency, interdisciplinarity, and triangulation, the hallmarks of cognitive translatology, underscore why this particular paradigm holds great potential as a unifying catalyst for advancing cognitive process research in T&I.

References

Albl-Mikasa, Michaela. 2013. "Developing and Cultivating Expert Interpreter Competence." *The Interpreters' Newsletter* 18: 17–34.

Alves, Fabio (ed.). 2003. *Triangulating Translation: Perspectives in Process Oriented Research*. Amsterdam: John Benjamins.

Alves, Fabio, and Jose Luis Vila Real Gonçalves. 2003. "A Relevance Theory Approach to the Investigation of Inferential Processes in Translation." In *Triangulating*

Translation. Perspectives in Process Oriented Research, Fabio Alves (ed.), 3–24. Amsterdam: John Benjamins.

——2007. "Modelling Translator's Competence. Relevance and Expertise under Scrutiny." In *Doubts and Directions in Translation Studies. Selected Contributions from the EST Congress, Lisbon 2004*, Yves Gambier, Miriam Shlesinger, and Radegundis Stolze (eds.), 41–55. Amsterdam: John Benjamins.

Alves, Fabio, and Tânia Liparini Campos. 2009. "Translation Technology in Time: Investigating the Impact of Translation Memory Systems and Time Pressure on Types of Internal and External Support." In *Behind the Mind. Methods, Models and Results in Translation Process Research*, Copenhagen Studies in Language 37, Susanne Göpferich, Arnt Lykke Jakobsen, and Inger M. Mees (eds.), 191–218. Copenhagen: Samfundslitteratur Press.

Angelelli, Claudia V. 2004. *Revisiting the Interpreter's Role*. Amsterdam: John Benjamins.

Angelone, Erik. 2013. "Watching and Learning from 'Virtual Professionals': Utilizing Screen Recording in Process-Oriented Translator Training." In *New Prospects and Perspectives for Educating Language Mediators*, Don Kiraly, Silvia Hansen-Schirra, and Karin Maksymski (eds.), 139–55. Tübingen: Günther Narr.

Baddeley, Alan D., and Graham J. Hitch. 1974. "Working Memory." In *The Psychology of Learning and Motivation*, vol. 8, Gordon H. Bower (ed.), 47–90. New York: Academic Press.

Bell, Roger T. 1991. *Translation and Translating. Theory and Practice*. London: Longman.

Berk-Seligson, Susan. 1990. The Bilingual Courtroom. Court Interpreters in the Judicial Process. Chicago: University of Chicago Press.

Bialystok, Ellen. 1992. "Selective Attention in Cognitive Processing: The Bilingual Edge." In *Cognitive Processing in Bilinguals*, Richard J. Harris (ed.), 501–13. Amsterdam: North Holland.

Broadbent, Donald. 1958. *Perception and Communication*. London: Pergamon Press.

Camps, Joaquim. 2003. "Concurrent and Retrospective Verbal Reports as Tools to Better Understand the Role of Attention in Second Language Tasks." *International Journal of Applied Linguistics* 13(2): 201–21.

Canale, Michael, and Merrill Swain. 1981. "A Theoretical Framework for Communicative Competence." In *The Construct Validation of Tests of Communicative Competence*, Adrian S. Palmer, Peter J. M. Groot, and George A. Trosper (eds.), 31–36. Washington: TESOL.

Cao, Deborah. 1996. "A Model of Translation Proficiency." *Target* 8(2): 325–40.

Carl, Michael, Barbara Dragsted, and Arnt Lykke Jakobsen. 2011. "A Taxonomy of Human Translation Styles." *Translation Journal* 16(2). Available online at http://translationjournal.net/journal/56taxonomy.htm (last accessed 16/04/2015).

Chesterman, Andrew. 2013. "Models of What Processes?" *Translation and Interpreting Studies* 8(2): 155–68.

Chomsky, Noam. 1965. *Aspects of the Theory of Syntax*. Cambridge, MA: The MIT Press.

Colina, Sonia. 2003. *Translation Teaching: From Research to the Classroom*. New York, San Francisco: McGraw Hill.

Danks, Joseph H., and Jennifer Griffin. 1997. "Reading and Translation. A Psycholinguistic Perspective." In *Cognitive Processes in Translation and Interpreting*, Joseph H. Danks, Gregory M. Shreve, Stephen B. Fountain, and Michael K. McBeath (eds.), 161–75. Thousand Oaks, CA: SAGE Publications, 1997.

de Bot, Kees. 1992. "A Bilingual Production Model. Levelt's Speaking Model Adapted." *Applied Linguistics* 13(1): 1–24.

de Groot, Annette M. B. 1997. "The Cognitive Study of Translation and Interpretation. Three Approaches." In *Cognitive Processes in Translation and Interpreting*, Joseph H. Danks, Gregory M. Shreve, Stephen B. Fountain, and Michael K. McBeath (eds.), 25–56. Thousand Oaks, CA: SAGE Publications.

de Groot, Annette M. B., and Judith F. Kroll (eds.). 1997. *Tutorials in Bilingualism*. Mahwah, NJ: Lawrence Erlbaum.

Dragsted, Barbara. 2004. *Segmenting in Translation and Translation Memory Systems: An Empirical Investigation of Cognitive Segmentation and Effects of Integrating a TM System into the Translation Process*. Copenhagen: Samfundslitteratur.

Dragsted, Barbara, and Inge Gorm Hansen. 2008. "Comprehension and Production in Translation: A Pilot Study on Segmentation and the Coordination of Reading and Writing Processes." In *Looking at Eyes. Eye-Tracking Studies of Reading and Translation Processing*, Copenhagen Studies in Language 36, Susanne Göpferich, Arnt L. Jakobsen, and Inger M. Mees (eds.), 9–29. Copenhagen: Samfundslitteratur.

Ehrensberger-Dow, Maureen, and Alexander Künzli. 2010. "Methods of Accessing Metalinguistic Awareness: A Question of Quality?" In *New Approaches in Translation Process Research*, Copenhagen Studies in Language 39, Susanne Göpferich, Fabio Alves, and Inger M. Mees (eds.), 113–32. Copenhagen: Samfundslitteratur.

Ehrensberger-Dow, Maureen, and Gary Massey. 2013. "Indicators of Translation Competence: Translators' Self-concepts and the Translation of Titles." *Journal of Writing Research* 5(1): 103–31. Available online at http://pd.zhaw.ch/publikation/upload/204294.pdf (last accessed 16/04/2015).

——2014. "Cognitive Ergonomic Issues in Professional Translation." In *The Development of Translation Competence: Theories and Methodologies from Psycholinguistics and Cognitive Science*, John Schwieter and Aline Ferriera (eds.), 58–86. Newcastle upon Tyne: Cambridge Scholars Publishing.

Elming, Jakob, Laura Winther-Balling, and Michael Carl. 2014. "Investigating User Behaviour in Post-editing and Translation Using the CASMACAT Workbench." In *Post-editing of Machine Translation: Processes and Applications*, Sharon O'Brien, Laura Winther Balling, Michael Carl, Michael Simard, and Lucia Specia (eds.), 147–70. Newcastle upon Tyne: Cambridge Scholars Publishing.

Englund Dimitrova, Birgitta. 2005. *Expertise and Explicitation in the Translation Process*. Amsterdam: John Benjamins.

Ericsson, K. Anders. 1996. "The Acquisition of Expert Performance: An Introduction to Some of the Issues." In *The Road to Excellence: The Acquisition of Expert Performance in the Arts and Sciences, Sports and Games*, K. Anders Ericsson (ed.), 1–50. Mahwah, NJ: Lawrence Erlbaum Associates.

——2006. "The Influence of Experience and Deliberate Practice on the Development of Superior Expert Performance." In *The Cambridge Handbook of Expertise and Expert Performance*, K. Anders Ericsson, Neil Charness, Paul J. Feltovich, and Robert R. Hoffman (eds.), 683–704. Cambridge: Cambridge University Press.

Ericsson, K. Anders, and Herbert A. Simon. 1984/1993. *Protocol Analysis. Verbal Reports as Data*. Rev. ed. Cambridge, MA: The MIT Press.

Gile, Daniel. 1995. *Basic Concepts and Models for Interpreter and Translator Training*. Amsterdam: John Benjamins.

——2009. *Basic Concepts and Models for Interpreter and Translator Training*. Rev. ed. Amsterdam: John Benjamins.

Göpferich, Susanne. 2008. *Translationsprozessforschung: Stand – Methoden – Perspektiven.* Tübingen: Narr.

——2009. "Towards a Model of Translation Competence and Its Acquisition: The Longitudinal Study 'TransComp'." In *Behind the Mind: Methods, Models and Results in Translation Process Research*, Copenhagen Studies in Language 37, Susanne Göpferich, Arnt L. Jakobsen, and Inger M. Mees (eds.), 11–37. Copenhagen: Samfundslitteratur.

——2013. "Translation Competence. Explaining Development and Stagnation from a Dynamic Systems Perspective." *Target* 25(1): 61–76.

Grosjean, François. 1997. "Processing Mixed Language: Issues, Findings, and Models." In *Tutorials in Bilingualism: Psycholinguistic Perspectives*, Annette M.B. de Groot and Judith F. Kroll (eds.), 225–54. Mahwah, NJ: Lawrence Erlbaum Associates.

Gutt, Ernst-August. 1991. *Translation and Relevance: Cognition and Context*. Oxford: Blackwell.

Hansen, Gyde. 2003. "Controlling the Process. Theoretical and Methodological Reflections on Research into Translation Processes." In *Triangulating Translation. Perspectives in Process Oriented Research*, Fabio Alves (ed.), 25–42. Amsterdam: John Benjamins.

——2006. "Retrospection Methods in Translator Training and Translation Research." *The Journal of Specialised Translation* 5: 2–41. Available online at www.jostrans.org/issue05/art_hansen.pdf (last accessed 16/04/2015).

Holmes, James S. 1972/2004. "The Name and Nature of Translation Studies." In *The Translation Studies Reader*, second edition, Lawrence Venuti (ed.), 180–92. London: Routledge.

Hymes, Dell H. 1972. "On Communicative Competence." In *Sociolinguistics*, John B. Pride and Janet Holmes (ed.), 269–93. Baltimore, MD: Penguin Books.

Ivanova, Adelina. 1999. "Discourse Processing during Simultaneous Interpreting: An Expertise Approach." Unpublished Ph.D. dissertation. University of Cambridge.

Jääskeläinen, Riitta. 1999. *Tapping the Process. An Explorative Study of the Cognitive and Affective Factors Involved in Translating*. Joensuu: University of Joensuu Press.

——2000. "Focus on Methodology in Think-aloud Studies on Translating." In *Tapping and Mapping the Processes of Translation and Interpreting: Outlooks on Empirical Research*, Sonja Tirkkonen-Condit and Riitta Jääskeläinen (eds.), 71–82. Amsterdam: John Benjamins.

——2002. "Think-aloud Protocol Studies into Translation: An Annotated Bibliography." *Target* 14(1): 107–36.

——2010. "Are All Professionals Experts? Definitions of Expertise and Reinterpretation of Research Evidence in Process Studies." In *Translation and Cognition*, Gregory Shreve and Erik Angelone (eds.), 213–27. Amsterdam: John Benjamins.

Jakobsen, Arnt L. 2002. "Orientation, Segmentation, and Revision in Translation." In *Empirical Translation Studies: Process and Product*, Copenhagen Studies in Language 27, Gyde Hansen (ed.), 191–204. Copenhagen: Samfundslitteratur.

——2003. "Effects of Think Aloud on Translation Speed, Revision and Segmentation." In *Triangulating Translation: Perspectives in Process Oriented Research*, Fabio Alves (ed.), 69–95. Amsterdam: John Benjamins.

——2005. "Investigating Expert Translators' Processing Knowledge." In *Knowledge Systems and Translation – Text, Translation and Computational Processing 7*, Helle van Dam, Jan Engberg, and Heidrun Gerzymisch-Arbogast (eds.), 173–89. Berlin: Mouton de Gruyter.

Jensen, Kristian. 2011. "Distribution of Attention between Source Text and Target Text during Translation." In *Cognitive Explorations of Translation*, Sharon O'Brien (ed.), 215–36. London: Continuum.

Kalina, Sylvia. 2000. "Interpreting Competences as a Basis and a Goal for Teaching." *The Interpreters' Newsletter* 10: 3–32.

Kiraly, Donald. 1995. *Pathways to Translation: Pedagogy and Process.* Kent, OH: Kent State University Press.

Kohn, Kurt, and Silvia Kalina. 1996. "The Strategic Dimension of Interpreting." *Meta* 41(1): 118–38.

Krings, Hans Peter. 1986. *Was in den Köpfen von Übersetzern vorgeht. Eine empirische Untersuchung zur Struktur des Übersetzungsprozesses an fortgeschrittenen Französischlernern.* Tübingen: Narr.

——2001. *Repairing Texts: Empirical Investigations of Machine Translation Post-Editing Processes*, trans. by Geoffrey Koby, Gregory Shreve, Katjz Mischerikow, and Sarah Litzer, Geoffrey Koby (ed.). Kent, OH: Kent State University Press.

Künzli, Alexander. 2004. "Risk Taking: Trainee Translators vs. Professional Translators. A Case Study." *The Journal of Specialised Translation* 2: 34–49. Available online at www.jostrans.org/issue02/art_kunzli.pdf (last accessed 16/04/2015).

——2007. "The Ethical Dimension of Translation Revision. An Empirical Study." *The Journal of Specialised Translation* 8: 42–56. Available online at www.jostrans.org/issue08/art_kunzli.pdf (last accessed 16/04/2015).

Leow, Ronald P., and Kara, Morgan-Short. 2004. "To Think Aloud or Not to Think Aloud: The Issue of Reactivity in SLA Research Methodology." *Studies in Second Language Acquisition* 16: 35–57.

Levelt, Willem J. M. 1983. "Monitoring and Self-repair in Speech." *Cognition* 14: 41–104.

Lörscher, Wolfgang. 1991. *Translation Performance, Translation Process, and Translation Strategies. A Psycholinguistic Investigation.* Tübingen: Narr.

Malakoff, Marguerite, and Kenji Hakuta. 1991. "Translation Skill and Metalinguistic Awareness in Bilinguals." In *Language Processing and Language Awareness by Bilingual Children*, Ellen Bialystok (ed.), 141–66. Oxford: Oxford University Press.

Massey, Gary, and Maureen Ehrensberger-Dow. 2011a. "Technical and Instrumental Competence in the Translator's Workplace: Using Process Research to Identify Educational and Ergonomic Needs." *ILCEA Revue* 14. Available online at http://ilcea.revues.org/index1060.html (last accessed 16/04/2015).

——2011b. "Commenting on Translation: Implications for Translator Training." *Journal of Specialised Translation* 16: 26–41. Available online at http://www.jostrans.org/issue16/art_massey_ehrensberger_dow.pdf (last accessed 16/04/2015).

Moser-Mercer, Barbara. 1997/2002. "Process Models in Simultaneous Interpretation." In *The Interpreting Studies Reader*, Franz Pöchhacker and Miriam Shlesinger (eds.), 148–61. London: Routledge.

——2000. "Simultaneous Interpreting: Cognitive Potential and Limitations," *Interpreting* 5(2): 83–94.

Moser-Mercer, Barbara, Ulrich H. Fraunfelder, Beatriz Casado, and Alexander Künzli. 2000. "Searching to Define Expertise in Interpreting." In *Language Processing and Simultaneous Interpreting: Interdisciplinary Perspectives*, Birgitta Englund Dimitrova and Kenneth Hyltenstam (eds.), 107–31. Amsterdam and Philadelphia: John Benjamins.

Mossop, Brian. 2007. "Empirical Studies of Revision: What We Know and Need to Know. *The Journal of Specialised Translation* 8: 5–20. Available online at www.jostrans.org/issue08/art_mossop.pdf (last accessed 16/04/2015).

Muñoz Martín, Ricardo. 2010a. "On Paradigms and Cognitive Translatology." In *Translation and Cognition*, Gregory M. Shreve and Erik Angelone (eds.), 169–87. Amsterdam: John Benjamins.

——2010b. "Leave No Stone Unturned: On the Development of Cognitive Translatology." *Translation and Interpreting Studies* 5(2): 145–62.

——2012. "Just a Matter of Scope. Mental Load in Translation Process Research." *Translation Spaces* 1: 169–88.

——2013. "More than a Way with Words: The Interface between Cognitive Linguistics and Cognitive Translatology." In *Cognitive Linguistics and Translation: Advances in Some Theoretical Models and Applications*, Ana Rojo and Iraida Ibrarretxe-Antuñano (eds.), 75–96. Berlin: De Gruyter.

——2014. "Situating Translation Expertise: A Review with a Sketch of a Construct." In *The Development of Translation Competence: Theories and Methodologies from Psycholinguistics and Cognitive Science*, John Schwieter and Aline Ferriera (eds.), 3–21. Newcastle upon Tyne: Cambridge Scholars Publishing.

O'Brien, Sharon. 2012. "Translation as Human-computer Interaction." *Translation Spaces* 1: 101–22.

——2013. "The Borrowers: Researching the Cognitive Aspects of Translation." *Target* 25(1): 5–17.

O'Brien, Sharon, Laura Winther Balling, Michael Carl, Michel Simard, and Lucia Specia (eds.). 2014. *Post-editing of Machine Translation: Processes and Applications*. Newcastle upon Tyne: Cambridge Scholars Publishing.

PACTE. 2000. "Acquiring Translation Competence. Hypotheses and Methodological Problems in a Research Project." In *Investigating Translation*, Allison Beeby, Doris Ensinger, and Marisa Presas (eds.), 99–106. Amsterdam: John Benjamins.

——2003. "Building a Translation Competence Model." In *Triangulating Translation: Perspectives in Process Oriented Research*, Fabio Alves (ed.), 43–66. Amsterdam: John Benjamins.

——2005. "Investigating Translation Competence: Conceptual and Methodological Issues." *Meta* 50(2): 609–19.

Paradis, Michel. 1997. "The Cognitive Neuropsychology of Bilingualism." In *Tutorials in Bilingualism*, Annette M. B. de Groot and Judith F. Kroll (eds.), 331–54. Mahwah, NJ: Lawrence Erlbaum.

——2004. *A Neurolinguistic Theory of Bilingualism*. Amsterdam: John Benjamins.

Pavlović, Nataša, and Goranka Antunović. 2013. "The Effect of Interpreting Experience on Distance Dynamics: Testing the Literal Translation Hypothesis." *Translation and Interpreting Studies* 8(2): 233–52.

Pym, Anthony. 2003. "Redefining Translation Competence in an Electronic Age. In Defence of a Minimalist Approach." *Meta* 48(4): 481–97.

Risku, Hanna. 2010. "A Cognitive Scientific View on Technical Communication and Translation: Do Embodiment and Situatedness Really Make a Difference?" *Target* 22(1): 94–111.

Rojo, Ana, and Iraida Ibarretxe-Antuñano. 2013. "Cognitive Linguistics and Translation Studies: Past, Present and Future." In *Cognitive Linguistics and Translation. Advances in Some Theoretical Models and Applications*, Ana Rojo and Iraida Ibarretxe-Antuñano (eds.), 3–30. Berlin: de Gruyter Mouton.

Seeber, Kilian G. 2011. "Cognitive Load in Simultaneous Interpreting. Existing Theories – New Models." *Interpreting* 13(2): 176–204.

——2013. "Cognitive Load in Simultaneous Interpreting. Measures and Methods." *Target* 25(1): 18–32.

Seleskovitch, Danica. 1968. *L'interprète dans les conférences internationales: Problèmes de langage et de communication.* Paris: Minard.

Seleskovitch, Danica, and Marianne Lederer. 1984. *Interpréter pour traduire.* Paris: Didier Érudition.

Sharmin, Selina, Oleg Špakov, Kari-Jouko Räihä, and Arnt L. Jakobsen. 2008. "Where on the Screen Do Translation Students Look While Translating, and For How Long?" In *Looking at Eyes. Eye-Tracking Studies of Reading and Translation Processing*, Copenhagen Studies in Language 36, Susanne Göpferich, Arnt L. Jakobsen, and Inger M. Mees (eds.), 31–51. Copenhagen: Samfundslitteratur.

Shreve, Gregory M. 1997. "Cognition and the Evolution of Translation Competence." In *Cognitive Processes in Translation and Interpreting*, Joseph H. Danks, Gregory M. Shreve, Stephen B. Fountain, and Michael K. McBeath (eds.), 120–36. Thousand Oaks, CA: SAGE Publications.

——2006. "The Deliberate Practice: Translation and Expertise." *Journal of Translation Studies* 9(1): 27–42.

Smith, Jacqui, and K. Anders Ericsson. 1991. *Towards a General Theory of Expertise: Prospects and Limits.* Cambridge: Cambridge University Press.

Sperber, Dan, and Deirdre Wilson. 1986. *Relevance: Communication and Cognition.* Oxford: Blackwell.

——1995. *Relevance: Communication and Cognition.* Second edition. Oxford: Blackwell.

Toury, Gideon. 1995. *Descriptive Translation Studies – and Beyond.* Amsterdam: John Benjamins.

——2012. *Descriptive Translation Studies – and Beyond.* Rev. ed. Amsterdam: John Benjamins.

van Dijk, Teun, and Walter Kintsch. 1983. *Strategies of Discourse Comprehension.* New York: Academic Press.

Wadensjö, Cecilia. 1998. *Interpreting as Interaction.* London: Longman.

Wilss, Wolfgang. 1996. *Knowledge and Skills in Translator Behavior.* Amsterdam: John Benjamins.

4 Collaborative and volunteer translation and interpreting

Miguel A. Jiménez-Crespo

Overview

Collaboration and volunteerism can be found in all types and modalities of translation and interpreting. In the context of translation research, these two phenomena have recently gained popularity thanks to the emergence of new web-based translation communities, although collaborative practices can be traced back to ancient times (O'Brien 2011). In interpreting, volunteerism represents a key area of research, mostly connected to intrasocial, non-professional, and activist contexts (i.e., Baker 2006; Boeri 2008). Collaboration is also present in interpreting insofar as simultaneous conference interpreting requires collaboration among the two or more professionals staffing the booth, who must switch at specific intervals and collaborate offline in case of difficulties, and also before and after the communicative event. The two notions under study here are therefore at the core of contemporary TIS research, with translation research focusing mainly on collaborative and volunteer practices mediated through the web, and interpreting research focusing mainly on volunteerism, specifically related to activism and the social turn in Translation Studies.

Theoretical foundations

Despite the existence of collaborative practices in translation and interpreting since antiquity, it was not until the emergence of action (Holz-Mänttäri 1984) and functionalist theories (Reiss and Vermeer 1984; Nord 1997) that the collaborative nature of translation was widely acknowledged and placed at the center of a theory of translation. These approaches helped change the previous focus from linguistics-inspired equivalence paradigms to an understanding of the translator and interpreter as experts in intercultural mediation operating within a specific social context. Within that social context, translators, like interpreters, collaborate with any number of agents, who necessarily influence the translators' decision-making processes. Collaboration in functionalist and action approaches starts with initiators, or commissioners, who request translations (companies, publishers, institutions, individuals, etc.), which are subsequently undertaken by one or more translators. The translation product is then reviewed and delivered to a client(s), whose implicit and explicit expectations play a decisive role in shaping the translation product. Collaboration understood in this way fits in with the broad definition of translation collaboration provided by O'Brien (2011). Nord's (1997) "function plus loyalty" model modified the powerful initial function bias of the early functionalist models (Reiss and Vermeer 1984), placing the translator at the center of a networked process in which the expectations of the users and the function of the translation are counterbalanced by their loyalty to the demands of the initiators or clients. According to this theoretical model, collaboration in translation involves clients, translators, revisers, and end users. Today it can be considered one of the most influential theories in TIS and in TIS training since it facilitated the move in translation theory from static individualistic models of translation based on linguistic equivalence to more dynamic models, in which the translator(s) is empowered as an intercultural broker who mediates among the various agents within a network. In the 2000s, more professionally oriented models of translation, such as the project model presented in the works of Gouadec (2007), continued to expand our understanding of the collaborative nature of the translation process by dissecting every translation profile into sub-components, or steps, in which different agents collaborate to create a final product. Therefore, the final translation typically represents the result of a vast network of interrelated tasks produced by several agents, such as initiators, translation managers, terminologists, translators, reviewers, proofreaders, Desktop Publishing (DTP) specialists, and localization engineers. The emergence of such collaborative networks is partly due to the rapid growth of the language industry in recent years, which has instigated greater diversification of the labor force in the field, creating new professional profiles that did not exist before.

Detailed analysis of these translation networks is at the core of another theoretical approach in the discipline: situated and embodied cognition applied to translation (Risku and Dickinson 2009; Risku and Windhanger 2013). These approaches developed from the introduction of social cognition theories to the study of translational phenomena within what is known as "cognitive translatology" (Muñoz Martín 2010). Situated and extended cognition approaches claim that the mind alone cannot be understood as the sole determinant of mental activity. Rather, the focus of study must be extended to include the interactions between the translator/interpreter's body, his/her environment, and the social contexts in which cognitive activity occurs. Risku and Windhanger (2013) conceptualize the professional interactions between all subjects in the process, as well as the interaction between the translations themselves, as social artifacts that influence the subjects and institutions involved. Following this approach, researchers have studied, for example, the interactions between translators in professional forums (Risku and Dickinson 2009).

Volunteerism, mostly related to social activism, has been the focus of a number of studies in interpreting. This research trend was initiated by Baker in her study of interpreting "communities set up outside the mainstream institutions of society," in which she focuses on the "narrative framework within which the work of communities of translators and interpreters who may be involved in political or social agendas may be explained and critiqued" (2006: 462). Boeri (2008, 2010, 2012) has studied the case of Babel, a pro-bono community of conference interpreters that contributes to and arranges conference interpreting in the World Social Forum. Boeri's study focuses on the "narratives that circulate among members of the conference interpreting community, especially those relating to issues of volunteering, activism and professionalism" (Boeri 2008: 29). In her analysis of the positioning of professional conference interpreters, Boeri rejects traditional binary models in favor of a network-like constellation of positionings that are available to and taken up by members of the conference interpreting community. Hokkanen (2012) focuses on simultaneous interpreting in Pentecostal churches in Finland, describing the type of volunteer interpreting performed as a twofold service, both to the members of the community and to God. This has implications for the education/training of interpreters, as well as for the expectations of the service they render. Aguilar-Solano (2012), using Bourdieu's theory of practice as a theoretical framework, focused on volunteer medical interpreting in public hospitals. This study used a methodology based on ethnographic approaches in which data was triangulated using participant observation of volunteer interpreters, audio-recorded interpreter-mediated interaction, and focus-group interviews with volunteer interpreters.

Evolution of the topic in TIS

In general, collaboration, as an object of theorizing in TIS, is defined in two distinct ways. On the one hand, collaboration is broadly defined as a general process in which "two or more agents collaborate in some form to produce a translation" (O'Brien 2011: 17), with possible agents including publishers, editors, translators, institutions, etc. It is also more narrowly understood as "the situation in which two or more translators work together to produce a translation" (2011: 17). Other definitions reflect the new technological scenarios that facilitate volunteer practices, that is, "group translating where the work is largely voluntary (i.e., unpaid in financial terms)" (Pym 2011: 77). Volunteer translation and interpreting can be defined as practices "conducted by people exercising their free will to perform translation work that is not remunerated, is formally organized, and is for the benefit of others" (Olohan 2014: 19). This last definition can easily be applied to interpreting scenarios since the main drive behind volunteer interpreting tends to be the desire to benefit others, both in one's own society or in an international context, as with such organizations as Ecos and Babels (Boeri 2008, 2012).

Tracing research on collaborative and volunteer phenomena involves important epistemological challenges related to the fuzziness and interrelatedness of the objects of study. Interpreting has a more defined trajectory of research on "volunteer interpreting" due to the abundant literature on community interpreting. The study of these phenomena in translation, however, has suffered from a definitional fuzziness due to the interrelated nature of several phenomena, such as "community translation," "social translation," "non-professional translation," and "volunteer translation" (Pym 2011; McDonough Dolmaya 2012). Oftentimes in TIS publications these terms are used interchangeably although they represent different constructs. One possible source of this fuzziness is that all these terms can be considered superterms, or what Vandepitte in her ontology of Translation Studies refers to as "umbrella terms" (Vandepitte 2008). The concepts of collaborative and volunteer translation do not fully overlap, in the sense that volunteerism does not necessarily involve collaborative translation. Moreover, due to the emergence of online cloud collaborative translation platforms (see Babych et al. 2012), collaborative processing between two or more professional translators, as well as terminologists or reviewers, is becoming the norm rather than the exception in professional settings. "Community translation" is often considered a synonym of "collaborative translation," which is currently used in scholarly publications to refer to any web-enabled practices. In Australia, however, due to the influence of community interpreting research, collaborative translation is considered a case of intrasocial translation.

The emergence of new phenomena enabled by the Internet, such as "crowdsourcing," "fansubbing," and "romhacking," have added a new level of complexity to this terminological issue, and all these new terms can be considered subordinate or hyponyms of those mentioned above. Figure 4.1 attempts to represent graphically the conceptual overlapping of volunteer and collaborative notions that appear in TIS literature.

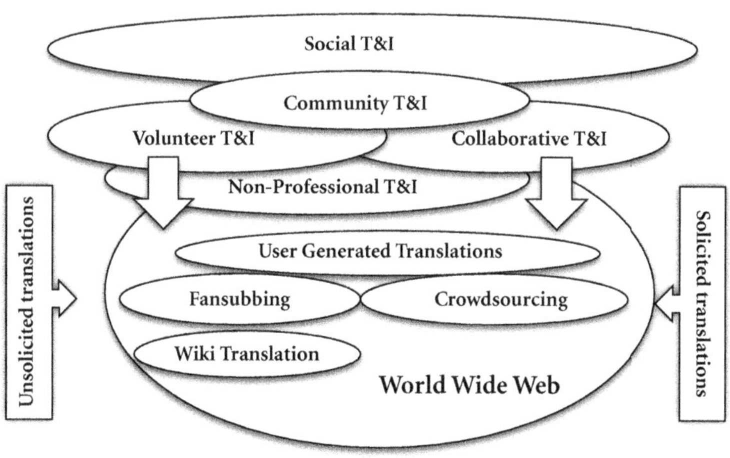

Figure 4.1 Mapping concepts related to volunteer and collaborative translation.

In this map, phenomena related to translational practices that occur both with and without web-mediation are posited as superterms. "Social translation" in TIS research can be considered the top-level concept as it encompasses volunteer, collaborative, and community translations, and all of the latter are instances of the former. Currently this term is being used in two distinct senses in Tanslation Studies (TS), with some TS scholars placing social translation closer to activist approaches to translation (Newark 2003; O'Hagan 2013), while in the context of technology it is now often used as a synonym for crowdsourcing (Austermühl 2011; O'Brien 2011).

Figure 4.1 lists concepts that pertain to the translation contexts, practices, and phenomena that emerged with participatory Web 2.0 technologies. The medium of the Internet, therefore, represents the main difference between the general practices and those listed below them. "User generated translations" (Perrino 2009) can be considered a generic term, as most, but not all, collaborative practices on the web tend to be done by the end users, the "prosumers" (O'Hagan 2013) of translations. Furthermore, all instances of "user generated translation" on the web can be divided between two distinctive models, "solicited" and "unsolicited" ones (O'Hagan 2009). These two attributes have been placed on both sides of the graph to represent the two possible ways a project can be started. The former refers to cases in which a call to the community to complete a specific localization task is issued by a company, such as Facebook, Skype, Adobe, or Twitter (Jiménez-Crespo 2011, 2013; Mesipuu 2012), or by an institution or non-profit, such as the Rosetta Foundation (Anastasiou and Schäler 2010; O'Brien and Schäler 2010) or Kotoba no Volunteer (Kageura et al. 2011). This is what is popularly known as "crowdsourcing," defined by O'Hagan (2013) as volunteer or community translation produced in some form of collaboration by a group of Internet users forming an online community. The "non-solicited model" refers to cases in which self-selected collectives of users undertake self-organized translation tasks without a specific organized request. The results are later distributed through the web via websites, blogs, subtitling, tweets, romhacking of videogames, fansubs, scanlations, or any other type of digital text.

Key studies

Translation crowdsourcing on the web, which typically, but not always, involves both volunteerism and collaboration, has been the focus of a number of empirical studies. Crowdsourcing was first defined by Howe (2006) as "the act of taking a job traditionally performed by a designated agent … and outsourcing it to an undefined, generally large group of people in the form of an open call" (2006: np). In TS, it usually refers to volunteer or community translation produced in some form of collaboration by a group of Internet users who form an online community (O'Hagan 2013). McDonough Dolmaya (2012: 169) stresses the role of professionals in crowdsourcing communities, which she describes as "collaborative efforts to translate content … either by enthusiastic amateurs ... or by professional translators." Other terms in TS literature referring to this type of digital collaborative translation include "crowdtranslation" (Kageura et al. 2011), "user-generated" (O'Hagan, 2009; Perrino, 2009), "open" (Cronin 2010), "community" (Ray and Kelly 2011), "volunteer" (Pym 2011), or "hive" (García 2009). The concept of crowdsourcing, which applies to web-mediated environments, and not to any other type of collaborative translation, can be traced back to the early 2000s when Shimohata et al. (2001) started to research how to use "collaborative translation on the web" in the context of machine translation training. For the sake of clarity, the research approaches of greatest interest for the purposes of this chapter will be divided into (1) machine translation-computational linguistics and (2) TIS approaches.

Machine translation (MT), computational linguistics, and natural language processing represent the most productive approaches in researching translation crowdsourcing. Machine translation researchers first attempted to take advantage of online volunteers in the late 1980s and early 1990s in order to improve instant online MT output, such as the case of Yukishite.net (Shimohata et al. 2001). Over the last decade a large amount of research has been devoted to the development and testing of crowdsourcing models or the use of crowdsourcing as a tool to produce translations in order to feed and improve MT engines (Zaidan and Callison-Burch 2011; Zbib et al. 2013). In the latter line of research, studies have focused on the production of translations whose final destination is not human consumption but the expansion and improvement of MT engines. This type of research has proven that crowdsourcing can produce, for the purposes of MT training, results similar to those produced by professional translators at one-fifth of the cost (Zbib et al. 2013). O'Hagan (2013) identifies these "feedback translations," that is, human post-edited MT output which is later used to feed MT engines, as one of the main areas of collaboration between computational linguistics and TS. Related to this line of research are applied studies on the development of online platforms to facilitate translation crowdsourcing (Bey et al. 2006; Désilets et al. 2009; Babych et al. 2012). This phenomenon is reaching a mature stage in which platforms for specific purposes have been developed, such as those for nonprofit purposes (Anastasiou and Schäler 2010; Kageura et al. 2011). Applied research in this area has also focused on adapting crowdsourcing platforms for translation training, as is the case of the platform MNH-TT (Babych et al. 2012).

TIS studies of collaboration have dealt mostly with two basic research questions: (1) What are the motivations and profiles of translation volunteers? and (2) What is the quality of translations produced through crowdsourcing? These studies have been, for the most part, inspired by the "sociological turn" in the discipline (Wolf 2010; Angelelli 2012), or what Chesterman (2009) calls "translator studies," reflecting a new focus on "the social role of the translators and the translators' profession, translation as a social practice" and "people and their observable actions" (2007: 173–74). In this context, apart from motivation, studies have also focused on the ethical implications of volunteer translation on the web (Drugan 2011). Methodologically, these studies have used a variety of methods, such as (1) interactionist methods involving online surveys and online interviews; (2) ethnographic or "netnographic" approaches, in which the informant immerses him/herself in the online community (Kozinets 2010); (3) mixed methods (Creswell and Plano Clark 2012), combining interactionist methods and "netnographic" approaches (Dombek 2013); and (4) a triangulation of corpus-based and experimental research methods to study the features of translated language in crowdsourced websites (Jiménez-Crespo 2013).

Survey-based methods are among the most widely used to research volunteer motivation. Studies have focused on cases of translators working in non-profit organizations (O'Brien and Schäler 2010), such as TED Open Translation Initiative (Camara forthcoming) or Wikipedia (McDonough Dolmaya 2012). In one study on the motivation of volunteers who contribute to the non-profit Rosetta Foundation, surveys were administered to 139 participants and it was found that the main incentive for the volunteers was the desire to support the causes to which the organization was committed (O'Brien and Schäler 2010). As with the other studies, O'Brien and Schäler found that subjects were also interested in improving their translation skills. Volunteers were also asked what would make them more engaged in the future, which is one of the main concerns of the organizations and companies that have set up crowdsourcing activities (Ray and Kelly 2011). The possibility of getting professional feedback for their translations was the most popular response. McDonough Dolmaya (2012), using an online survey completed by 75 respondents, researched the motivation of Wikipedia volunteer translators. A survey used in a previous study (Lakhani and Wolf 2005) to research motivation on FOSS (Free and Open-Source Software) was adapted in McDonough Dolmaya's study to identify the specific motivations of volunteer translators. The possible motivations were divided into intrinsic (self-improvement or enjoyment) and extrinsic ones (personal benefit, potential economic gains). Participants were then divided into groups of non-professional and professional translators, and the results were compared with studies in FOSS. This allowed her to identify differences between professional participation in these two practices. McDonough Dolmaya's findings indicate that, while intrinsic motivations were the more significant, volunteers were led to participate by a combination of motivations. Motivations such as making the content available in other languages and supporting the initiative were among the most significant, although among the professional translators that participated, gaining status or clients was also an important motivation. In line with the findings of the previous study (Lakhani and Wolf 2005), translation participants noted that gaining experience and feedback from others was an important factor. McDonough Dolmaya also found empirical proof of what other researchers (Ray and Kelly 2011) had only conjectured, namely, that volunteers do not view all initiatives equally and consider some to have higher status than others.

Two studies have focused on the motivation of volunteers in TED Open Translation Initiative (Olohan 2014; Camara forthcoming), a series of short talks that were distributed online and subtitled in a large number of languages. Camara's study used online surveys with a wide sample, while Olohan (2014) studied the motivation of volunteers by using a qualitative methodology with data obtained from blog entries in which the main contributors were asked by the organization: "Why do you translate?" Only 11 blog entries were available and so this corpus cannot be considered to be representative of the over 8000 translators in TED. However, the researcher claims, "the aim here is not to uncover all possible motivations … but rather to assess the usefulness of a qualitative analysis of data of this kind in studying motivation" (Olohan 2014: 23). In line with previous research, this study found a combination of motivations behind the volunteers' efforts, such as support for the cause behind TED, "ideas worth spreading," or the opportunity to be part of a community. One of the more interesting results of Camara's study is the fact that professional translators, who generally make up around 17 percent of the volunteers both in TED and in Wikipedia (McDonough Dolmaya 2012), are often assigned higher responsibilities in the translation community, serving as managers or reviewers.

The only in-depth mixed-method approach in TS is the one by Dombek on the motivations of volunteer Polish translators at Facebook (2013). The research questions for this doctoral dissertation concerned the profile and motivation of the volunteers and the impact of technology platforms on volunteerism (2013: 259). The study used several theoretical frameworks from neighboring disciplines, such as (1) self-determination theory (SDT); (2) functional approach to volunteer motivation; (3) theories of motivation of volunteers; and (4) gamification. The study combines netnographic methods developed by Kozinets (2010), in which the researcher participates in discussion forums and the Facebook page for the community, with interactionist methods, including online surveys to gain insight into the characteristics of the collective being researched and their motivations to participate in the process, as well as remote interviews, and with observational research methods, including remote analysis of translation processes followed by Think Aloud Protocals (TAPs), which were recorded and played back to the subjects. The objective of this third method was to analyze the human–machine interaction framework provided by the translation application built by Facebook for crowdsourcing. For this third method, the researcher adapted Activity Checklist approaches (Kaptelinin and Nardi 2012), a methodology used to handle the interpretation of empirical evidence about complex phenomena related to the technological mediation of everyday practices. The results of the study show that the motivations for this group of Polish Facebook translators were varied. For example, respondents reported that participating in FB: (1) promoted their feelings of competence, autonomy, and relatedness; (2) met their expectations of personal and social benefit; (3) produced a sense of reciprocity, self-efficacy, group commitment, and reputation gain; and (4) was perceived as fun and enjoyable. In addition, the observational part of the study showed that the technological platform designed by FB "often constrained attaining users' goals instead of facilitating them" (Dombek 2013: 262), which was often a source of frustration for the volunteers. The shortcomings identified by the subjects in the study were detrimental to the motivation of the volunteers in all four of the motivations identified above. Finally, it is worth mentioning that this netnographic study showed that the collaborative communicative platforms and discussion forums served as a means for the volunteers to arrive at solutions to the technological problems they faced.

The quality of crowdsourced translations has also been the object of empirical studies (Perez and Carreira 2011; Jiménez-Crespo 2013). Jiménez-Crespo (2013) used product-oriented corpus-based approaches to study collaborative translation on the web, as well as a multimethod approach in which corpus-based studies were triangulated with experimental studies (Jiménez-Crespo forthcoming). The research questions for these studies, related to previous corpus studies on the "language of translation" (Baker 1995), attempt to identify whether crowdsourcing can produce "natural-sounding" translations and whether translation or voting on different translation proposals is the more effective way to reach that goal. In the first study Jiménez-Crespo used consolidated comparable corpus-based methods in TS in order to research whether the Spanish version of Facebook included the most frequent lexical items in the potential range of variation in non-translated or original Spanish social networking sites. The comparable corpus included a translational section with 142 lexical items in interactive segments in the crowdsourced Spanish version of Facebook. The non-translational comparable section included all the interactive and navigation segments in the 25 most popular Spanish social networking sites. The results showed that the localized version of Facebook included the most frequent lexical units for each communicative purpose used in the research study and that the degree of naturalness was therefore achieved.

New directions

Interest in both collaborative translation and volunteer interpreting continues to increase as evidenced by the proliferation of international conferences on the topic, such as the 2014 European International Association for Translation and Intercultural Studies (IATIS) conference on collaborative translation or the 2014 conference on non-professional translation and interpreting in Germersheim, Germany. The field, however, remains wide open to future research from different perspectives. Currently, most studies, both on translation and interpreting, assume a sociological perspective, while the opportunity for additional research from a product-based or cognitive perspective could also contribute to the body of knowledge of the "language of translation" and of issues related to translation competence. In this last area, cognitive studies have often focused on non-professionals as tertium comparationis (Jääskeläinen et al. 2011). Cognitive studies in which volunteers and professionals participate could add to the knowledge of how non-structured practice outside training institutions contributes to the acquisition of translation/interpreting competence. This can also help with trends in applied research that focus on using collaborative and volunteer practices as training grounds both in translation (i.e., O'Hagan 2008; Babych et al. 2012) and interpreting (Boeri 2010). From a product-based perspective, collaborative and volunteer translation products represent what Chesterman identifies as a "translation subtype" against which to test potential general tendencies of translation (Chesterman 2004). Crowdsourcing will continue to attract the attention of scholars, with a myriad of unanswered research questions related to ethical, political, ideological, and quality issues.

References

Aguilar-Solano, Maria. 2012. "Positioning of Volunteer Interpreters in the Field of Public Service Interpreting in Spanish Hospitals: A Bourdieusian Perspective." Unpublished Ph.D. dissertation. University of Malaga, Spain.

Anastasiou, Dimitra, and Reinhart Schäler. 2010. "Translating Vital Information: Localisation, Internationalisation, and Globalisation." *Synthèses* 3: 11–25.

Angelelli, Claudia (ed.). 2012. "The Sociological Turn in Translation and Interpreting Studies." Special issue. *Translation and Interpreting Studies* 7(2).

Austermühl, Frank. 2011. "Of Clouds and Crowds: Current Developments in Translation Technology", *T21T.* Available online at: www.t21n.com/homepage/articles/T21N-2011-09-Austermuehl.pdf (accessed June 20, 2014).

Babych, Bogdan et al. 2012. "MNH-TT: A Collaborative Platform for Translator Training." *Translating and the Computer* 34. Available online at www.mt-archive.info/Aslib-2012-Babych.pdf (accessed June 20, 2014).

Baker, Mona. 1995. "Corpora in Translation Studies: An Overview and Some Suggestions for Future Research." *Target* 7: 223–43.

——2006. "Translation and Activism: Emerging Patterns of Narrative Community." *The Massachusetts Review* 47(3): 462–84.

Bey, Youcef, Christian Boitet, and Kyo Kageura. 2006. "The TRANSBey Prototype: An Online Collaborative Wiki-based CAT Environment for Volunteer Translators." In *Proceedings of the Third International Workshop on Language Resources for Translation Work, Research & Training (LR4Trans-III)*, Elia Yuste (ed.), 49–54. Paris: ELRA.

Boeri, Julie. 2008. "A Narrative Account of the Babels vs. Naumann Controversy. Competing Perspectives on Activism in Conference Interpreting." *The Translator* 14: 21–50.

——2010. "Emerging Narratives of Conference Interpreters' Training: A Case Study of Ad Hoc Training in Babels and the Social Forum." *Puentes* 9: 61–70.

——2012. "Translation/Interpreting Politics and Praxis: The Impact of Political Principles on Babels' Interpreting Practice." *The Translator* 18: 269–90.

Camara, Lidia. Forthcoming. "Motivation for Collaboration in TED Open Translation Project." *International Journal of Web Based Communities.*

Chesterman, Andrew. 2004. "Beyond the Particular." In *Translation Universals. Do they Exist?*, Anna Mauranen and Pekka Kujamäki (eds.), 33–49. Amsterdam and Philadelphia: John Benjamins.

——2007. "Bridge concepts in Translation Sociology". In M. Wolf, Michaela and A. Fukari (eds.), *Constructing a Sociology of Translation*. Amsterdam-Philadelphia: John Benjamins, pp. 171–183.

——2009. "The Name and Nature of Translator Studies." *Hermes—Journal of Language and Communication Studies* 42: 13–22.

Creswell, John W., and Vicky L. Plano Clark. 2012. *Designing and Conducting Mixed Methods Research*. Second edition. California, CA: Thousand Oaks: SAGE Publications.

Cronin, Michael. 2010. "The Translation Crowd." *Tradumàtica* 8. Available online at. www.fti.uab.es/tradumatica/revista/num8/articles/04/04central.htm (accessed June 10, 2014).

Désilets, Alain et al. 2009. "Building a Collaborative Multilingual Terminology System." *ASLIB Translating and the Computer*, November 29–30, 2009, London, UK. Available online at http://wiki-translation.com/tiki-download_wiki_attachment.php?attId=57 (accessed June 20, 2014).

Dombek, Magdalena. 2013. "A Study into the Motivations of Internet Users Contributing to Translation Crowdsourcing: The Case of Polish Facebook User-Translators." Unpublished Ph.D. dissertation. Dublin City University.

Drugan, Joanna. 2011. "Translation Ethics Wikified: How Do Professional Codes of Ethics and Practice Apply to Non-Professionally Produced Translation." *Linguistica Antverpiensia* 10: 97–111.

García, I. (2009) "Beyond Translation Memory: Computers and the Professional Translator." *Jostrans: The Journal of Specialized Translation* 12: 199–214.

Gouadec, Daniel. 2007. *Translation as a Profession*. Amsterdam and Philadelphia: John Benjamins.

Hokkanen, Sari. 2012. "Simultaneous Church Interpreting as Service." *The Translator* 18(2): 291–309.

Holz-Mänttäri, Justa. 1984. *Translatorisches Handeln. Theorie und Methode*. Helsinki: Suomalainen Tiedeakatemia.

Howe, Jeff. 2006. "Crowdsourcing: A Definition. Crowdsourcing: Tracking the Rise of the Amateur." Available online at http://crowdsourcing.typepad.com/cs/2006/06/crowdsourcing_a.html (accessed June 20, 2014).

Jääskeläinen, Rita, Pekka Kujamaki, and Jukka Mäkisalo. 2011. "Towards Professionalism – or against It? Dealing with the Changing World in Translation Research and Translation Education." *Across Languages and Cultures* 12(2): 143–56.

Jiménez-Crespo, Miguel A. 2011. "From Many One: Novel Approaches to Translation Quality in a Social Network Era." *Linguistica Antverpiensia, New Series* 12: 153–74.

——2013. "Crowdsourcing, Corpus Use, and the Search for Translation Naturalness: A Comparable Corpus Study of Facebook and Non-Translated Social Networking Sites." *Translation and Interpreting Studies* 8: 23–49.

——Forthcoming. "Testing Explicitation in Translation: Triangulating Corpus and Experimental Studies." *Across Languages and Cultures*.

Kaptelinin, Victor, and Bonnie A. Nardi. 2012. *Activity Theory in HCI: Fundamentals and Reflections*. San Francisco, CA: Morgan & Claypool.

Kageura, Kyo et al. 2011. "Has Translation Gone Online and Collaborative? An Experience from Minna no Hon'yaku." *Linguistica Antverpienisia* 10: 47–72.

Kozinets, Robert V. 2010. *Netnography: Doing Ethnographic Research Online*. London: SAGE Publications.

Lakhani, Karim R., and Robert G. Wolf. 2005. "Why Hackers Do What They Do: Understanding Motivation and Effort in Free/Open Source Software Projects." In *Perspectives in Free and Open Source Software*, Joseph Feller, Brian Fitzgerald, Scott Hissam, and Karim Lakhani (eds.), 3–22. Cambridge, MA: MIT Press.

McDonough Dolmaya, Julie. 2012. "Analyzing the Crowdsourcing Model and Its Impact on Public Perceptions of Translation." *The Translator* 18(2): 167–91.

Mesipuu, Marit. 2012. "Translation Crowdsourcing and User-translator Motivation at Facebook and Skype." *Translation Spaces* 1: 33–53.

Muñoz Martín, Ricardo. 2010. "On Paradigms and Cognitive Translatology." In *Translation and Cognition*, Gregory M. Shreve and Erik Angelone (eds.), 169–87. Amsterdam and Philadelphia: John Benjamins.

Newark, Peter. 2003. "No Global Communication without Translation." In *Translation Today*, Gunilla M. Anderman and Margaret Rogers (eds.), 55–68. Buffalo, NY: Multilingual Matters.

Nord, Christiane. 1997. *Functionalist Approaches Explained*. Manchester: St. Jerome.

O'Brien, Sharon. 2011. "Collaborative Translation." In *Routledge Handbook of Translation Studies*, volume 2, Carmen Millán-Varela and Francesca Bartrina (eds.), 17–20. London: Routledge.

O'Brien, Sharon, and Reinhart Schäler. 2010. "Next Generation Translation and Localization. Users Are Taking Charge." *Translating and the Computer Conference*, November 17–18, 2010, London. Available online at http://doras.dcu.ie/16695/1/Paper_6.pdf (accessed June 20, 2014).

O'Hagan, Minako. 2008. "Fan Translation Networks: An Accidental Translator Training Environment?" In *Translator and Interpreter Training: Issues, Methods and Debates*, John Kearns (ed.), 158–83. London: Continuum.

——2009. "Evolution of User-Generated Translation: Fansubs, Translation Hacking and Crowdsourcing." *The Journal of Internationalization and Localization* 1: 94–121.

——2013. "The Impact of New Technologies on Translation Studies: A Technological Turn?" In *Routledge Handbook of Translation Studies*, Carmen Millán-Varela and Francesca Bartrina (eds.), 503–18. London: Routledge.

Olohan, Maeve. 2014. "Why Do You Translate? Motivation to Volunteer and TED Translation." *Perspectives: Studies in Translatology* 7(1): 17–33.

Perez, Estefanía, and Oliver Carreira. 2011. "Evaluación del Modelo de Crowdsourcing Aplicado a la Traducción de Contenidos en Redes Sociales: Facebook." In *La Traductología Actual: Nueva Vías de Investigación en la Disciplina*, E. Calvo Encinas et al. (eds.), 99–118. Granada: Comares.

Perrino, Saverino. 2009. "User-Generated Translation: The Future of Translation in a Web 2.0 Environment." *The Journal of Specialised Translation* 12: 55–78.

Pym, Anthony. 2011. "Translation Research Terms: A Tentative Glossary for Moments of Perplexity and Dispute." In *From Translation Research Projects 3*, Anthony Pym (ed.), 75–110. Tarragona: Intercultural Studies Group.

Ray, Rebecca, and Natalie Kelly. 2011. *Crowdsourced Translation: Best Practices for Implementation*. Lowell, MA: Common Sense Advisory.

Reiss, Katharina, and Hans J. Vermeer. 1984. *Grundlegung einer Allgemeinen Translationstheorie*. Tubinga: Niemeyer.

Risku, Hanna, and Angela Dickinson. 2009. "Translators as Networkers: The Role of Virtual 76 Communities." *Hermes* 42: 49–70.

Risku, Hanna, and Florian Windhanger. 2013. "Extended Translation: A Sociocognitive Research Agenda." *Target* 13: 33–45.

Shimohata, Sayori et al. 2001. "Collaborative Translation Environment on the Web." *Proceedings from MT Summit VIII*: 331–34. Available online at www.mt-archive.info/MTS-2001-Shimohata.pdf (accessed July 10, 2012).

Vandepitte, Sonia. 2008. "Remapping Translation Studies: Towards a Translation Studies Ontology." *Meta* 53(3): 569–88.

Wolf, Michaela. 2010. "Translation 'Going Social'? Challenges to the (Ivory) Tower of Babel." *MonTI* 2: 29–46.

Zaidan, Omar F., and Chris Callison-Burch. 2011. "Crowdsourcing Translation: Professional Quality from Non-Professionals." In *Proceedings of the 49th Annual Meeting of the Association of Computational Linguistics*, 1120–29. Available online at www.cs.jhu.edu/%7Eozaidan/AOC/turk-trans_Zaidan-CCB_acl2011.pdf (accessed June 20, 2014).

Zbib, Rahib et al. 2013. "Systematic Comparison of Professional and Crowdsourced Reference Translations for Machine Translation." In *Proceedings of NAACL-HLT 2013*, 612–16. Available online at http://clair.eecs.umich.edu/aan/paper.php?paper_id=N13-1069#pdf (accessed June 20, 2014).

5 Fictional representations of translators and interpreters

Klaus Kaindl

Overview

Translation is a ubiquitous phenomenon. The notion of translation features widely in a variety of disciplines, but it is also well known outside of academia as a concept that can be applied in a wide range of societal contexts. It is perhaps its broad definition that has made translation a "travelling concept" (Bal 2002), which in the last 20 years has become an analogy for various forms of transfer and interaction in an increasingly globalized world: "translation has become a kind of master metaphor epitomizing our present *condition humaine* in a globalized and centerless context, evoking the human research for a sense of self and belonging in a puzzling world full of change and difference" (Delabastita 2009: 111). In particular, we find that the tension between homogenizing and diversifying societal, political, economic, and cultural forces, which characterizes the dynamics of globalization, is reflected in translation and interpreting. Assimilation versus differentiation, acculturation versus transculturation, change versus preservation, standardization versus fragmentation, and integration versus marginalization are but a few of the oppositions that translation/interpreting and globalization have in common.

It is therefore no coincidence that translation and interpreting have in recent years become a recurring theme in film and literature to depict a changing world and explore different aspects of globalization. We find fictional translators and interpreters across virtually all genres: historical novels (e.g., *Malinche* by Laura Esquivel) and science fiction films (*Star Wars* by George Lucas), romance novels (*Translator's Kiss* by Doug Murphy) and thrillers (*The Mission Song* by John Le Carré), LGBT fiction (*In Translation* by Annamarie Jagose) and westerns (*Dances with Wolves* by Kevin Costner), postmodern literature (*Le désert mauve* by Nicole Brossard) and experimental films (*The Task of the Translator* by Lynne Sachs), plays (*Interpreters* by Ronald Harwood) and silent films (*The Dragoman* by Edward Sloman), novellas and television series (*Game of Thrones*), poems (Chrétien de Troyes' *Cligès*) and musicals (*Truth in Translation* by Michael Lessac and Hugh Masekela). If we were to include non-fictional works, we could add (auto)biographies and memoirs of translators and interpreters (*A Foreign Affair* by Valerie Barnes), as well as documentaries on the topic of translation and interpreting (*The Whisperers* by David Bernet).

The frequent appearance of translation as a literary and filmic theme, however, should not blind us to the fact that translators and interpreters have been fictionalized throughout the centuries across nearly all literary periods from the Middle Ages to the Romantic Age, as well as throughout the entire history of film (cf. Hagedorn 2006 and Kaindl 2014a: 5–10). Writers and directors employ the concept of translation in a variety of ways. It can be used as a means to symbolize cultural, social, or religious values, to highlight the problematic relationship of fiction and reality, or to raise philosophical questions about literature. The topic of translation is placed into a fictional space transporting it into a new and larger context that goes beyond the concrete working and living situation of the translator or interpreter. Writers and directors harness both the humorous and the dramatic, and above all the sociopolitical potential of the process of translation and the figure of the translator or interpreter.

The strong presence of translators and interpreters in films and novels has undoubtedly contributed to the new visibility of translators and interpreters and their work, as Strümper-Krobb (2009) and Ben-Ari (2010) point out. Fictionalized representations of translators and interpreters also contribute to the public image of the profession, making these representations a topic of interest for Translation and Interpreting Studies insofar as they provide insight into the societal implications of translation. However, it is only since the turn of the millennium that this area of research has received consistent scrutiny.

Theoretical foundations

The phrase "fictional turn," first coined by Else Vieira (1995: 50), denotes an approach that explores how fictional representations of translators and interpreters can contribute to our theoretical understanding of translation phenomena. This approach implies that translation fiction does not function only as a primary but also as a secondary source of information for Translation Studies. Such a claim, however, raises the problematic question of the epistemological relationship between fiction and scientific method.

The notion that our knowledge about the world is ultimately always subjective and greatly influenced by how it is conveyed to us has been at the center of many philosophical debates since Plato's famous Allegory of the Cave. Many scholars have since expressed their views on this topic. Walter Benjamin, for example, in his essay "On the Program of the Coming Philosophy" (1989), explored how the concept of experience and the concept of knowledge relate to each other and how associations can be made between them. The fictionalization of translators and interpreters as a source of information for academic analysis touches directly upon the conflict described by Benjamin to the extent that works of fiction portray translation phenomena from a point of view that is always subjective, whereas the scientific method is considered objective and non-judgmental.

Therefore, it seems that fictional representations in literature and film must be clearly distinguished from scientific representations, based on their different approaches to reality. While fiction depicts the world through aesthetic, poetic, visual, and rhetorical means, science uses different methods—of an empirical and theoretical nature—designed to obtain verifiable, intersubjectively comprehensible knowledge about social reality. However, as Rockwell (1974: 4) points out, fiction is also always related to the real world: "fiction can give us two types of information about society: first in a descriptive way, facts about the state of technology, laws, customs, social structure and institutions. Second, more subtle and less easily obtained information about values and attitudes." Even if they are only vaguely and loosely related to reality, novels and films can have a major impact on society due to their popularity. The movie *The Interpreter*, starring Nicole Kidman, for example, has perhaps influenced public opinion about interpreters more than any scientific study. Similarly, Translation Studies draws on fictional assumptions to formulate its hypotheses, or as Spitzl puts it: "translation and interpreting studies is in itself based on a variety of fictional assumptions, such as the circuit diagrams of modelling communication … the practice of backtranslation in court, or the basic assumption of equidistance in asymmetric settings" (2014a: 365f).

The blurring of the boundaries between reality (represented by scholarship) and fiction is, however, not an exclusively postmodern phenomenon. Foucault indicates that literary texts were for a long time considered to be authentic and accurate depictions and so were regularly used as sources of information. It was only in the seventeenth and eighteenth centuries that "scientific texts were accepted on their own merits and positioned within an anonymous and coherent conceptual system of established truths and methods of verifications" (1980: 126).

A variety of disciplines recognized the potential of fictional texts for theoretical and conceptual research early on. In his book *Sociology through Literature* (1963), Lewis Coser describes literary texts as a "key form of social evidence and testimony" (1963: xvi), which sociology should utilize as a source of information and to broaden the horizon of research. Disciplines such as ethnography (e.g., Gupta 2005) and legal studies (Scheiber 2007) also draw on fictional texts as sources of information; philosophy in particular seems to be committed to exploring the filmic medium. For example, in the introduction to their volume *Philosophy and Film*, Freeland and Wartenberg conclude: "film also can challenge philosophy to think of itself and its questions in a new way" (1995: 2). Accordingly, film can also become "a stage in a philosophic argument" (1995: 7). Litch (2002) in turn proposes to use the philosophical potential of the film medium in the teaching of students since it can make philosophical questions available in a generally accessible form and thus "can even make the transition to philosophical thinking easier" (2002: 2).

Similar approaches to translation fiction can be found in Translation and Interpreting studies. According to Pagano (2002: 97), "fiction represents a genre that informs translation thinking from a comprehensive perspective, sensitive to relationships and movements difficult to capture through more orthodox analyses." Arrojo, too, argues for the "powerful role of fiction as theory" (2014: 37), as it has the capacity to anticipate or initiate theoretical developments and thus can serve as a source of inspiration in Translation and Interpreting Studies. Finally, Cronin views the filmic representation of translators and interpreters as "a rich intertextual resource" (2009: xi), which can be used to initiate discussion with students of issues concerning loyalty, (un)translatability, invisibility, foreignizing and domesticating translation strategies, etc.

However, this is not to say that the analysis of fictional texts as a source of theoretical information can be a substitute for knowledge gained through scientific methods. Rather science can harness the creative potential of fictional texts in order to gain new perspectives and insights into translation and interpreting phenomena. In this sense, fiction can help science to expand and broaden its perspective as is demonstrated by the different research orientations of the "fictional turn."

Evolution of the topic in TIS

The first comprehensive studies of the representation of fictional translators and interpreters were conducted in the fields of literary studies and linguistics and centered mainly on the theme of machine translation in the science fiction genre (e.g., Plank 1959; Krueger 1968). These studies focused particularly on the plausible portrayal of such translations given that plausibility is an important feature of this genre (Meyers 1980: 124). Plausibility here, as measured against the state of the art of machine translation and the so-called "magic decoder," is seen as a "touchstone for the validity of the strong form of the plausibility theory" (1980: 126), although Meyers observes that the majority of novels do not meet this plausibility criterion.

In the field of Translation and Interpreting Studies, Steiner, Arrojo, Welt Trahan, and Kurz are among the pioneers in the study of fictional translators and interpreters and their work. Their studies deal with various issues that would evolve into separate lines of research in the 1990s. In *After Babel*, Steiner examines Borges' short story *Pierre Menard* (1975: 70–73), considering it "the most acute, most concentrated commentary anyone has offered on the business of translation. What studies of translation there are, … could, in Borges's style, be termed a commentary on his commentary" (1975: 70). Arrojo (1986: 11–22) goes even further, incorporating Borges' short story into her deconstructivist analysis of the relationship between the original and the translation or the author and the translator. Both demonstrate the explanatory potential literary works can have for translation theory. In her essay on the Arabic translator in *Don Quixote*, Welt Trahan (1984) opens up another perspective for Translation Studies, one that is closer to literary studies, examining the narrative and, consequently, metaphorical function of translators and literature. Kurz (1987) employs a third approach, using Doris Lessing's novel *The Summer before the Dark* as a starting point for comparing the description of interpreters in fiction with reality. Her interest is in whether the fictional portrayal of the profession is realistic. In a way, she transfers the criterion of plausibility used in the study of science fiction novels to fiction in general. These three pioneering works paved the way for the main lines of research in transfiction, which developed in the 1990s and have become more diverse in recent years.

Translation theory through fiction

The study of fictional texts for the purposes of enhancing our theoretical understanding of translation phenomena focuses on different areas. A number of scholars are interested in the new theoretical perspectives on translation that can be opened up to scientific investigation through an examination of fictional texts. The central focus of this research is on Latin-American authors, most notably Borges, Cortázar, and Guimarães Rosa (see also Pagano 2002; Arrojo 2004). These authors deal with the complex relationship between the original and translation(s). At a time when translation theory was still in its infancy, the above-mentioned authors developed the psychological, semiotic, deconstructivist, and feminist foundations of translation theory, which to this day inspire theoretical reflection.

Lavieri (2007) expands this approach. Interested in how works of literature can become a source of theoretical knowledge about translation, he also analyzes the influence fictional representations of translations may have on how translation is practiced in a society. In contrast to Wakabayashi (2011: 100), who draws a clear distinction between reality and fiction, he assumes that these two domains can never be clearly separated from each other, as we do not experience reality in an immediate way; it is always indirectly mediated through symbols, language, and texts. As a result, literary texts can also become a possible source for the creation of translational knowledge. Thus, this fictional poetry of translation opens up a new dimension for translation research: the interplay between fictional representations and actual translation practice.

A third approach that explores works of fiction as a source of translation theory examines the translation theories that are explicitly or implicitly discussed in novels and films. For example, Apostolou (2014) and Kaindl (2014b) investigate how Benjamin's philosophy of translation is taken up in short stories by authors such as Hasak-Lowy and Tawada.

The metaphorical potential of translation in fiction

The second movement posits translation as a metaphor, analyzing it from a literary point of view in order to reflect on a variety of social and communicative processes. There are various focal points within this movement. In numerous films and books translators and interpreters assume the distinctive roles or are used to address questions of identity against the backdrop of social upheaval, such as migration, war, political and religious conflict, and other ethically and morally charged situations. The character of the translator and the process of translating and interpreting can be deployed to portray a variety of communicatively tense situations, which may involve understanding and misunderstanding, the formation and mediation of meaning, issues of "the foreign" and "the domestic," and the encounter of languages and cultures. These concepts are then developed to address fundamental existential questions. The resulting identity constructs of fictional translators and interpreters are explored in a variety of studies that draw on imagological concepts (e.g., Andres 2008), as well as methods from literary studies, such as "close reading" (e.g., in Wilhelm 2010).

Waisman (2005) and Gentzler (2008) expand the metaphorical approach to translators and interpreters by examining the connection between fictional representations of translation and the formation of national identities in Latin America. "Translation in South America is much more than a linguistic operation; rather, it has become one of the means by which an entire continent has come to define itself" (Gentzler 2008: 108). Building on this assumption, Gentzler analyzes translation-related themes in works of fiction with a view to their role in the construction of cultures, demonstrating how, for example, Borges' view of literary translation can be read as a rebellion against the colonial powers of Europe (2008: 115).

Over the last several years there has been a growing interest in works where social processes are linked to the concept of cultural translation as defined by Bhabha (1994). As Wilson, who studies the "translational identity" (2011: 235) of characters in translingual narratives, emphasizes, cultural translation can be applied not only to real transcultural communication processes but also to fiction (2011: 235). This perspective, which is rooted in cultural studies, is, for example, used by Lüsebrink (2009) in his analysis of Eva Hofmann's *Lost in Translation*, where he sees the exile of the narrator as a translation process. Steiner (2009) assumes a postcolonial perspective when he studies migration as cultural translation in the works of Sudanese and Tanzanian authors. Parker (2005), Maier (2006), Brodzki (2007), Baer (2014), and Beuren (2014) discuss the use of fictional translators to question normative categories of gender and sexuality. Similarly, the interpreter in Amadou Hampâté Bâ's novel *L'étrange destin de Wangrin* can be seen as a symbol or embodiment of (post)colonial tension (see Spitzl 2014b). Andres (2009: 14) takes this idea even further, describing literary and filmic representations of fictional interpreters as a "collective metaphor" for issues related to language and identity.

Translation fiction and translation reality

Parallel to the study of translation fiction with a view to its theoretical and metaphorical potential, a third direction has emerged, which focuses on contrasting real and fictional translation and interpreting situations or translators and interpreters. The volumes edited by Kurz and Kaindl (2005) and Kaindl and Kurz (2008) do not seek to examine the mimetic realism of fiction; rather they address the question of whether these fictional characterizations could be realistic even though they have not yet occurred in reality (see Kaindl and Kurz 2005: 11). The reason behind this approach is that the interest on the part of a given profession in books and films portraying that profession is usually not merely literary. Instead, such fiction is nearly always compared to reality insofar as reading, Luhmann contends, enables the reader to "locate oneself in the world as it is portrayed" (2000: 62). Fictional depictions also provide insights into the ideas, clichés, and stereotypes of translating and interpreting that exist in a given society and can therefore be used as a source for the study of popular theories concerning translation and interpreting.

Key studies

Arrojo provides us with a number of studies that analyze literary texts as a source for translation theory (e.g., 2003, 2004, 2006). In her article "The Power of Fiction as Theory" (2014), she uses the literary works of Jorge Luis Borges to illustrate a practical approach to the analysis of literary texts in order to enhance our theoretical understanding of translational phenomena. She links aesthetic and literary considerations with poetological, philosophical, historico-cultural, sociological, and political concerns, thus providing us with a deeper insight into the history of ideas that connects translation, culture, and society.

The majority of studies analyze the metaphoric potential of translation phenomena. The first comprehensive study in this area is the collection by Delabastita and Grutman (2005), which aims to provide a systematic overview of the diverse portrayals of fictionalized translators and interpreters and, at the same time, to examine the topic in the wider context of multilingualism. Hagedorn (2006) provides us with the only monograph to date on fictional translation as a literary device. As he shows in his diachronic study of fictitious translation, which spans a 400-year period and begins with Miguel Cervantes' *Don Quixote*, fictitious translation has assumed increasingly multilayered functions over the centuries. The ways in which fictitious translation is portrayed are similarly varied. Fictional translations can be introduced in the preface or afterword of a work, in footnotes, or as part of the actual narrative. The functions of fictitious translation range from providing intertextual references, introducing a layer of irony and humor, to posing philosophical questions about the nature of literature.

A third area of investigation involves the comparison of the literary world with social reality, for which Klaus Kaindl (2008) proposes a method of investigation based on Bourdieu's field-habitus theory. Following an examination of the fields in which translators and interpreters work, the habitus constructs of fictionalized translators and interpreters are analyzed on a physical (appearance, features), psychological (emotional and mental state), and cognitive (translation practice, professionalism) level, and are then compared to the real-world public image of the profession. This approach is particularly useful for the analysis of biographies and documentaries about translators, as demonstrated by Plassard (2013) in her analysis of the documentary *The Woman with Five Elephants*, about Svetlana Geier, a translator of Dostoevsky into German.

New directions

The massive fictionalization of translators and interpreters is seen primarily as a phenomenon of globalization. As a result, very few historical studies exist. An exploration of the fictional representations of translation phenomena throughout history and how they were linked to questions of identity and loss of identity could shed light on the interconnectedness of translation and social phenomena. Furthermore, an analysis of historical works of literature could yield important information on the translation practice and working conditions of translators and interpreters. Bachleitner (1989) is the first to provide us with a study in this area, drawing on the fictional representation of translation processes in literary texts from the first part of the nineteenth century. This study offers a kind of social history of the profession and gives us an idea of the professional everyday life of the translator.

With the growing interest in the literary and filmic portrayal of translators and interpreters came the need to organize research approaches according to their methodologies. In this regard, frameworks pertaining to literary and film studies can offer valuable guidance. While most studies to date are restricted to the interpretation of texts, D'hulst (2010) proposes a widening of the scope of research to include narrative structural points of reference. He uses the linguist Benveniste's differentiation between the act of uttering (*énonciation*) and the utterance (*énoncé*) as a starting point (2010: 54f). Applied to the theme of translation and interpreting, this corresponds to the distinction between works in which concrete acts of translation or interpreting take place (*énonciation*) and works that tell about translation and interpreting (*énoncé*). Another distinction would be whether the translation or act of interpreting in question is intra or interlingual. The different aspects of narrative presentation, such as the narrator's position (do the narrator and the narrative belong to the same world or not?) and narrator types (extradiegetic vs. intradiegetic), although only mentioned in passing in D'hulst's work, may also be productive distinctions. Narratological studies, such as those by Genette (1988) and Bal (1997), are very helpful for the analysis of narrative structural aspects both in literature and in film. So far, very few studies have employed narratological categories of character analysis, such as the classification of the portrayal of translators and interpreters as heroes, villains, or helpers, or the distinction between static and dynamic or between one-dimensional and multidimensional characters. The same can be said of cinematographic categories, such as the visual and acoustic, which are both equally important in the construction of fictional characters. The portrayal of a character or his/her actions is greatly influenced by camera work, film editing, image composition, lighting, etc.—criteria that have been given little consideration so far as they relate to fictional translators and interpreters.

Derrida (1999) proposes another area of investigation that would widen the scope of the fictional turn by viewing translation as a general matrix for interpreting literary texts. He uses Shakespeare's *Merchant of Venice* to demonstrate that the play can be read as a general description of the translator's task and interprets the individual storylines as reflecting key aspects of translation theory. For example, he interprets Portia's attempt to convince her father, the merchant Shylock, to depart from the literal (Jewish) interpretation of the contract and to accept the (Christian) interpretation as a confrontation between two translation principles, the literal, on the one hand, and the assimilating, on the other. Ost (2010) refers to this approach as the "paradigme traductif," in which translation moves away from being the object of investigation to become a tool for the analysis of fictional texts.

References

Andres, Dörte. 2008. *Dolmetscher als literarische Figuren: von Identitätsverlust, Dilettantismus und Verrat*. München: Weidenbauer.

——2009. "Dolmetscher in fiktionalen Werken – von Verirrung, Verwirrung und Verführung." *Germanistisches Jahrbuch Russland – Das Wort*: 11–24.

Apostolou, Fotini. 2014. "Walter Benjamin Revisited: A Literary Reading of Todd Hasak-Lowy's Short Story 'The Task of This Translator'." In *Transfiction. Research into the Realities of Translation Fiction*, Klaus Kaindl and Karlheinz Spitzl (eds.), 69–86. Amsterdam and Philadelphia: John Benjamins.

Arrojo, Rosemary. 1986. *Oficina de Tradução – A Teoría na Práctica*. São Paulo: Àtica.

——2003. "The Power of Originals and the Scandal of Translation – A Reading of Edgar Allan Poe's 'The Oval Portrait'." In Maria Calzada Pérez (ed.), *Apropos Ideology: Translation Studies on Ideology – Ideologies in Translation Studies*, 165–80. Manchester: St. Jerome.

——2004. "Tradução, (in)fidelidade e gênero num conto de Moacyr Scliar." *Revista Brasileira de Lingüística Aplicada* 4(1): 27–36.

——2006. "Translation and Impropriety: A Reading of Claude Bleton's *Les nègres du traducteur*." *Translation and Interpreting Studies* 1(2): 91–109.

——2014. "The Power of Fiction." In *Transfiction. Research into the Realties of Translation Fiction*, Klaus Kaindl and Karlheinz Spitzl (eds.), 37–49. Amsterdam and Philadelphia: John Benjamins.

Bachleitner, Norbert. 1989. "'Übersetzungsfabriken'. Das deutsche Übersetzungswesen in der ersten Hälfte des 19. Jahrhunderts." *Internationales Archiv für Sozialgeschichte der deutschen Literatur* 14(1): 1–49.

Baer, Brian J. 2014. "Interpreting 'Daniel Stein': Or What Happens When Fictional Translators Get Translated." In *Transfiction. Research into the Realities of Translation Fiction*, Klaus Kaindl and Karlheinz Spitzl (eds.), 157–75. Amsterdam and Philadelphia: John Benjamins.

Bal, Mieke. 1997. *Narratology: Introduction to the Theory of Narrative.* Toronto: Toronto University Press.

——2002. *Travelling Concepts in the Humanities: A Rough Guide.* Toronto: Toronto University Press.

Ben-Ari, Nitsa. 2010. "Representations of Translators in Popular Culture." *Translation and Interpreting Studies* 5(2): 220–42.

Benjamin, Walter. 1989. "On the Program of the Coming Philosophy." In *Benjamin: Philosophy, Aesthetics, History,* Gary Smith (ed.), 1–12. Chicago: University of Chicago Press.

Beuren, Daniela. 2014. "Neither Is a Translator, Unless They're Transauthers: Confusion and (Re-)gendering in Feminist Fiction/translation." In Klaus Kaindl and Karlheinz Spitzl (eds.), *Transfiction. Research into the Realities of Translation Fiction,* 315–27. Amsterdam and Philadelphia: John Benjamins.

Bhabha, Homi. 1994. *The Location of Culture.* London and New York: Routledge.

Brodzki, Bella. 2007. *Can These Bones Live? Translation, Survival, and Cultural Memory.* Stanford, CA: Stanford University Press.

Coser, Lewis A. (ed.). 1963. *Sociology through Literature. An Introductory Reader.* Englewood Cliffs, NJ: Prentice Hall.

Cronin, Michael. 2009. *Translation Goes to the Movies.* London and New York: Routledge.

Delabastita, Dirk. 2009. "Fictional Representations." In *The Routledge Encyclopedia of Translation Studies,* Mona Baker and Gabriela Saldanha (eds.), 109–12. London: Routledge.

Delabastita, Dirk, and Rainer Grutman. 2005. "Introduction. Fictional Representations of Multilingualism and Translation." In *Fictionalising Translation and Multilingualism,* Dirk Delabastita and Rainer Grutman (eds.). *Linguistica Antverpiensia* 4: 11–34.

Derrida, Jacques. 1999. "Qu'est-ce qu'une traduction 'relevante'?" In *Quinzièmes Assises de la Traduction littéraire* (Arles 1998), 21–48. Arles: Gallimard.

D'hulst, Lieven. 2010. "La traduction mise en scène dans la prose francophone et hispanophone moderne: de la narrativisation à la métalepse." In *Translatio in fabula, enjeux d'une rencontre entre fictions et traductions,* Sophie Klimis et al. (eds.), 51–62. Brussels: Facultés Universitaires Saint-Louis.

Foucault, Michel. 1980. "What Is an Author." In *Language, Counter-Memory, Practice: Selected Essays and Interviews by Michel Foucault,* Donald F. Bouchard (ed.), 113–38. Ithaca, NY: Cornell University Press.

Freeland, Cynthia A., and Thomas E. Wartenberg. 1995. *Philosophy and Film.* New York/London: Routledge.

Genette, Gérard. 1988. *Narrative Discourse Revisited.* New York: Cornell University Press.

Gentzler, Edwin. 2008. *Translation and Identity in the Americas. New Directions in Translation Theory.* London and New York: Routledge.

Gupta, Akhil. 2005. "Narratives of Corruption: Anthropological and Fictional Accounts of the Indian State." *Ethnography* 6(1): 5–34.

Hagedorn, Hans Christian. 2006. *La traducción narrada: el recurso narrativo de la traducción ficticia.* Cuenca: Ediciones de la Universidad de Castilla-La Mancha.

Kaindl, Klaus. 2008. "Zwischen Fiktion und Wirklichkeit: TranslatorInnen im Spannungsfeld von Wissenschaft, Literatur, Realität." In *Translationskultur – ein innovatives und produktives Konzept,* Larisa Schippel (ed.), 307–33. Berlin: Franke & Timme.

——2014a. "Going Fictional! Translators and Interpreters in Literature and Film: An Introduction." In *Transfiction. Research into the Realties of Translation Fiction*, Klaus Kaindl and Karlheinz Spitzl (eds.), 1–26. Amsterdam and Philadelphia: John Benjamins.

——2014b. "Of Dragons and Translators: Foreigness as a Principle of Life." In *Transfiction. Research into the Realties of Translation Fiction*, Klaus Kaindl and Karlheinz Spitzl (eds.), 87–101. Amsterdam and Philadelphia: John Benjamins.

Kaindl, Klaus, and Ingrid Kurz. 2005. "Einleitung." In *Wortklauber, Sinnverdreher, Brückenbauer? DolmetscherInnen und ÜbersetzerInnen als literarische Geschöpfe*, Ingrid Kurz and Klaus Kaindl (eds.), 9–18. Vienna: LIT Verlag.

——(eds.) 2008. *Helden, Verräter, Gaukler? Das Rollenbild von TranslatorInnen im Spiegel der Literatur*. Münster: LIT Verlag.

Krueger, John R. 1968. "Language and Techniques of Communication as Theme or Tool in Science-fiction." *Linguistics. An International Review* 39: 68–86.

Kurz, Ingrid. 1987. "Conference Interpreting – Myth and Reality." In *Proceedings of the 28th Annual Conference of the American Translators Association, Albuquerque, New Mexico, October 8–11, 1987*, K. Kummer (ed.), 315–20. Medford, NJ: Learned Information.

Kurz, Ingrid, and Klaus Kaindl (eds.). 2005. *Wortklauber, Sinnverdreher, Brückenbauer? DolmetscherInnen und ÜbersetzerInnen als literarische Geschöpfe*. Vienna: LIT Verlag.

Lavieri, Antonio. 2007. *Translatio in fabula. La letteratura come practica teorica del tradurre*. Rome: Editori Riuniti.

Litch, Mary M. 2002. *Philosophy through Film*. New York and London: Routledge.

Luhmann, Niklas. 2000. *The Reality of Mass Media*. Stanford, CA: Stanford University Press.

Lüsebrink, Hans-Jürgen. 2009. "'Lost in Translation': Übersetzung und Exilerfahrung bei Eva Hoffman (Polen/Kanada/USA) und Jacques Poulin (Québec, Kanada)." In *Kultur übersetzen. Zur Wissenschaft des Übersetzens im deutsch-französischen Dialog*, Alberto Gil and Manfred Schmeling (eds.), 97–106. Berlin: Akademie Verlag.

Maier, Carol. 2006. "The Translator as Theôros. Thoughts on Cogitation, Figuration and Current Creative Writing." In *Translating Others Vol. 1*, Theo Hermans (ed.), 163–80. Manchester: St. Jerome.

Meyers, Walter Earl. 1980. *Aliens and Linguistics. Language Study and Science Fiction*. Athens: University of Georgia Press.

Ost, François. 2010. "La traduction dans la fiction. Du pareil à l'autre." In *Translatio in fabula, enjeux d'une rencontre entre fictions et traductions*, Sophie Klimis et al. (eds.), 21–50. Brussels: Facultés Universitaires Saint-Louis.

Pagano, Adriana S. 2002. "Translation as Testimony: On Official Histories and Subversive Pedagogies in Cortázar." In *Translation and Power*, Maria Tymoczko and Edwin Gentzler (eds.), 80–98. Amherst: University of Massachusetts Press.

Parker, Emma. 2005. "Lost in Translation: Gender and the Figure of the Translator in Contemporary Queer Fiction." In *The Poetics of Transubstantiation: From Theology to Metaphor*, Douglas Burnham and Enrico Giaccherini (eds.), 118–25. Aldershot: Ashgate.

Plank, Robert. 1959. "Communications in Science Fiction." In *Our Language and Our World*, S.I. Hayakawa (ed.), 272–78. New York: Harperer.

Plassard, Freddie. 2013. "Portrait d'une traductrice dans le film *La femme aux cinq éléphants*." *Forum* 11(1): 203–21.

Rockwell, Joan. 1974. *Fact in Fiction. The Use of Literature in the Systematic Study of Society.* London: Routledge.
Scheiber, Oliver (ed.). 2007. *Auf dem Scheiterhaufen der Paragraphen – Richter als literarische Geschöpfe.* Vienna: LIT Verlag.
Spitzl, Karlheinz. 2014a. "Fiction as a Catalyst: Some Afterthoughts." In *Transfiction. Research into the Realties of Translation Fiction*, Klaus Kaindl and Karlheinz Spitzl (eds.), 363–68. Amsterdam and Philadelphia: John Benjamins.
——2014b. "Taking Care of the Stars: Interpreted Interaction in Amadou Hampâté Bâ's 'L'étrange destin de Wangrin'." In *Transfiction. Research into the Realties of Translation Fiction*, Klaus Kaindl and Karlheinz Spitzl (eds.), 103–12. Amsterdam and Philadelphia: John Benjamins.
Steiner, George. 1975. *After Babel. Aspects of Language and Translation.* Oxford: Oxford University Press.
Steiner, Tina. 2009. *Translated People, Translated Texts.* Manchester: St. Jerome.
Strümper-Krobb, Sabine. 2009. *Zwischen den Welten. Die Sichtbarkeit des Übersetzers in der Literatur.* Berlin: Weidler.
Vieira, Else Ribeiro Pires. 1995. "(In)visibilidades na tradução: Troca de olhares teóricos e ficcionais." *Com Textos* 6: 50–68.
Waisman, Sergio. 2005. *Borges and Translation: The Irreverence of the Periphery.* Cranbury, NJ: Associated University Press.
Wakabayashi, Judith. 2011. "Fictional Representations of Author-Translator Relationships." *Translation Studies* 4(1): 87–102.
Welt Trahan, Elisabeth. 1984. "The Arabic Translator in *Don Quixote*: His Master's Voice and Victim." In *Translation Perspectives: Selected Papers, 1982–1983*, Marilyn Gaddis Rose (ed.), 71–85. Binghampton, NY: SUNY Press.
Wilhelm, Christine. 2010. *Traduttore traditore – Vermittler durch Verrat. Eine Analyse literarischer Translatorfiguren in Texten von Jorge Luis Borges, Italo Calvino und Leonardo Sciascia.* Trier: WVT.
Wilson, Rita. 2011. "Cultural Mediation through Translingual Narrative." *Target* 23(2): 235–50.

6 Gender and sexuality

Brian James Baer and Françoise Massardier-Kenney

Overview

Interest in issues related to gender and sexuality in Translation Studies arose in the 1970s, reflecting the rise of the women's movement and LGBT movements in many Western societies, which occurred simultaneously with the spread of post-structuralist or postmodern theoretical approaches to the study of social identities. For this reason, research on the topics of gender and sexuality in translation and interpreting contexts has often had an activist bent, that is, it was designed to draw attention to and to some extent redress the imbalance of power in traditional patriarchal societies, where masculinity and heterosexuality are the privileged embodiment of gender/sexuality. The study of issues related to gender and sexuality has been extremely productive in the field of Translation Studies, resulting in a number of theoretical writings on the relationship between gender/sexual identity and textual authority, case studies treating female- and/or gay-identified translators and interpreters and the translation of literary and other works related to gender and sexuality, as well as more large-scale historical studies meant to make visible female and gay translators. In so doing, the study of gender and sexuality reassesses the role of translation in the development of literary and political movements.

Theoretical foundations

Key works in the development of gender studies include de Beauvoir's *Second Sex* (1953), whose influence can be felt both in the works of the proponents of *écriture féminine* (what is called French feminism in the US and represented in particular by Hélène Cixous and Luce Irigaray), and in that of materialist feminists, such as Monique Wittig and, more recently, Judith Butler. De Beauvoir's notion that one is not born a woman but becomes one and her study of patriarchal oppressive practices have led to a view of gender as a cultural construction that is both the expression of oppressive gender norms and the locus (the embodiment) of possibilities for personal agency and transformation, providing escape from a long tradition of oppression and victimization. Luce Irigaray followed de Beauvoir's study of patriarchal practices but used a

Lacanian psychoanalytic model mixed with a Marxist one in *This Sex Which Is Not One* (1977); and *Speculum of the Other Woman* (1974) to argue that in a patriarchal culture—"a phallic economy"—women function like a currency and are used by men based on their exchange value. Similarly, Hélène Cixous, a prolific poet, scholar, playwright, and theorist, especially known for her essay "Laugh of the Medusa" (1976), combines Derridean deconstruction and Lacanian psychoanalysis to critique Western logocentrism through the concept of *écriture feminine*, a mode of writing that is inscribed in a feminine libidinal economy rather than a masculine one. Cixous, too, was very interested in literature as a transnational phenomenon and wrote extensively on transgressive writing practices, focusing on authors who have "strangered their own language" (O'Grady 1996–97: 9).

Rather than focusing on sexual difference or *écriture féminine*, Butler developed the notion of performativity, that is, the idea that notions of gender and sex come into being through repeated discursive practices that reflect deeply ingrained cultural norms. The concept of performativity, derived from Austin's theory of speech acts, is a fundamentally *linguistic* concept (Ehrlich and Meyerhoff 2014: 37) and has influenced TIS in major ways. Monique Wittig's work pushes the interrogation of gender even further, toward the very abolition of the concept. Rather than a binary opposition male/female, she proposes a view of subjects whose identity is formed outside of gender norms. Her self-identification as a radical lesbian was a way to invent a new category outside of heterosexual and gender concepts. In her works of fiction, such as *L'Opoponax* (1964), *Les Guérillères* (1969), or *The Lesbian Body* (1973), she invents a language that escapes the formations of patriarchal language. The influence of these feminist thinkers in gender research in TIS is often under-acknowledged but deep-seated and informs the major research approaches in the field.

The dual origins of gender and sexuality studies—in libertarian movements and the academy—has produced a theoretical tension between a minoritarian, or civil rights, model, which posits the existence of more or less stable and discrete categories of gay/straight, and a universalist model, according to which sexual desire is polymorphous. And so, while minoritarian models seek to validate, and in so doing reaffirm, gay and lesbian identities, post-structuralist or postmodern approaches to the study of sexuality developed in the academy seek to deconstruct the oppressive logic upon which the exclusive, asymmetrical categories of gay/straight are built by exposing "the incoherencies in the allegedly stable relations between chromosomal sex, gender and sexual desire" (Jagose 1996: 3). In addition to the term *queer*, post-structuralist approaches to the study of sexuality have generated a number of other non-essentializing terms to describe same-sex phenomena, such as same-sex desire, same-sex contact, men who sleep with men, gay-identified individuals, and the conglomeration LGBTIQ (Lesbian, Gay, Bisexual, Transgender, Intersex, and Queer). Minoritarian approaches, on the other hand, see those categories as the necessary ground for resisting oppression (see Bersani 1995).

The view of (homo)sexuality as a social construct was first elaborated in the late 1960s and 1970s in such seminal works as Mary MacIntosh's "The Homosexual Role" (1968), Kenneth Plummer's *Sexual Stigma* (1975), and volume one of Michel Foucault's *History of Sexuality* (1976–78). These works posited homosexuality as a discursive construct, produced through specific legal, medical, religious, and other discourses. A defining moment in the history of homosexuality, Foucault argues, occurred in the late nineteenth century when the legal and medical discourses of industrial societies "produced" homosexuality as a totalizing identity, rather than, as in pre-modern societies, a set of specific sex acts (the sodomite). For Foucault, the modern discursive construction of homosexuality reflected the increasing intrusion of the modern state in individuals' lives, while also providing the conditions for resisting that intrusion. The relationship of "homosexuality" to the modern policing of gender/sexual norms (i.e., heteronormativity), and, specifically, to the internalization of those norms as homophobia, was elaborated by Guy Hocquenghem's *Homosexual Desire* (1972/1978) and by Eve Kosofsky Sedgwick in *Between Men* (1985), where she developed the notion of homosexual panic. To the extent that, in a constructivist paradigm, the birth of the homosexual necessitated the birth of its defining other—the heterosexual—homosexual panic represented for Sedgwick the internalized policing of sexual norms in patriarchal societies when the imperative to create strong homosocial bonds was problematized by the emergence of the exclusive binary opposition of homosexual/heterosexual.

The influence of the constructivist approach on the study of (homo)sexuality has been profound. Whereas histories of homosexuality and anthologies of gay and lesbian literature produced by the early gay rights movement assumed a unified and consistent identity across time and space, queer histories acknowledged the conceptual inconsistencies and differences in the various cultural constructions of homosexuality, as elaborated by David Halperin in *How to Do the History of Homosexuality* (2002). The suspicion of universalizing claims, metanarratives, and nationalist frames encouraged the production of pluralized histories, such as Stephen O. Murray's *Homosexualities* (2000), and typologies of the various social constructions of homosexuality (see Adam 1979), as well as microhistories, in which the construction of homosexuality is analyzed within a specific locale at a specific moment in time. Some exemplary microhistories include George Chauncey's *Gay New York* (1994), David Higg's edited volume *Queer Sites: Gay Urban Histories since 1600* (1999), and Florence Tamagne's *Histoire de l'homosexualité en Europe: Berlin, Londres, Paris, 1919–1939* (2000). More recently, scholars have attempted to redress the almost exclusive focus on large urban centers by studying homosexuality in rural contexts (e.g., Howard 2001; Johnson 2013; Fisher et al. 2014). In *Sexual Citizenship*, David T. Evans (1993) offers an important corrective to earlier constructivist studies of homosexuality, stressing the importance of the material contexts in which sexualities are made.

More recently, queer scholars have studied the construction of homosexuality at the intersection of the local and the global, of the national and the transnational (Altman 2001; Binnie 2004; Puar 2007). The constructivist view of sexuality within the context of postcolonial studies has produced a number of works documenting the social construction of (homo)sexuality in societies outside the developed West (Schmitt and Sofer 1992; Murray and Roscoe 1997; Essig 1999; Vanita 2002; Ze'evi 2006) and in pre-modern Western societies (e.g., Bray 1982/1995; Halperin 1990; Fradenburg and Freccero 1996). Works such as Ronald Hyam's *Empire and Sexuality* (1990), Robert Aldrich's *Colonialism and Homosexuality* (2003), and Joseph Allen Boone's *The Homoerotics of Orientalism* (2014) explore the role played by homosexuals, homosexuality, and same-sex desire in European colonization, complicating earlier models of the relationship between the East and West.

Evolution of the topic in TIS

Several scholars in the field of Translation and Interpreting Studies were quick to draw an analogy between the theoretical deconstruction of the biological body as the transcendent signifier of gender identity (gender as genitalia)—see Foucault's *The History of Sexuality* (1978) and Thomas Laqueur's *Making Sex* (1990)—and the deconstruction of the source text as transcendent signifier of meaning (the original as origin). If there is no transcendent reality knowable outside of language, then the sexual body, no less than the textual corpus, is a discursive construction and so must be studied within the regime of knowledge/power that assigns meaning to it. Another productive analogy was drawn by Lori Chamberlain in her seminal essay "The Metaphorics of Translation," in which she traced the overlapping of the categories of gender and translation in traditional discourse on translation, which served to mutually reinforce the subordinate position of women and translators in patriarchal societies. Early scholars working on issues of gender and sexuality also treated as mutually reinforcing the relationship between national and gender identities, specifically in the context of French Canada (see Simon 1996).

Gender has become such a complex and contested concept that a number of scholars in TIS now resort to using the term "women" to describe all kinds of practices at the risk of invoking traditional, essentialist definitions of women and men (see von Flotow 2011). This tendency has its own perils, especially considering the rise of transgender as a category and the problematization of the category "woman." As early as 1996, Maier (with Massardier-Kenney) pointed out that gender definitions were local, fluid, and evolving concepts, which need to be interrogated, especially in light of the bond that, in the West at least, translation has had with woman and the subaltern Other. As Massardier-Kenney later cautioned, one could use the feminine as a privileged element of identity without isolating it from other processes of devalorization (social or symbolic), such as class, racialization, or nationalization (Massardier-Kenney 1997: 56). This approach coincided with what is now called "third-wave feminism" and is exemplified in Kadish and Massardier-Kenney's *Translating Slavery: Gender and Race in French Abolitionist Writing, 1780–1830*, which showed that translation, gender, and race had been inextricably linked in the writing of the women involved in the antislavery movement.

Recent studies involving gender use a variety of approaches, some of which are specific to a feminist *engagé* approach as it was developed by French theoreticians of difference, such as Irigaray and Cixous, or in the Canadian context by such critics and translators as Godard (1990) and de Lotbinière-Harwood (1991). The latter sought to make women "visible in the text" (Lotbinière-Harwood 1991: 101) by emphasizing feminine difference, while others focus on recovery (the study of little known women translators or the study of women translators as a social category) or on the effect of a translator's gender/sexuality on the translation process. Still others focus on the strategies used to translate gendered language. Some scholars have adopted the "memoir approach," i.e., when women scholars or translators reflect on the ways in which their gender identification and that of the source-text author influence their practice.

While many studies in the field of sexuality acknowledge the importance of language, few of those studies prioritize what David Damrosch refers to as the "problematics of translation" (Damrosch 2009: 8). Conversely, in TIS, issues of sexuality remain under-studied, which is somewhat surprising given the fact that one of the founding figures of the modern discipline of Translation Studies, James Holmes, was a self-identified homosexual, whose gay-themed poetry and translations of queer texts and authors formed a significant part of his creative oeuvre (Larkosh 2011a: 1–4).

The research that has been done on sexuality and translation in Translation Studies and related fields, such as Comparative Literature, can be generally divided into two categories:

1. Case studies of translation of gay-themed literary works that highlight various incongruities between the source and target cultures related to their conceptualizations of sexuality and sexual identities, social tolerance, and morality. Censorship—be it political, market, or self-imposed—often plays an important role in shaping the translations of such texts. When works with overt homosexual content are translated, the translations may, Berlina (2012: 450) argues, function as "a litmus test for the target culture's relation to homosexuality." Drawing a direct relationship between the treatment of homosexual content and a culture's overall relationship to homosexuality is, however, not a simple task as the treatment of homosexuality in translated literature can take many forms, ranging from excision (covert or overt) and substitution (changing homosexual references to heterosexual ones) to highlighting the text's gay thematics, or, conversely, to toning them down or adapting them to target culture scripts and frames (see Tyulenev 2014). Those themes may or may not be treated in paratextual material and in the bindings of the translation (see Harvey 2003a; Baer

2014; Mazzei 2014). Taken all together, these treatments may form a coherent representation of homosexuality or may instead appear to contradict one another, underscoring the position of translated texts "as interfaces between competing ideological positions" (Harvey 2003a: 43).

2. Case studies of gay-identified translators who *queer* their translations, that is, express, intentionally or not, their own same-sex desire or make visible the homosexuality of the source text and/or of the source-text author. Some notable examples of this line of research include Keenaghan (1998), Larkosh (2007), and Baer (2014).

Key studies

In the study of gender and translation, an early example of historical recovery is Delisle's edited volume *Portraits de traductrices* (1999/2002), which includes portraits of several women translators, some well-known (Anne Dacier, Eleanor Marx), others less so (Ekaterina Karavelova, Anne de la Roche-Guilhem). While the volume provides biographical sketches of these women translators, Delisle cautions the reader not to make them into early feminists or women's rights activists; however, he points out that translation was a way for these women to overcome the limits imposed on them by their patriarchal society and to show their intellectual worth at a time when they were not accepted as the equal of men.

In a recent volume titled *Translating Women* (2011), edited by Luise von Flotow, several essays also focus on the work of women translators (e.g., Martin on Eliza P. Reid and Jane Haldimand Marcet, and Barker on Helen Maria Williams). Other works focusing on the history of women translators include Tyulenev's 2011 study of Russian women translators and Woods' 2011 reassessment of Willa Muir, the wife of poet Edwin Muir and his co-translator of Kafka's works.

Another important contribution to the historiography of women translators is Julie Candler Hayes (2009). Her chapter on Anne Dacier demonstrates the importance of Dacier's work for the development of translation theory in France, in particular her "sense of the incapacity of conventional poetic forms to capture the energy she experiences through texts from another time and place" (140). Hayes points out that translation projects were essential in providing women with an apprenticeship in literary culture when authorship was defined as an exclusively male domain, and she provides an overview of many women translators (both French and British) during the period 1600 to 1800. Hayes' work belongs to a now significant body of research on women translators in pre-modern Europe, before the advent of Romanticism and its cult of originality, that connect gender with historical constructions of authorship (see Goldberg 1997; Kronitiris 1997; White 2011; and Goodrich 2013).

Wolf (2005) studies the historical conditions that shaped the "oppressive situations" (21) in which two German translators from the eighteenth century,

Luise Gottsched and Therese Huber, worked. Wolf parallels her historical study of the formation of these women's individuality through translation with a contemporary overview, based on questionnaires and interviews with translators and publishers on the status of feminist translation and the situation of feminist translators. Her findings show that much remains to be done to make women more visible discursively: literary translators work at home, publishers are not committed to inclusive language and seek fluency, paratexts such as forewords and footnotes are discouraged, and feminist translation is restricted to very specific genres (lesbian novels and female detective novels) and to a female readership.

Another line of inquiry consists in studying translation strategies and attempting to determine whether the gender of the translator influences the translation choices made. These studies range from the translation by women of patriarchal texts and of feminist texts: Rim Hassen on woman translators of the Quran (2011), Leonardi and Federici's study (2012) of the translation of Woolf's canonical "feminist" text *A Room of One's Own* into Italian, James Underhill's study of translations of Emily Dickinson's poetry into French (2011), and Henitiuk's (2011) work on the role of gender in translations of *The Pillow Book*, written by a woman in Japan's Hein court.

Vanessa Leonardi's monograph *Gender and Ideology in Translation: Do Women and Men Translate Differently?* (2007) hypothesizes that the gender of translators affects the process as well as the product of translation. In order to test her hypothesis, she compares the strategies used in the translation of four twentieth-century Italian novels into English by male and female translators, making use of critical constrastive text linguistics analysis (CCTL), as well as analysis of the translators' paratexts. The fact that Leonardi's corpus is very small and that there are no translations of the same source text by both a male and a female translator does not allow her to validate her hypothesis, but her use of CCTL could fruitfully be applied to larger corpora and provides a useful methodology to investigate the impact of the translator's gender on translated texts.

Several essays that appeared in the volume *Gender, Sex and Translation* (2005), edited by José Santaemilia, address some of the general questions posed by earlier scholars. For instance, von Flotow surveys the role of gender and contexts in determining translation discourse (the translation of the Bible by Julia Evelina Smith, or the translation of eighteenth-century abolitionist discourse of French women in late twentieth-century America, or gay literature) while Godayol questions the possibility of building a feminist theory of translation when different groups use different definitions of concepts such as gender, sex, and identity. Similarly, Martín reflects on the risks of essentialism and the necessity of adopting normative, static meanings. These works suggest that translating as/like a woman, to use Godayol's term, means questioning the existence of a "feminine" subject/translator as a fixed category and returning to Carol Maier's solution of considering the translator as "woman-identified" to avoid such pitfalls.

A variation on the study of the effect of a translator's gender positioning involves a focus on translating gendered language, that is, the use of language specifically aimed at revealing gender construction. For instance, Sardin (2011) analyzes Tahar Ben Jelloun's novel *The Sand Child*, noting that the translation erases the ambiguity around grammatical gender, normalizing the author's linguistic creativity. Likewise, in her study of translations/dubbing of chick lit from English into French, which represents subversive "non-traditional features of female sexuality" (184), Feral (2011) discovers a pattern of deletion and a weakening in the representation of sexually autonomous women. Furukawa (2010) studies three Japanese versions of *Bridget Jones's Diary* in terms of their handling of dialogue. Other important discussions of the impact of the translator's gender identification on the practice of translation include Espasa (2003), Askehave and Korning Zethsen (2013), and Castro (2013).

Another approach to the study of gender involves self-reflection by translators on the influence of gender in their translation. The most noticeable, developed, and nuanced example of this line of research is Maier, who works from the concept of positioning as "woman-identified" to that of "woman-interrogated," and moves from a gender-based identity to a questioning of the very notion of gender and its implications for writing and translating (1985, 1998). Using her own translation work as an object of study, Maier acknowledges the ways in which her social (if not biological) identity as a woman has influenced her translation process but without adopting the interventionist translation strategies developed by the Canadian school theorists, such as Godard and de Lotbinière-Harwood. Other examples of self-reflection include Fisher's (2010) interrogation of the influence of the work of German feminist linguists on her translation of Scottish poet Carol Ann Duffy's collection *Mean Time*.

The study of sexuality and/in translation is somewhat less developed than the study of gender, although the two concepts remain in many ways intertwined. One of the most sophisticated studies of the interconnection of homosexuality and translation is Harvey's *Intercultural Movements:* American Gay *in French Translation* (2003b). Harvey's earlier work in sociolinguistics on the sub-cultural language of gay and lesbian communities prepared him for this study of the translation of American gay fiction into French. Harvey focused in particular on "camp" talk, a sub-cultural dialect used by many gay men in the US, which was heavily represented in the novels chosen for analysis. Through a series of close readings, Harvey identifies significant shifts in the translation of camp talk into French that flattened or normalized the talk. Harvey then interpreted these shifts as a product of resistance on the part of the French to the idea of a separate gay culture, in favor of a more universalist conception of (national) identity. Harvey's work stands out for its convincing connection of textual features with cultural beliefs and dispositions, and for inscribing his study of these translations within a larger study of key individuals who served as cultural mediators between the gay cultures of the US and France.

Also important from a theoretical and methodological point of view is Keenaghan's 1998 study, in which he examines the translation of Lorca's

"Ode to Whitman" done by the translator and writer Jack Spicer, situating Spicer's interventionist approach both in his aesthetic beliefs—poetry as disclosure—and in his political positioning—as a gay activist. Keenaghan discusses Spicer's decision to use sexually explicit language in his translation as an "in your face" act that makes Lorca's often coded, euphemistic allusions to homosexuality visible to a small readership of San Francisco avant-garde artists and writers. In analyzing Spicer's intervention, Keenaghan refers to Lee Edelman's concept of homographesis, which describes the ways in which gay-identified writers are compelled by hegemonic institutions and mainstream audiences to inscribe their homosexuality into their writing in ways that are easily recognized and, therefore, contained. "The appeal of applying this theory of homographesis to translation studies," Keenaghan writes, "lies in Edelman's insistence that the process of reading entails a rewriting, a dual process that is actualized in the very practice of translation" (1998: 282).

Another interesting study (Parker 2005) connects the queer take on sexuality with the postmodern view of translation as interpretation in the figure of the translator in Barbara Wilson's *Gaudí Afternoon* (1990) and Jeanette Winterson's *Written on the Body* (1992). In these novels, Parker writes, "the figure of the translator is employed as a metaphor for the subversion of the binary sex-gender system that underpins the hetero-patriarchal ideology endorsed by mainstream Christianity" (118). Kinloch (2011) is unique for bringing together minority sexual and ethnic identities.

In Interpreting Studies there is a surprising dearth of research focusing on gender and sexuality. An exception is Angelelli (2004b), who used gender as a category of analysis to study interpreters' attitudes toward their perceptions of roles and behaviors in practice. The quantitative study was conducted in Canada, Mexico, and the United States across interpreters working in three different settings: conference, court, and healthcare. She found no significant differences between female and male interpreters in terms of visibility (i.e., agency operationalized as interpreters' alignment with the parties; establishing trust/facilitating mutual respect; communicating affect as well as message; explaining cultural gaps/interpreting culture as well as language; establishing communication rules during the conversation). Angelelli (2004a) discusses gender and empathy in this study of medical interpreting at California Hope.

New directions

Translation and Interpreting Studies has made a significant contribution to the study of gender mostly in terms of the recovery of female translators and the construction of a strong tradition of both female translators and woman-identified ones. However, the impact of a translator's gender on translation will require further documentation. Many more case studies are needed in order to generate a corpus of texts that can be analyzed with some of the tools provided by CCTL. Larger scale studies using corpora could also benefit from computational linguistics methods such as latent semantic analysis.

Greater attention to the complexity of identity formations would also allow scholars to avoid essentializing or isolating one aspect of identity (gender or sexual orientation) from other components. Despite the enormous body of work in sociolinguistics on gender, sexuality, and language, issues of gender and sexuality have received surprisingly little attention to date in Interpreting Studies. Osman and Angelelli (2007) hint at the role gender might have played in the interpreted communicative events discussed but do not explicitly study the issue. Angelelli 2004a and 2004b are among the few studies to analyze the role of gender in interpreted communicative events. There is, therefore, much still to be done regarding the role of gender in interpreting, ranging from the use of gendered language to the impact of gender on turn taking.

Recently, greater attention has been paid to the topic of sexuality and translation, as evidenced by a special issue of the journal *Comparative Literature Studies* (51.2 [2014]) and an international conference at the University of Vienna, "Queering Translation – Translating the Queer" (March 2015). Comparatists, however, often use the term *translation* as a metaphor and ignore much of the work already done in Translation Studies, specifically, approaches like Harvey's that connect concrete textual evidence with larger social concerns and dispositions. That being said, some of the questions for future research would be the study of the translation of theoretical texts on gender and sexuality, including paratextual material, as well as more sociologically informed studies of queer translators. There is much still to be done in studying the translation of Western "gay" literature in other cultures and of the translation of texts depicting same-sex desire or eroticism from cultures outside the developed West. As William Spurlin (2014a: 205) suggests, "translation studies may be broadened through the pressures of queer theoretical orientations, while problematizing the still existent monolingualism, and largely Anglophonic biases, of contemporary academic queer studies, thereby opening up new spaces of dissidence in both disciplines."

References

Adam, Barry. 1979. "A Social History of Gay Politics." In *Gay Men: A Sociology of Male Homosexuality*, Martin P. Levine (ed.), 285–300. New York: Harper & Row.

Aldrich, Robert. 2003. *Colonialism and Homosexuality*. New York: Routledge.

Altman, Dennis. 2001. *Global Sex*. Chicago: University of Chicago Press.

Angelelli, Claudia V. 2004a. *Medical Interpreting and Cross-cultural Communication*. Cambridge: Cambridge University Press.

——2004b. *Re-visiting the Interpreter's Role*. Amsterdam: John Benjamins.

Askehave, Inger, and Karen Korning Zethsen. 2013. "Talking Translation: Is Gender an Issue?" Special issue, *Gender, Language and Translation at the Crossroads of Disciplines*, Olga Castro (ed.). *Gender and Language* 7(1): 117–34.

Baer, Brian James. 2014. "Interpreting *Daniel Stein*: Or What Happens When Fictional Translators Get Translated?" In *Transfiction: Research into the Realities of Translation Fiction*, Klaus Kaindl and Karlheinz Spitzl (eds.), 157–75. Amsterdam: John Benjamins.

Barker, Anna. 2011. "Helen Maria Williams' *Paul and Virginia* and the Experience of Mediated Alterity." In *Translating Women*, Luise von Flotow (ed.), 57–70. Ottawa: University of Ottawa Press.

Berlina, Aleksandra. 2012. "Homosexuality in the Russian Translation of *The Hours*." *Sexuality and Culture: An Interdisciplinary Quarterly* 16(4): 449–66.

Bersani, Leo. 1995. *Homos*. Cambridge, MA: Harvard University Press.

Binnie, Jon. 2004. *The Globalization of Sexuality*. London: SAGE Publications.

Boone, Joseph Allen. 2014. *The Homoerotics of Orientalism*. New York: Columbia University Press.

Bray, Alan. 1982/1995. *Homosexuality in Renaissance England*. London: Gay Men's Press.

Bucholtz, Mary 2014. "The Feminist Foundations of Language, Gender, and Sexuality Research." In Ehrlich, Meyerhoff and Holmes (eds.) 23–47. Chichester: John Wiley & Sons.

Butler, Judith. 1990. *Gender Trouble: Feminism and the Subversion of the Body*. New York: Routledge.

Castro, Olga. 2013. "(Re)examining Horizons in Feminist Studies of Translation: Towards a Third Wave?" In *A (Self)-critical Perspective of Translation Theories/ Una visión (auto)crítica de los estudios de traducción*, Javier Franco Aixelá, María del Carmen Africa, and Vidal Claramonte (eds.). *MonTI* 1: 59–86.

Chamberlain, Lori. 1988. "Gender and the Metaphorics of Translation" *Signs* 13.3: 454–72.

Chauncey, George. 1994. *Gay New York. Gender, Urban Culture, and the Making of the Gay Male World, 1890–1940*. New York: Basic Books.

Cixous, Hélène. 1976. "The Laugh of the Medusa." Trans. by Keith and Paula Cohen. *Signs* 1(4): 875–93.

Damrosch, David (ed.). 2009. "Introduction: All the Time in the World." In *Teaching World Literature*, David Damrosch (ed.), 1–11. New York: MLA.

De Beauvoir, Simone. 1953 *The Second Sex*. Trans. by H. M. Parshley. New York: Knopf.

Delisle, Jean. 1999. *Portraits de traducteurs*. Ottawa: Presse de l'Université d'Ottawa.

Ehrlich, Susan, and Miriam Meyerhoff. 2014. "Introduction: Language, Gender, and Sexuality." In *The Handbook of Language, Gender, and Sexuality*, Susan Ehrlich, Miriam Meyerhoff, and Janet Holmes (eds.), 1–20. Chichester: John Wiley & Sons.

Espasa, Eva. 2003. "A Gendered Voice in Translation: Translating like a Feminist." In Género, lenguaje y traducción: actas del Primer Seminario Internacional sobre Género y Lenguaje (el género de la traduc*ción – la traducción del género; Valencia*) 16–18 octubre 2002, José Santaemilia (ed.), 328–35. Valencia: Guada Impresores.

Essig, Laurie. 1999. *Queer in Russia. A Story of Sex, Self, and the Other*. Durham, NC: Duke University Press.

Evans, David T. 1993. *Sexual Citizenship. The Material Construction of Sexualities*. New York: Routledge.

Feral, Anne-Lise. 2011. "Sexuality and Femininity in Translated Chick Texts." In *Translating Women*, Luise von Flotow (ed.), 183–202. Ottawa: University of Ottawa Press.

Fisher, Christopher, Jay Irwin, and Jason Coleman (eds.). 2014. Special issue on Rural LBGT Health. *Journal of Homosexuality* 61.8.

Fisher, Lina. 2010. "Theory and Practice of Feminist Translation in the 21st Century." In *Translation: Theory and Practice in Dialogue*, Rebecca Hyde Parker, Karla Guadarrama Garcia, and Antoinette Fawcett (eds.), 67–84. London and New York: Continuum.

Foucault, Michel. 1978. *The History of Sexuality. Volume I. An Introduction*. Trans. by Ed. Alain. New York: Vintage.

Fradenburg, Louise, and Carla Freccero (eds.). 1996. *Premodern Sexualities.* New York: Routledge.
Furukawa, Hiroko. 2010. "Rendering Female Speech as a Male or Female Translator: Constructed Femininity in the Japanese Translations of *Pride and Prejudice* and *Bridget Jones's Diary.*" In *Translation: Theory and Practice in Dialogue*, Rebecca Hyde Parker, Karla Guadarrama Garcia, and Antoinette Fawcett (eds.), 181–200. London and New York: Continuum.
Godard, Barbara. 1990. "Theorizing Feminist Discourse/Translation." In *Translation, History and Culture*, Susan Bassnett and André Lefevere (eds.), 87–96. London: Pinter.
Goldberg, Jonathan. 1997. *Desiring Women Writing. English Renaissance Examples.* Stanford, CA: Stanford University Press.
Goodrich, Jaime. 2013. *Faithful Translators. Authorship, Gender and Religion in Early Modern England.* Evanston, IL: Northwestern University Press.
Halperin, David M. 1990. *100 Years of Homosexuality and Other Essays on Greek Love.* New York: Routledge.
——2002. *How to Do the History of Homosexuality.* Chicago: University of Chicago Press.
Harvey, Keith. 2003a. "'Events' and 'Horizons': Reading Ideology in the 'Bindings' of Translations." In *Apropos of Ideology*, Maria Caldaza-Perez (ed.), 43–69. London and New York: Routledge.
——2003b. *Intercultural Movements.* American Gay *in French Translation.* Manchester: St. Jerome.
Hassen, Rim. 2011. "English Translation of the Quran by Women: The Challenges of 'Gender Balance' in and through Language." In *Woman and Translation: Geographies, Voices and Identities / Mujer y traducción: geografías, voces e identidades*, Luise von Flotow and José Santaemilia (eds.). Special issue of Mon*TI* 3: 211–30.
Hayes, Julie Candler. 2009. *Translation, Subjectivity and Culture in France and England, 1600–1800.* Stanford, CA: Stanford University Press.
Henitiuk, Valerie. 2011. "Prefacing Gender: Framing Sei Shônagon for a Western Audience, 1875–2006." In *Translating Women*, Luise von Flotow (ed.), 239–62. Ottawa: University of Ottawa Press.
Hocquenghem, Guy. 1978. *Homosexual Desire.* Daniella Dangoor (trans.). London: Allison and Busby.
Howard, John. 2001. *Men Like That: A Southern Queer History.* Chicago: University of Chicago Press.
Hyam, Ronald. 1990. *Empire and Sexuality.* Manchester: Manchester University Press.
Irigaray, Luce. 1974/1985. *Speculum of the Other Woman.* Trans. by Gillian C. Gill. Cornell, NY: Cornell University Press.
——1977/1985. *This Sex Which Is Not One.* Trans. by Catherine Porter and Carolyn Burke. Cornell, NY: Cornell University Press.
Jagose, Annamarie. 1996. *Queer Theory. An Introduction.* New York: New York University Press.
Johnson, Colin. 2013. *Just Queer Folks: Gender and Sexuality in Rural America.* Philadelphia: Temple University Press.
Kadish, Doris and Françoise Massardier-Kenney, eds. 1994. *Translating Slavery.* Kent: Kent State University Press.
Keenaghan, Eric. 1998. "Jack Spicer's Pricks and Cocksuckers. Translating Homosexuality into Visibility." *The Translator* 4(2): 273–94.

Kinloch, David. 2011. "A Queer Glaswegian Voice." In *Translation and Opposition*, Dimitris Asimakoulas and Margaret Rogers (eds.), 129–45. Bristol and Buffalo, NY: Multilingual Matters.

Kronitiris, Tina. 1997. *Oppositional Voices: Women as Writers and Translators in the English Renaissance*. New York and London: Routledge.

Laqueur, Thomas. 1990. *Making Sex: Body and Gender from the Greeks to Freud*. Cambridge, MA: Harvard University Press.

Larkosh, Christopher. 2007. "The Translator's Closet. Editing Identities in Argentine Literary Culture." *TTR* 21(2): 63–88.

——2011a. "Introduction: Re-engendering Translation." In *Re-engendering Translation: Transcultural Practice, Gender/Sexuality and the Politics of Alterity*, Christopher Larkosh (ed.), 1–10. Manchester: St. Jerome.

——2011b. "Two in Translation: The Multilingual Cartographies of Nestor Perlongher and Caio Fernando Abreu." In *Re-engendering Translation: Transcultural Practice, Gender/Sexuality and the Politics of Alterity*, Christopher Larkosh (ed.), 72–90. Manchester: St. Jerome.

Leonardi, Vanessa. 2007. *Gender and Ideology in Translation: Do Women and Men Translate Differently?* Oxford: Peter Lang.

Leonardi, Vanessa, and Eleonora Federici. 2012. "Using and Abusing Gender in Translation. The Case of Virginia Woolf's *A Room of One's Own* Translated into Italian." *Quaderns* 19: 183–98.

Lotbinière-Harwood, Susanne de. 1991. *Re-belle et infidèle: La traduction comme pratique de réécriture au féminin* [*The body bilingual: Translation as a re-writing in the feminine*]. Montréal: Les Éditions du Remue-Ménage.

MacIntosh, Mary. 1968. "The Homosexual Role." *Social Problems* 16(2): 182–92.

Maier, Carol. 1985. "A Woman in Translation, Reflecting." *Translation Review* 17: 4–8.

——1996. "Gender in/and Literary Translation" (with Françoise Massardier-Kenney). In *Translation Horizons. Beyond the Boundaries of "Translation Spectrum" (Translation Perspectives IX)*, Marilyn Gaddis Rose (ed.), 243–68. Binghamton, NY: Center for Research in Translation. SUNY Binghamton.

——1998. "Issues in the Practice of Translating Women's Fiction." *Bulletin of Hispanic Studies* 75(1): 95–108.

Massardier-Kenney, Françoise. 1997. "Towards a Redefinition of Feminist Translation Practice." *The Translator* 3(1): 55–69.

Mazzei, Christiano A. 2014. "How Adolfo Caminha's *Bom-Crioulo* Was 'Outed' through Its Translated Paratext." In *A Companion to Translation Studies*, Sandra Bermann and Catherine Porter (eds.), 310–22. Chichester: Wiley-Blackwell.

Murray, Stephen O. 2000. *Homosexualities*. Chicago: University of Chicago Press.

Murray, Stephen O., and Will Roscoe. 1997. *Islamic Homosexualities: Culture, History, and Literature*. New York: New York University Press.

O'Grady, Kathleen. 1996–97. "Guardian of Language: Interview with Hélène Cixous." *Women's Education des Femmes* 12(4): 6–10.

Osman, Ghada, and Claudia Angelelli. 2007. "'A Crime in Another Language?' An Analysis of the Interpreter's Role in the Yousry Case." *Translation and Interpreting Studies* 2(1): 47–82.

Parker, Emma. 2005. "Lost in Translation: Gender and the Figure of the Translator in Contemporary Queer Fiction." In *The Poetics of Transubstantiation: From Theology to Metaphor*, Douglas Burnham and Enrico Giaccherini (eds.), 118–25. Aldershot: Ashgate.

Plummer, Kenneth. 1975. *Sexual Stigma*. Boston: Routledge & Keegan Paul.

Puar, Jaspir K. 2007. *Terrorist Assemblages. Homonationalism in Queer Times.* Durham, NC: Duke University Press.

Santaemilia, José (ed.). 2005. *Gender, Sex and Translation: The Manipulation of Identities.* Manchester: St. Jerome.

Sardin, Pascale. 2011. "'Gender Trouble' in the American Translation of Tahar Ben Jelloun's *L'Enfant de sable.*" In *Translating Women*, Luise von Flotow (ed.), 205–26. Ottawa: University of Ottawa Press.

Schmitt, Arno, and Jehoeda Sofer (eds.). 1992. *Sexuality and Eroticism among Males in Moslem Societies.* New York: The Haworth Press.

Sedgwick, Eve Kosofsky. 1985. *Between Men: English Literature and Male Homosocial Desire.* New York: Columbia University Press.

Simon, Sherry. 1996. *Gender in Translation: Cultural Identity and the Politics of Transmission.* London and New York: Routledge.

Spurlin, William. 2014. "Introduction. The Gender and Queer Politics of Translation: New Approaches." *Comparative Literary Studies* 51(2): 201–214

Tamagne, Florence. 2000. *Histoire de l'homosexualité en Europe: Berlin, Londres, Paris, 1919–1939.* Paris: Seuil.

Tyulenev, Sergey. 2011. "Women-Translators in Russia." *Woman and Translation: Geographies, Voices and Identities/Mujer y traducción: Geografías, voces e identidades. MonTI* 3: 75–105.

——2014. "Strategies of Translating Sexualities as Part of the Secularization of Eighteenth- and Early Nineteenth-century Russia." *Comparative Literature Studies* 51(2): 253–76.

Underhill, James W. 2011. "Echoes of Emily Dickinson: Male and Female French Translators Listening to the Poet." In *Translating Women*, Luise von Flotow (ed.), 203–38. Ottawa: University of Ottawa Press.

Vanita, Ruth (ed.). 2002. *Queering India: Same-sex Love and Eroticism in Indian Culture and Society.* New York: Routledge.

von Flotow, Luise. (ed.). 2011. Translating Women. Ottawa: University of Ottawa Press.

White, Micheline (ed.). 2011. *English Women, Religion, and Textual Production, 1500–1625.* Farnham: Ashgate.

Wilson, Barbara. 1990. *Gaudí Afternoon.* Seattle, Wash.: Seal Press.

Winterson, Jeanette. 1992. *Written on the Body.* London: Jonathan Cape.

Wittig, Monique. 1964. *L'Opoponax.* Paris: Editions de Minuit.

——1969. *Les Guérillères.* Paris: Editions de Minuit.

——1973. *Le Corps lesbien.* Paris: Editions de Minuit.

Wolf, Michaela. 2005. "The Creation of a 'Room of One's Own': Feminist Translators as Mediators between Cultures and Genders." In *Gender, Sex and Translation: The Manipulation of Identities*, José Santaemilia (ed.), 15–25. Manchester: St. Jerome.

Woods, Michelle. 2011. "Reassessing Willa Muir. Her Role and Influence in the Kafka Translations." *Translation Studies* 4(1): 58–71.

Ze'evi, Dror. 2006. *Producing Desire. Changing Sexual Discourse in the Ottoman Middle East, 1500–1900.* Berkeley: University of California Press.

7 History and historiography

María Manuela Fernández Sánchez

Overview

The increasing interest in historical studies of translation and translators over the last 30 years is reflected in the many books, articles, anthologies, international conference proceedings, special volumes of academic journals, and encyclopedia entries that have been produced on this topic. Pym (1998) and D'hulst (2001: 22) discuss the importance of historical knowledge in advancing our understanding of the structure and development of the discipline, while others document and explain translation discourses, as well as the lives and activities of translators and interpreters, from the past. More interestingly, the discussion of the potential of historical studies of translation to enrich historical knowledge in general and provide insights into other social sciences is taking place against the backdrop of a profound rethinking of the epistemological status of historical research, which raises a number of methodological questions (Hermans 1999; D'hulst 2010b; Rundle, St-Pierre, Hermans, and Delabastita 2012). As a result, translation scholars working in the field today have become more methodologically aware and have adopted conceptual tools from modern historiography and other closely related disciplines. They are also open to pursuing historical research in order to "correct" the historical record (Payàs 2006; Hokenson 2013) and to meet the challenge of acquisition of knowledge in a new global context (Mignolo 2002; Cronin 2003; Tymoczko 2009).

Theoretical foundations

In the field of historiography, or the study of how historical knowledge "was gained and communicated, and how it developed through time" (Swiggers 1990: 21), the work of Ancient Greek and Roman historians continues to have a profound influence. According to British historian Arthur Marwick (2001: 52), there are at least three reasons to read the works of early classical historians. The first is their value as primary sources, placing us in direct contact with ideas and values not generally our own. The second is the richness of the legacy of historical concepts, methods, and solutions that have been handed down to us by historians of the past. Finally, Marwick argues that the historical work of ancient times can still provide useful ideas that might be missed if our exclusive focus were on recent texts.

The writings of Thucydides (*c*. 455 BC–*c*. 400 BC), one of the most important historians in Ancient Greece, are, for example, still relevant to historians today. His historical narrative of the Peloponnesian War serves as a model of the classical conception of 'educational history' as Thucydides is concerned with exploring both the events that occurred and the facets of human nature exposed by war. Moreover, like his predecessor Herodotus (*c*. 484 BC–*c*. 425 BC), Thucydides draws on various sources to ensure the veracity of his account of the war. In the opinion of many experts (Alegre Gorri 2005: 31), Thucydides as a historian is ahead of his time because of his conviction that historical facts are the result of human actions, a belief that vividly contrasted with the religious thinking of his contemporaries who believed in the agency of divine intervention or fate. Furthermore, Thucydides was deeply committed to the quest for certainty (τὸ σαφές), or at least a certain guarantee of reliability (εἰκός), when gathering information from sources.

A basic distinction should be made at this point between reality (ὄν) and the words used to express reality (λόγος). Recording history necessarily highlights the essential distance between these two concepts (Alegre Gorri 2005: 30). Consequently, in the Western tradition, Herodotus and Thucydides are regarded as pioneers because of their historical consciousness, which led them to separate experience from writing, or a plurality of memories from a particular written representation. Another relevant tenet of these ancient historians is the requirement of estrangement from one's homeland (*apolis*) as a condition for writing its history. This concept of neutrality would remain, for many centuries, a core ethical principle in the practice of writing history (Koselleck 2004: 114).

Roman historians made a similar distinction between *res gestae*, or the events of the past, and *historia rerum gestarum*, or a certain arrangement of historical events based on a plan or an idea. The English word 'history' and the corresponding terms in Romance languages, however, designate both realities. Generally speaking, the term 'history' covers a wide range of activities: the things that happened in the past, the account of those past events in a narrative form, and the activities and writings of historians. For professional historians, 'history' mainly signifies the specialized work of historians and their scholarly activities, whereas 'historiography' refers to the study of historical knowledge, that is, how histories are produced, which includes the study of the works of individual historians. According to D'hulst, a third level in historical research is 'metahistoriography,' or "the explicit reflection on the concepts and methods to write history and also on epistemological and methodological problems that are related to the use of these concepts and methods" (2010a: 398).

To the extent that history is concerned with change over time, the concept of 'history' has always been sensitive to the effects of tumultuous events and acute social tensions (i.e., revolutions, wars, migrations, postcolonialism, and globalization). For example, one of the effects of the French Revolution was the emergence of a new conception of history. Though very productive (Koselleck 2004: 77), this model was less able to predict future historical events. The concept of history as *magistra vitae* was no longer viable, which opened the door to the possibility of many different histories, each unique and not subject to comparison.

The interwar period again brought far-reaching changes in historiographical methods and in the concept of history itself. Indeed, this was the time when the foundations were laid for history as an autonomous discipline. A number of things precipitated this reconceptualization of history: (1) the critique levelled by the French *Annales* school at academic historical positivism, as represented by the work of German historian Leopold von Ranke; (2) the demand for precision and objectivity made by economists and economic historians; and (3) the theoretical and empirical contributions of Marxist scholars.

According to Martínez Shaw (2004: 26), the convergence of these three currents of thought resulted in an acknowledgement of the need to study "total history," which, instead of focusing primarily on political and military events (the main interest of positivist schools of history), would be open to all topics. Still another result of this historiographical turn was the dialogue established with the other social sciences (e.g., sociology, anthropology, and psychology). This dialogue was two-sided and would be a determining factor in the development of the contemporary social sciences (Martínez Shaw 2004: 28). Historical research accepted concepts and categories from other academic disciplines, and, in turn, those other disciplines enriched their modes of analysis by adding a temporal dimension. Consequently, after the 1930s, history definitively became a social science and its object of study included all levels of social reality (Braudel 1958).

Over the last 40 years, there has been a succession of paradigms representing the different ways of understanding and recording historical knowledge. Nevertheless, what all of them have in common is the criticism of traditional historiography (centered on the paradigm of the nation-state), as well as the belief in the possibility of multiple histories. In fact, one of the turning points in the critical conceptualization of history was the linguistic turn that began to define the social sciences in the 1970s. Perhaps more than any of his contemporaries, American historian Hayden White (1973) stands out for his conceptualization of works of history as narrative prose discourse, "the content of which is as much imagined (the modes of figurative emplotments, metaphorical tropologies, argumentative devices, ideological positioning) as found (the evidential facts)" (Jenkins and Munslow 2004: 198).

Placing in doubt the traditional idea that historians can objectively explain the past by inferring the facts from the historical evidence, this new conceptualization of history writing posits that the past can only be known through the historical discourse of historians, which comes to us mostly in the form of a narrative and from a particular point of view. The revival of narrative as a form of historical explanation, however, coexists with other modes of historical writing, such as structural history and analysis on three time scales (long, medium, and short term), as reflected in the work of Braudel.

Despite the eclecticism that now pervades historiographical practice, it is widely accepted among modern historians that the purpose of their work is not to 'construct' or 'reconstruct' the past, but rather to make accessible the most likely explanation of past events and human intentions. History is an empirical discipline supported by evidence and by conceptual tools imported from many other disciplines. Rather than explaining the past objectively "by inferring the 'facts' from the evidence" (Munslow 1997: 1), historians focus on selecting, inventorying, organizing, checking, and understanding a wide range of historical material in order to provide a written representation of the past. As Marwick (2001: 40) writes, "it is never, naturally, the whole past, but always just some limited aspect which the historian has chosen to investigate." Bloch (2001: 79) claims that since historical knowledge is neither instantaneous nor direct, historians must adapt to this limitation and accept the fact that historical knowledge consists of traces and remnants. When historians embark on a certain research path, therefore, they must identify and arrange available evidence according to specific objectives, research questions, and epistemological assumptions, while acknowledging the possible diversity of historical explanations in reference to the same event.

As for the contemporary functions of historical knowledge, the instrumentalization of the past in modern society through *museification*, the entertainment industry, and media events, as well as the public use of memory in commemorations and other memorial practices, requires that we acknowledge the diverse political and cultural contexts that shape the representation and reception of the past. Similarly, postcolonial perspectives have drawn attention to issues related to access to knowledge and the representation of ethnic and cultural differences. As Mignolo and Schiwy (2003: 18) note, "Today we are witnessing a desubalternization or a decolonization of knowledge that places translation/transculturation into a new epistemological context and structure of power."

As argued by Cronin (2003: 79), the critical perspective of globalization also has direct consequences on translation history. In regard to the past, historical activism "can allow hidden histories to emerge that are often neglected or obscured by histories that are bounded by the paradigm of the nation-state." Similarly, professional groups can find in a historical approach a space for revindication and legitimatization. For example, as Adam and Stone (2011) point out, the official history of organizations for the Deaf generally consists of the stories of founders and benefactors (usually the non-deaf), excluding individuals who served as language brokers within Deaf communities. As these authors contend: "by examining early interpreting work undertaken in the Deaf community, interpreting professionals are better able to understand how they have arrived at this point in their history" (Adam and Stone 2011: 225).

Evolution of the topic in TIS

Over the last fifteen years, the historiography of translation and interpreting has experienced a thematic expansion into emerging areas of research, often supported by compilatory bibliographic work (Singerman 2002; Gallén, Lafarga, and Pegenaute 2010). Other major tendencies are the internationalization of historical studies (Chan 2004; Cheung 2006; Wakabayashi 2012) and new interest in interpreting history, whether it be research on the history of the profession (Takeda 2010), on the role of interpreting in the colonial history of Latin America (Grupo Alfaqueque 2010; HISTAL Group 2014), or on interpreters in settings of conflict (Baker 2010; Baigorri-Jalón 2011).

As a consequence, historical research in T&I Studies reflects great methodological diversity, which has resulted in a wide array of genres, ranging from more traditional national translation histories (Ruiz Casanova 2000), to case studies (Sturge 2010; Wakabayashi 2013), to empirical and quantitative work (Poupaud, Pym, and Torres Simón 2009). Such research has also taken the form of microhistory (Adamo 2006; Zarrouk 2006), as well as large-scale descriptive studies by international teams, which focus on the theory and practice of translation beyond national boundaries (Chevrel, D'hulst, and Lombez 2012). There are also oral histories (Arias Torres and Feria García 2012), historiographical work on translation anthologies (Sabio Pinilla and Ordóñez López 2012; Seruya, D'hulst, Assis Rosa, and Lin Moniz 2013), historical studies of the many "agents" involved in the translation, publication, circulation, and reception of translated texts (Milton and Bandia 2009), and work that highlights exclusions and little-known historical translation and interpreting experiences that may not be included in a general history of translation and interpreting (Santoyo 2006; Seruya 2010). In addition, an entire sub-field has emerged on the "hidden" history of women translators (Delisle 2002; Hayes 2008; von Flotow 2011), especially in the English Renaissance (Goldberg 1997; Kronitiris 1997; White 2011; Goodrich 2013).

The relative sophistication of contemporary historical studies in T&I stems primarily from the prolific activity of its founders and of the first generation of translation scholars. Evidence of this is the fact that in bibliographies on translation and interpreting, the same names invariably appear as the authors of publications on a wide range of topics. These scholars were in many ways ahead of their time, and their multidisciplinary origins have had a positive impact on the development of the field by embracing alternative historical paradigms, such as "history from below" and new gender, sociological, and postcolonial perspectives, which have greatly enriched historical studies of translation and interpreting. Another innovative approach to translation and interpreting history involves the use of photographs to document the life and work of translators and interpreters through history (Fernández-Ocampo and Wolf 2014).

Key studies

Although interpreting history is not an altogether new research area, there are many aspects that have yet to be explored. One of the emerging areas of research involves interpreting during the Cold War period, namely in military and diplomatic negotiations, and at high-level political encounters. In the first study on this topic, Baigorri-Jalón and Fernández Sánchez (2010) explored why and to what extent interpreting was decisive in maintaining international dialogue in a bipolar world order. Since a variety of official and extra-official communication channels contributed to the prevention of war, it was necessary to examine the ones that were open during this era. It was also important to identify the interpreters in these early meetings and to document the unique demands placed upon them in those very sensitive settings.

The theoretical foundations for such historical studies were laid by works that investigated issues of ideology and power (Tymoczko and Gentzler 2002; Baker 2006). These works provided the tools for interpreting historians to analyze the ambivalent position of high-level interpreters (in negotiating professional and personal agendas) and to focus on interpreting as a crucial instrument in foreign policy (as a site to negotiate power relations). Indeed, the practice of interpreting became a delicate art in a context steeped in rivalry and suspicion.

Subsequent investigations studied military and diplomatic settings (Fernández Sánchez 2011, 2012, 2013), taking into account new primary sources, particularly interpreters' testimonies. In order to incorporate subjective and emotional experience into the research, it was first necessary to carefully verify the historical information provided by the testimonies. The next step involved a careful analysis of personal experiences in order to acquire an in-depth understanding of the practical concerns experienced by interpreters in certain settings.

Other examples of historical work are grounded in postcolonial approaches to T&I Studies. Such approaches focus on the sociopolitical background of translators and interpreters, revealing how translation practices are implicated in colonial expansion and domination, as well as in resistance to that domination. Postcolonial studies often challenge theoretical assumptions that might otherwise be taken for granted. A relevant example is *Los traductores de árabe del Estado español. Del Protectorado a nuestros días* (Arabic translators of the Spanish government: From the protectorate to modern times) by Arias Torres and Feria García (2012). This book tells the story of the Spanish translators and interpreters who worked in the Spanish protectorate in Morocco (1912–57) and were later involved in colonial diplomacy until the independence of Morocco and the end of the Spanish Sahara (1957–76). This is the first extensive study on the topic, totalling over 600 pages.

This book is important for many reasons, one of which is that it reveals the uncommon use of pseudotranslations, a practice actively encouraged by the Spanish colonial government. Pseudotranslation is usually employed as a literary strategy, or in contexts of official censorship (Rabadán Álvarez 2000). However, the use of pseudotranslations in this specific colonial context was unique in that it belonged to a broader oppressive translation policy supported by the unequal status of the language and culture of the colonized, the Arabic and the African local population, and the language and culture of the colonizer, the Spanish colonial administration. The logic behind this manipulation is rather perverse. As the authors cautiously observe (342), there is little need for the colonizers to directly produce an official text in the dominated language that will need to be translated afterwards into the language of prestige and power by an official translator. It is much easier to dictate the official text directly to the translator and ask him/her to write the same text in Arabic based on the rhetorical conventions of that time. The resulting text reads as a translated text, while as an official translation, it carries the authorship of the translator.

Additionally, in this marginalized colonial context, it would not occur to the general public or to dissident groups to seek access to the original text. There is no reason for this since the text is written in a marginalized language and thus not widely known. The consequences of this manipulative strategy go beyond the desire for domination inherent in a colonial nation and raise questions about who controls the past and the historical truth.

Another interesting example provided by this impressive historical study is the phenomenon of "fictitious directionality," which refers to the translation of the bilingual publication known as *Boletín Oficial de la Zona* (Official Gazette of the Zone). This publication supposedly contained original legal texts in Arabic. In reality, however, they were actually Arabic translations of Spanish texts produced by colonial authorities.

The previous discussion is just one example of the contributions made by sound historical research. After patiently revising historical and personal archives, the authors were able to track down and interview ten surviving Spanish interpreters, among other oral sources. They also managed to compile a corpus of 67 photographic documents of interpreters from the 1920s to 2009. The photographs record contemporary events, particularly those regarded as important from a professional or personal point of view. In this way, they document the persistent presence of Spanish interpreters working with the Arabic language in various settings, including political encounters at the highest level. The invaluable services of interpreters, however, were ignored for many years until terrorist attacks in Madrid on March 11, 2004, brought to the forefront the crucial need for professional Arabic interpreters.

In addition, Delisle and Woodsworth (2012) is extremely informative for students and scholars alike. It is also a collected work providing a broad range of examples of the contributions made by translators and interpreters in all areas of cultural history. Also of interest is the special issue of *Translation Studies* titled "Rethinking Methods in Translation History," edited by Carol O'Sullivan (2012). This issue encourages scholars to reconsider recurring methodological questions and the epistemological status of historical research.

New directions

This schematic overview of individual historical studies offers a limited number of examples which document and analyze the involvement of translators and interpreters in the political agenda of their principals and in the Spanish colonial administration. As Cronin observes (2006: 93): "Part of the task of translation studies is to show that translation questions arise often when they are least expected." Historical research in T&I Studies has the potential to provide relevant data, which could help to promote comparative studies in many areas, focusing on the influence of political and cultural government agendas in the distribution of knowledge, to name a pressing issue in our time.

To conclude, it is assumed that history needs to be periodically rewritten according to the imperatives of the present. In this light, the internationalization of the discipline seeks to rediscover new types of primary sources, new regions, as well as additional languages and cultural traditions (Gentzler 2008), which require the writing of new histories.

References

Adam, Robert, and Christopher Stone. 2011. "Through a Historical Lens. Contextualizing Interpreting Research." In *Advances in Interpreting Research*, Brenda Nicodemus and Laurie Swabey (eds.), 225–39. Amsterdam and Philadelphia: John Benjamins.

Adamo, Sergia. 2006. "Microhistory of Translation." In *Charting the Future of Translation History*, Georges L. Bastin and Paul F. Bandia (eds.), 81–100. Ottawa: University of Ottawa Press.

Alegre Gorri, Antonio. 2005. "El mundo griego: tiempo e historia." In *Filosofía de la Historia*, Reyes Mate (ed.), 21–32. Madrid: Trotta.

Arias Torres, Juan Pablo, and Manuel C. Feria García. 2012. *Los traductores de árabe del Estado español. Del Protectorado a nuestros días*. Barcelona: Bellaterra.

Baigorri-Jalón, Jesús. 2011. "Wars, Languages and the Role(s) of Interpreters." In *Les liaisons dangereuses: Langues, traduction, interprétation*, Henri Awaiss and Jarjoura Hardane (eds.), 173–204. Beirut: Université Saint Joseph.

Baigorri-Jalón, Jesús, and María Manuela Fernández Sánchez. 2010. "Understanding High-Level Interpreting in the Cold War: Preliminary Notes." *FORUM* 8(2): 1–29.

Baker, Mona. 2006. *Translation and Conflict. A Narrative Account*. New York: Routledge.

——2010. "Interpreters and Translators in the War Zone: Narrated and Narrators." *The Translator* 16(2): 197–222.

Bloch, Marc. 2001. *Apología para la historia o el oficio de historiador*. Trans. by María Jiménez and Danielle Zaslavsky. México: Fondo de Cultura económica.

Braudel, Ferdinand. 1958. "Histoire et sciences sociales. La longue durée." *Annales* 23 (4): 725–53.

Chan, Leo Tak-hung. 2004. *Twentieth-Century Chinese Translation Theory*. Amsterdam and Philadelphia: John Benjamins.

Cheung, Martha (ed.). 2006. *From Earliest Times to the Buddhist Project. An Anthology of Chinese Discourse on Translation*. Vol. 1. Manchester: St. Jerome.

Chevrel, Yves, Lieven D'hulst, and Christine Lombez (eds.). 2012. *Histoire des traductions en langue française: XIX siècle, 1815–1914*. Lagrasse: Verdier.
Cronin, Michael. 2003. *Translation and Globalization*. London and New York: Routledge.
——2006. *Translation and Identity*. Manchester: St. Jerome.
Delisle, Jean (ed.). 2002. *Portraits de traductrices*. Ottawa: Ottawa University Press.
Delisle, Jean, and Judith Woodsworth (eds.). 2012. *Translators through History*. Rev. ed. Amsterdam and Philadelphia: John Benjamins.
D'hulst, Lieven. 2001. "Why and How to Write Translation Histories?" *CROP* 6: 21–32.
——2010a. "Translation History." In *Handbook of Translation Studies*, Yves Gambier and Luc van Doorslaer (eds.), 397–405. Amsterdam and Philadelphia: John Benjamins.
——2010b. "*Translation Studies* Forum: Cultural Translation." *Translation Studies* 3(3): 353–56.
Fernández-Ocampo, Anxo, and Michaela Wolf (eds.). 2014. *Framing the Interpreter. Towards a Visual Perspective*. London: Routledge.
Fernández Sánchez, María Manuela. 2011. "Interpreting in the Cold War: Military, Political and Diplomatic Settings." In *Interpreting Naturally. A Tribute to Brian Harris*, M. J. Blasco Mayor and M.A. Jiménez Ivars (eds.), 163–91. Bern: Peter Lang.
——2012. "A Bilingual Officer Remembers Korea: A Closer Look at Untrained Interpreters in the Korean War." In *Languages and the Military. Alliances, Occupation and Peace Building*, Hilary Footitt and Michael Kelly (eds.), 115–30. Basingstoke: Palgrave Macmillan.
——2013."Sobre un eslabón clave en la historia política y militar. Una perspectiva traductológica." *Cuadernos de ALDEEU* 25: 89–108.
Gallén, Enric, Francisco Lafarga, and Luis Pegenaute (eds.). 2010. *Traducción y autotraducción en las literaturas ibéricas*. Bern: Peter Lang.
Gentzler, Edwin. 2008. *Translation and Identity in the Americas. New Directions in Translation Theory*. Abingdon: Routledge.
Goldberg, Jonathan. 1997. *Desiring Women Writing. English Renaissance Examples*. Stanford, CA: Stanford University Press.
Goodrich, Jaime. 2013. *Faithful Translators. Authorship, Gender and Religion in Early Modern England*. Evanston, IL: Northwestern University Press.
Grupo Alfaqueque. 2010. *Los límites de Babel. Ensayos sobre la comunicación entre lenguas y culturas*. Madrid and Frankfurt: Iberoamericana and Vervuert.
Hayes, Julie. 2008. *Translation, Subjectivity, and Culture in France and England, 1600–1800*. Stanford, CA: Stanford University Press.
Hermans, Theo. 1999. *Translation in Systems. Descriptive and Systemic Approaches Explained*. Manchester: St. Jerome.
HISTAL Group. 2014. Available online at www.histal.ca (accessed May 25, 2014).
Hokenson, Jan. 2013. "History and the Self-Translator." In *Self-Translation: Brokering Originality in Hybrid Culture*, Anthony Cordingley (ed.), 39–60. London: Bloomsbury.
Jenkins, Keith, and Alun Munslow. 2004. *The Nature of History Reader*. London and New York: Routledge.
Koselleck, Reinart. 2004. *historia/Historia*. Trans. by Antonio Gómez Ramos. Madrid: Trotta.
Kronitiris, Tina. 1997. *Oppositional Voices: Women as Writers and Translators in the English Renaissance*. New York and London: Routledge.
Martínez Shaw, Carlos. 2004. "La historia total y sus enemigos en la enseñanza actual." In *Aprender y pensar la historia*, Mario Carretero and James F. Voss (eds.), 25–46. Buenos Aires and Madrid: Amorrortu.

Marwick, Arthur. 2001. *The New Nature of History. Knowledge, Evidence, Language.* Basingstoke: Palgrave.

Mignolo, Walter. 2002. "The Geopolitics of Knowledge and the Colonial Difference." *The South Atlantic Quarterly* 101(1): 57–96.

Mignolo, Walter D., and Freya Schiwy. 2003. "Double Translation." In *Translation and Ethnography. The Anthropological Challenge of Intercultural Understanding*, Tullio Maranhão and Bernhard Strek (eds.), 3–29. Tucson: The University of Arizona Press.

Milton, John, and Paul Bandia (eds.). 2009. *Agents of Translation.* Amsterdam and Philadelphia: John Benjamins.

Munslow, Alun. 1997. *Deconstructing History.* Florence, KY: Routledge.

O'Sullivan, Carol (ed.). 2012. "Rethinking Methods in Translation History." Special issue. *Translation Studies.* 5(2).

Payàs, Gertrudis. 2006. "Lorsque l'histoire de la traduction sert à réviser l'histoire." *TTR* 19(2): 15–36.

Poupaud, Sandra, Anthony Pym, and Ester Torres Simón. 2009. "Finding Translations. On the Use of Bibliographical Databases in Translation History." *Meta* 54(2): 264–78.

Pym, Anthony. 1998. *Methods in Translation History.* Manchester: St. Jerome.

Rabadán Álvarez, Rosa. 2000. *Traducción y censura inglés-español: 1939–1985. Estudio preliminar.* León: Universidad de León.

Ruiz Casanova, José Francisco. 2000. *Aproximación a una historia de la traducción en España.* Madrid: Cátedra.

Rundle, Christopher, Paul St-Pierre, Theo Hermans, and Dirk Delabastita. 2012. "*Translation Studies* Forum: Translation and History." *Translation Studies* 5(2): 232–48.

Sabio Pinilla, José Antonio, and Pilar Ordóñez López. 2012. *Las antologías sobre la traducción en el ámbito peninsular. Análisis y estudio.* Bern: Peter Lang.

Santoyo, Julio-César. 2006. "Blank Spaces in the History of Translation." In *Charting the Future of Translation History*, Georges L. Bastin and Paul F. Bandia (eds.), 11–43. Ottawa: Ottawa University Press.

Seruya, Teresa. 2010. "Translation in Portugal during the *Estado Novo* Regime." In *Translation under Fascism*, Christopher Rundle and Kate Sturge (eds.), 117–44. Basingstoke: Palgrave.

Seruya, Teresa, Lieven D'hulst, Alexandra Assis Rosa, and Maria Lin Moniz. 2013. *Translation in Anthologies and Collections (19th and 20th Centuries).* Amsterdam and Philadelphia: John Benjamins.

Singerman, Robert. 2002. *Jewish Translation History. A Bibliography of Bibliographies and Studies.* Amsterdam and Philadelphia: John Benjamins.

Sturge, Kate. 2010. "'Flight from the Programme of National Socialism'? Translation in Nazi Germany." In *Translation under Fascism*, Christopher Rundle and Kate Sturge (eds.), 51–83. Basingstoke: Palgrave.

Swiggers, Pierre. 1990. "Reflections on (Models for) Linguistic Historiography." In *Understanding the Historiography of Linguistics. Problems and Projects*, W. Hüllen (ed.), 21–34. Münster: Nodus Publikationen.

Takeda, Kayoko. 2010. *Interpreting the Tokyo War Crimes Tribunal. A Sociopolitical Analysis.* Ottawa: University of Ottawa Press.

Tymoczko, Maria. 2009. "Why Translators Should Want to Internationalize Translation Studies." *The Translator* 15(2): 401–21.

Tymoczko, Maria, and Edwin Gentzler. 2002. *Translation and Power.* Amherst and Boston: University of Massachusetts Press.

von Flotow, Luise. 2011. *Translating Women*. Ottawa: Ottawa University Press.
Wakabayashi, Judy. 2012. "Japanese Translation Historiography: Origins, Strengths, Weaknesses and Lessons." *Translation Studies* 5(2): 172–88.
——2013. "Evaluating Historical Views on Translation: A Case Study of Motoki Ryōei, Early Japanese Theorist." *MonTI* 5: 167–91.
White, Hayden. 1973. *Metahistory: The Historical Imagination in Nineteenth Century Europe*. Baltimore, MD: The Johns Hopkins University Press.
White, Micheline (ed.). 2011. *English Women, Religion, and Textual Production, 1500–1625*. Farnham: Ashgate.
Zarrouk, Mourad. 2006. "Microhistoria e historia de la traducción." *Sendebar* 17: 5–20.

8 Translation and interpreting pedagogy

Sonia Colina and Claudia V. Angelelli

Overview

Current research related to translation and interpreting (T&I) pedagogy includes both pure and applied research. Applied research is conducted directly on issues related to teaching, learning, or testing, in classrooms or virtual environments, on persons, materials, or activities, with the goal of having a direct impact on pedagogical practice (see Chapter 12, "Action research"). Pure research includes studies of cognitive processing (see Chapter 3, "Cognitive processes") which have an indirect impact on T&I learning environments. In other words, the implications of such research for T&I pedagogy are not always obvious. The focus of this chapter will be primarily on applied research in T&I pedagogy.

Since the 1950s pedagogical practices have been used to help TIS students acquire in an optimally efficacious and efficient way the skills necessary to perform as translators and interpreters. Pedagogy is intertwined with education. In education in general, and in language or TIS education in particular, pedagogy has evolved from a teacher-centered to a learner-centered model. Based on the Vygotskian model of social constructivism, notions of scaffolding in education have impacted, to different degrees, pedagogies in all fields. TIS is no exception.

In the maps of Translation Studies proposed by Holmes (1972/1988) and Toury (1995), still widely accepted in the field, T&I pedagogy belongs in the applied branch (applied extensions), along with translator aids and translation criticism, and in opposition to the pure disciplines (theoretical and descriptive). Although neither Holmes nor Toury refer to interpreting per se, Translation Studies for them was inclusive of interpreting and therefore one may assume that the same applies to interpreting pedagogy. Like all applied branches, T&I pedagogy is informed by theoretical models and is dependent on descriptive data, as well as on research findings from Translation Studies and related fields. A crucial aspect of T&I pedagogy is how to bridge the distance between the applied and theoretical branches so that the former can be truly informed by the latter. In Toury's (1995: 17) view, the question of how to convert or bridge the findings or concepts of the pure branches to the applied ones, such as pedagogy, is left to the teachers.

An alternative view considers this responsibility to be shared (Colina 2003a; Roy 2006; Angelelli 2008). Teachers/practitioners are responsible for their own professional development and for keeping up to date in the field. Researchers/scholars, on the other hand, are responsible for making research findings available to practitioners. It is only when there is dialogue between theory/research and teaching/practice that fields can make progress. Indeed, the last two decades have shown that at the intersection of the pure and applied branches lie research questions of considerable relevance for T&I pedagogy that should attract the interest of researchers and scholars. Among them are the nature of T&I, specifically, what constitutes T&I competence, or expert behavior, how it is acquired and what facilitates its acquisition, what acquisitional or learning stages apprentice translators/interpreters go through, how linguistic competence impacts T&I ability and acquisition, and how teacher and student attitudes and roles affect their teaching and learning in the translation or interpreting classroom. Also of interest are the applied extensions in research areas outside of TIS, such as educational theories, theories of second language acquisition and teaching, cognitive processes research, and translation process research. Furthermore, the classroom is a perfect environment for action research (see Chapter 12, "Action research"), i.e., research carried out by teachers that helps them solve teaching problems or improve/refine their teaching. This chapter makes reference to many of the above-mentioned research topics and the methodologies commonly used to investigate and address them.

Theoretical foundations

T&I pedagogy, as studied today, draws from various theoretical sources, in accordance with the interdisciplinary nature of Translation and Interpreting Studies. Here we focus on those that, from our perspective, have had a greater impact on the field, namely education and educational theories, Translation and Interpreting Studies, and second language acquisition and teaching.

In the realm of educational theory, T&I pedagogy research relies heavily on learning theory and on epistemological theories that debate the nature of knowledge, ranging from objectivist, modernist theories to more recent postmodern, constructivist approaches, which see knowledge and learning as essentially dialogic, constructed in social interaction, rather than as an objective reality that can be transmitted. These theories, specifically Vygotsky's notions of social constructionism and scaffolding (1997) and Nunan's student-centered curriculum design (1993), constitute the theoretical foundations for T&I pedagogy (as developed, for example, by Kiraly 1995, 2000 and 2015). In addition, educational theory underlies scholarly discussions of teaching objectives, goals, and assessment in T&I pedagogy.

Most research in T&I pedagogy today also has its foundation in modern theories and conceptualizations of both translation and interpreting, solidly rooted in Translation Studies. Until relatively recently, conceptualizations of

T&I were reflected only implicitly and indirectly in the T&I classroom through teachers' own views. Today, however, most T&I research is guided by some general notion of translation theory and Translation Studies. For instance, the majority of non-literary translation classrooms are inspired by functionalist theories of translation (Nord 1997), guided by translation briefs and contextual considerations surrounding the target text. In interpreting classrooms we see the use of role plays as learning activities that promote interaction and discussion. Scripts based on empirical data promote discussions of different renderings appropriate to different settings, as well as discussions of possible interpretations and of the complexity of the interpreter's role (Angelelli 2006; Roy 2006). Simultaneously, the sociological turn in T&I Studies and the shift of emphasis from the translation to the translator, and from the message rendered to the role played by the interpreter rendering it (and to the community of practice), means that learners and learners' profiles take center stage in the T&I classroom. Consequently, serious consideration is increasingly given to the study of student competencies and student behavior in preparation for specific T&I programs, as well as outcomes and the assessment of outcomes, all intended to better align student qualifications with professional and market demands. These are matters generally investigated through empirical methods that can range from case studies to experimental studies with larger groups of subjects. Some experimental studies involve researching multiple aspects of competence over an extended period of time, such as the work of the PACTE research group.

From communicative methodologies to more constructivist and socially oriented ones, it is obvious that T&I pedagogy owes much to acquisition theories and teaching methodologies developed either for general use or specifically for the teaching of language. From applied linguistics TIS pedagogy has acquired approaches to teaching and learning that focus on input and output, process and product orientations, developing and assessing learners' competence, classroom management, testing and measurement, and teacher education/supervision, as well as the interaction between bi/multilingualism and the acquisition of translational competence in multilingual and multicultural learning environments. Research methodologies are also adopted and adapted from applied linguistics, involving experimental and case studies, as well as action research conducted by teachers in their classrooms.

Evolution of the topic in TIS

Until very recently (the last couple of decades), research related to T&I pedagogy relied almost entirely on anecdotal accounts, case studies at best, detailing how translation/interpreting was taught in a particular institution or program. The few studies produced at the time were void of reflection on or discussion of any research on translation teaching, learning, or other relevant fields (see, for instance, the articles in the series *Teaching Translation and Interpreting*, edited by Cay Dollerup and Anne Loddegaard, published by John Benjamins). They reflected the instructors' use of their observations to 'inform' their teaching, accompanied perhaps by some ideas or modifications derived therefrom. Epistemologically, these practices revealed dominant positivist views, according to which knowledge is an objectifiable reality that can be transmitted to the student in a linear fashion. Accordingly, teaching is seen as a transmissionist activity in which teachers are experts in possession of the knowledge that is to be passed on. Not surprisingly in this context, research (empirical or theoretical) on T&I learning, acquisition, cognitive processing, and translation processes was rarely applied to inform T&I pedagogy.

Interpreting pedagogy to some extent followed its own trajectory. Following World War II, the need to communicate across linguistic boundaries became a pressing need within the international community (Angelelli 2004b). Interpreting entered academia to meet a pragmatic need (rather than as an object of study). Thus, research questions about T&I pedagogy were deferred in order to address the immediate market or professional needs of practitioners. Logistical questions related to the conducting of "training" took priority over questions that addressed what a well-rounded education of interpreters should look like and how it might account for the different settings in which interpreters work (i.e., community, conference, legal, and medical). For example, based on instructors' personal experience and opinions rather than on empirical research, many programs that taught interpreting did little more than teach terminology relevant to the field.

The 1990s and the beginning of the twenty-first century saw a surge in research contributions with pedagogical implications. These studies, often using think-aloud protocols, investigated, among other issues, differences in the translation processes of professional translators and students (e.g., Kiraly 1995; Kussmaul 1995; and many others), or of novice and expert interpreters (Degueldre 2002; Englund Dimitrova 2005). In interpreting, scholars began to investigate, with the help of discourse analysis, such issues as turn-taking or adjacent pairs (Davidson 1998; Baraldi and Gavioli 2012), role, and agency (Metzger 1999; Davidson 2000 and 2001; and Angelelli 2004a and 2004b, to name a few). Studies inspired by research models and methods in second language acquisition and teaching also made their debut during this decade. This research continues today. Some of the relevant topics include: the nature and relevance of communicative translation pedagogies (Kiraly 1990; Colina 2003a), the nature of translation competence (Cao 1996; Campbell 1998), and the effects of translation directionality (Campbell 1998). This period was also characterized by calls for translation pedagogy to be better informed by empirical research findings (Colina 2003a and 2003b).

It is also during this time that functionalist theories took hold in translator education. In opposition to the previous read-and-translate methods, in which students are given sentences from a text devoid of context, functionalist methods place the text in its communicative and functional context. They provide instructions for the translation with respect to the purpose and other situational features of the target text (e.g., audience, motive, and time and place of reception), thus establishing the theoretical foundation for textual analysis research (e.g., features of text types and genres in specific languages). In Translation Studies, a general shift toward the translator (and toward other agents in the translation process) was brought about by new theoretical frameworks and viewpoints, such as the sociological turn and cultural studies approaches, which, in addition to functionalism, fostered increased interest in the student translator and therefore in research into areas that could be applied to pedagogy, such as cognitive and translation process research.

The last two decades have also seen an explosion in the kind of empirical and applied research that started in the 1990s. Among the topics of these studies are: the sociocultural context of the translation/interpreted rendition, professional and student qualifications, linguistic competence of T&I students (Angelelli and Degueldre 2002; Beeby 2004), translation competence (Pym 2003; PACTE Group 2008; Malmkjær 2009), translation/interpreting directionality and the native speaker translator/interpreter (Pokorn 2005, 2009), cognitive and expertise studies (Shreve 2006; Shreve and Angelone 2010; Muñoz-Martín 2014a, 2014b), task-based instruction in T&I teaching (González-Davies 2004), and T&I quality assessment (Colina 2008, 2009; Angelelli and Jacobson 2009). The relationship between language teaching and translation remains a topic of interest, in particular the role of translation in the language classroom (see Laufer and Girsai 2008; Witte, Harden, and Harden 2009; Carreres and Noriega-Sánchez 2011; Kim 2011; and Laviosa 2014).

The surge in T&I programs has also fostered action research case studies and research drawing on student feedback and questionnaires. For instance, Shih (2011) reports on action research aimed at investigating the effect of learning translation theories on student practice; the findings—based on data collected through student journals and questionnaires—suggest that students view translation theories as guidelines, methods, or techniques. Journals have also been found to be a valuable tool to foster student learning. Case studies undertaken by teachers and teacher/researchers have investigated, for example, the use of comparable corpora to identify textual features (Laursen and Arinas Pellón 2012) and of specific approaches and techniques for a particular course (e.g., Kenny 2008; Qiujin 2010). Technological advances have made it possible for researchers to examine large corpora and undertake large-scale textual studies that have important implications for T&I pedagogy (e.g., Jiménez-Crespo 2010, 2013). Translation process research has also benefited from innovative methodologies made available by new technologies, such as eye-tracking and keystroke logging (cf. Muñoz-Martín 2014b). The findings of these studies are often relevant to the teaching of translation and interpreting.

In recent years, cognitive studies and translation process research (TPR) have made significant contributions to translation and interpreting pedagogy. Examples of lines of research in this area include: writing process research, investigations of translation processes in student and expert translators using keystroke logging and eye-tracking, retrospection and process research methodologies, and expertise studies, among others. Examples of these studies can be found in special issues of *Translation and Interpreting Studies* (8.2 [2013] and 9.1 [2014]) and *MonTI* (2014).

Key studies

Two back-to-back special issues of *Translation and Interpreting Studies* (*TIS* 8:2 [2013] and 9:1 [2014]) offer fine examples of pure and applied research, respectively. Issue 8.2, "Describing Cognitive Processes in Translation: Acts and Events," is devoted to process-oriented research in translation and interpreting. It includes studies on translation as a cognitive act, on processes related to translation acts, and processes related to the sociological translation event, which have implications for teaching and learning of translation. Issue 9.1, "The Development of Professional Competence," is devoted to translation process research and to particular aspects of professional translation and interpreting competence, such as directionality of translation, revision, use of background and cultural information, search behavior, self-awareness, and grammatical (de) metaphorization. While all studies in this volume address professional competence, some also explicitly compare experts to novices and students.

Another example of process-oriented research is the special issue of *MonTI*, edited by Muñoz-Martín (2014a), entitled "Minding Translation. Con la traducción en mente." This issue presents a collection of studies on process-oriented research using a variety of research methodologies (eye-tracking, key logging, screen recording, retrospective protocols, talk-aloud protocols, ethnographic methods, etc.) and with a focus on cognitive processes. Although most articles in the volume have implications for translation pedagogy, some address specific aspects of teaching and learning, such as translation competence acquisition (PACTE Group 2008), translation in the language classroom, and data collection from participants with different levels of expertise. Another example of process-oriented research is Alves, *Triangulating Translation. Perspectives in Process Oriented Research* (2003). It is a collection of empirical and theoretical studies on process-oriented research promoting the benefits of using several methods of data gathering and analysis (i.e., triangulation) when researching the process of translation. The articles in Part III, in particular, use triangulation to study the learning processes (e.g. dictionary use), comparing them with those of learners of foreign languages and those of experienced translators. Englund Dimitrova (2005) offers another example of triangulation in her exploration of linguistic and behavioral data. In this study of professional competence and expertise in translation, the author explores translation as a text-reproduction task focusing on participants with different degrees of translation experience. The research triangulates Russian–Swedish translation data with Talk-aloud protocols (TAPs), a research method of data collection in which participants are asked to think aloud as the translate and computer logging. And lastly, in the area of TAPs, Kussmaul's, *Training the Translator* (1995) must be mentioned, despite its earlier date, as one of the first studies in Translation Studies to connect research findings to teaching methodologies.

The author presents the results of a think-aloud protocol study, which identifies successful student strategies (and unsuccessful ones) that should be considered when designing lessons and methodologies.

In a completely different line of research, Valdés et al. (2003) is a study of circumstantial bilinguals and their capacity to perform as language mediators. Based on a five-year ethnographic study of Latino bilingual youngsters interpreting for their families and immediate communities, this study sheds light on bilinguals' behaviors and strategies used while interpreting and translating, which has implications for the teaching of translation to heritage learners.

New directions

As the world becomes more complex, so too do translation, interpreting, and their respective pedagogies. A broader view of translation/interpreting, referred to in some circles as language mediation or language brokering, points in the direction of increasingly porous divisions between pedagogies geared toward language acquisition and T&I teaching and learning. In light of this, we anticipate that translation or interpreting pedagogy research will focus increasingly on serving the needs of more diverse student populations, characterized by varying levels of language proficiency and translation or interpreting competence. Research may also focus on fine-tuning preparation for more complexly defined translation/interpreting tasks. In other words, the generalizations (i.e., oversimplifications) of the past, such as the idea that translation or interpreting should not be taught until students are fully bilingual and/or that translation/interpreting should only be carried out into the L1, are now seen as inadequate and descriptively inaccurate. Consequently, teachers and scholars are more interested in learning how to teach translation/interpreting to students with various levels of linguistic proficiency and how to create reasonable outcomes and evaluation methods for a variety of student profiles. Along those lines, a new direction (already seen in dissertations in progress) will focus on teacher qualifications and teacher profiles, the various roles and definitions of translation/interpreting in the language classroom, and the role of language (and language enhancement) in the translation or interpreting classroom/program.

Current studies based on empirical data have triggered discussions of ethics, standards, and certification that ultimately call into question unsupported claims regarding the teaching and testing of T&I. Therefore, we should see more research studies in fields like testing, certification, and standards, which will provide a more empirically based foundation for T&I pedagogy. Additionally, the use of action research (see Chapter 12, "Action research") provides an ideal environment in which to reflect on teachers' practices, beliefs, and behaviors. Furthermore, the explosion of programs using blended approaches or distance learning for both teaching and testing raises a host of questions related to T&I pedagogy in areas such as motivation, community of learners, teacher/student and student/student interaction, and discourse in the virtual classroom, all of which need further study. And last but not least, technological developments that have entered translation/interpreting classes, such as software localization (including the translation of text strings deprived of context), computer-assisted translation or machine translation, as well as remote interpreting or the use of stylus pens that record speech for interpreters to play back, are also posing new issues and opportunities for researchers to explore.

References

Alves, Fabio. 2003. *Triangulating Translation Perspectives in process oriented research.* Amsterdam/Philadelphia: John Benjamins

Angelelli, Claudia V. 2004a. *Medical Interpreting and Cross-cultural Communications.* Cambridge: Cambridge University Press.

——2004b. *Revisiting the Interpreter's Role: A Study of Conference, Court and Medical Interpreters in Canada, Mexico, and the United States.* Amsterdam and Philadelphia: John Benjamins.

——2006. "Designing Curriculum for Healthcare Interpreting Education: A Principles Approach." In *New Approaches to Interpreter Education*, Cynthia Roy (ed.), 23–46. Washington DC: Gallaudet University Press.

——2008. "Longitudinal Studies and the Development of Assessment for Advanced Competencies." In *The Longitudinal Study of L2 Advanced Capacities*, Lourdes Ortega and Heidi Byrnes (eds.), 264–78. Second Language Acquisition Research Series. New York: Routledge.

Angelelli, Claudia V., and Christian Degueldre. 2002. "Bridging the Gap between Language for General Purposes and Language for Work: An Intensive Superior-level Language/skill Course for Teachers, Translators, and Interpreters." In *Developing Professional-Level Language Proficiency*, Betty Lou Leaver and Boris Shekhtman (eds.), 77–95. Cambridge: Cambridge University Press.

Angelelli, Claudia V., and Holly E. Jacobson (eds.). 2009. *Testing and Assessment in Translation and Interpreting Studies: A Call for Dialogue between Research and Practice.* American Translators Association Scholarly Monograph Series XIV. Amsterdam and Philadelphia: John Benjamins.

Baraldi, Claudio, and Laura Gavioli (eds.). 2012. *Coordinating Participation in Dialogue Interpreting.* Amsterdam and Philadelphia: John Benjamins.

Beeby, Allison. 2004. "Language Learning for Translators: Designing a Syllabus." In *Translation in Undergraduate Degree Programmes*, Kirsten Malmkjær (ed.), 39–66. Amsterdam and Philadelphia: John Benjamins.

Campbell, Stuart. 1998. *Translation into the Second Language.* London and New York: Longman.

Cao, Deborah. 1996. "A Model of Translation Proficiency." *Target* 8(2): 325–40.

Carreres, Angeles, and María Noriega-Sanchez. 2011. "Translation in Language Teaching: Insights from Professional Translator Training." *Language Learning Journal* 39(3): 281–97.

Colina, Sonia. 2003a. *Translation Teaching: From Research to the Classroom.* New York: McGraw Hill.

——2003b. "Towards an Empirically-based Translation Pedagogy." In *Beyond the Ivory Tower: Rethinking Translation Pedagogy*, Brian James Baer and Geoffrey Koby (eds.), 29–59. American Translators Association Monograph Series, Vol. XII. Amsterdam: John Benjamins.

——2008. "Translation Quality Evaluation: Empirical Evidence for a Functionalist Approach." *The Translator* 14(1): 97–134.

——2009. "Further Evidence for a Functionalist Approach to Translation Quality Evaluation." *Target* 21(2): 215–44.

Davidson, Brad. 1998. "Interpreting Medical Discourse: A Study of Cross-Linguistic Communication in the Hospital Clinic." Unpublished Ph.D. dissertation, Stanford University, Stanford, CA.

——2000. "The Interpreter as Institutional Gatekeeper: The Social-linguistic Role of Interpreters in Spanish-English Medical Discourse." *Journal of Sociolinguistics* 4: 379–405.

——2001. "Questions in Cross-linguistic Medical Encounters: The Role of the Hospital Interpreter." *Anthropological Quarterly* 74: 170–78.

Degueldre, Christian. 2002. "Le rôle de l'imagerie dans la communication réalisée par un interprète." *META* 47(1): 58–86.

Dollerup, Cay, and Anne Loddegaard (eds.). 1992. *Teaching Translation and Interpreting: Training, Talent and Experience.* Philadelphia and Amsterdam: John Benjamins.

Englund Dimitrova, Brigitta. 2005. *Expertise and Explicitation in the Translation Process.* Amsterdam and New York: John Benjamins.

González-Davies, María. 2004. *Multiple Voices in the Translation Classroom.* Amsterdam and New York: John Benjamins.

Holmes, James. 1972/1988. "The Name and Nature of Translation Studies." In *Translated! Papers on Literary Translation and Translation Studies*, James Holmes (ed.), 67–80. Amsterdam: Rodopi.

Jiménez-Crespo, Miguel. 2010. "The Intersection of Localization and Translation: A Corpus Study of Spanish Original and Localized Web Forms." *Translation and Interpreting Studies* 5(2): 186–207.

——2013. "Crowdsourcing, Corpus Use, and the Search for Translation Naturalness: A Comparable Corpus Study of Facebook and non-Translated Social Networking Sites." *Translation and Interpreting Studies* 6(1): 62–86.

Kenny, Mary Ann. 2008. "Discussion, Cooperation, Collaboration: The Impact of Task Structure on Student Interaction in a Web-based Translation Exercise Module." *The Interpreter and Translator Trainer* 2(2): 139–64.

Kim, Eun-Young. 2011. "Using Translation Exercises in the Communicative EFL Writing Classroom." *English Language Teaching Journal* 65(2): 154–60.

Kiraly, Donald. 1990. "A Role for Communicative Competence and the Acquisition-Learning Distinction in Translator Training." In *Second Language Acquisition/Foreign Language Learning*, Bill Van Patten and James Lee (eds.), 207–15. Bristol, PA and Clevedon: Multilingual Matters.

——1995. *Pathways to Translation: Pedagogy and Process.* Kent, OH: Kent State University Press.

——2000. *A Social Constructivist Approach to Translator Education: Empowerment from Theory to Practice.* Manchester: St. Jerome.

——2015. "Occasioning Translator Competence: Moving beyond Social Constructivism towards a Postmodern Alternative to Instructionism." Special issue. *Translation and Interpreting Studies* 10(1).

Kussmaul, Paul. 1995. *Training the Translator.* Amsterdam and Philadelphia: John Benjamins.

Laufer, Batia, and Nany Girsai. 2008. "Form-focused Instruction in Second Language Vocabulary Learning: A Case for Contrastive Analysis and Translation." *Applied Linguistics* 29(4): 694–716.

Laursen, Anne Lise, and Ismael Arinas Pellón. 2012. "Text Corpora in Translator Training. A Case Study of the Use of Comparable Corpora in Classroom Teaching." *The Interpreter and Translator Trainer* 6(1): 45–70.

Laviosa, Sara. 2014. *Translation and Language Education. Pedagogic Approaches Explored.* New York: Routledge.

Malmkjær, Kirsten, 2009. "What Is Translation Competence?" *Revue française de linguistique appliquée* 14(1): 121–34.

Metzger, Melanie. 1999. *Sign Language Interpreting: Deconstructing the Myth of Neutrality.* Washington DC: Gallaudet University Press.

Muñoz-Martín, Ricardo (ed.). 2014a. "Minding Translation. Con la traducción en mente." Special issue. *MonTI* 1.

——2014b. "A Blurred Snapshot of Advances in Translation Process Research." *MonTI* 1: 49–84.

Nord, Christiane. 1997. *Translating as a Purposeful Activity: Functionalist Approaches Explained.* Manchester: St. Jerome.

Nunan, David. 1993. *Designing Tasks for the Communicative Classroom.* Cambridge Language Teaching Series. Cambridge: Cambridge University Press.

PACTE Group. 2008. "First Results of a Translation Competence Experiment: 'Knowledge' of Translation and 'Efficacy' of the Translation." In *Translator and Interpreter Training. Issues, Methods and Debates*, John Kearns (ed.), 104–26. London: Continuum.

Pokorn, Nike K. 2005. *Challenging the Traditional Axioms.* Amsterdam and Philadelphia: John Benjamins.

——2009. "Natives or Non-natives? That Is the Question ... Teachers of Translation into Language B." *The Interpreter and Translator Trainer* 3(2): 189–208.

Pym, Anthony. 2003. "Redefining Translation Competence in an Electronic Age: In Defence of a Minimalist Approach." *Meta* 48(4): 481–97.

Qiujin, Chen. 2010. "The Application of Text Type in Non-Literary Translation Teaching." *Translation and Interpreting Studies* 5(2): 208–19.

Roy, Cynthia (ed.). 2006. *New Approaches to Interpreter Education.* Washington DC: Gallaudet University Press.

Shih, Claire Y. 2011. "Learning from Writing Reflective Learning Journals in a Theory-based Translation Module: Students' Perspectives." *The Interpreter and Translator Trainer* 5(2): 309–24.

Shreve, Gregory M. 2006. "The Deliberate Practice: Translation and Expertise." *Journal of Translation Studies* 9(1): 27–42.

Shreve, Gregory M., and Erik Angelone (eds.). 2010. *Translation and Cognition.* Amsterdam and Philadelphia: John Benjamins.

Toury, Gideon. 1995. *Descriptive Translation Studies and Beyond.* Amsterdam and Philadelphia: John Benjamins.

Valdés, Guadalupe, Cristina Chávez, Claudia Angelelli, Kerry Enright, Dania Garcia, and Marisela Gonzalez. 2003. "The Study of Young Interpreters: Methods, Materials and Analytical Challenges." In *Expanding Definitions of Giftedness. The Case of Young Interpreters from Immigrant Communities*, Guadalupe Valdés (ed.), 99–118. Mahwah, NJ: Lawrence Erlbaum Associates, Inc.

Vygotsky, Lev. 1997. *Thought and Language.* Cambridge, MA: MIT Press.

Witte, Arnd, Theo Harden, and Alessandra Ramos de Oliveira Harden (eds.). 2009. *Translation in Second Language Learning and Teaching.* Oxford: Peter Lang.

9 Power and conflict

Anna Strowe

Overview

One of the contributions of descriptive Translation Studies, and of the various cultural and sociological approaches it initiated, is the recognition that translation and interpreting are connected not merely to linguistic concerns but also to a wide range of other issues. An approach that encourages the analysis of translations and interpreted communicative events (ICEs) within their social, cultural, and political contexts leads almost inevitably to the conclusion that translation and interpreting, like any other socially embedded process, are shaped by vectors of power that influence communicative choices on the part of language mediators, as well as the reception of both the source and target texts. While translation and interpreting are indispensable to the functioning of international law and governmental systems, and of media reporting and oversight, T&I events are also shaped by asymmetries of power at a more individual level, arising from the competing institutional, linguistic, and cultural affiliations of the language professional and the other parties involved, as well as from the dynamics of the event itself.

The intersection of systems of power and T&I processes and products is visible at many levels and with many permutations. Power can be exercised and expressed in T&I at various operative levels, by individuals and institutions (see Strowe 2013). Exercises of individual power include the choices of language professionals, commissioners, and consumers of T&I, as well as those of other participants in T&I events. Aggregated, these choices form trends that contribute to the construction and functioning of textual norms in T&I (Hermans 1996) and the shaping of market preferences, which in turn influence publishers' attitudes toward translated texts (e.g., Venuti 2008: 9–13). Institutional or cultural power can also function in a top-down fashion, dictating individual practice. Such exercises of power include governmental language and censorship policies (Ní Cuilleanáin et al. 2009; Angelelli 2012a; and more widely Spolsky 2012), as well as non-governmental rules and norms concerning T&I (Angelelli 2006; McDonough Dolmaya 2011). Issues of language bias or linguicism, for example, create power dynamics (Phillipson 2012: 214) that affect T&I events (Berk-Seligson 2008), as do questions of class, race, and immigration status (Angelelli 2004a: 19–20 et passim). The very structure of ICEs also inherently gives power to language professionals (Roland 1999: 165–66), who may use it to act either as advocates or institutional gatekeepers, depending on the role they occupy in the ICE (e.g., Davidson 2001; Angelelli 2004b; Jacquemet 2005). Moreover, power dynamics within academia itself affect the ways in which scholars and others discuss and study T&I (e.g., Chamberlain 2004; Cheung 2006).

Similarly, conflict can manifest itself at different levels of T&I products and processes. The very rationale for T&I assumes a degree of conflict between the needs and demands of the interested parties, as well as the capacities of the languages and cultures themselves (see Catford 1965: chs. 4–7 on asymmetrical grammatical and lexical rules; and Jakobson 2004: 141 on what language "must" convey). In fact, many early formulations of conflict in translation explore cases of cultural conflict involving T&I mediation of linguistic and cultural differences. More recent scholarship on conflict in TIS has focused on T&I in situations of violent conflict. T&I in these situations can serve a variety of functions. The products and processes of linguistic mediation can create conflict, support or oppose particular views or sides in an existing conflict, resolve conflict, or describe and document conflict.

Theoretical foundations

Many theorists and scholars of translation who treat questions of power and conflict do so using practical rather than theoretical definitions of the terms. There are, however, a number of theorists who have articulated ideas about power and conflict that are relevant to discussions in TIS. This section provides a brief examination of some of those approaches, as well as an overview of the types of practical definitions that are often employed in TIS.

Steven Lukes (2005) proposes a three-pronged model for analyzing power as a force in social and political life, focusing in particular on the dynamics of power in American politics. Lukes describes as "one-dimensional" any analysis that explores power as the force or ability that allows actor A to cause actor B to make decisions contrary to B's self-interest. As Lukes observes (2005: 19), this situation implies the pre-existence of conflict between particular decisions in order for B to make a decision that is or is not contrary to B's own interests. A "two-dimensional" analysis, such as that of Peter Bachrach and Morton Baratz (1962), allows for non-decisions to be factored into exercises of power. This model also allows for an analysis of forms of power that function pre-emptively to prevent even the discussion of issues that might give rise to the level of conflict; thus, power can be viewed not only in situations of present conflict but also in the processes that allow or prevent such situations. Lukes notes that neither the one-dimensional nor the two-dimensional model allows for analysis of power that does not focus on observable behavioral outcomes, and both fail to account for systemic rather than individual manifestations of power. What Lukes describes as "three-dimensional" analysis treats forms of control over the political agenda that are not only based on decision-making but also on the pre-decision formation of bias and desire. This model posits the ability of power to affect situations of potential or latent conflict while recognizing a distinction between the subjective and the real, or objective, interests of the agents.

Although Mona Baker (2006) draws on the work of Lukes to provide a foundation for her discussion of power, TIS scholars far more commonly cite the works of Michel Foucault and Pierre Bourdieu. Tejaswini Niranjana's exploration of postcolonial translation begins with the Foucauldian equation of knowledge and power in order to examine the asymmetries of power in colonial translational contexts (1992: 1; on the relationship between knowledge and power, see Foucault 1976/1990). Michaela Wolf explicitly takes Foucault's early work on power as her main framework, defining power "as a means of control, of subjection, and of repression" that is intertwined with discursive practices (1995: 124; see also Foucault's work on madness and medicine [*History of Madness* 1961/2006; *The Birth of the Clinic* 1963/2003], on oppressive and repressive forms of power [*Discipline and Punish* 1975/1991], and on the subject ["The Subject and Power" 1982]). Ian Mason and Wen Ren (2012) draw on Foucault's view of power as a multivalent strategy in analyzing the complex power dynamics of ICEs. In a note, Baker observes that Foucault, like Lukes, "downplays the issue of observable conflict, acknowledges that power takes many forms, and further locates the exercise of power in the way the social and political order structures reality for us" (2006: 173n1).

The discussions of power and social structure in sociology are another source for TIS research. It is worth noting that this is a reciprocal relationship; the journal *Social Semiotics*, for example, published a special issue titled "Translation and Conflict" (Salama-Carr 2007a). The work of Bourdieu is particularly relevant to questions of language and power (see Bourdieu 1991), but scholars in TIS also regularly draw on the work of Niklas Luhmann (1995) and Erving Goffman (on the possibility of using Goffman as a theorist of power, see Richard Jenkins [2008]). Wolf (2011) connects TIS to Bourdieu and Luhmann in her treatment of power; Wolf (2012) also explores how Bourdieu's notion of *habitus* is connected to activism in T&I. Also relevent here is the collected volume *Constructing a Sociology of Translation* (Wolf and Fukari 2007). Two recent special issues of TIS journals focus on the application of sociology in TIS: one on the "sociological turn" from *Translation and Interpreting Studies* (Angelelli 2012b) and one more specifically on Bourdieu from *The Translator* (Inghilleri 2005). Sergey Tyulenev's *Applying Luhmann to Translation Studies* (2012) includes specific discussions of power in relation to Luhmann's work and translation.

The concern in all these approaches with the constructive power of discourse is reflected in Norman Fairclough's book *Language and Power* (1989), which explores the role language plays in "the production, maintenance, and change of social relations in power," as well as the ways in which language and power form systems of domination in society (1989: 1). Fairclough situates his work on language and power among existing sub-disciplines in linguistics, advocating critical language study as an approach that acknowledges relationships between language and power, while drawing on the expertise of those fields. Although these fields have evolved since Fairclough's book, his clear and concise articulation of the relationships among language, power, and ideology remains relevant, and critical discourse analysis (CDA) remains an important tool for many scholars in TIS (on CDA in general, see also Fairclough [2010] and Michael Toolan [2002]; on CDA and power, see Teun van Dijk [2008]). CDA has been used to analyze the ways in which discourse serves to construct identity in an ICE (see, for example, Mason 2005; Tipton 2008; Merlini 2009; Angelelli 2011) and how narrative is used to represent both conflict and the parties involved (Baker 2006). Other works examine specific discourse markers, such as those associated with politeness (Krouglov 1999), or features of discourse in particular settings (Berk-Seligson 1990 and 2009; Angelelli 2004a) to track the workings of power.

Conflict clearly figures into these articulations of power, but it is also a topic of research and theorization on its own. Two main conceptualizations of conflict figure into contemporary research in Translation and Interpreting studies: social, economic, and cultural studies that address "conflict theory," and Studies that articulate the causes and effects of violent conflict. Theorizations of conflict in TIS research are often not explicitly referenced, although approaches taken by scholars in TIS often align with thinking in these areas.

Conflict theory is a term that designates approaches to social questions predicated on the notion that much of society is based on particular forms of conflict. The conflict model begins with inequality—e.g., economic, social, or gendered—as the basis of a social conflict with the potential to lead to changes in society. Movements based to some extent on this model include Marxism and feminism, as well as many contemporary social justice movements (see Sears and Cairns 2010: 20–24). Many theorizations of T&I as inherently related to cultural or linguistic conflict reflect this approach, as do articulations more directly related to Marxist, feminist, or postcolonial thought.

Of particular interest in TIS are social conflicts involving language and access to translation and interpreting services, including access to public services and biases against speakers of other languages, which are often associated with issues of immigration (e.g., Angelelli 2004a: 19–20). Brad Davidson (2000 and 2001) examines the dynamics of language-based prejudice in the medical sphere by analyzing ICEs involving Spanish-speaking patients and English-speaking care providers.

Identifying individual theories of violent conflict that contribute to TIS is difficult because of the wide variety of conflict situations, as well as the multiple roles that T&I can play in such situations. Studies in TIS that treat particular aspects of T&I in conflict situations, such as the ethics of embedded interpreters (e.g., Inghilleri 2009 and 2010) or the role of translation in the preservation of cultural memory and narratives of trauma (e.g., Kuhiwczak 2007 and Nikolaou 2007), benefit from theoretical works in philosophy and cultural studies on ethics, trauma studies, and cultural memory. Thus far, however, no one particular mode of thinking about violent conflict stands out as fundamental to approaching conflict in TIS.

In her introduction to *Globalization, Political Violence and Translation*, Esperanza Bielsa grounds her analysis on Zygmunt Bauman's articulation of "negative globalization," defined as globalization that has facilitated the growth of exploitation and violence more than the growth of any necessary correctives (Bielsa and Hughes 2009: 1–2). Bielsa describes the violence this type of globalization brings by using Mary Kaldor's term "new wars" (cited in Bielsa and Hughes 2009: 3) and Arjun Appadurai's analysis of "large-scale cultural violence" (4). Bielsa points to globalized forms of violence that are both the product and cause of economic decline, that transcend national boundaries and include non-state actors, and that have come to form a permanent part of globalized society (5).

TIS scholars also frame their approaches to translation and conflict in less theoretical terms. In the introduction to *Translation and Power*, for example, Maria Tymoczko and Edwin Gentzler (2002: xvii) simply refer to the *Oxford English Dictionary* definitions of power in order to establish the semantic range of the word so as to frame the case studies in the volume. Baker refers briefly to Lukes and Foucault in her elaboration of power, but her working definition of conflict is more practical: "In its broadest meaning, conflict refers to a situation in which two or more parties seek to undermine each other because they have incompatible goals, competing interests, or fundamentally different values … This book adopts the broader definition of conflict but draws extensively – though not exclusively – on examples of political, armed conflict in elaborating its theoretical premises" (Baker 2006: 1). Similarly, Myriam Salama-Carr, in her introduction to *Translating and Interpreting Conflict*, takes a relatively non-theoretical view of conflict, distinguishing the types of conflict she addresses from more metaphorical uses of the term: "Throughout these essays 'conflict' refers to those situations of political, cultural and ideological confrontation in which the translator and the interpreter can be involved" (2007b: 1).

The variety of theoretical approaches to power and conflict across disciplines, as well as the many ways in which T&I are related to power and conflict, mean that there is still much work to be done in connecting disciplines and articulating theoretical frameworks for the study of power and conflict in TIS. This work has begun, largely by relating specific theoretical notions to particular case studies, but this work neither exhausts existing models nor describes the entire range of cases available in T&I.

Evolution of the topic in TIS

Discussions of power and conflict in TIS largely begin with articulations of cultural conflict in text and language. Salama-Carr (2013) observes that many traditional formulations of the problems of T&I employ a rhetoric of opposition, juxtaposing two supposedly conflicting views or approaches to a text that create a tension addressed by TIS scholars. This oppositional phrasing is visible from St. Jerome's distinction between translating "word for word" and "sense for sense" through twentieth- and twenty-first-century discussions of T&I, such as foreignizing vs domesticating strategies or adequacy vs acceptability.

Recognition of the position of T&I within wider cultural power structures also has a long history. Cicero (translated in Robinson 2002: 7–12) describes Latin translations of Greek oratory as a way to contest Greek cultural superiority in oratory. This concern with cultural dominance and the relative superiority of particular languages finds expression in a variety of cultural contexts related to translation. Joachim du Bellay, for example, uses translation to argue that French can be as expressive as Latin (translated in Robinson 2002: 102–6). These examples depend on the relative power of particular cultural or linguistic groups, as well as affecting the role of the translator or interpreter, enhance or diminishing the power of that role.

A conceptualization of translation as an essentially conflictual activity, the site of cultural and linguistic conflict, extends well into contemporary TIS, as well as into the meta-discourse of TIS. George Steiner discusses translation as an aggressive, appropriative act (1975: 297–98). Lawrence Venuti also sees translation as a fundamentally violent act, referring to the "violence that resides in the very purpose and activity of translation" and observing that this relationship is "always configured in hierarchies of dominance and marginality" (2008: 14).

One of the more significant shifts in research over the last few decades has been away from metaphorical and philosophical notions of power and conflict in T&I toward investigations of the intersections between social and political power relations and conflicts and the practices of T&I. Feminist and postcolonial scholars, for example, explore how power structures and conflicts related to gender or colonial politics are created, maintained, and represented through T&I (e.g., Niranjana 1992; Bassnett and Trivedi 1999; Chamberlain 2004; Bugnot 2012). In Interpreting Studies, in particular, scholars have examined the functioning of the immediate forms of interpersonal and institutional power in real time in the ICE. Such research can examine interpreters' roles as mediators, advocates, gatekeepers, and participants in a medical context (Davidson 2001; Angelelli 2004a; Hsieh 2006) or in a juridical setting (Berk-Seligson 1990; Pöllabauer 2004; Inghilleri 2012).

Corresponding to this developing concern with translation and the workings of power is a shift toward the study of violent conflict. Several conferences and publications over the past two decades have taken as their focus the role of T&I in situations of violent conflict. Salama-Carr's articulation of the focus of her volume on violent conflict, quoted above, marks a shift in the field (Boéri 2010: 365). Although significant, this shift does not replace other approaches to the issues of power and conflict; scholars continue to conduct studies examining all the aspects of power and conflict discussed above.

Key studies

Some of the most influential studies on the role of power in translation come from postcolonial scholars interested in the roles played by T&I in projects of colonization and de-colonization. These studies often address the power dynamics involved in these projects, as well as the violent conflicts engendered by them (see, for example, Rafael 1988; Niranjana 1992; Cheyfitz 1997; Bassnett and Trivedi 1999). A more recent volume that includes postcolonial concepts but aims to provide a broader view of how power can relate to T&I is *Translation and Power* (2002), edited by Tymoczko and Gentzler. Studies of institutional power include examples of dominant political or cultural institutions that use T&I to support existing power structures, as well as those that use T&I to resist those structures (see Tymoczko 2010; Wolf 2012). This concern with the dynamics of power and how power intersects with T&I extends into other areas of investigation, such as economic globalization, media coverage, cultural colonization, and, of course, violent conflict and war.

Several specific conflicts have attracted considerable attention. The war, ethnic cleansing, and peacekeeping mission in the former Yugoslavia (see Dragovic-Drouet 2007; Baker 2010; Jones 2010; Stahuljak 2010; Elias-Bursac 2011 and 2012) and the American involvement in Iraq (see Palmer 2007; Inghilleri 2009 and 2010) have each generated a significant body of research. Terrorism as a form of non-state conflict has also attracted attention in TIS (see Bielsa and Hughes 2009; Hess 2012; Rafael 2012), as has T&I during and after World War II (see Takeda 2009 and 2010; Tobia 2010; Footitt and Tobia 2013; Wolf 2013). Several longer studies have drawn from these areas and others to discuss wider questions of T&I related to conflict and power, including Emily Apter's *The Translation Zone* (2006), Mona Baker's *Translation and Conflict* (2006), and Moira Inghilleri's *Interpreting Justice* (2012). These studies of T&I investigate not only large-scale trends related to T&I in conflict situations but also the ways in which individual language professionals support or resist existing power structures and perpetuate or resolve conflict. Another study of interest is Nitsa Ben-Ari's (2012) work on early-twentieth-century Palestinian political dissidents who became translators, editors, and publishers.

Research in Interpreting Studies also shows the ways in which dynamics of power and conflict are manifested in ICEs outside of violent situations. The language professional is able to exert a certain type of power in his or her capacity as interpreter, that is, as the person with the necessary linguistic competence to facilitate communication, as well as to guide the communication into specific channels (see Roland 1999: 165–66; Zimányi 2013). The structure of the ICE is also able to enhance or detract from the interpreters' perceived power, in both physical (e.g., Morris 1999: 10–12) and institutional ways (e.g., Takeda 2008). Further work on the role of the language professional includes Angelelli (2004a, 2011, and 2012a) and Davidson (2000 and 2001) on medical ICEs, Susan Berk-Seligson (2009) on discourse in bilingual police interrogations, and Erik Camayd-Freixas' (2011) first-hand account of the intersection of power, politics, ethics, and interpreting in a controversial US immigration case.

New directions

A number of potential new directions present themselves in relation to translation, power, and conflict. Some scholars have already begun to examine T&I ethics in conflict situations (see Monacelli and Punzo 2001; Inghilleri 2009 and 2010); questions of ethics also raise associated issues of translator/interpreter education. How can T&I programs respond to the complex ethical demands of the situations discussed in the recent scholarship? Similarly, given that many of the translators and interpreters in conflict situations have no formal education, what does this reveal about professional hierarchies?

These questions of training are also tied to trends in global information and communication technology that have become increasingly relevant in recent conflicts. With more and more of the world networked, what is the role of the civilian in the transmission of information? The events of the Arab Spring and the ongoing conflict in Syria have been significantly affected by the presence of images, video footage, and narratives created by civilians, and the dissemination of this media has depended partly on so-called amateur translators and interpreters (on non-professional T&I, see Susam-Sarajeva and Pérez-González 2012). These questions connect as well to research on the use of children as interpreters for immigrant parents or relatives (e.g., Angelelli 2010).

Another fruitful area related to new technologies will likely derive from the new systems of state surveillance and information-gathering. Revelations in the US about wiretapping and communications monitoring by the Department of Homeland Security raise new questions about T&I in intelligence gathering regarding the exercise of power, methods of monitoring conflict and potential conflict, and the relationship between data collection and transmission, including T&I, and the public.

Related to more metaphorical concepts of conflict in T&I, an expansion of investigations into non-Western thought would be a productive contribution to narratives of tension and conflict in T&I. Such an investigation would have to take into consideration the fact that the notion of "theory" itself is not universal (see Susam-Sarajeva 2002 and Cheung 2006). Nevertheless, it could complicate the notion of conflict and power in T&I in important and productive ways.

References

Angelelli, Claudia. 2004a. *Medical Interpreting and Cross-Cultural Communication*. Cambridge: Cambridge University Press.

——2004b. *Revisiting the Interpreter's Role: A Study of Conference, Court, and Medical Interpreters in Canada, Mexico, and the United States*. Amsterdam: John Benjamins.

——2006. "Validating Professional Standards and Codes: Challenges and Opportunities." *Interpreting* 8(2): 175–93.

——2010. "A Professional Ideology in the Making: Bilingual Youngsters Interpreting for Their Communities and the Notion of (No) Choice." In "Profession, Identity and Status: Translators and Interpreters as an Occupational Group," Rakefet Sela-Sheffy and Miriam Shlesinger (eds.). Special issue. *Translation and Interpreting Studies* 5(1): 94–108.

——2011. "Can You Ask Her about Chronic Illnesses, Diabetes and All That?" In *Methods and Strategies of Process Research: Integrative Approaches in Translation Studies*, Cecilia Alvstad, Adelina Hild, and Elisabet Tiselius (eds.), 231-46. Amsterdam/Philadelphia: John Benjamins.

——2012a. "Language Policy and Management in Service Domains: Brokering Communication for Linguistic Minorities in the Community." In *The Cambridge Handbook of Language Policy*, Bernard Spolsky (ed.), 243–61. Cambridge: Cambridge University Press.

——(ed.) 2012b. "The Sociological Turn in Translation and Interpreting Studies." Special issue. *Translation and Interpreting Studies* 7(2).

Apter, Emily. 2006. *The Translation Zone: A New Comparative Literature.* Princeton, NJ: Princeton University Press.

Bachrach, Peter, and Morton S. Baratz. 1962. "Two Faces of Power." *The American Political Science Review* 56(4): 947–52.

Baker, Catherine. 2010. "The Care and Feeding of Linguists: The Working Environment of Interpreters, Translators, and Linguists during Peacekeeping in Bosnia-Herzegovina." *War & Society* 29(2): 154–75.

Baker, Mona. 2006. *Translation and Conflict: A Narrative Account.* London: Routledge.

Bassnett, Susan, and Harish Trivedi. eds. 1999. *Post-colonial Translation: Theory and Practice.* London: Routledge.

Ben-Ari, Nitsa. 2012. "Political Dissidents as Translators, Editors, and Publishers." In "The Sociological Turn in Translation and Interpreting Studies." Special issue. *Translation and Interpreting Studies* 7(2): 144–60.

Berk-Seligson, Susan. 1990. *The Bilingual Courtroom: Court Interpreters in the Judicial Process.* Chicago and London: University of Chicago Press.

——2008. "Judicial Systems in Contact: Access to Justice and the Right to Interpreting/Translating Services among the Quichua of Ecuador." *Interpreting* 10(1): 9–33.

——2009. *Coerced Confessions: The Discourse of Bilingual Police Interrogations.* Berlin: De Gruyter.

Bielsa, Esperanza, and Christopher Hughes (eds.). 2009. *Globalization, Political Violence and Translation.* London: Palgrave Macmillan.

Boéri, Julie. 2010. "Review of *Translating and Interpreting Conflict*, Myriam Salama-Carr (ed.)." *The Translator* 16(2): 364–69.

Bourdieu, Pierre. 1991. *Language and Symbolic Power.* Cambridge, MA: Harvard University Press.

Bugnot, Marie-Ange. 2012. "Traduction des discours sur l'islam dans la presse de France et d'Espagne." In "Journalisme et traduction/Journalism and Translation," Roberto Valdeón (ed.) Special issue. *Meta* 57(4): 977–96.

Camayd-Freixas, Erik. 2011. "Court Interpreter Ethics and the Role of Professional Organizations." *Interpreting in a Changing Landscape. Proceedings of the 6th International Critical Link Conference.* Amsterdam: John Benjamins.

Catford, J. C. 1965. *A Linguistic Theory of Translation*. Oxford: Oxford University Press.

Chamberlain, Lori. 2004. "Gender and the Metaphorics of Translation." In *The Translation Studies Reader*, 2nd edition, Lawrence Venuti (ed.), 306–21. New York and London: Routledge.

Cheung, Martha P. Y. 2006. "From 'Theory' to 'Discourse': The Making of a Translation Anthology." In *Translating Others*, vol. 1, Theo Hermans (ed.), 87–101. Manchester: St. Jerome.

Cheyfitz, Eric. 1997. *The Poetics of Imperialism: Translation and Colonization from The Tempest to Tarzan*. Philadelphia: University of Pennsylvania Press.

Davidson, Brad. 2000. "The Interpreter as Institutional Gatekeeper: The Socio-Linguistic Role of Interpreters in Spanish-English Medical Discourse." *Journal of Sociolinguistics* 4(3): 379–405.

——2001. "Questions in Cross-Linguistic Medical Encounters: The Role of the Hospital Interpreter." *Anthropological Quarterly* 74(4): 170–78.

Dragovic-Drouet, Mila. 2007. "The Practice of Translation and Interpreting during the Conflicts in the Former Yugoslavia (1991–99)." In *Translating and Interpreting Conflict*, Myriam Salama-Carr (ed.), 29–40. Amsterdam: Rodopi.

Elias-Bursac, Ellen. 2011. "Translating at the War Crimes Tribunal in the Hague." *The Fuse*. Available online at http://artsfuse.org/33537/fuse-commentary-translating-at-the-war-crimes-tribunal-in-the-hague/ (last accessed January 28, 2015).

——2012. "Shaping International Justice: The Role of Translation and Interpreting at the ICTY in The Hague." *Translation and Interpreting Studies* 7(1): 34–53.

Fairclough, Norman. 1989. *Language and Power*. Harlow: Longman.

——2010. *Critical Discourse Analysis*. 2nd edition. London: Routledge.

Footitt, Hilary, and Simona Tobia. 2013. *"War Talk": Foreign Languages and the British War Effort in Europe 1940–46*. Basingstoke: Palgrave Macmillan.

Foucault, Michel. 1982. "The Subject and Power." *Critical Inquiry* 8(4): 777–95.

——1990. *The Will to Knowledge: The History of Sexuality I*. Trans. by Robert Hurley. Harmondsworth: Penguin.

——1991. *Discipline and Punish*. Trans. by Alan Sheridan. Harmondsworth: Penguin.

——2003. *The Birth of the Clinic: An Archeology of Medical Perception*. Trans. by A. M. Sheridan. London: Routledge.

——2006. *History of Madness*. Trans. by Jonathan Murphy and Jean Khalfa. Jean Khalfa (ed.). London: Routledge.

Hermans, Theo. 1996. "Norms and the Determination of Translation. A Theoretical Framework." In *Translation Power Subversion*, Román Álvarez and M. Carmen-África Vidal (eds.), 25–51. Clevedon: Multilingual Matters.

Hess, Maya. 2012. "Translating Terror: The (Mis)application of US Federal Prison Rules in the Yousry Case." *The Translator* 18(1): 23–46.

Hsieh, Elaine. 2006. "Conflicts in How Interpreters Manage Their Roles in Provider-Patient Interactions." *Social Science and Medicine* 62(3): 721–30.

Inghilleri, Moira (ed.). 2005. "Bourdieu and the Sociology of Translation and Interpreting." Special issue. *The Translator* 11(2).

——2009. "Translators in War Zones: Ethics under Fire in Iraq." In *Globalization, Political Violence and Translation*, Esperanza Bielsa and Christopher Hughes (eds.), 207–21. London: Palgrave Macmillan.

——2010. "'You Don't Make War Without Knowing Why': The Decision to Interpret in Iraq." Special issue. *The Translator* 16(2): 175–96.

——2012. *Interpreting Justice: Ethics, Politics, and Language*. London: Routledge.

Inghilleri, Moira, and Sue-Ann Harding (eds.). 2010. "Translation and Violent Conflict." Special issue. *The Translator* 16(2).

Jacquemet, Marco. 2005. "The Registration Interview: Restricting Refugees' Narrative Performances." In *Dislocations/Relocations: Narratives of Displacement*, Mike Baynham and Anna De Fina (eds.), 197–220. Manchester: St. Jerome.

Jakobson, Roman. 2004. "On Linguistic Aspects of Translation." In *The Translation Studies Reader*. 2nd edition. Lawrence Venuti (ed.), 138–43. New York and London: Routledge.

Jenkins, Richard. 2008. "Erving Goffman: A Major Theorist of Power?" *Journal of Power* 1(2): 157–68.

Jones, Francis. 2010. "Poetry Translation, Nationalism and the Wars of the Yugoslav Transition." Special issue. *The Translator* 16(2): 223–53.

Krouglov, Alexander. 1999. "Police Interpreting: Politeness and Sociocultural Context." *The Translator* 5(2): 285–302.

Kuhiwczak, Piotr. 2007. "The Grammar of Survival. How Do We Read Holocaust Testimonies?" In *Translating and Interpreting Conflict*, Myriam Salama-Carr (ed.), 61–73. Amsterdam: Rodopi.

Luhmann, Niklas. 1995. *Social Systems*. Stanford, CA: Stanford University Press.

Lukes, Steven. 2005. *Power: A Radical View*. 2nd edition. New York: Palgrave Macmillan.

Mason, Ian. 2005. "Projected and Perceived Identities in Dialogue Interpreting." In *Translation and the Construction of Identity*. IATIS Yearbook 2005, Juliane House, M. Rosario Martín Bueno, and Nicole Baumgarten (eds.), 30–52. Manchester: St. Jerome.

Mason, Ian, and Wen Ren. 2012. "Power in Face-to-Face Interpreting Events." Special issue. *Translation and Interpreting Studies* 7(2): 234–53.

McDonough Dolmaya, Julie. 2011. "Moral Ambiguity: Some Shortcomings of Professional Codes of Ethics for Translators." *The Journal of Specialised Translation* 15: 28–49.

Merlini, Raffaela. 2009. "Seeking Asylum and Seeking Identity in a Mediated Encounter: The Projection of Selves through Discursive Practices." *Interpreting* 11(1): 57–92.

Monacelli, Claudia, and Roberto Punzo. 2001. "Ethics in the Fuzzy Domain of Interpreting: A 'Military' Perspective." In "The Return to Ethics." Special issue. *The Translator* 7(2): 265–82.

Morris, Ruth. 1999. "The Gum Syndrome: Predicaments in Court Interpreting." *International Journal of Speech Language and the Law* 6(1): 6–29.

Ní Cuilleanáin, Eiléan, Cormac Ó Cuilleanáin, and David Parris. 2009. *Translation and Censorship*. Dublin: Four Courts Press.

Nikolaou, Paschalis. 2007. "The Troy of Always: Translations of Conflict in Christopher Logue's *War Music*." In *Translating and Interpreting Conflict*, Myriam Salama-Carr (ed.), 75–95. Amsterdam: Rodopi.

Niranjana, Tejaswini. 1992. *Siting Translation: History, Post-Structuralism, and the Colonial Context*. Berkeley: University of California Press.

Palmer, Jerry. 2007. "Interpreting and Translation for Western Media in Iraq." In *Translating and Interpreting Conflict*, Myriam Salama-Carr (ed.), 13–28. Amsterdam: Rodopi.

Phillipson, Robert. 2012. "Imperialism and Colonialism." In *The Cambridge Handbook of Language Policy*, Bernard Spolsky (ed.), 201–25. Cambridge: Cambridge University Press.

Pöllabauer, Sonja. 2004. "Interpreting in Asylum Hearings." *Interpreting* 6(2): 143–80.

Rafael, Vicente. 1988. *Contracting Colonialism: Translation and Christian Conversion in Tagalog Society under Early Spanish Rule.* Ithaca, NY: Cornell University Press.
——2012. "Translation and the US Empire: Counterinsurgency and the Resistance of Language." *The Translator* 19(1): 1–22.
Robinson, Douglas. 2002. *Western Translation Theory from Herodotus to Nietzsche.* 2nd edition. Manchester: St. Jerome.
Roland, Ruth. 1999. *Interpreters as Diplomats: A Diplomatic History of the Role of Interpreters in World Politics.* Ottawa: University of Ottawa Press.
Salama-Carr, Myriam (ed.). 2007a. "Translation and Conflict." Special issue. *Social Semiotics.* 17(2).
——2007b. *Translating and Interpreting Conflict.* Amsterdam: Rodopi.
——2013. "Translation and Conflict." In *The Handbook of Translation Studies,* vol. 4, Yves Gambier and Luc van Doorslaer (eds.), 31–35. Amsterdam: John Benjamins.
Sears, Alan, and James Cairns. 2010. *A Good Book, in Theory: Making Sense Through Inquiry.* 2nd edition. Toronto: University of Toronto Press.
Spolsky, Bernard (ed.). 2012. *The Cambridge Handbook of Language Policy.* Cambridge: Cambridge University Press.
Stahuljak, Zrinka. 2010. "Minor Empires: Translation, Conflict, and Postcolonial Critique." Special issue. *The Translator* 16(2): 255–74.
Steiner, George. 1975. *After Babel: Aspects of Language and Translation.* Oxford: Oxford University Press.
Strowe, Anna. 2013. "Power and Translation." In *Handbook of Translation Studies,* vol. 4, Yves Gambier and Luc van Doorslaer (eds.), 134–41. Amsterdam: John Benjamins.
Susam-Sarajeva, Şebnem. 2002. "A 'Multilingual' and 'International' Translation Studies?" In *Crosscultural Transgressions: Research Models in Translation Studies II: Historical and Ideological Issues,* Theo Hermans (ed.), 193–207. Manchester: St. Jerome.
Susam-Sarajeva, Şebnem, and Luis Pérez-González (eds.). 2012. "Non-Professionals Translating and Interpreting. Participatory and Engaged Perspectives." Special issue. *The Translator* 18(2).
Takeda, Kayoko. 2008. "Interpreting at the Tokyo War Crimes Tribunal." *Interpreting* 10(1): 65–83.
——2009. "The Interpreter, the Monitor and the Language Arbiter." *Meta* 54(2): 191–200.
——2010. *Interpreting the Tokyo War Crimes Tribunal: A Sociopolitical Analysis.* Ottowa: University of Ottowa Press.
Tipton, Rebecca. 2008. "Reflexivity and the Social Construction of Identity in Interpreter-mediated Asylum Interviews." *The Translator* 14(1): 1–19.
Tobia, Simona. 2010. "Crime and Judgement: Interpreters/Translators in British War Crimes Trials, 1945–49." Special issue. *The Translator* 16(2): 275–93.
Toolan, Michael (ed.). 2002. *Critical Discourse Analysis: Critical Concepts in Linguistics.* 4 vols. London: Routledge.
Tymoczko, Maria (ed.). 2010. *Translation, Resistance, Activism.* Amherst: University of Massachusetts Press.
Tymoczko, Maria, and Edwin Gentzler (eds.). 2002. *Translation and Power.* Amherst: University of Massachusetts Press.
Tyulenev, Sergey. 2012. *Applying Luhmann to Translation Studies.* London: Routledge.
van Dijk, Teun. 2008. *Discourse and Power.* Houndmills: Palgrave Macmillan.
Venuti, Lawrence. 2008. *The Translator's Invisibility.* 2nd edition. London: Routledge.

Wolf, Michaela. 1995. "Translation as a Process of Power: Aspects of Cultural Anthropology in Translation." In *Translation and Intercultural Communication: Selected Papers from the EST Congress-Prague 1995*, Mary Snell-Hornby, Zuzana Jettmarová, and Klaus Kaindl (eds.), 123–33. Amsterdam: John Benjamins.

——2011. "Mapping the Field: Sociological Perspectives on Translation." *International Journal of the Sociology of Language* 207: 1–28.

——2012. "The Sociology of Translation and Its 'Activist Turn.'" Special issue. *Translation and Interpreting Studies* 7(2): 129–43.

——2013. "'German Speakers, Step Forward!': Surviving through Interpreting in Nazi Concentration Camps." *Translation and Interpreting Studies* 8(1): 1–22.

Wolf, Michaela, and Alexandra Fukari. 2007. *Constructing a Sociology of Translation*. Amsterdam: John Benjamins.

Zimányi, Krisztina. 2013. "'Somebody Has to Be in Charge of a Session': On the Control of Communication in Interpreter-Mediated Mental Health Encounters." *Translation and Interpreting Studies* 8(1): 94–111.

10 Profession, identity, and status

Rakefet Sela-Sheffy

Overview

With increasing academic interest in sociological perspectives on translation and interpreting, questions of identity and status have begun attracting attention in Translation Studies. The new sociological perspectives in TS have brought to the fore issues of power and ideology, role and ethics (e.g., Pym 2002; Calzada-Perez 2003; Angelelli 2004; Diriker 2004; Inghilleri 2005; Wolf 2006; Pym et al. 2006; Wolf and Fukari 2007; Bandia and Milton 2009; Diaz Fouces and Monzó 2010), as well as problems of translation fields and markets (e.g., Heilbron 1999; Heilbron and Sapiro 2002; Buzelin 2007, 2014; Amit 2008). They also include the emerging discussion of translators' habitus (Simeoni 1998; Inghilleri 2003; Sapiro 2004b; Gouanvic 2005; Sela-Sheffy 2005; Torikai 2009; Buzelin 2011; Meylaerts 2011; Vorderobermeier 2014), and that of translators' agency and networks (e.g., Bogic 2010; Kinunnen and Koskinen 2010; Buzelin 2011; Abdallah 2014). Notwithstanding earlier attempts (Schwarz 1975; Henderson 1987; Tseng 1992; Hammond 1994; Archibald 1997; Robinson 1997), it is only recently that research has been consistently devoted to the social formations of translators and interpreters as specific professional groups subject to their own social constraints, with their particular access to resources, their status struggles, and sense of professional selves (Choi and Lim 2002; Sapiro 2004a; Sela-Sheffy 2006, 2008, 2010, 2013, 2014; Gouadec 2007; Wadensjö et al. 2007; Dam and Zethsen 2008, 2010, 2011, 2012; Salaets and Van Gucht 2008; Chan 2009; Pan et al. 2009; Monzó 2011; Setton and Lianglang 2011; Grbić 2011; Ferreira-Alves 2011; Katan 2011b; Arocha and Joyce 2013; Volland 2014). In such studies, professional identities and status refer to the experience of the people who work in the different translatorial jobs and the ways they understand their occupation and make sense of it as part of their social world so as to locate themselves and maintain dignity as professionals in specific social spaces.

Theoretical foundations

Identity has become a buzzword in the humanities and the social sciences. Conceived not as a given entity but rather as a dynamic and multilayered cultural construct, collectively produced and reproduced through social struggles in transforming cultural settings, it has everything to do with status and self-esteem (Stryker et al. 2000; Sela-Sheffy 2014). Surprisingly, however, this important aspect of social life has been as yet relatively little discussed with reference to the occupational context. While academic studies and public debates over identity focus primarily on typically political categories of stereotypization and hierarchy, such as ethnicity, race, gender, or religion, the occupational dimension is given scant attention. However, the role of occupations or professions in shaping identities can hardly be overstated – work, after all, is what many people do during large parts of their lives. Not only do occupations constitute major components of people's understanding of their lives, but they often create fields of action in which cultural repertoires are constantly constructed and negotiated (Davis 1994). That is, they serve as important social spaces where group identity, patterns of action, and values are maintained and perpetuated or transformed, thereby building people's perception of themselves and their world (Stryker et al. 2000). Thinking about occupations in this way opens many fascinating directions for the study of human agency in creating, maintaining, and changing immediate and broader social environments, and the ways in which the individuals themselves are created and transformed while moving in these spaces.

The sociological literature on professions offers a body of theoretical and historical research on the formation of modern professions, their institutions, forms of knowledge, career patterns, education and jurisdiction (e.g., Larson 1977; Abbott 1988; Torstendahl and Burrage 1990; Freidson 1994; Macdonald 1995; Evetts 2003). Concentrating on institutional and formal factors, these studies are largely embedded in the context of the more traditionally institutionalized and prestigious liberal professions known as the "success stories" of professionalism, notably medicine, law, and accounting (see, however, Noordegraaf 2007; Muzio 2011). However, from a culture-oriented viewpoint, precisely the "failed professionalizing" occupations (Elsaka 2005) or the underrated ones offer exciting cases in that they reveal more acutely strategies of coping with threatened status (Sela-Sheffy 2010, 2014). Among other occupational groups that are to varying extents underprofessionalized or marginalized, such as journalists, school teachers, craft-artists, or therapists, translators and interpreters serve as a quintessential case for examining how an occupational group deals with its own indeterminacy and marginality.

Unlike mainstream sociology of the professions, which assigns much weight to formal, institutional, and economic factors, studies of the codes of behavior, attitudes, and values shared by members of an occupation so as to maintain it as a functioning social *figuration* (Elias 1993, 1996) are still marginal. The latter aspects stand at the heart of the culture-oriented *practice theory* developed mainly by Bourdieu (1980, 1979/1986) and followers, a theory designed to deal with all kinds of sociocultural formations, and especially those lacking clear institutionalized boundaries. According to this theory, social dynamics are governed less by formal procedures and means of control than by sets of distinguishing mental and bodily dispositions (habituses), which are internalized and exercised by groups of individuals to the extent that they become their second nature (Bourdieu 1986; also Jenkins 1992; Sheffy 1997; Lahire 2003; Sapiro 2004a; Guanvic 2005; Buzelin 2011). While in Elias' view, these are large-scale, long-term processes that produce enduring sociocultural formations (notably, that of "Western Culture"), Bourdieu's conceptualization focuses on the mutually distinguishing peculiarities of coexisting groups that produce and reproduce persistent social tensions and splits (Sela-Sheffy 2005). Typically, Bourdieu's theoretical framework has drawn its examples from fields that defy professionalization or are hardly defined as occupations at all, such as the intellectual field or the arts. To a great extent, such fields (notably the literary field) serve as models for status dynamics in the field of translation (Sela-Sheffy 2006, 2008, 2010).

While the sociological theory of occupational prestige highlights economic achievements as parameters of prestige evaluation (Treiman 1977; Nam and Powers 1983), the practice-oriented approach draws attention to the *cultural resources* that endow an occupation with symbolic values, beyond material and economic constraints. These values, constantly negotiated and redefined, are what is at stake for any given group of actors competing with other groups in every field of action (Bourdieu 1985). Understanding translation as a site of social action in this sense emphasizes the personal dispositions of its practitioners and their group relations. How these individuals position themselves, what kind of capital they pursue, how they struggle to achieve it, and what their cultural resources are, all these questions are at the core of current research into status and the profession in TIS.

All this naturally raises important methodological questions. Often, studies into these aspects draw on quantitative, survey-based studies. The bulk of such recent studies has already produced an impressive body of knowledge on translators and interpreters as a profession in different parts of the world (see below). Serving still as a major tool of sociological research, this quantitative method poses, however, intriguing challenges for cultural analysis. A well-known problem in analyzing surveys is that the respondents' replies cannot be taken at face value, as if they were reporting the unmediated reality of their life and attitudes. The fact is often disguised that, like any other communicative practice, responding to questionnaires is motivated by the need to maintain dignity. As Bourdieu argued in his classic criticism of public opinion polls (1972/1983), people will only provide what they assume to be an expected, respectable reply in the given context, according to their own cultural models. However, since the predesigned questionnaires are inevitably structured and formulated in categories that reflect the researchers' own knowledge and values, they are liable to create alienation vis-à-vis the respondents' world. This means that respondents are very often faced with the request to address questions to which they do not have ready-made answers as part of their own symbolic maps (Lamont and Molnár 2002) or cultural toolkit (Swidler 1986). This point may be particularly tricky in the realm of Translation Studies, where the researchers are often translators themselves and therefore have recourse to inside knowledge of the field they study. However, their sense of affinity with their subject of study may often be misleading in light of the diversity of translatorial sectors, of which only very specific factions, mainly those of literary translators, may share the same intellectual-oriented mindset and cultural baggage of the scholar-translators.

Moreover, as Bourdieu argues further, the problem with questionnaires also lies in the very procedure of using, in the name of scientific accuracy, the same template for studying dissimilar communities that differ in habitus factors such as age, gender, ethnicity, educational background and proficiencies, and many other aspects of people's life. It so happens that respondents often select what seem to them to be the least politically "harmful" pregiven replies, or refrain from replying at all. As a result of all the above, the findings of such surveys may often remain enigmatic, concealing more than revealing, and ratifying – rather than problematizing – academic presuppositions.

Bearing all this in mind, however, surveys are still an important tool for collecting large-scale rich evidence, which can reveal certain patterns of the practitioners' commonly accepted attitudes toward their professions. Nevertheless, a growing awareness of the need to complement this line of study by an in-depth look at the practitioners' own viewpoint is reflected by recent studies that use a variety of qualitative methods, from biographical and text analysis through in-depth interviews to ethnographies in workplaces (see below). All these qualitative-oriented studies attempt to tackle in more detail questions related to translators' own sense of their occupational world and its role in organizing their lives. Obviously, such studies are more attentive to the nuances of how the practitioners actively shape and negotiate their identity and status in the different translatorial communities. Employing microlevel analyses, they are designed to capture the multilayered narratives people construct to give meaning to their work experience and distinguish themselves from other groups, "above" and "below" them (Lamont 2000; Grbić 2011), and the complex, often conflicting, moral contents they allocate to their job to justify their impaired status or to claim higher status. All of which inevitably escape survey-based studies.

Evolution of the topic in TIS

The professional profile(s) and status of translators and interpreters is a constant concern of people working in these fields, as is voiced by its proliferating associations and training programs. This concern "from below" is certainly an important motivation for academic research on these issues, given that many scholars in TIS are closely associated with these fields of practice. However, the major impetus to this scholarly agenda was given by the theoretical landscape that has developed as a natural trajectory of TIS. On the one hand, the bulk of writing on translation *norms* in recent decades has already established the importance of cultural factors and systemic relations in constraining the performance of translators and interpreters (Toury 1978, 1999, 2012; Shlesinger 1989, 1999; Schäffner 1998; Hermans 1999; Lambert 2006; Meylaerts 2008; Sapiro 2008). On the other hand, critical writings have offered assessments of the alleged invisibility and submissiveness of translators (Venuti 1995, 1998). A common denominator of all these discussions has been the (implicit or explicit) assumption that the majority of translators, in many different social settings, suffer from an inferior status (Simeoni 1998). In this context, the problem is usually deduced from translation output (mostly of literary texts), which reveal a tendency to conform to *domestic* cultural norms rather than revolutionize them. This tendency is usually interpreted as resulting from the translators' reluctance to claim active agency in cultural change (exceptions are periods of concentrated efforts of culture planning where translators stand out as important agents of change: Even-Zohar 1990; Paker 2002; Toury 2002). Having emerged historically from the traditions of philology, linguistics, and literary studies, the leading paradigm of TIS that endorses this view of translation as an underrated profession has mainly focused on analysis of literary translations and their communicative contexts. Discussions of this issue thus remained, by and large, confined to the inside agendas and ideologies of the field of translation and its scholarly criticism, removed from the broader sociological context of identity and status struggles, and failing to draw inspiration from relevant theories and comparable cases in other professional settings.

Translation is, however, a most fruitful field for studying precisely the kind of social creativity that propels professional dynamics and the related processes of status and identity construction. It is the contradiction between the potential power of translators and interpreters as cultural mediators (Bandia and Milton 2009), on the one hand, and their obscure professional definition and alleged sense of submissiveness, on the other, that makes them such an intriguing occupational group. Their insecure status as a profession is especially paradoxical today when so much attention is being devoted to cross-cultural processes such as globalization, migration, and trans-nationalism, as well as "cultural translation" in general. While the agency of translators may seem less pivotal in settled cultural contexts with highly established, self-assured cores of hegemonic cultural traditions (such as the Anglo-American ones; e.g., Gentzler 2002), its consequences seem much more evident in multicultural, peripheral, or emerging social settings (e.g., their role in the making of modern Turkey is a paradigmatic example: Ayluçtarhan 2007; Tahir-Gürçağlar 2008; Demircioğlu 2009). Even in the former environments, with their overpowering mechanism of naturalization and anti-foreignization tendencies, knowledge of (certain) foreign languages and borrowing from (certain) foreign cultures are warmly welcomed and are valued as important symbolic resources. In the latter environments, however, which depend more acutely on translation work for their maintainability and prospering, translators' position as a profession would have been expected to be much stronger and more visible.

Nevertheless, all the evidence shows that the professional status of translators and interpreters is, as a rule, ambivalent and insecure. Reports are copious about translators and interpreters being poorly treated, underpaid, and underrated manpower in the industry of text production and business firms, or in community service contexts. They are often described as a "transparent medium," "servants" of a higher authority, and as those who belong "behind the scenes" (Jänis 1996) and are unaware of their own power (Chesterman and Wagner 2002). This does not mean that all translators and interpreters in all the relevant sectors are submissive and lacking occupational pride, nor does it mean that they are always at the bottom of the occupational prestige ladder and payroll. Nonetheless, their self-perception and dignity as an occupation remain vague and constantly questioned, negotiated or fought for.

This identity problem is doubtless an important incentive for expanding the landscape of TIS to encompass broader sociocultural perspectives on the conditions and prospects of translation as a profession. Not only does this problem bear directly on translators and interpreters' job performance, it also makes their self-imaging work and their use of cultural resources a pressing issue on which they depend for recognition. Moreover, such a broader sociocultural view on translation is also conducive to our understanding of the processes of professionalization and anti-professionalization in general, and of the formation of professions, topics which lie at the heart of the sociology of the professions. From the latter perspective, translators and interpreters are thus an extreme example of an under-studied semi-professional occupation. Given that, as mentioned above, the sociology of the professions tends to focus on highly regarded, fully institutionalized occupations at the top of the professional prestige ladder, such status problems, connected with suspended professionalization, appear as marginal. By contrast, these problems emerge as central in the context of research on lower-status occupations, such as teaching in schools, alternative therapy, nursing, childcare, and the like. In light of this, research on the status constraints and effects of status in the realm of translation and interpreting can contribute considerably to filling this lacuna in the sociological study of professions at large.

Key studies

In line with the above, it is only recently that an increasing interest has developed within TIS in the social *agents* of translation and their professional environments. The study of the professional status and identity of translators and interpreters began in earnest only in the second half of the 2000s (see, however, earlier attempts such as Karamitroglou 2000, on the status of subtitlers in Greece; and Choi and Lim 2002, addressing the status of translators and interpreters of Korean). From then on, research into these topics has expanded. Let me mention briefly some important studies.

In the vast Chinese- and Korean-speaking worlds, a lot of work is now accumulating on the professional status, work conditions, and job-related satisfaction and expectations of practicing translators and interpreters. This is occurring against the backdrop of growing demand for their services in an era of massive globalization in these countries (Chan 2009; Pan et al. 2009; Setton and Lianglang 2011; Liu 2013; Volland 2014). All in all, these studies point to a burgeoning professionalization process with a pragmatic attitude prevalent among practitioners, as well as a downplaying of aspirations to the role of cultural mediator. In Europe, similar interest emerged in the status of translators and related questions of professionalism, roles, and identity, with the ongoing project of Dam and Zethsen (2008, 2010, 2011, 2012, and more) on status factors that vary among different classes of business translators and interpreters in Denmark leading the way. In Israel, Sela-Sheffy (2006, 2008, 2010, 2013), and Sela-Sheffy and Shlesinger (2008, 2011) introduced a nationwide project of mapping the identities of translators and interpreters in different sectors as a factor of their suspended professionalization. Among other things, it reveals the role of literary translators' identity in perpetuating an inverse ratio between high status and professionalization level. Katan (2011a), drawing on hundreds of online questionnaires, offered a worldwide survey of translators and interpreters' perception of their work and occupational concerns, with special insight into the lesser impact of theory and academic training on their professional mindsets. Similar to findings of other projects, it reveals intricate identity work on the part of translators, who, despite awareness of their lower status, are reluctant to change their occupational status quo.

At the same time, Angelelli (2004) in North America, Rudvin (2007) in Italy, Wadensjö et al. in Sweden (2007), among many others, initiated investigation into the complexity of roles and identities of interpreters, and their relations with the community, in view of their acute deprofessionalization and low status. The status problems and enigmatic roles of community and court interpreters are also explored at length by other scholars around the world. Monzó's analysis on professional struggles between legal interpreters in Spain (2011) is one example, and Grbić's on boundary making by sign-language interpreters in Austria (2011) is another, to mention two studies that are profoundly informed by the theory of professionalization and symbolic capital. Whereas the latter projects are qualitatively oriented, Pöchhacker (2011) provides an overview of the ample survey research on conference interpreters as a source of knowledge about their perception of their professional role and occupational concerns.

Meanwhile, discussion of the translator's habitus gained impetus with Inghilleri's edited volume on Bourdieu's perspective (2005), as a continuation of earlier attempts, and with that of Vorderobermeier (2014) among the recent contributions. This discussion triggers and has been triggered by specific empirical case studies which proceed from two complementary perspectives. Some of these studies use the habitus concept in analyzing large samples to identify shared group dispositions and self-images characterizing and distinguishing between different translator factions (e.g., Inghilleri 2003; Sapiro

2004a; Wolf 2007; Sela-Sheffy 2008, 2010; Amit-Kochavi 2011, to mention just a few). Others, by contrast, used this concept to reveal social patterns through micro-scale analyses of individual trajectories and life-stories (e.g., Torikai 2009; Meylaerts 2011; Buzelin 2014; Vorderobermeier 2014). From yet another perspective, in other emerging centers of TIS research, notably Finland, Kinunnen and Koskinen (2010) have promoted ethnographic studies of the workplace, with the aim of identifying the networks and active agency of translators and interpreters in shaping their social environment and maintaining their professional status (e.g., Koskinen 2009; Abdallah 2012).

This rich and diverse body of work, which accelerated throughout the course of the decade, culminated in the publication of an edited volume on the topic *Identity and Status in the Translatorial Professions* (Sela-Sheffy and Shlesinger 2011), containing some of the above-mentioned studies.[1] Cutting across occupational and geographical arenas, the articles in this volume report mainly empirical studies, wavering between survey-based (including online questionnaires) quantitative analyses and miscellaneous qualitative methodologies, including narrative and biographical analysis and in-depth interviews. Another milestone in the study of the status and agency of translators, mainly in the realm of the production of literary and other texts, was the collected volume *Agents of Translation* (Bandia and Milton 2009). Works in this collection expand their study beyond the translator to include, in historical perspective, the professional networks in which translators work and the various agents responsible for the selection, publication, and reception of translated texts. From a more professionalization-oriented perspective, a state-of-the-art collection of contributions on the topic of *The Translation Profession: Centers and Peripheries*, edited by Helle Dam and Kaisa Koskinen, is currently forthcoming as a special issue of *JoSTrans*.

New directions

This attempt to look at translators from a broader, external angle, as a field of cultural production, should contribute to furthering a systematic integration of sociocultural insights and working tools in the currently accepted frameworks of studying translation within complex cultural contexts. By analogy to other interdisciplinary research frameworks, such as, notably, sociolinguistics, cultural sociology, or sociological history, such integration is expected to be productive for our understanding of the *work of translating* itself. That is, concentrating attention on the practitioners as active social agents should also give rise to valuable insights into the ways these individuals *act and perform as translators* (Toury 2012).

Future research will advance access to and better use of existing culture-oriented theoretical frameworks. An integrated view on the works cited above and many others in TIS reveal two major focal points in these theoretical frameworks, namely: (1) the *agents' dispositions to action* and *value scales*, which define and distinguish between the different groups of translators and interpreters; and (2) the *repertoire* on which these agents draw in their professional and extraprofessional activities—that is, the multilayered and diversified stocks of working patterns and everyday conduct available in specific fields, constraining the action of those who play in these fields.

Finally, a culture-oriented approach should also contribute to the critical discourse on translators' ethics and ideology and the activist demand for a reformulation of the translator's and interpreter's social role and for greater social engagement on the part of translators and interpreters. Such research is intended to provide a better idea about the *people who do* the translation and interpreting jobs, their background and cultural orientations, their hopes and feelings, as well as their social spaces and specific constraints, in order to effectively address questions of the translator's and interpreter's agency and empowerment.

Note

1 A previous version of this volume appeared as a double special issue of the journal *Translation and Interpreting Studies*, guest edited by Sela-Sheffy and Shlesinger, under the title "Profession, Identity and Status: Translators and Interpreters as an Occupational Group" (2009, 2010). The individual issues were dedicated to the topics of status and the profession, and to the topic of role and identity, respectively.

References

Abbott, Andrew. 1988. *The System of Professions. An Essay on the Division of Expert Labor*. Chicago and London: University of Chicago Press.

Abdallah, Kristiina. 2012. "Translators in Production Networks: Reflections on Agency, Quality and Ethics." Ph.D. Dissertation, University of Eastern Finland.

——2014. "The Interface between Bourdieu's Habitus and Latour's Agency: The Work Trajectories of Two Finnish Translators." In *Remapping Habitus in Translation Studies*, Gisella Vorderobermeier (ed.), 111–34. Amsterdam and New York: Rodopi.

Amit, Yuval. 2008. "The Export of Israeli Culture – Formal Institutions' Activities in Translating Literature from the Hebrew." Unpublished Ph.D. dissertation, Tel Aviv University [Hebrew].

Amit-Kochavi, Hannah. 2011. "The People Behind the Words – Professional Profiles and Activity Patterns of Translators of Arabic Literature into Hebrew (1896–2009)." *Translation and Interpreting Studies* 5(1): 41–58.

Angelelli, Claudia V. 2004. *Revisiting the Interpreter's Role: A Study of Conference, Court, and Medical Interpreters in Canada, Mexico, and the United States*. Amsterdam and Philadelphia: John Benjamins.

Archibald, James. 1997. "The Pragmatics of Professionalism: Translation and Interpretation in Puerto Rico and Quebec." *Meta* 42(4): 649–60.

Arocha, Izabel S., and Linda Joyce. 2013. "Patient Safety, Professionalization, and Reimbursement as Primary Drivers for National Medical Interpreter Certification in the United States." *Translation & Interpreting* 5(1): 127–42.

Ayluçtarhan, Sevda. 2007. "Dr. Abdullah Cevdet's Translations (1908–1910): The Making of a Westernist and Materialist 'Culture Repertoire' in a 'Resistant' Ottoman Context." M.A. thesis, Boğaziçi University.

Bandia, Paul, and John Milton (eds.). 2009. *Agents of Translation*. Amsterdam and Philadelphia: John Benjamins.

Bogic, Anna. 2010. "Understanding the Hidden Actors with the Help of Latour: The 'Making' of the Second Sex." In "Applied Sociology in Translation Studies," Esther Monzó and Oscar Díaz Fouces (eds.). Special issue. *MonTI* 2: 173–92.

Bourdieu, Pierre. 1980. "Quelques propriétés des champs." In *Questions de Sociologie*, 113–20. Paris: Edition de Minuit.

——1972/1983. "Public Opinion Does Not Exist." *Communication and Class Struggle*, vol.1, Armand Mattelart and Seth Siegelaub (eds.), 124–30. New York: International General.

——1971/1985. "The Market of Symbolic Goods." *Poetics* 14: 13–44.

——1979/1986. *Distinction: A Social Critique of the Judgment of Taste*. London and New York: Routledge and Kegan Paul.

Buzelin, Hélène. 2007. "Translations in the Making." In *Constructing a Sociology of Translation*, Michaela Wolf and Alexandra Fukari (eds.), 135–69. Amsterdam and Philadelphia: John Benjamins.

——2011. "Agents of Translation." In *Handbook of Translation Studies*, Yves Gambier and Luc Van Doorslaer (eds.), 6–12. Amsterdam and Philadelphia: John Benjamins.

——2014. "How Devoted Can Translators Be?" *Target* 26(1): 63–97.

Calzada-Perez, Maria (ed.). 2003. *Apropos of Ideology*. Manchester: St. Jerome.

Chan, Andy Lung Jan. 2009. "Perceived Benefits of Translator Certification to Stakeholders in the Translation Profession: A Survey of Vendor Managers." *Across Languages and Cultures* 11(1): 93–113.

Chesterman, Andrew, and Emma Wagner. 2002. *Can Theory Help Translators? A Dialogue between the Ivory Tower and the Wordface*. Manchester: St. Jerome.

Choi, Jungwha, and Hyang-Ok Lim. 2002. "The Status of Translators and Interpreters in Korea." *Meta* 47(4): 627–35.

Dam, Helle V., and Karen Korning Zethsen. 2008. "Translator Status: A Study of Danish Company Translators." *The Translator* 14(1): 71–96.

——2010. "Translator Status: Helpers and Opponents in the Ongoing Battle of an Emerging Profession." *Target* 22(2): 194–211.

——2011. "The Status of Professional Business Translators on the Danish Market: A Comparative Study of Company, Agency and Freelance Translators." *Meta* 56(4): 976–97.

——2012. "Translators in International Organizations: A Special Breed of High-status Professionals? Danish EU Translators as a Case in Point." *Translation and Interpreting Studies* 7(2): 212–33.

Davis, John. 1994. "Social Creativity." In *When Culture Accelerates: Essays on Rapid Social Change, Complexity and Creativity*, C. N. Hann (ed.), 95–110. London and Atlantic Highlands, NJ: The Athlone Press.

Demircioğlu, Cemal. 2009. "Translating Europe: The Case of Ahmed Midhat as an Ottoman Agent of Translation." In *Agents of Translation*, John Milton and Paul Bandia (eds.), 131–59. Amsterdam and Philadelphia: John Benjamins.

Diaz Fouces, Oscar, and Esther Monzó (eds.). 2010. "Applied Sociology in Translation Studies – Sociologia aplicada a la traducció." Special issue. *MonTI* 2.

Diriker, Ebru. 2004. *De-/Re-Contextualizing Conference Interpreting*. Amsterdam and Philadelphia: John Benjamins.

Elias, Norbert. 1993. *Mozart: Portrait of a Genius.* Polity Press.

——1996. *The Germans: Power Struggles and the Development of Habitus in the Nineteenth and Twentieth Centuries.* New York: Columbia University Press.

Elsaka, Nadia. 2005. "New Zealand Journalists and the Appeal of 'Professionalism' as a Model of Organization: An Historical Analysis." *Journalism Studies* 6(1): 73–86.

Even-Zohar, Itamar. 1990. "The Position of Translated Literature within the Literary Polysystem." "Polysystem Studies." Special issue. *Poetics Today* 11(1): 45–52.

Evetts, Julia. 2003. "The Sociological Analysis of Professionalism: Occupational Change in the Modern World." *International Sociology* 18(2): 395–415.

Ferreira-Alves, Fernando. 2011. "Job Perceptions, Identity-Building and Interpersonal Relations among Translators as a Professional Group in Northern Portugal." *ILCEA* 14. Available online at http://ilcea.revues.org/index1119.html (accessed April 20, 2015).

Freidson, Eliot. 1994. *Professionalism Reborn.* Chicago: University of Chicago Press.

Gentzler, Edwin. 2002. "What's Different about Translation in the Americas?" *CTIS Occasional Papers* 2: 7–19.

Gouadec, Daniel. 2007. *Translation as a Profession.* Amsterdam and Philadelphia: John Benjamins.

Gouanvic, Jean-Marc. 2005. "A Bourdieusian Theory of Translation, or the Coincidence of Practical Instances: Field, 'Habitus', Capital and 'Illusion.'" *The Translator* 11(2): 147–66.

Grbić, Nadja. 2011. "'Boundary Work' as a Concept for Studying Professionalization Processes." In *Identity and Status in the Translatorial Professions*, Rakefet Sela-Sheffy and Miriam Shlesinger (eds.), 247–62. Amsterdam and Philadelphia: John Benjamins.

Hammond, Deanna L. (ed.). 1994. *Professional Issues for Translators and Interpreters.* Amsterdam and Philadelphia: John Benjamins.

Heilbron, Johan. 1999. "Towards a Sociology of Translation: Book Translation as a Cultural World-System." *European Journal of Social Theory* 2(4): 429–45.

Heilbron, Johan, and Gisèle Sapiro (eds.). 2002. "Traduction: les échanges littéraires internationaux. " Special issue. *Actes de la recherche en sciences sociales* 144(3).

Henderson, J. A. 1987. *Personality and the Linguist: Comparison of the Personality Profiles of Professional Translators and Conference Interpreters.* Bradford: University of Bradford Press.

Hermans, Theo. 1999. *Translation in Systems, Descriptive and System-Oriented Approaches Explained.* Manchester: St. Jerome.

Inghilleri, Moira. 2003. "Habitus, Field and Discourse. Interpreting as a Socially Situated Activity." *Target* 15(2): 243–68.

——(ed.). 2005. "Bourdieu and the Sociology of Translation and Interpreting." Special issue. *The Translator* 11(2).

Jänis, Marja. 1996. "What Translators of Plays Think about Their Work." *Target* 8(2): 341–64.

Jenkins, Richard. 1992. "Practice, Habitus and Field." In *Pierre Bourdieu*, Richard Jenkins (ed.), 66–102. London: Routledge.

Karamitroglou, Fotios. 2000. "The Subtitler and the Cook, or Don't Shoot the Subtitler: The Status of Subtitling Profession in Greece." Available at www.geocities.ws/karamitroglou/cookeng.html (accessed October 13, 2014).

Katan, David. 2011a. "Occupation or Profession. A Survey of the Translators' World." In *Identity and Status in the Translatorial Professions*, Rakefet Sela-Sheffy and Miriam Shlesinger (eds.), 65–88. Amsterdam and Philadelphia: John Benjamins.

——2011b. "Status of Translators." In *Handbook of Translation Studies*, Yves Gambier and Luc van Doorslaer (eds.), 146–52. Amsterdam and Philadelphia: John Benjamins.

Kinunnen, Tuija, and Kaisa Koskinen (eds.). 2010. *Translators' Agency.* Tempere: Tempere University Press.

Koskinen, Kaisa. 2009. "Going Localized, Getting Recognized. The Interplay of the Institutional and the Experienced Status of Translators in the European Commission." *Hermes* 42: 93–110.

Lahire, Bernard. 2003. "From the Habitus to an Individual Heritage of Dispositions/ Towards a Sociology at the Level of the Individual." *Poetics* 31: 329–55.

Lambert, Jose. 2006 (1995). "Translation, Systems and Research: The Contribution of Polysystem Studies to Translation Studies." In *Functional Approaches to Culture and Translation: Selected Papers by José Lambert*, Dirk Delabastita, Lieven D'hulst, and Reine Meylaerts (eds.), 105–30. Amsterdam and Philadelphia: John Benjamins.

Lamont, Michèle. 2000. *The Dignity of Working Men: Morality and the Boundaries of Race, Class, and Immigration.* Cambridge, MA: Harvard University Press; and New York: Russell Sage Foundation.

Lamont, Michèle, and Virág Molnár. 2002. "The Study of Boundaries in the Social Sciences." *Annual Review of Sociology* 28: 167–95.

Larson, Magli Sarfatti. 1977. *The Rise of Professionalism. A Sociological Analysis.* Berkeley, Los Angeles, and London: University of California Press.

Liu, Fung-ming Christy. 2013. "A Quantitative Enquiry into the Translator's Job-related Happiness: Does Visibility Correlate with Happiness?" *Across Languages and Cultures* 14(1): 123–47.

Macdonald, Keith M. 1995. *The Sociology of the Professions.* London: SAGE Publications.

Meylaerts, Reine. 2008. "Translators and (Their) Norms: Towards a Sociological Construction of the Individual." In *Beyond Descriptive Translation Studies: Investigations in Homage to Gideon Toury*, Anthony Pym, Miriam Shlesinger, and Daniel Simeoni (eds.), 91–102. Amsterdam and Philadelphia: John Benjamins.

——2011. "Habitus and Self-Image of Native Literary Author-Translators in Diglossic Societies." In *Identity and Status in the Translatorial Professions*, Rakefet Sela-Sheffy and Miriam Shlesinger (eds.), 135–54. Amsterdam and Philadelphia: John Benjamins.

Monzó, Esther. 2011. "Legal and Translational Occupations in Spain: Regulation and Specialization in Jurisdictional Struggles." In *Identity and Status in the Translatorial Professions*, Rakefet Sela-Sheffy and Miriam Shlesinger (eds.), 11–30. Amsterdam and Philadelphia: John Benjamins.

Muzio, Daniel. 2011. "Introduction: Professions and Organizations – A Conceptual Framework." *Current Sociology* 1(59): 389–405.

Nam, Charles B., and Mary G. Powers. 1983. *The Socioeconomic Approach to Status Measurement. With a Guide to Occupational and Socioeconomic Scores.* Houston: Cap and Gown Press.

Noordegraaf, Mirko. 2007. "From 'Pure' to 'Hybrid' Professionalism: Present-Day Professionalism in Ambiguous Public Domains." *Administration & Society* 39(6): 761–85.

Paker, Saliha (ed.). 2002. *Translations: (Re)shaping of Literature and Culture.* Bogaziçi Istanbul: Bogaziçi University Press.

Pan, Jun, Sun Zhi-Xiang, Wang Hong-Hua. 2009. "Professionalization in Interpreting: Current Development of Interpreting in Shanghai and Jiangsu Province." *Journal of PLA University of Foreign Languages* 6: 81–85, 101.

Pöchhacker, Franz. 2011. "Conference Interpreting: Surveying the Profession." In *Identity and Status in the Translatorial Professions*, Rakefet Sela-Sheffy and Miriam Shlesinger (eds.), 49–64. Amsterdam and Philadelphia: John Benjamins.
Pym, Anthony. 2002. "Introduction: The Return to Ethics in Translation Studies." *The Translator* 7(2): 129–38.
Pym, Anthony, Miriam Shlesinger, and Zuzana Jettmarova (eds.). 2006. *Sociocultural Aspects of Translating and Interpreting*. Amsterdam and Philadelphia: John Benjamins.
Robinson, Douglas. 1997. *Becoming a Translator: An Accelerated Course*. London and New York: Routledge.
Rudvin, Mette. 2007. "Professionalism and Ethics in Community Interpreting." *Interpreting* 9(1): 47–69.
Salaets, Heidi, and Jan Van Gucht. 2008. "Perceptions of a Profession." In *Crossing Borders in Community Interpreting: Definitions and Dilemmas*, Carmen Valero-Garcés and Anne Martin (eds.), 267–87. Amsterdam and Philadelphia: John Benjamins.
Sapiro, Gisèle. 2004a. "Une liberté contrainte. La formation de la théorie de l'habitus" [followed by an interview with Pierre Bourdieu]. In *Pierre Bourdieu, sociologue*, P. Champagne, L. Pinto, and G. Sapiro (eds.), 49–91. Paris: Fayard.
——2004b. "Translation and Identity: Social Trajectories of the Translators of Hebrew Literature in French." Paper presented at the conference "Institutions, Habituses and Individuals: Social, Historical and Political Aspects of Cultural Exchange," Tel Aviv, May 2–5, 2004.
——2008. "Normes de traduction et contraintes sociales." In *Beyond Descriptive Translation Studies: Investigations in Homage to Gideon Toury*, Anthony Pym, Miriam Shlesinger, and Daniel Simeoni (eds.), 199–208. Amsterdam and Philadelphia: John Benjamins.
Schäffner, Christina. 1998. "The Concept of Norms in Translation Studies." *Current Issues in Language & Society*. 5(1/2): 2–9.
Schwarz, Hans. 1975. "Der Status des Übersetzers" [Translator status]. *Babel* 21(1): 5–15.
Sela-Sheffy, Rakefet. 2005. "How to Be a (Recognized) Translator: Rethinking Habitus, Norms, and the Field of Translation." *Target* 17(1): 1–26.
——2006. "Strategies of Image-Making and Status Advancement of Translators and Interpreters as a Marginal Occupational Group." In *Beyond Descriptive Translation Studies: Investigations in Homage to Gideon Toury*, Anthony Pym, Miriam Shlesinger, and Daniel Simeoni (eds.), 79–90. Amsterdam and Philadelphia: John Benjamins.
——2008. "The Translators' Personae: Marketing Translatorial Images as Pursuit of Capital." *Meta* 53(3): 609–22.
——2010. "'Stars' or 'Professionals': The Imagined Vocation and Exclusive Knowledge of Translators in Israel." In "Applied Sociology in Translation Studies," Esther Monzó and Oscar Díaz Fouces (eds.). Special issue. *MonTI* 2: 131–52.
——2013. "Elite and Non-elite Translatorial Manpower: The Non-professionalized Culture in the Translation Field in Israel." Paper presented at the 7th EST Congress, Germersheim (Germany), August 29–September 1, 2013.
——2014. "Translators' Identity Work: Introducing Micro-sociological Theory of Identity to the Discussion of Translators' Habitus." In *Remapping Habitus in Translation Studies*, Gisella Vorderobermeier (ed.), 43–55. Amsterdam and New York: Rodopi.
Sela-Sheffy, Rakefet, and Miriam Shlesinger. 2008. "Strategies of Image-Making and Status Advancement of Translators and Interpreters as a Marginal Occupational Group." In *Beyond Descriptive Translation Studies: Investigations in Homage to*

Gideon Toury, Anthony Pym, Miriam Shlesinger, and Daniel Simeoni (eds.), 79–90. Amsterdam and Philadelphia: John Benjamins.

——(eds.). 2009, 2010. "Profession, Identity and Status: Translators and Interpreters as an Occupational Group." Double special issue. *Translation and Interpreting Studies* 4(2), 5(1).

——(eds.). 2011. *Identity and Status in the Translatorial Professions*. Amsterdam and Philadelphia: John Benjamins.

Setton, Robin, and Alice G. Lianglang. 2011. "Attitudes to Role, Status and Professional Identity in Interpreters and Translators with Chinese in Shanghai and Taipei." In *Identity and Status in the Translatorial Professions*, Rakefet Sela-Sheffy and Miriam Shlesinger (eds.), 89–118. Amsterdam and Philadelphia: John Benjamins.

Sheffy, Rakefet. 1997. "Models and Habituses as Hypotheses in Culture Analysis." *Canadian Review of Comparative Literature / Revue Canadienne de Littérature Comparée* 24(1): 35–47.

Shlesinger, Miriam. 1989. "Extending the Theory of Translation to Interpretation: Norms as a Case in Point." *Target* 1(1): 111–15.

——1999. "Norms, Strategies and Constraints: How Do We Tell Them Apart?" In *Anovar/ Anosar: Estudios de Traduccion E Interpretacion*, A. A. Lugri and A. F. Ocampo, (eds.), 65–77. Vigo: Universidade de Vigo.

Simeoni, Daniel. 1998. "The Pivotal Status of the Translator's Habitus." *Target* 10(1): 1–39.

Stryker, Sheldon, Timothy J. Owens, and Robert W. White (eds.). 2000. *Self, Identity and Social Movements*. Minneapolis and London: University of Minnesota Press.

Swidler, Ann. 1986. "Culture in Action." *American Sociological Review* 51: 273–86.

Tahir-Gürçağlar, Şehnaz. 2008. *The Politics and Poetics of Translation in Turkey, 1923–60*. Amsterdam: Rodopi.

Torikai, Kumiko. 2009. *Voices of the Invisible Presence: Diplomatic Interpreters in Post-World War II Japan*. Amsterdam and Philadelphia: John Benjamins.

Torstendahl, Rolf, and Michael Burrage. 1990. *The Formation of Professions*. London: Sage Publications.

Toury, Gideon. 1978. "The Nature and Role of Norms in Literary Translation." In *Literature and Translation: New Perspectives in Literary Studies*, James S. Holmes, José Lambert, and Raymond van den Broeck (eds.), 83–100. Leuven: Acco.

——1999. "A Handful of Paragraphs on 'Translation' and 'Norms.'" In *Translation and Norms*, Christina Schäffner (ed.), 10–32. Clevedon: Multilingual Matters.

——2002. "Translation as a Means of Planning and the Planning of Translation: A Theoretical Framework and an Exemplary Case." In *Translations: (Re)shaping of Literature and Culture*, Saliha Paker (ed.), 148–65. Bogaziçi Istanbul: Bogaziçi University Press.

——2012. "A Bilingual Speaker Becomes a Translator. A Sketch of a Developmental Model." In *Descriptive Translation Studies and Beyond*, Gideon Toury (ed.), 277–94. Amsterdam and Philadelphia: John Benjamins.

Treiman, Donald J. 1977. *Occupational Prestige in Comparative Perspective*. New York: Academic Press.

Tseng, Joseph. 1992. "Interpreting as an Emerging Profession in Taiwan. A Sociological Model." Unpublished M.A. thesis, Fu Jen Catholic University, Taiwan.

Venuti, Lawrence. 1995. *The Translator's Invisibility: A History of Translation*. London and New York: Routledge.

——1998. *The Scandals of Translation: Towards an Ethics of Difference.* London and New York: Routledge.

Volland, Nicolai. 2014. "The Birth of a Profession: Translators and Translation in Modern China." In *Modern China and the West: Translation and Cultural Mediation*, Hsiao-yen Peng and Isabelle Rabut (eds.), 126-150. Leiden: Brill.

Vorderobermeier, Gisella M. 2014. "The (Re)construction of the Habitus: Literary Translators' Trajectories Put into Methodological Perspective." In *Remapping Habitus in Translation Studies*, Gisella Vorderobermeier (ed.), 149–62. Amsterdam and New York: Rodopi.

Wadensjö, Cecilia, Birgitta Englund Dimitrova, and Anna-Lena Nilsson (eds.). 2007. *The Critical Link 4: Professionalisation of Interpreting in the Community.* Selected papers from the 4th International Conference on Interpreting in Legal, Health and Social Service Settings, Stockholm, Sweden, May 20–23, 2004. Amsterdam and Philadelphia: John Benjamins.

Wolf, Michaela. 2006. "Translating and Interpreting as a Social Practice – Introspection into a New Field." In *Übersetzen – Translating – Traduire: Towards a "Social Turn,"* Michaela Wolf (ed.), 9–19. Münster, Hamburg, Berlin, Vienne and London: LIT Verlag.

——2007. "Bourdieu's 'Rules of The Game': An Introspection into Methodological Questions of Translation Sociology." *Matraga* 14(20): 130–45.

Wolf, Michaela, and Alexandra Fukari (eds.). 2007. *Constructing a Sociology of Translation.* Amsterdam and Philadelphia: John Benjamins.

11 Reader response and reception theory

Leo Tak-hung Chan

Overview

Since the discipline of Translation Studies was semi-officially inaugurated three decades ago with the publication of James Holmes' well-known essay, "The Name and Nature of Translation Studies", there have been surprisingly few studies conducted on the reading of translations, other than those of an evaluative nature done in the name of translation criticism. But just as the audience has recently come to occupy a pivotal position in communication studies, so too the real or historical reader is garnering increasing attention in Translation Studies. This reader should not be confused with the "addressee" (at whom the translation is targeted) or the translator-as-reader (who first reads the text before doing a translation). Indeed, much has been written about how translators can better serve the target addressees, i.e., readers, in the translator-oriented research that has long been dominant in the field. Text-oriented research, which constructs an image of the reader from the text, has also received a good deal of attention. The recent profusion of research on reader response and audience response in literary and cultural studies, however, has produced new methodologies and terminologies, which, when transferred to translation research, open up new possibilities for the study of the real, rather than the imagined, reader.

In discussing text-reader interaction, "response," "interpretation," and "reception" are terms that are frequently used, sometimes interchangeably. In research on the reading of translations, two distinctions need to be made. First, response is not to be equated with interpretation. Interpretations of original texts may be applicable to their translations, but readers are also free to reinterpret whatever is translated as if it were written originally in their language. Second, reception may overlap, but is not synonymous, with response. The former is a word with more general connotations, as seen in its recent application in communication and audience studies. A situation where reception enters the discussion is when one writes about the history of readers' reactions toward a given text. Producing an interpretation of a novel, therefore, represents a particular response to that text, and accumulated responses allow us to write a history of reception over time.

Theoretical foundations

Albeit in a rather limited way, several strands of research on reader response and reception have shaped research on translation, each exerting its impact in a different manner. First among these is the Western theoretical tradition of thinking about readers' relationships to the text. A comprehensive account by Andringa (2006) traces the line of descent from the Russian Formalists through Czech Structuralists, such as Mukařovsky and Vodicka, to German *Rezeptionsästhetik*, thence to Bourdieu, and, finally, to polysystems scholars, such as Even-Zohar. Briefly stated, our age has witnessed, consequent upon the "death of the author" (à la Barthes), the inevitable "rise of the reader." But the ascendancy of the reader was also effected through a shift of interpretive focus away from the text. Textualists, as represented for instance by the American New Critics, had an interest in the way in which readers' understanding is structured by texts, but it is only with the German theorists (and, later, those of the Chicago School) that the "uni-actional" emphasis on the text as containing a core of fixed meanings to be detected, decoded, or deciphered is finally superseded by a belief in the readers' participatory role (Iser 1974; Jauss 1982). How this "inter-actional" or "trans-actional" emphasis can be made relevant to translation is an issue for translation research to address.

Another important shift in the history of reader response theory was the rise of the "communal reader," which occurred in the 1980s when Fish (1980) introduced the concept of "interpretive communities." Fish's position represents a "sociological turn" in the field and is linked conceptually to the later proliferation of studies on book clubs and reading sub-cultures (Radway 1984). As unique communities bound together by such identity factors as race, nation, and language, readers share certain preoccupations that significantly affect not only their reading choices but also the meaning they derive from these texts. With regard to translations, readers from a monolingual community actually engage in a unique kind of cross-cultural reading.

Since one inherent difficulty in studying reader response is how to ascertain what readers actually "feel" (Keen 2007), not only as individuals but as members of a community, an empirical approach has obvious advantages (Tötösy de Zepetnek and Sywenky 1997). In seeking to validate certain hypotheses about responses, such an approach contributes to reception studies by making available a wide range of scientific tools and methods, including think-aloud protocols, content analysis, discourse analysis, and so on. Even in the simplest of cases, survey-based research, as well as ethnographic studies (see Part III of this volume), will yield usable results, which may disprove, support, or substantiate impressionistic observations. In relation to translations, in addition to surveying readers' comments and web reviews, researchers can also investigate sales figures, print runs, production and distribution, literacy rates, etc., which serve as a barometer of how a work has been received.

Studies of reader response have also derived energy from cultural studies. Viewing earlier theorists like Iser and Jauss as "traditional," scholars in the field of cultural studies adopt a more radical, even oppositional, stance while broadening the scope of investigation to include a variety of media forms, in effect aligning themselves with mass communications studies. In addition to analyzing literary texts, cultural studies approaches include film, television, newspapers, magazines, and a variety of other cultural products; at the same time, the response of the "audience" often attracts attention, eclipsing that of the "reader." The subtle theoretical permutations in this sub-field are exemplified by work done by John Fiske, Janet Staiger, and John Frow, among others (see Machor and Goldstein 2001), while the increasing prominence of the approach is epitomized by the launching of two journals in the last decade: *Participations*, a "journal of audience and reception studies," and *Reception: Texts, Readers, Audiences, History*. The explosion of research in audience reception studies has led to new paradigms, such as "reading formations" and "uses-and-gratifications studies," but perhaps most important of all is a revised perception of the reader as more than a passive receptor, as the Frankfurt School would have it. These post-structuralist reconfigurations of the reader will inevitably impact translation research on reading practices.

A final source of inspiration has come from book history studies. Usually dated to the appearance of Robert Darnton's essay in 1982 (in Finkelstein and McCleery 2002), this approach has brought with it an added perspective. For book historians, readers are worth studying not only in terms of their meaning-making activity; they are also of interest as living human beings, as a driving force behind what gets published. In such studies, readers are "actual," not idealized or implied, and get involved with texts at specific moments in history. As the publishing studies scholar Squires (2007) has demonstrated with reference to contemporary British popular fiction, in their reading of books readers are implicated in a distinct "field" (in Bourdieu's sense) of human activity—a "network of communication circuits in which writers, publishers, printers, distributors, reviewers and readers collaborate" (according to Darnton). The history of the book, and of publishing, is also a history of reading, in which social and economic factors (especially the latter) play a crucial role. In this light, the reception of a literary or non-literary work cannot be explained simply as a text-and-reader affair.

Evolution of the topic in TIS

Translation theorists have always had a place for the reader (or some such person) in their ruminations, although the reader constructed in many theories is in fact the translator, whose interpretation, or reading, of the source text definitively shapes the translation. Among the early discussions, the most prominent is Nida's concept of "dynamic equivalence." In opposing the philologists who believe that meaning is inherent in the text, Nida argues that equivalence obtains where the target text (TT) receptor responds to the translation in exactly the same way that the source text (ST) receptor does to the source text. Significantly, his concern is with the achievement of better translation results through closer attention to the receptor or reader. There was also some concern with reading in the early theorizations, although it was largely confined to the sub-field of translation criticism, in particular, in work done by Reiss (2000) and Wilss (1982). Yet critical evaluation of translated works remains only one mode of reading, deployed by bilingual experts, and has little to do with the experience of the overwhelming majority of monolingual readers.

It may be thought that, with its valorization of target reception, the descriptive approach would be conducive to reader-oriented studies, methodologically, as well as theoretically. As Hermans notes in *Translation in Systems*, questions surrounding reception have occupied a prominent place in work of the descriptive school (1999: 44). A great many reception studies have been carried out in the descriptivist mode, but the target text—not the target reader—is often at the core. Hermans (1996), however, delineates the different roles of the biographical reader, the implied reader, and the narratee, although his subject is the translator's presence, which he analyzes by way of a translated Dutch novel, *Max Havelaar*. In the same issue of *Target* in which Hermans' article appears, Schiavi (1996) further elaborates on the complexity of the reader's role. Beginning with textual exegesis, Schiavi problematizes the nature of the reader, advancing the notions of an implied author, an implied translator (who is at the same time an implied reader), and an implied reader of the translation.

Building on Hermans and Schiavi, Assis Rosa (2006) reconceptualizes three sets of relationships between (a) the actual translator and the actual TT reader, (b) the implied translator and the implied TT reader, and (c) the implied author and the implied ST reader. For her, the target text reader has two dimensions—the actual/real versus the ideal/implied. She counters the habitual orientation toward the translator in translation research, in which the general readership is important only inasmuch as it impinges on the translator's choice of translation strategies and foregrounds the text's actual, historically situated readership. For her, too much attention has been given to textually encoded readers, even though the implied reader is not completely irrelevant in her opinion. In noting that the "realness" of the target reader is not to be neglected if a correct estimation of translation norms is to be arrived at, she is still very much a descriptivist.

Despite these theoretical forays, the conventional translator-oriented approach has found a new proponent in Littau (1997), who gives it a new twist. Beginning with the observation that the twin activities of translation and reading are now more closely intertwined than ever before, with electronic media threatening to displace print media, Littau argues that there are now two kinds of translators/readers, as well as two modes of translating/reading: "*To read is therefore also to translate*," which, according to Littau, not only allows the translator to "flaunt the signs of her manipulation of the text," but also allows the interactive reader-cum-translator at her PC to become someone actively participating in the production of meaning (1997: 92). The authorized translator thus co-exists with the new breed of reader-cum-translators.

Key studies

Apart from the theoretical studies discussed in the previous section, much research in recent years has deepened our understanding of the actual readers of translated texts, their reading practices, and the history of their changing tastes. Here one should begin by considering a terminological issue. An array of terms has been deployed in the field to refer to the reader, who has been characterized positively, negatively, and neutrally, described alternately as "sophisticated," "naïve," "average," "mass," "ordinary," "common," and even "uncommon." The easy semantic slippage between terms like ordinary, common, and average gives rise to confusion, as do theoretical terms, such as Booth's ideal reader, Iser's implied reader, Fish's informed reader, Eco's model reader, Riffaterre's superreader, Culler's qualified reader, and so on. Chan (2010) explores the many vistas opened up by these terms in translation research, and settles for the theoretical construct of a "target reader," which allows for further sub-division into the monolingual, uninformed "general reader" and the bilingual, critical "special reader," thus highlighting one key difference between research on translations and research on non-translations.

While Hermans, Schiavi, and Assis Rosa have focused largely on the practice of reading as it pertains to a hypothetical reader, Eoyang (1993) and O'Neill (2005) propose tripartite reading models meant to explain the various scenarios of text-reader interaction, using examples from literary translations in China and Europe, respectively. Eoyang distinguishes three kinds of translated texts—surrogate, contingent, and coeval—and the corresponding modes of reading them, while O'Neill posits three modes of translation reading in reference to the European translations of Joyce: the prototextual, the metatextual, and the intertextual (or transtextual). Offering a more comprehensive view, Eoyang and O'Neill recognize the different practices of different readerships, especially those of actual readers.

Such readers, belonging to specific "interpretive communities," have figured in various studies that adopt empirical or historical perspectives. The communal reader is the subject of Safiullina (2009), which, utilizing letters sent by readers to a translation journal published in Stalinist Russia from 1938–40, analyzes the worldview of "creative readers" who depart from the party line. A comparable study is Dollerup, Reventlow, and Hansen (2006), which presents a collection of statistical data on readers' responses to translated folktales—part of the experimental project Copenhagen Studies in Reader Response. In contrast to the minimal attempts at empirical investigation in this field, studies of a historical nature, devoted to particular countries or regions, are many. A few examples will suffice here. Godayol (2014) narrates the history of reception of Betty Friedan's *The Feminine Mystique* in 1965, through the Catalan translation by Jordi Solé-Tura, which sparked interest in feminist thinking during the years of Franco's dictatorship. Baer (2014) emphasizes the heightened agency of readers under conditions of censorship, as they read across cultures and between the lines when encountering translations of foreign literature in Stalinist Russia. Chan (2009), in his analysis of readers' comments from printed and electronic sources, suggests reasons for the overwhelming success of the translations of Haruki Murakami's fiction in East Asia in the 1990s, against a background of globalization. And Munday (1998), making use of published reviews and interviews, details English readers' "misunderstanding" of Gabriel García Márquez in translation. Scholars of reception history from a translation perspective will also glean much that is useful from the book series from Bloomsbury Publishing titled "The Reception of British and Irish Authors in Europe," in which translations into European languages of the works of authors such as Scott, Lawrence, Burns, Austen, Byron, Woolf, and Dickens (Hollington 2013) are discussed in individual anthologies. Such histories of reception of foreign authors and works are a staple of many anthologies (e.g., Tötösy de Zepetnek and Sywenky 1997), although the role played by translations is often not given much prominence.

Other notable studies include Adeaga (2006), who examines the translation of Third World literature in relation to reader expectations and nation-building motivations, paying attention at the same time to the often neglected elements of publishing, promotion and distribution. Carter (2014) uses quantitative surveys to study the contrasting responses of New Zealanders and Frenchmen toward a novel about Maori culture written in French by a "cultural outsider" that is translated into English.

Drawing on the perspectives of translation theory and reader response, Leong (2010) analyzes the writing of manga and anime fan fiction based on Japanese originals, and advances the idea of fan readers/writers as "partial translators," while Hickey (2003) distinguishes between two kinds of translation evaluation undertaken differently by "professional" and "lay" readers, focusing attention on the latter group. Through a statistical analysis based on an English-language survey of 478 readers and an Italian-language survey of 313 readers, Pagliassotti (2008) studies non-Asian readers' reactions to translated male homoerotic comics, produced originally for women readers in Japan.

New directions

As mentioned earlier, while translation research oriented toward the reader as TT receptor is something that began long ago, efforts to characterize translation readers in terms of their relation to the author and the text have received a fresh impetus from reader response and reception studies. Research of the latter kind will hopefully move beyond attempts at identifying the presence or functions of the reader to exploring issues of reader subjectivity. How does this reader cross cultural and linguistic borders, and what motivates the reading of translations? What new forms of knowledge, supra- as well as inter-cultural, are acquired as readers move between two worlds, one well known and the other less so? In this connection, attention should be given to new readerships in the age of globalization. To bring translation research in line with current developments in other fields, one should study the reader's relationship not only to translated literature but also to non-literary genres, especially new media forms (like comics and animated films). This opens up for consideration other types of readers and their diverse motivations. In contrast to the recreational reading of literature, for instance, readers can be seen to engage in informational reading (of websites and manuals), occupational reading (when learning a second language or teaching a subject at school), devotional reading (of the Buddhist scriptures or the Bible), environmental reading (of signs and notices), and so on. How do such reading situations "make" the translation reader?

For some time now, it has been observed that Translation Studies has taken a sociological turn. The rise of the communal reader, as mentioned above, has presaged a new sociology of reading, although the exact trajectory of the work initiated in this direction has yet to be explored. How do book clubs online (like the Australian and New Zealand Literature Lovers Bookclub) and offline (like the US Book-of-the-Month Club) facilitate the dissemination of translated literature? The phenomenon of "very active" readers who not only produce work in imitation of their favorite authors but also undertake to translate their favorite books—often collectively—has been exemplified by the online *Harry Potter* translation phenomenon (see, for example, the "Harry in Deutsch" Internet Club). The impact of non-professional reader-translators, which was unimaginable as little as 10 years ago, will require scholars to change the way they write. Although reception has never been completely ignored, in most translation histories the reader has been largely relegated to a secondary, if not marginal, position. Most translation histories to date have also focused more on what translators do to texts than on why and how translated texts are read. Perhaps we will see, at long last, some shift in the writing of reception history, away from the translator who reads toward the reader who translates.

References

Adeaga, Tomi. 2006. *Translating and Publishing African Languages(s) and Literature(s): Examples from Nigeria, Ghana and Germany*. Frankfurt am Main: IKO.

Andringa, Els. 2006. "Penetrating the Dutch Polysystem: The Reception of Virginia Woolf, 1920–2000." *Poetics Today* 27(3): 501–68.

Assis Rosa, Alexandra. 2006. "Defining Target Text Reader: Translation Studies and Literary Theory." In *Translation Studies at the Interface of Disciplines*, Joao Ferreira Duarte, Alexandra Assis Rosa, and Teresa Seruya (eds.), 99–109. Amsterdam and Philadelphia: John Benjamins.

Baer, Brian J. 2014. "Translated Literature and the Role of the Reader." In *A Companion to Translation Studies*, Sandra Bermann and Catherine Porter (eds.), 333–45. Chichester: Wiley Blackwell.

Carter, Ellen. 2014. "Imagining Place: An Empirical Study of How Cultural Outsiders and Insiders Receive Fictional Representations of Place in Caryl Fèrey's *Utu*." *Imaginations: Journal of Cross-cultural Image Studies* 5.1. Available online at www3.csj.ualberta.ca/imaginations/?p=5231 (accessed August 29, 2014).

Chan, Tak-hung Leo. 2009. "Reading the Global: The Reader-Consumer and the Murakami Translation Phenomenon." *Translation Quarterly* 53/54: 1–46.
——2010. *Readers, Reading and Reception of Translated Fiction in Chinese: Novel Encounters.* Manchester: St. Jerome.
Dollerup, Cay, Ivan Reventlow, and Rosenberg Hansen. 2006. "Readers' Response to Translated Narratives: Statistical Findings from the 'Folktale' Project." *Translation Quarterly* 40: 40–59.
Eoyang, Eugene. 1993. *The Transparent Eye: Reflections on Translation, Chinese Literature, and Comparative Poetics.* Honolulu: University of Hawaii Press.
Finkelstein, David, and Alistair McCleery (eds.). 2002. *Book History Reader.* London and New York: Routledge.
Fish, Stanley. 1980. *Is There a Text in This Class? The Authority of Interpretive Communities.* Cambridge: Cambridge University Press.
Godayol, Pilar. 2014. "Feminism and Translation in the 1960s: The Reception in Catalunya of Betty Friedan's *The Feminine Mystique.*" *Translation Studies* 7(3): 267–83.
Hermans, Theo. 1996. "The Translator's Voice in Translated Narrative." *Target* 8(1): 23–48.
——1999. *Translation in Systems: Descriptive and Systemic Approaches Explained.* Manchester: St. Jerome Publishing.
Hickey, Leo. 2003. "The Reader as Translation Assessor." *Studies in Translation* 1(1): 59–92.
Hollington, Michael (ed.). 2013. *The Reception of Charles Dickens in Europe.* London: Bloomsbury Academic.
Iser, Wolfgang. 1974. *The Implied Reader: Patterns of Communication in Prose Fiction from Bunyan to Beckett.* Baltimore, MD and London: Johns Hopkins University Press.
Jauss, H. R. 1982. *Toward an Aesthetic of Reception.* Trans. by Timothy Bahti. Brighton: Harvester Press.
Keen, Suzanne. 2007. *Empathy and the Novel.* New York: Oxford University Press.
Leong, Jane Ying Yieng. 2010. "Selling the Sweatdrop: The Translation of 'Japaneseness' in Manga and Anime Fan Fiction." Unpublished Ph.D. dissertation. University of Western Australia.
Littau, Karin. 1997. "Translation in the Age of Postmodern Production: From Text to Intertext to Hypertext." *Forum for Modern Language Studies* 33(1): 82–96.
Machor, James L., and Philip Goldstein (eds.). 2001. *Reception Study: From Literary to Cultural Studies.* London and New York: Routledge.
Munday, Jeremy. 1998. "The Caribbean Conquers the World? An Analysis of the Reception of García Márquez in Translation." *Bulletin of Hispanic Studies* 75(1): 137–44.
O'Neill, Patrick. 2005. *Polyglot Joyce: Fictions of Translation.* Toronto: University of Toronto Press.
Pagliassotti, Dru. 2008. "Reading Boy's Love in the West." *Particip@tions* 5(2). Available online at www.participations.org/Volume%205/Issue%202/5_02_pagliassotti.htm (accessed September 2, 2014).
Radway, Janice A. 1984. *Reading the Romance: Women, Patriarchy, and Popular Literature.* Chapel Hill: University of North Carolina Press.
Reiss, Katharina. 2000. *Translation Criticism – The Potentials and Limitations: Categories and Criteria for Translation Quality Assessment.* Manchester: St. Jerome Publishing.

Safiullina, Nailya. 2009. "Window to the West: From the Collection of Readers' Letters to the journal *Internatsional'naia Literatura*." *Slavonica* 15(2): 128–61.
Schiavi, Guiliana. 1996. "There Is Always a Teller in a Tale." *Target* 8(1): 1–22.
Squires, Claire. 2007. *Marketing Literature: The Making of Contemporary Writing in Britain*. New York: Palgrave Macmillan.
Tötösy de Zepetnek, Steven, and Irene Sywenky (eds.). 1997. *The Systemic and Empirical Approach to Literature and Culture as Theory and Application*. Edmonton and Seigen: University of Alberta Research Institute for Comparative Literature and Cross-Cultural Studies and Seigen University Institute for Empirical Literature and Media Research.
Wilss, Wolfram. 1982. *The Science of Translation: Problems and Methods*. Tübingen: G. Narr.

Part III

Research methods

12 Action research

Brenda Nicodemus and Laurie Swabey

Definition

Action research is an approach for investigating questions and finding solutions to problems that people confront in their everyday lives (Moen and Solvberg 2012; Stringer 2014). Although most frequently associated with educational research, action research is practiced within a number of diverse disciplines (Sagor 2011; Shanks, Miller, and Rosendale 2012; Mills 2014). Action research serves as an umbrella term for several approaches that have emerged from different research traditions, and researchers and educators have differing perspectives about what it is, what it is for, and who can do it (Whitehead and McNiff 2006). Reason and Bradbury offer the following definition:

> Action research is a family of practices of living inquiry that aims, in a great variety of ways, to link practice and ideas in the service of human flourishing. It is not so much a *methodology* as an *orientation* to inquiry that seeks to create participative communities of inquiry in which qualities of engagement, curiosity and question posing are brought to bear on significant practical issues.
>
> (Reason and Bradbury 2008: 1)

In contrast to other research approaches, action research shifts the locus of control from "objective" professional or academic researchers to individuals who traditionally have been the subjects of research (Herr and Anderson 2005). Action research often takes the form of a partnership between a practitioner and a researcher working together to solve a problem. Studies may also be conducted by *practitioner-researchers*, in which practitioners are regarded not only as *do-ers* (people who are competent in a practice), but also as *thinkers* (people who are competent in debating knowledge and generating ideas) (Stringer 2014). Practitioner-researchers raise questions about problems or issues in their environment with the goal of creating contextually relevant solutions. In this way practitioner-researchers hold themselves accountable for their work within the environment in which they are engaged. Further, practitioner-researchers strive to generate theories in order to transform this knowledge into new learning that will benefit others (McNiff and Whitehead 2011).

The types of questions that practitioner-researchers ask include:

- What is my concern about my practice?
- Why am I concerned?
- How do I gather evidence to show reasons for my concern?
- What can I do about the situation?
- How do I test the validity of my claims to knowledge?
- How can I check whether any conclusions I come to are reasonably fair and accurate?
- How do I modify my practice in light of my evaluation?
- How do I explain the significance of my work to others?

At its core, the goal of action research is for people to increase the effectiveness of the work in which they are personally engaged (Stringer 2014). This is achieved by examining the particular dynamics present in a local setting, taking a specified action within that setting, and evaluating the results of that action. This process of planning, taking action, and evaluating leads to further planning, action, and evaluation (Burns 1999; Coghlan and Brannick 2010). Throughout this process, community and organizational members collectively reflect upon the descriptions and explanations that emerge. In a recursive manner, new actions are then planned and taken, which are once again reviewed (Kemmis, McTaggart, and Nixon 2014).

Action research is regarded as a qualitative approach to inquiry. A number of textbooks describe how to conduct action research projects (e.g., Brydon-Miller, Greenwood, and Maguire 2003; Craig 2009; Mills 2014), and there has been an increase in the number of Master's theses and dissertations that use an action research approach (Lee and Wang 2012). Data in action research projects are generally taken from a variety of sources (e.g., observations, scores, interviews, survey responses, grades, and conversations) and commonly involve three phases: (1) pre-study planning, (2) implementation of action, and (3) post-study analysis (Craig 2009).

When proposing an action research study, Institutional Review Boards may show resistance to aspects of the approach that are non-traditional, such as participation by the researcher, a cyclical approach to inquiry, and shared organizational and community involvement (Herr and Anderson 2005). The practical and participatory nature of action research is lauded for the concrete outcomes that can emerge in local settings, but some argue that a weakness of the approach is its localism (Brydon-Miller et al. 2003). It is typically perceived as impossible to take on large-scale social change efforts with the action research approach, although others have argued against this bias (Martin 2008). Action research has also been criticized as lacking in rigor (Chapman, Paterson, and Medves 2011), a claim that can be countered with careful research design and implementation. Therefore, those who adopt an action research approach should be prepared to address the concerns that surround it.

Origins

It is generally accepted that action research emerged in the United States during the 1940s through the work of social psychologist Kurt Lewin. In his work, Lewin (1946) promoted shared decision-making by stakeholders in the workplace and the establishment of community action programs. While others, including John Collier and Jacob Moreno, have also been credited with the rise of action research, it was Lewin's work and reputation that gave impetus to action research movements in many different disciplines. In the 1950s, action research was taken up in educational circles, specifically by the teaching profession, and was advanced by Stephen Corey in his book *Action Research to Improve School Practices* (1953). Use of action research went into decline in the United States in the late 1950s, perhaps because of a focus on new research models and technical excellence in the "space age." In contrast, the approach began to gain momentum in the UK only in the 1970s, mainly through the influence of Lawrence Stenhouse, who was working in the context of teacher education. Stenhouse argued that teachers in classrooms should be supported by higher education personnel and wrote that the "fruitful development in the field of curriculum and teaching depends upon evolving styles of co-operative research by teachers and using full-time researchers to support the teachers' work" (1975: 162).

Another researcher, Stephen Kemmis, became active in action research in Australia and gained worldwide influence by developing ideas with a critical and participatory focus. Through Kemmis' contributions, action research became recognized as a form of practical research that legitimized teachers' attempts to understand their work from their own point of view. Instead of learning about the disciplines and applying those theories to their work in a sterile, objective manner only, teachers were encouraged to explore what they were doing and propose ways of improving it by using a hands-on approach.

Although action research initially flourished in the field of education, this approach to inquiry is now widely accepted across disciplines and recognized for its potential to contribute to knowledge and theory generation. The adoption of action research by various disciplines produced a number of variants of its basic tenets. The variants include *cooperative inquiry* (Reason and Rowan 1981; Heron 1988), *participatory action research* (Goodnough 2008; McIntyre 2008; Sappington, Baker, Gardner, and Pacha 2010), and *action science* (Argyris and Schön 1978). Variations of action research approaches also exist within educational settings (Elliott 1991; Hollingsworth 1997; Atweh, Kemmis, and Weeks 1998; Noffke and Somekh 2005; Greenwood and Levin 2007), including approaches known as *teacher research* (Cochran-Smith and Lytle 1993; Burnaford, Fischer, and Hobson 2001; Kincheloe 2012), *reflective practice* (Evans 2002), and *community service learning* (Wade and Anderson 1996; Zeichner and

Melnick 1996; Angelelli 1998; Kaye 2004). The use of action research in educational settings has contributed significantly to the development of more "democratic" teaching practices that are linked to students' and teachers' everyday lives.

Feminist theory has also spawned alternate forms of action research through its refusal to accept theories, research, and perspectives that devalue or erase women's lives, experiences, and contributions to research (Reinharz 1992; Morawski 1994; Stewart and Franz 1994; Wilkinson and Kitzinger 1996; Collins 2000; hooks 2000). One of the strengths of action research is that the fundamental principles that undergird the approach are universal, while emerging variants are able to emphasize particular aspects of the process.

Uses

Given the roots of action research in education, it is not surprising to find a parallel in Translation and Interpreting Studies. The use of this approach in T&I is relatively new and primarily appears in the literature on interpreter education and translator education. However, the literature contains more musings about the potential for this type of research than published studies that actually use this approach. Liu (2011), in a methodological review of 48 articles published in the journal *Interpreting* during the period of 2004–9, identified only one article that used action research as an approach, and it was a study related to educating interpreters. She pointed out the need for action research to identify new problems and additional questions. Pöchhacker (2011) also commented on the promising possibilities of action research, both for interpreting practice and for the development of techniques to use in teaching interpreting. Other references alluding to the importance and potential of action research are found earlier in the signed language interpreting literature (Napier 2005b; Turner 2005).

Action research has also been discussed in the translation literature, particularly in regard to translator education, where it is becoming more widely used to identify problems and answer a variety of practical questions. Fraser (2004) is often quoted, suggesting the need for a better model for translation research. Perhaps, Fraser states, "we need to start from practice and work back from it to theory" (2004: 59) and, in doing so, more aptly mirror the actual work of practitioners. In his recent book *Teaching and Researching Translation*, Basil Hatim carries this idea further, proposing "action research as an ideal methodology with which to study translation, and thus question the assumption that theory and practice are separate and distinct" (2013: 3).

Cravo and Neves (2007) identified benefits to using action research in Translation Studies that are similar to those identified in interpreter education and Interpreting Studies, including narrowing the gap between theory and practice, identifying new issues or practices, and making connections between scholars and practitioners. They described the benefits of researchers and translators working together, while also identifying some of the challenges and problems of this particular approach.

Angelelli (2008) suggested that action research projects conducted collaboratively between researchers and interpreting associations could advance the profession. One example of a project suggested by Angelelli is the exploration of how interpreters enact their roles based on professional codes of conduct in a variety of settings. Professional codes of conduct promulgated by interpreting organizations are based on a theoretical model that constructs the interpreter (or translator) as a neutral conduit of the source text; thus quality of the interpretation or translation is based on its "closeness" to the source text. However, studies of actual interpreter behavior suggest that such a model is neither possible nor desirable. As a result, practitioners may feel conflicted when attempting to follow the standards promoted by their professional organizations. An action research approach could provide opportunities for researchers and practitioners to work together on studies that examine actual and prescribed roles of interpreters.

The debate about how interpreters and translators should be educated is ongoing, yet within this debate there is a growing belief that action research holds promise for both teaching and practice (Kiraly 2000; Cravo and Neves 2007; Pöchhacker 2010; Hatim 2013). In addition to contributing to effective methods of instruction, action research has other potential applications in interpreter/translator education, including the investigation of processes and practices for selecting students for admission to programs, as well as the assessment of student learning. As with collaboration between researchers and practitioners, collaboration between teachers and students promises great benefits for all parties involved. Both Gile (2004) and Pöchhacker (2010), however, caution that such partnerships require mutual trust, the capacity for self-reflection, and an understanding of teaching and learning that transcends the traditional "sage on the stage" approach, which is more teacher-centered than student- or learner-centered. Kiraly, a proponent of the social-constructivist approach to translator education, advocates strongly for action research in the classroom, stating, "Adopting the role of teacher as researcher is, I believe, the key to innovation in our field" (2000: 122).

Sample studies

This section highlights three studies that use action research to examine and improve interpreter education. Although the three studies tackle different problems, they share a number of features. Each describes a real-world problem in a classroom, program, or community, and the pursuit of a solution relevant to the stakeholders. The research was not conducted "on" a randomly selected group of participants. Rather, the researchers were directly involved in the programs or classrooms described. For example, one researcher (Napier) not only conducted the study but also established the program, taught courses in the program, and served as the program coordinator. Each study exemplifies the cyclical nature of action research, with every stage in the process—planning, taking action, and evaluation—influencing the next cycle.

Two of these studies (Napier 2005a; Slatyer 2006) were undertaken purposefully as action research projects. In the third study, Hansen and Shlesinger (2007) report that they did not begin their project with an action research approach. Instead, they described seeing the "action research spiral" emerge almost inadvertently as they planned, developed, implemented, and evaluated interventions for their program, and then, based on insights and evidence, started the cycle again. These three studies also exemplify other common characteristics of action research: the studies were all practical and participatory; they were all conducted in the local environment; data collection was from a variety of sources (e.g., scores, focus groups, teacher evaluations, grades); the process was iterative; evaluation, and making changes based on evaluation, was key; and each study involved collaboration with stakeholders, including students, teachers, and, in the case of the first study, community partners.

Two of the studies described here are about interpreting curriculum development and change that came out of Australia. The first is an example of action research with the aim of collaboratively developing a curriculum for teaching ad hoc interpreters of languages of lesser diffusion (Slatyer 2006). The problem investigated was the use of untrained interpreters, often other community members, for new and emerging migrant and refugee language groups. Although Australia has a well-developed system for providing interpreting service for most languages, serving emerging language communities, as well as individuals who use languages of limited diffusion, is an ongoing challenge. In this project, collaboration was key and was achieved by inviting the major stakeholders—the service providers that hire interpreters, the professional interpreting organization, migrant and refugee groups, and educators—to provide input on the curriculum planning and pilot course delivery. A three-phase interpreting curriculum was developed and piloted, which included a week of intensive instruction on campus, a six-week period of mentored and supervised fieldwork, and then another week of intensive instruction on campus. Slatyer described the benefits of using an action research approach, citing, in particular, the ongoing collection and analysis of data from a variety of sources, including the end-users of the curriculum. The cycles of planning, information gathering, implementation, and evaluation provided evidence for modifications of the pilot curriculum. The project resulted in a model curriculum that allowed novice interpreters to achieve the minimum level of competence needed for professional practice.

In another study from Australia, Napier (2005a) used an action research approach to make effective changes in a curriculum and delivery mode for a postgraduate diploma program for signed language interpreters. The specific problems that motivated the study were both external and systemic, with a need to reach potential students from all parts of Australia who were unable to attend the program in a more traditional format. The proposed solution involved making changes to the curriculum and format (e.g., teaching/learning strategies, materials, locations, modes) so that the program could be effectively offered in a distance mode. After establishing this objective, an action plan was established with four phases: (1) sensing (identifying the need for change), (2) reading (literature review, focus groups with faculty/staff stakeholders, student questionnaires), (3) matching (recommendations for change), and (4) acting (implementation of change). Evaluation was cited by Napier as an important reason for choosing an action research approach, and a variety of formative and summative assessments were used to evaluate the revised educational delivery format (e.g., teacher evaluations of workload for each unit, the amount of student participation online, and evaluation of student grades for each unit). Students also evaluated the revised delivery format after each teaching block, with changes implemented in the next block. At the end of the semester, all teacher and student evaluations were analyzed to make further changes in future course offerings. As the program grows, the faculty will monitor the need for additional changes.

A final example of action research in interpreter education (at the Copenhagen School of Business) comes from Hansen and Shlesinger (2007). The specific problems that motivated this study included a high rate of failure on final exams and ineffective student self-study materials. The proposed solution involved revamping the language lab to increase its versatility and functionality, as well as improving the availability of innovative self-study materials. The researchers implemented an experimental selection and range of teaching and learning materials for the language lab, including unique uses of technology for practice and assessment. Data was collected and analyzed from a variety of sources, including student self-study logs and course evaluations. The positive evaluations by students were supported by interpreting performance exam scores that were considerably higher than those from previous years. After possible confounding variables were ruled out, results indicated that the new learning materials and the versatility of the lab contributed significantly to improving the students' competence. This particular study illustrates the depth and scope of an action research project and highlights the real world challenges in developing innovative materials to improve student performance without increasing students' anxiety.

In addition to the studies reviewed above, Cravo and Neves (2007: 92–107) acknowledge the complexity of using action research in Translation Studies and address many of the issues encountered in using this new approach in studies of translation, translator education, and translator teacher education. Furthermore, Fraser (2004: 57–61) looks broadly at translation and interpreting research and makes a strong case for the incorporation of action research, particularly in order for theory to reflect more accurately the experience of practitioners.

Conclusion and new directions

Action research is a participatory approach to inquiry that couples action and reflection in the pursuit of practical solutions to issues of pressing concern within a community. In this chapter we provided an overview and history of the action research approach and three examples from T&I research. Gile (2004) alludes to action research as a trend in T&I Studies and identifies both the positive aspects of this research, including access to interpreters and direct observation of their work, and the challenges, including the possibility of bias.

In all disciplines, it is important to select a suitable approach for investigating identified questions. While action research is one of many approaches that could be considered, practitioners should be aware that action research does have a set of fundamental principles and practices that must be adhered to in order to make publishable, defensible claims. Although the term "action research" seems practical, accessible, and inviting, students and interpreter/translator practitioners should not undertake this approach lightly but should fully consider the rigor that it requires.

The gap between theory and practice in both Translation and Interpreting Studies is frequently lamented in the literature. Action research offers one approach for reducing this gap by developing partnerships among practitioners, researchers, and community members to investigate, evaluate, and implement *concrete* solutions to the problems they face. In action research, problems are investigated in a more embedded, contextualized manner, with stakeholders assuming more engaged roles than in traditional "objective" approaches to research. The most significant influence of the action research approach may be on the content and delivery of interpreter and translator education.

Further reading

McNiff and Whitehead (2011) and Stringer (2014) provide clear guidelines that enable novice practitioner-researchers to move through the process of action research inquiry. Craig (2009) offers a practical blueprint of action research based on her experiences with students. Herr and Anderson (2005) give a useful start-to-finish description of the research process for doctoral students using an action research approach.

Reason and Bradbury's (2008) extensive (over 700 pages) edited volume contributes numerous perspectives on the grounding, practices, and skills needed, as well as "exemplars" of action research projects. Noffke and Somekh (2005) describe action research within the context of social science research as a welcome approach that can impact local communities.

References

Angelelli, Claudia. 1998. "A Service-Learning Component in a Translation Course: A Report from Stanford University." In *Proceedings of the 38th Annual Conference of the American Translators Association*, Muriel M. Jerome-O'Keeffe (ed.), 375–380. Alexandria, VA: American Translators Association.

——2008. "The Role of the Interpreter in the Healthcare Setting: A Plea for a Dialogue between Research and Practice." In *Crossing Borders in Community Interpreting*,

Carmen Valero-Garcés and Anne Martin (eds.), 147–65. Amsterdam and Philadelphia: John Benjamins.

Argyris, Chris, and Donald A. Schön. 1978. *Organizational Learning: A Theory of Action Perspective*. Reading, MA: Addison-Wesley.

Atweh, Bill, Stephen Kemmis, and Patricia Weeks (eds.). 1998. *Action Research in Practice: Partnerships for Social Justice in Education*. New York: Routledge.

Brydon-Miller, Mary, Davydd Greenwood, and Patricia Maguire. 2003. "Why Action Research?" *Action Research* 1: 9–28.

Burnaford, Gail E., Joseph Fischer, and David Hobson. 2001. *Teachers Doing Research: The Power of Action through Inquiry*. Mahwah, NJ: Erlbaum.

Burns, Anne. 1999. *Collaborative Action Research for English Language Teachers*. Cambridge: Cambridge University Press.

Chapman, Christine, Margo Paterson, and Jennifer M. Medves. 2011. "The QUIP-PED Project: Exploring Relevance and Rigor of Action Research Using Established Principles and Criteria." *The Qualitative Report* 16: 208–28.

Cochran-Smith, Marilyn, and Susan Landy Lytle. 1993. *Inside Outside: Teacher Research and Knowledge*. New York: Teachers College Press.

Coghlan, David, and Teresa Brannick. 2010. *Doing Action Research in Your Own Organization*. London: SAGE Publications.

Collins, Patricia Hill. 2000. *Black Feminist Thought: Knowledge, Consciousness, and the Politics of Empowerment*. 2nd edition. New York: Routledge.

Corey, Stephen M. 1953. *Action Research to Improve School Practices*. New York: Bureau of Publications, Teachers College, Columbia University.

Craig, Dorothy Varcarcel. 2009. *Action Research Essentials*. San Francisco: Jossey-Bass.

Cravo, Ana, and Joselia Neves. 2007. "Action Research in Translation Studies." *The Journal of Specialised Translation* 7: 92–107.

Elliott, John. 1991. *Action Research for Educational Change*. Buckingham: Open University Press.

Evans, Linda. 2002. *Reflective Practice in Educational Research: Developing Advanced Skills*. London: Continuum.

Fraser, Janet. 2004. "Translation Research and Interpreting Research: Pure, Applied, Action or Pedagogic?" In *Translation Research and Interpreting Research: Traditions, Gaps and Synergies*, Christina Schäffner (ed.), 57–61. Clevedon: Multilingual Matters.

Gile, Daniel. 2004. "Translation Research versus Interpreting Research: Kinship, Differences and Prospects for Partnership." In *Translation Research and Interpreting Research: Traditions, Gaps and Synergies*, Christina Schäffner (ed.), 10–35. Clevedon: Multilingual Matters.

Goodnough, Karen. 2008. "Dealing with Messiness and Uncertainty in Practitioner Research: The Nature of Participatory Action Research." *Canadian Journal of Education* 31: 431–58.

Greenwood, Davydd J., and Morten Levin. 2007. *Introduction to Action Research: Social Research for Social Change*. 2nd edition. Thousand Oaks, CA: SAGE Publications.

Hansen, Inge, and Miriam Shlesinger. 2007. "The Silver Lining: Technology and Self-Study in the Interpreting Classroom." *Interpreting* 9(1): 95–118.

Hatim, Basil. 2013. *Teaching and Researching Translation*. Harlow, Essex: Pearson Education Limited.

Heron, John. 1988. "Impressions of the Other Reality: A Co-operative Inquiry into Altered States of Consciousness." In *Human Inquiry in Action: Developments in New Paradigm Research*, Peter Reason (ed.), 182–98. London: SAGE Publications.

Herr, Kathryn, and Gary L. Anderson. 2005. *The Action Research Dissertation: A Guide for Students and Faculty*. Thousand Oaks, CA: SAGE Publications.

Hollingsworth, Sandra (ed.). 1997. *International Action Research: A Casebook for Educational Reform*. London: Routledge.

hooks, bell. 2000. *Feminist Theory: From Margin to Center*. London: Pluto Press.

Kaye, Cathryn Berger. 2004. *The Complete Guide to Service Learning: Proven, Practical Ways to Engage Students in Civic Responsibility, Academic Curriculum, and Social Action*. Minneapolis, MN: Free Spirit Publishing.

Kemmis, Stephen, Robin McTaggart, and Rhonda Nixon. 2014. *The Action Research Planner: Doing Critical Participatory Action Research*. Singapore: Springer.

Kincheloe, Joe L. 2012. *Teachers as Researchers: Qualitative Paths to Empowerment*. New York: Routledge.

Kiraly, Don. 2000. *A Social Constructivist Approach to Translator Education: Empowerment from Theory to Practice*. Manchester: St. Jerome.

Lee, Young Ah, and Ye Wang. 2012. "Searching for New Directions: Developing MA Action Research Project as a Tool for Teaching." *US–China Education Review* 8: 697–709.

Lewin, Kurt. 1946. "Action Research and Minority Problems." *Journal of Social Issues* 2: 34–46.

Liu, Minhua. 2011. "Methodology in Interpreting Studies: A Methodological Review of Evidence-based Research." In *Advances in Interpreting Research: Inquiry in Action*, Brenda Nicodemus and Laurie Swabey (eds.), 85–120. Amsterdam: John Benjamins.

Martin, Ann W. 2008. "Action Research on a Large Scale: Issues and Practices." In *The SAGE Handbook of Action Research: Participative Inquiry and Practice*, 2nd edition, Peter and Hilary Bradbury (eds.), 394–406. London: SAGE Publications.

McIntyre, Alice. 2008. *Participatory Action Research*. Thousand Oaks, CA: SAGE Publications.

McNiff, Jean, and Jack Whitehead. 2011. *All You Need to Know about Action Research*. 2nd edition. London: SAGE Publications.

Mills, Geoffrey E. 2014. *Action Research: A Guide for the Teacher Researcher*. 5th edition. Boston: Pearson.

Moen, Torill, and Astrid M. Solvberg. 2012. "The Power of Words: A Crucial Conversation at the Launch of an Action Research Project." *U.S.–China Review* 6: 557–67.

Morawski, Jill G. 1994. *Practicing Feminisms, Reconstructing Psychology: Notes on a Liminal Science*. Ann Arbor: University of Michigan Press.

Napier, Jemina. 2005a. "Making Learning Accessible for Sign Language Interpreters: A Process of Change." *Educational Action Research* 13(4): 505–24.

——2005b. "Linguistic Features and Strategies of Interpreting: From Research to Education to Practice." In *Sign Language Interpreting and Interpreter Education: Directions for Research and Practice*, Marc Marschark, Rico Peterson, and Elizabeth Winston (eds.), 84–111. New York: Oxford University Press.

Noffke, Susan E., and Bridget Somekh. 2005. "Action Research." In *Research Methods in the Social Sciences*, Bridget Somekh and Cathy Lewin (eds.), 89–96. Thousand Oaks, CA: SAGE Publications.

Pöchhacker, Franz. 2010. "The Role of Research in Interpreter Education." *Translation & Interpreting* 2: 1–10.

——2011. "Researching Interpreting: Approaches to Inquiry." In *Advances in Interpreting Research: Inquiry in Action*, Brenda Nicodemus and Laurie Swabey (eds.), 5–26. Amsterdam and Philadelphia: John Benjamins.

Reason, Peter, and Hilary Bradbury (eds.). 2008. *The SAGE Handbook of Action Research: Participative Inquiry and Practice*. 2nd edition. London: SAGE Publications.

Reason, Peter, and John Rowan. 1981. *Human Inquiry: A Sourcebook of New Paradigm Research*. Chichester: Wiley.

Reinharz, Shulamit. 1992. *Feminist Methods in Social Research*. New York: Oxford University Press.

Sagor, Richard. 2011. *The Action Research Guidebook: A Four-stage Process for Educators and School Teams*. 2nd edition. Thousand Oaks, CA: SAGE Publications.

Sappington, Neil, Paul J. Baker, Dianne Gardner, and Joe Pacha. 2010. "A Signature Pedagogy for Leadership Education: Preparing Principals through Participatory Action Research." *Planning and Changing* 41: 249–73.

Shanks, Joyce, Lauren Miller, and Susannah Rosendale. 2012. "Action Research in a Professional Development School Setting to Support Teacher Candidate Self-efficacy." *SRATE Journal* 21: 26–32.

Slatyer, Helen. 2006. "Researching Curriculum Innovation in Interpreter Education." In *New Approaches to Interpreter Education*, Cynthia Roy (ed.), 47–65. Washington DC: Gallaudet University Press.

Stenhouse, Lawrence. 1975. *An Introduction to Curriculum Research and Development*. London: Heinemann.

Stewart, Abigail J., and Carol E. Franz (eds.). 1994. *Women Creating Lives: Identities, Resilience, and Resistance*. Boulder, CO: Westview Press.

Stringer, Ernest T. 2014. *Action Research*. 4th edition. Thousand Oaks, CA: SAGE Publications.

Turner, Graham. 2005. "Toward Real Interpreting." In *Sign Language Interpreting and Interpreter Education: Directions for Research and Practice*, Marc Marschark, Rico Peterson, and Elizabeth Winston (eds.), 29–56. New York: Oxford University Press.

Wade, Rahima C., and Jeffrey B. Anderson. 1996. "Community Service-learning: A Strategy for Preparing Human Service-oriented Teachers." *Teacher Education Quarterly* (Fall): 59–74.

Whitehead, Jack, and Jean McNiff. 2006. *Action Research: Living Theory*. Thousand Oaks, CA: SAGE Publications.

Wilkinson, Sue, and Celia Kitzinger (eds.). 1996. *Representing the Other: A Feminism and Psychology Reader*. London: SAGE Publications.

Zeichner, Kenneth, and Susan Melnick. 1996. "The Role of Community Field Experiences in Preparing Teachers for Cultural Diversity." In *Currents of Reform in Pre-service Teacher Education*, Kenneth Zeichner, Susan Melnick, and Mary Louise Gomez (eds.), 176–98. New York: Teachers College Press.

13 Bibliometric studies

Luc van Doorslaer

Definition

Because of the recent success and relatively frequent use of bibliometric methods, some would argue that the (sub)field of bibliometrics has now become more than a method itself and could even be seen as "an empirical branch of the social studies of science" (Grbić 2013: 20). The success is a direct consequence of the quantification of academic research production, a tendency that has recently also gained ground in the humanities. Bibliometric methods offer tools for measuring, quantitatively analyzing, and exploring academic literature and its impact. This impact can relate both to a (sub)discipline and to specific publications, individual researchers or research groups.

The term 'bibliometrics' was coined by Alan Pritchard of the National Computing Centre in Manchester in 1969. Pritchard was unsatisfied with the then widely used term 'statistical bibliography,' as it was "clumsy, not very descriptive, and can be confused with statistics itself or bibliographies on statistics" (Pritchard 1969: 348). He suggested that the term 'bibliometrics' be used to refer to "the application of mathematics and statistical methods to books and other media of communication" by analogy with similar terms like "the accepted, and analogous 'biometrics', 'econometrics', and 'scientometrics'" (1969: 349).

Origin of the method

Glänzel notes that statistical analysis of scientific literature had already begun half a century before the term 'bibliometrics' was coined, and mentions a couple of examples from the 1920s (2003: 6). However, this research remained relatively unnoticed. At that time much more traditional methods of information retrieval were sufficient, and there were no real financing systems for scientific research that needed sophisticated statistical methods. This only changed with the publication of Derek de Solla Price's seminal work *Little Science – Big Science* (1963), in which the author "analysed the recent system of science communication and thus presented the first systematic approach to the structure of modern science applied to the science as a whole" (Glänzel 2003: 8).

The book also introduced modern research-evaluation techniques, with major consequences for our understanding of science communication in the era of globalization and huge knowledge growth.

The (sub)disciplines of scientometrics and bibliometrics developed rapidly in the seventies and the eighties. Whereas in the first decades of the twentieth century, data collection had to be done manually, this changed with the development of computer technology. The availability of large bibliographical databases in machine-readable form has made metrics of science develop very rapidly over the last decades. Today three main application fields can be discerned: (1) basic bibliometric, mainly methodologically oriented research; (2) science information data about individual scientific disciplines; and (3) research evaluation used as a basis for science policy of institutional structures at the supranational, national, or regional level (see also Glänzel 2003: 9–10).

Although bibliometric methods originated in information science, they have now found wide application in a variety of research fields in the humanities as well. A recent book publication offering an overview of bibliometric and adjacent approaches is De Bellis' *Bibliometrics and Citation Analysis* (De Bellis 2009), which deals not only with the somewhat confusing terminological overlap between bibliometrics, informetrics, scientometrics, and cybermetrics, but also with approaches to the topic from empirical, mathematical, and even philosophical viewpoints. Frequently used bibliometric applications include citation and publication analysis, the measuring of term frequencies, and (social) network analysis.

Uses

Different types of bibliometric (sometimes scientometric) methods are described and largely illustrated by existing publications in T&I Studies. They vary from relatively "simple counting" approaches to studies based on the use of several types of statistical software. Grbić and Pöllabauer (2008a, 2008b) and Grbić (2013) focus on methods like (social) network analysis, word and co-word analysis, as well as on more obvious publication and citation counting.

Network analysis investigates the relations that exist among individual authors or researchers. This is a key technique in sociology and network theory. A whole range of (statistical) software programs are now available for visualizing such interconnections and the embeddedness of individuals in larger research groups or networks (see, for instance, PAJEK and UCINET in Grbić and Pöllabauer 2008a). Word analysis is a tool frequently used in text linguistics for conducting various kinds of quantitative corpus analysis. Co-word or co-occurrence analysis, in particular, focuses on the co-occurrence of word pairs. Here again, a variety of text analysis software programs (i.e., WordSmith Tools) is available to support this work.

Quantitative data can be counted and analyzed in several ways, depending on the categories in the available corpus. For impact studies, publication and citation counting are the most obvious ones. But other possible categories include affiliations of authors, the nature of the publications, the text types, the languages of publication, and the keywords.

The fact that more and more bibliometric approaches are being used in T&I Studies cannot be separated from the degree of institutionalization of the discipline. After more than half a century of scholarly research, T&I Studies has reached a stage at which it is worthwhile investigating developments, tendencies, and differences within the discipline. In modern knowledge-based societies, academic degrees, theoretical reflection, and scholarly production have raised the status of an activity like translation. After some time, institutionalized research arrives at a point where there is a need for metareflection about the discipline (see Gambier and van Doorslaer 2009). The past decades in T&I Studies have shown a (sometimes exponential) growth in the number of scholars, curricula, publishers, journals, book series, scholarly associations, conferences, summer schools, Ph.D. programs, etc. (see also Gile 2012). When the amount of knowledge grows, it is inevitable that this will lead to a need for knowledge-structuring, which explains why, at the beginning of the twenty-first century, T&I Studies has become very active in producing knowledge-structuring resources like historical surveys, handbooks, encyclopedias, textbooks, dictionaries, journals, terminologies, and (research) bibliographies. Bibliometric tools are pre-eminently used for investigating exactly the kind of material gathered in such resources.

Nadja Grbić confirms that "[b]ibliographical databases are essential sources of data for bibliometric and/or scientometric … studies" (2013: 21). As T&I journals are only very partially represented in the main citation indexes (e.g., the *Science Citation Index* [SCI], the *Social Sciences Citation Index* [SSCI], or the *Arts and Humanities Citation Index* [AHCI]), several bibliometric approaches start from the main online bibliographies of the discipline, like the *Translation Studies Bibliography* (TSB) (see Gambier and van Doorslaer 2013) or the online version of the *Translation Studies Abstracts* (TSA). It is to be noted that these two bibliographies use the term 'Translation Studies' as an umbrella concept for both Translation and Interpreting Studies, as is often done in the discipline, although the use is not universally accepted. A keyword-analysis based on a relatively early version of the TSB databases, and still without the use of statistical tools, can be found in van Doorslaer (2005), in which he investigates and compares the frequency of several of the more than 600 keywords in the online bibliography, focusing on the different types of discourse. In a recent contribution, Javier Franco Aixelá (2013) adds impact and citation counts based on the Alicante bibliography *Bitra*. He extracts the most cited works in the discipline from the database, with a view to arranging them in terms of chronology, authors, types of publications and sub-genres, among other things. In the following section dealing specifically with TIS research, a number of examples will be provided to illustrate the use of the different categories and methodological tools.

Sample studies

One of the first articles in the discipline to apply an explicit bibliometric approach did not deal with scholarly production as such but provided an analysis of the *Index Translationum*, the UNESCO database of translated books. Anatolij Šajkevič describes his paper as "an attempt to give a first general impression of the volume, dynamics, and structure of the world output of translated books" (1992: 67). His statistical analysis of the rich data of the *Index Translationum* resulted in very interesting correlations. Šajkevič included a wide variety of tables and graphs focusing on the average annual publication of translated books per country, the world linguistic spectrum, linguistic and thematic spectra per country, thematic evolution, the most translated authors, the proportion of translated books in relation to the size of the country, as well as linguistic and thematic clusters within the countries.

Bibliometric methods are appropriate for conducting partial or topical analyses, for instance, when focusing on specific sub-fields. A number of studies concentrate on particular branches of Interpreting Studies, such as Gile (2000) on Conference Interpreting Research (CIR). His quantitative analysis shows that, at the time of publication, the number of authors dealing with CIR had clearly increased, but only a very limited number of these authors displayed long-term activity. Moreover, much of CIR research seemed to be conducted independently of an academic institution. This example shows how purely quantitative data can provide unique insights into the particular features of a sub-field and its development.

Probably the most thorough bibliometric research in T&I Studies up to now has been conducted by Nadja Grbić and Sonja Pöllabauer. Their 2008 *Target* article is a case in point and shows how revealing well-conducted scientometric research can be when applied to a well-defined and limited corpus. Their study focuses on spoken and signed language community interpreting in German-speaking countries. Using several of the methodological tools outlined above (e.g., keyword, title word, and co-occurrence analysis), the study focuses on the type and nature of publications, the growth rates of specific sub-fields, the most common languages of publication, the disciplinary affiliation of the authors, the author- and co-authorships involved, as well as the topics touched upon. From a methodological point of view, it is interesting to note that the authors themselves gained "a wider perspective on the topic" by combining and triangulating different bibliometric methods. In so doing, "results which were obtained using one method could be underpinned with additional insights obtained through a different method" (Grbić and Pöllabauer 2008a: 326–27).

Though they do not make use of statistical software programs, some of the examples discussed below share similarities with a bibliometric approach. Much more limited in scope and elaboration is Bin and Mingjiong (2009), for instance, which concentrates on publications on simultaneous interpreting in the first decade of the twenty-first century, particularly those dealing with cognitive and empirical issues. The fields of sign language interpreting and educational interpreting are the object of Aquino Albres and Broglia Feitosa de Lacerda (2013), in which a national category is correlated with an international perspective. The authors cross-reference the references in international articles with those in local Brazilian research on the topic.

Although he does not use the terms 'bibliometric' or 'scientometric' himself, Gideon Toury has also delivered a quantitatively inspired study based on an analysis of the publications in the journal *Target* over the first 20 years of its existence. His observations about the development of one of the leading journals in the discipline are based on "parameters of potential interest for a sociocultural account" (Toury 2009: 206) of both the discipline and the journal. The categories he selects for analysis include the major contributing countries, distribution of the journal (subscriptions) per country, and the gender of the author. This contribution shows that selection criteria for bibliometric research are not necessarily topical but can also be based on the source of publication (for instance, a journal). Within the limits of these categories, a general perspective is provided on the development of the discipline as a whole. In this sense the approach is comparable to the analyses of general bibliographies mentioned earlier. Another recent example is van Doorslaer (forthcoming), in which the large databases of the TSB are used to measure both the geographical spread of T&I research activity (based on the academic affiliation of the authors) and the languages of publication.

The final example to be mentioned here is Rovira-Esteva and Orero (2011), who explicitly link their study to the growing role of research assessment in academic environments, in their case in Spain. They use a relatively limited corpus: three years of publication, with 71 volumes from nine journals dealing with T&I Studies or language as a form of communication. Although the authors are very cautious and self-critical in explaining the selection of their corpus, one wonders why one of the main publishers in the discipline (Benjamins) has none of their journals represented. This shows the risk of non-representativeness in any corpus created for bibliometric research. Rovira-Esteva and Orero list several averages (such as number of authors and number of pages) and compare them in interdisciplinary terms to other fields. They also have a partly national perspective, as they specifically count the number of Spanish authors in a separate category. An interesting finding emerges when studying the references, namely, that "books are by and large the most cited kind of contribution" (2011: 242). This confirms the hypothesis that several fields in the humanities, unlike in the hard sciences, rely much more on monographs and book chapters than on journal contributions, although monographs and book chapters are not counted among the "citable items" in the major databases, such as Scopus and Web of Knowledge.

Despite all the valuable research done with the methods described above, it cannot be denied that bibliometric approaches have their limitations and weaknesses. First of all, the focus on the quantitative data inevitably runs the risk of overshadowing qualitative peculiarities or nuances. Every type of quantitative approach can increase its relevance by adding qualitative refinement or differentiations. It is also obvious that the results of data-based research necessarily depend on the reliability of the data. For instance, in T&I Studies the quality of the UNESCO *Index Translationum* is often criticized. Databases always depend on the data-gathering qualities of the producers (in this case, the member-states of UNESCO) and on the type of categories defined. Under such circumstances, comparing data is often hazardous. Nevertheless Anthony Pym qualifies the *Index Translationum* as "a convenient low-effort first step" for bibliometric and bibliographical research (Poupaud, Pym, and Torres Simón 2009: 270).

Some of the qualities of bibliometric methods in the case studies discussed in this section imply risks for the researcher. If a well-defined and well-limited corpus can lead to revealing results, this also means that insufficiently defined or carelessly selected corpora can yield misleading results. Lack of representativeness is one of the pitfalls in the complex methodological, sometimes technical, process of bibliometric research. Therefore, it is difficult to recommend best practices, as best practices usually rely on best selection criteria, best definitions, and best categories. It is often the selection criteria and categorization practices that decide through which prism the quantitative data will be read and interpreted.

Conclusion and potential applications

It is undeniably the case that quantitative methods, and bibliometric methods in particular, have gained much more attention in recent years. One can now find quite a lot of "counting" approaches in T&I Studies, although not always using technological tools and statistical or mathematical software. In general the tendency to adopt more bibliometric approaches cannot be separated from the measuring of academic output, assessment of research impact, the "objectivization" of scientific activity, and the process of knowledge-structuring in a discipline in the process of institutionalization. No doubt the measuring of academic output has been stimulated by different types of research assessment and the well-known principle of "publish or perish." As is the case in most subfields of the humanities, such methods are often approached in a critical way in T&I Studies, as those methods are better at assessing quantity than quality. Nevertheless, bibliometric and scientometric approaches are valuable in providing a broader view of the development of the discipline itself. As a consequence of increasing levels of institutionalization and the growing amount of knowledge generated in T&I Studies, only recently has the field come to apply quantitative methods to this end. The knowledge structuring resources that are available today in T&I Studies (mainly online bibliographies) contain reliable data on many thousands of publications. Bibliometric methodologies make it possible to use these resources not only as search tools, but also as research tools. These resources and methods are thus not only valuable aids in supporting research; following systematic analysis of the data they contain, they also offer new insights into the development of the discipline. After more than half a century of scholarly work, T&I Studies has now reached a stage at which such meta-information can help in developing a new line of institutional research about the historical evolution of the discipline itself. Moreover, the use of bibliometric methods is in itself proof of a higher level of structure and institutionalization.

Bibliometrics remains essentially a quantitative method of investigation. As such it provides T&I Studies (and other humanities) with empirical data. The actual design of a study depends on the availability of data, the focus of the researcher, as shown in the selection and categorization of data, as well as on the available software for the data analysis. A qualitative refinement can add value to or relativize the data. The perspective on isolated figures may change through contextualization or triangulation with other available metrics. For example, though the available studies in TIS are limited, we know from research in other disciplines that one impact indicator may contradict another (like impact factors of journals vs number of downloads). Comparing data is often tricky because of the different methodologies used, but the different outcomes of quantitative studies show the limitations of bibliometrics if used as a counting-only method. In T&I Studies a variety of approaches based on bibliometric methods is now developing. The journal *Perspectives* has announced a special issue with the title "Bibliometrics in Translation Studies" for 2015, which will be exclusively devoted to contributions using bibliometric and scientometric methods.

In addition to more classical approaches, such as citation analysis or publication counting, future investigations of institutional research could concentrate on some of the categories available in the bibliographical databases, like geographical spread of research, gender disparity, or genre as research object. Particularly rewarding could be the analysis of networks of researchers in T&I Studies, both from a geographical and a topical point of view. For example, up to now data have shown that productivity in T&I research (in absolute figures) is highest in Europe. This tells us something about Europroductivity—nothing more, nothing less. More data about established and/or developing networks among researchers could relate such a simple figure to the hierarchy of ideas and paradigms, even to the "traveling" of theories and concepts. Such an approach could eventually tell us more about the existence (or non-existence) of the complex phenomenon of "Eurocentrism," or of other types of continental centrisms. More information about the social and professional networks would also strengthen our knowledge about the discipline itself.

References

Aquino Albres, Neiva de, and Cristina Broglia Feitosa de Lacerda. 2013. "Interpretação educacional como campo de pesquisa: estudo bibliométrico de publicações internacionais e suas marcas no campo nacional." *Cadernos de Tradução* 31(1): 179–204.

Bin, Gao, and Chai Mingjiong. 2009. "A Bibliometric Analysis of New Developments in Simultaneous Interpreting Studies in the West." *Chinese Translators Journal* (2): 17–21.

De Bellis, Nicola. 2009. *Bibliometrics and Citation Analysis: From the "Science Citation Index" to Cybermetrics*. Lanham, MD, Toronto, and Plymouth: The Scarecrow Press.

de Solla Price, Derek J. 1963. *Little Science – Big Science*. New York: Columbia University Press.

Franco Aixelá, Javier. 2013. "Who's Who and What's What in Translation Studies: A Preliminary Approach." In *Tracks and Treks in Translation Studies: Selected Papers from the EST Congress, Leuven 2010*, Reine Meylaerts, Catherine Way, Magdalena Bartlomiejczyk, and Sonia Vandepitte (eds.), 7–28. Amsterdam and Philadelphia: John Benjamins.

Gambier, Yves, and Luc van Doorslaer (eds.). 2009. *The Metalanguage of Translation*. Amsterdam and Philadelphia: John Benjamins.

——2013. *Translation Studies Bibliography*. 10th edition. Available at www.benjamins.com/online/tsb/ (last accessed October 16, 2014).

Gile, Daniel. 2000. "The History of Research into Conference Interpreting: A Scientometric Approach." *Target* 12(2): 297–321.

——2012. "Institutionalization of Translation Studies." In *Handbook of Translation Studies*, vol. 3, Yves Gambier and Luc van Doorslaer (eds.), 73–80. Amsterdam and Philadelphia: John Benjamins.

Glänzel, Wolfgang. 2003. *Bibliometrics as a Research Field. A Course on Theory and Application of Bibliometric Indicators*. Available at www.cin.ufpe.br/~ajhol/futuro/references/01%23_Bibliometrics_Module_KUL_BIBLIOMETRICS%20AS%20A%20RESEARCH%20FIELD.pdf (last accessed September 30, 2014).

Grbić, Nadja. 2013. "Bibliometrics." In *Handbook of Translation Studies*, vol. 4, Yves Gambier and Luc van Doorslaer (eds.), 20–24. Amsterdam and Philadelphia: John Benjamins.

Grbić, Nadja, and Sonja Pöllabauer. 2008a. "Counting What Counts: Research on Community Interpreting in German-speaking Countries. A Scientometric Study." *Target* 20(2): 297–332.

——2008b. "To Count or Not to Count: Scientometrics as a Methodological Tool for Investigating Research on Translation and Interpreting." *Translation and Interpreting Studies* 3(1/2): 87–146.

Poupaud, Sandra, Anthony Pym, and Ester Torres Simón. 2009. "Finding Translations. On the Use of Bibliographical Databases in Translation History." *Meta* 54(2): 264–78.

Pritchard, Alan. 1969. "Statistical Bibliography or Bibliometrics?" *Journal of Documentation* 25(4): 348–49.

Rovira-Esteva, Sara, and Pilar Orero. 2011. "A Contrastive Analysis of the Main Benchmarking Tools for Research Assessment in Translation and Interpreting: The Spanish Approach." *Perspectives* 19(3): 233–51.

Šajkevič, Anatolij J. A. 1992. "Bibliometric Analysis of 'Index Translationum'." *Meta* 37(1): 67–96.

Toury, Gideon. 2009. "Incubation, Birth and Growth. Observations on the First 20 years of *Target*." *Target* 21(1): 189–207.

Translation Studies Abstracts Online. Manchester: St. Jerome. Available at: www.stjerome.co.uk/tsa/ (last accessed October 16, 2014).

van Doorslaer, Luc. 2005. "The Indicative Power of a Key Word System: A Quantitative Analysis of the Key Words in the *Translation Studies Bibliography*." *Meta* 50(4) (on CD-ROM accompanying the volume).

——2014. "Knowledge Structuring in Translation Studies." *Innovative Infotechnologies for Science, Business and Education* 1(16): 22–5.

14 Case studies

Bernd Meyer

Definition

A case study is not a specific method but rather a research strategy (Yin 1981). Case studies investigate properties, actions, attitudes, and social structures of individuals, groups, or institutions by applying one or more methods, such as participant observation, interviews, and analysis of documents (Thomas 2010). Furthermore, case study research is characterized as an approach "that facilitates exploration of a phenomenon within its context using a variety of data sources" (Baxter and Jack 2008: 544). The philosophical background is a qualitative, constructivist paradigm, based on the claim that reality is socially constructed and can best be understood by exploring the tacit, i.e., experience-based, knowledge of individuals. Therefore, immersion and empathy are necessary conditions for case study research (Hammersley and Gomm 2000: 1; Stake 2000: 21; Baxter and Jack 2008: 545). Case studies are distinguished from other major types of social inquiry, such as experiments and survey studies, by their explorative nature, their use of various methods, and their bottom-up procedures (Hammersley and Gomm 2000: 2).

Although case studies aim at investigating a social phenomenon through the lenses of the involved actors, they nevertheless require some kind of prior categorization of the phenomenon. The previous identification and categorization of the phenomenon, or the case, distinguishes case studies from ethnographic research. There is always a broader, abstract, and more or less defined category that is applied to a specific, individual phenomenon, or a group of related phenomena. One could, for example, study different types of multilingual communication in German hospitals (i.e., categorized communicative practices) with reference to the concept of "inclusive multilingualism" (Backus et al. 2013). In this sense, "inclusive multilingualism" is taken as a defined concept, and the specific forms of multilingual communication (i.e., code-switching, interpreting, and translation) are labels for observable phenomena. Taking the concept of "inclusive multilingualism" as an example, one could study one hospital or more than one, or compare hospitals with other public service institutions, or compare German hospitals with Dutch clinics. In either case, the concept and its underpinnings create theoretical expectations, by which categorized phenomena are analyzed. Conversely, the concept itself is reflected and studied through the lenses of concrete and specific social phenomena, such as communicative practices in specific institutions. Thus, case studies do not have to be limited to individual cases. Rather, they may focus on a number of instances of a single case or even on different, though interrelated, cases. Furthermore, cases can be studied over time, or in relation to a specific historical moment—i.e., researchers may focus on developmental aspects in longitudinal projects—or they may be interested in the "here and now" of a specific social phenomenon.

Case studies aim at exploring a certain phenomenon or issue in depth. This leads researchers to limit the number and size of the cases under investigation. Another limitation is that case study research focuses on naturally occurring data, and therefore control of variables is not a major concern. The generalizability of results and observations is limited, and the primary goal is to develop an understanding of the case, and not the testing of theory-driven claims.

As case study data may come from a variety of sources, case studies are often, but not necessarily, based on different methods (mixed methods) and, as a consequence, different data sources. Yin (2012: 10) lists the following six common data sources: direct observations, interviews, archival records, documents, participant observation, and physical artifacts. For Translation and Interpreting Studies, additional sources may include source and target texts or transcriptions of authentic discourse (Meyer 1998).

Origins

Case study research originated in the social sciences. A major concern of case study research is to study a phenomenon within its social context. Thus, it is not just a technique (or set of techniques) but also an attitude that requires a willingness to come close to the object of inquiry. In this regard, it shares the features of other qualitative approaches in social and cultural sciences, such as Grounded Theory (Glaser and Strauss 1967), ethnomethodology (Garfinkel 1967/1984), and ethnography of communication (Hymes 1962), or interactional sociolinguistics (Gumperz 1982). Thus, the origins of qualitative research lie in an interest in social phenomena as embedded in and meaningful for a specific context. Therefore, Stake (2000: 21) positions case studies in an anti-positivist paradigm and argues that they aim at "perceptions and understanding that come from immersion in and holistic regard for the phenomena." In this sense, even outlier cases may be of interest because they allow insights into social realities that are otherwise not accessible and as yet unknown to the public and/or the scientific community. Although case study research does not follow the usual pattern of scientific reasoning, i.e., the formulation of theoretical claims and their empirical falsification, it may indeed lead to the revision of a concept or a claim if the study is able to demonstrate that the concept or theory makes false predictions. Single cases, i.e., one black swan, may provide enough evidence to demonstrate that strong claims, such as "all swans are white", are false (Popper 1934/1959).

Uses

In Translation and Interpreting Studies, many publications are based on case studies without explicit reference to the concept and the underlying presuppositions of case study research. Studies are rarely labeled as case studies, although individual authors or specific translations, translation strategies or translation processes are studied on the basis of naturalistic data and various non-experimental data sources. Research questions address interpreter roles in dialogue and simultaneous interpreting, effects of translation exercises on language acquisition, or the identification of ideological stance in different translations of the same source text. For examples of TIS studies that are labeled as case studies, see the following section.

Sample studies

Numerous studies in social sciences have the phrase "case study" in their titles without sharing the theoretical and methodological presuppositions of case study research. Rather, the notion "case studies" is used as a colloquial expression, referring to investigations that focus on an individual case. A brief and systematic description of how to do a case study in the terminological sense is Baxter and Jack (2008). Their text is especially helpful for novice researchers because it details the specific steps that should be taken in case study research. One important aspect highlighted in this paper is the prior categorization of the object of study, or "the case." According to Baxter and Jack, each case allows for specific research questions (2008: 546).

An example that illustrates the problem of case categorization is Yin's study on citizen patrols as a volunteer activity. As Yin (2012: 61) points out, citizen patrols are a social phenomenon that need to be defined and differentiated from similar activities, i.e., commercial security patrols or initiatives of shop owners. Thus, a case study on citizen patrols has to be based on prior analysis of the field, and it requires a definition of several similar, yet distinguishable activities.

Within TIS three studies are presented that have been explicitly labeled as case studies in their titles. The studies come from different frameworks and fields of investigation: Pöchhacker and Kadriç (1999) is a study on healthcare interpreting in a hospital in Vienna. The aim is to explore how the participation of ad hoc interpreters influences the course and content of a speech therapy session. Károly (2014) studies the effects of translation exercises on language learning, especially the development of awareness of textual norms and cultural backgrounds. Kuo and Nakamura (2005) compare different Chinese translations of an interview given in English by a Taiwanese political figure, which appeared in two Taiwanese newspapers. They apply Critical Discourse Analysis (CDA) to show how ideologies influence certain translational choices.

The Vienna study on healthcare interpreting starts with a look at statistical data to motivate the relevance of the study. Ad hoc interpreting was, and continues to be, the most widespread form of communication with non-German-speaking patients in Austrian and German hospitals. Although experts usually consider this type of interpreting to be problematic, few studies have been done to explore how such ad hoc interpreters (in this case, a female cleaner with Croatian as her heritage language) act in the therapeutic setting. The authors explain the data collection in detail, characterize the participants of the interaction, and even provide a visualization of the seating arrangement. The session plus parent briefing lasts about 47 minutes and each part of the session is briefly characterized and described. Then several excerpts from the session are presented together with detailed information about their temporal extension, i.e., start and end of each excerpt on the timeline.

The excerpts presented follow the course of the session, which starts with a greeting and welcome, followed by the session itself, the preparation of the patient for therapeutic exercises at home, and finally a briefing for the parents. For each section of the session, various excerpts illustrate typical problems of ad hoc interpreting in healthcare settings, such as the lack of continuous renditions and, conversely, the interpreters' intervention into the therapeutic process by providing comments and unauthorized information to the patient and his parents. Furthermore, the authors document conceptual and illocutionary shifts in the renditions, concluding that "the interpreter in many ways leaves the clients with both much less and much more than the therapists intended them to understand" (Pöchhacker and Kadriç 1999: 176). These observations corroborate the findings of other studies, as well as general concerns about ad hoc interpreting in hospitals. Finally, the authors assume that this study represents a typical case (177) and, furthermore, that it reveals the naïve approach of healthcare providers toward intercultural and multilingual communication. In contrast to typical case studies, this study does not approach the data from the perspective of the participants, but rather projects professional standards and concepts of interpreter performance onto the performance of an untrained interpreter. In this regard, it only partly follows the principle of creating a circular research process in which established categories are reflected and redefined by data analysis.

Károly (2014) argues for translation exercises and contrastive analyses of source and target texts as useful methods in foreign language teaching. The participants in the study are 12 Hungarian learners of English with little experience in translation. The aim of the study is to identify translation problems of novice students in order to orientate teachers in designing translation tasks. The theoretical framework is Nord's model of translation-oriented source text analysis (2005). Three texts are chosen for analysis: a commission press release, an answer given to a parliamentary question, and an online news report. All texts are extensively presented and their inherent properties are analyzed in order to single out the difficulties for the participants of the study. The author then presents the major translation problems encountered by the students. The analysis is based on their assignments, i.e., translations of the source texts into Hungarian. After the completion of the translation tasks, the author conducted semi-structured interviews with students to explore their individual problems in more detail.

The study reveals translation problems on various levels (lexical, syntactic, genre-related). Moreover, the post-translation interviews with the students show that they are more focused on lexical than on text-structural or syntactic properties of the source texts, and that they encountered several practical problems, such as access to and working with terminology databases. In addition, the interviews highlight the importance of background knowledge, i.e., the preparatory analysis of the source text in class, and the need for carefully planning the translation process. In general, the author claims that the "results of the research reported here, particularly the results of the interviews, seem to confirm the assumption that a functionalist approach, which is widely used in professional translator training, also has benefits in translation classes outside the professional context" (Károly 2014: 104). Furthermore, the author derives several practical recommendations from the study. For example, it is highlighted that students should read authentic parallel texts in the target language to develop a sense for genre-specific norms.

Unlike the Vienna study, this study is mainly motivated by theoretical assumptions about the translation process, and the theoretical framework is used to analyze the translations done by students and to categorize the problems they encountered. While the analysis of student translations and the overview of translation problems mainly confirm assumptions derived from the theoretical framework, the interviews with students reveal additional challenges, which have pedagogical implications. In this sense, the interviews are richer than the analyzed translations, as they reveal more about the students' view and go beyond illustrating theoretically motivated assumptions about the usefulness of translation exercises.

Kuo and Nakamura (2005) investigate an interview with Taiwan's former first lady, Wu Shu-chen. The interview was conducted in English, and Chinese translations of the English original appeared in two Taiwanese newspapers with opposing political orientations. The authors found several translational choices in the target texts which differed from one another. They argue that these differences are not arbitrary, but ideologically motivated. The authors use CDA as a framework and methodological tool to investigate "the relationship between language and ideology in media discourse" (Kuo and Nakamura 2005: 395) with regard to the different Chinese versions of the English source text. A typical CDA procedure to reveal power relations and ideological functions of media discourses is the comparison of different news reports and other media communications on the same event. This procedure serves as a model for the comparison of the two translations of one English interview, with the aim to identify ideologically motivated translational choices.

In the second section of their paper, the authors provide detailed information about the pre-history of the English interview of Wu Shu-chen, and on the historical-political background in which it took place. In the third section, the authors analyze different dimensions of the translated versions in comparison to the original text, such as deletions and additions, different lexical choices, and general text structures (paragraphs, headlines). In their conclusion, the authors state that "media institutions tend to construct reality in a manner congruent with their underlying ideological and political functions" (Kuo and Nakamura 2005: 411). This statement clearly shows that the study is primarily a case study on ideology in media discourse, and only secondarily one on media translation. From the viewpoint of Translation and Interpreting Studies, the process of producing the two versions and the decision-making processes of the translators involved would have been far more interesting than the fact that, for ideological or other reasons, two translations of the same source text exist. However, the study is typical in the sense that the notion of "case study" is applied here to an investigation of a single event, i.e., the translation of one interview.

Another example is Baraldi and Gavioli's (2012) volume on participation in dialogue interpreting in which several cases from authentic interactions are discussed. The chapters focus on the notion of "participation," i.e., the idea that dialogue interpreters are active participants who fulfill specific communicative tasks to keep the interaction going (Wadensjö 1998). Most of the authors in the volume base their claims or observations on transcriptions of interpreter-mediated conversations. Once again, however, the empirical cases presented in most chapters (including my own) mainly serve as illustrations of claims rather than as empirical anchors for scientific reasoning.

Conclusion and potential applications

The social sciences concept of "case study" is not widely used in Translation and Interpreting Studies, although it might be able to ameliorate and enrich studies in this field. Especially the non-normative stance, the application of mixed methods, and the interest in the views of participants (translators, interpreters, clients, institutional agents, etc.) have this potential, as many studies in the field of translation and interpreting are still biased by normative views about "good" translation, a lack of data triangulation, and an evaluative perspective on translators and interpreters. By adopting the analytical mentality of case study research, we may enhance our understanding of translation/interpreting processes and give a voice to the multitude of actors and practices in translation and interpreting.

Further reading

Gomm, Hammersley, and Foster (2000) is a collection of key methodological texts in case study research. The volume provides various chapters written by several authors on issues such as generalizability, or theoretical foundations of qualitative research in general and case studies in particular. Yin (2012) is a single-authored book on how to do case study research with some theoretical reflections and several examples from different fields. This book is of particular interest for novice researchers. It is focused and concisely written, which also makes it useful for teaching.

References

Backus, Ad, Durk Gorter, Karlfried Knapp, Rosita Schjerve-Rindler, Jos Swanenberg, Jan D. ten Thije, and Eva Vetter. 2013. "Inclusive Multilingualism: Concept, Modes and Implications." *European Journal of Applied Linguistics* 1(2): 179–215.

Baraldi, Claudio, and Laura Gavioli (eds.). 2012. *Coordinating Participation in Dialogue Interpreting*. Amsterdam: John Benjamins.

Baxter, Pamela, and Susan Jack. 2008. "Qualitative Case Study Methodology: Study Design and Implementation for Novice Researchers." *The Qualitative Report* 13(4): 544–59.

Garfinkel, Harold. 1967/1984. *Studies in Ethnomethodology*. Malden, MA: Polity Press/Blackwell Publishing.

Glaser, Barney G., and Anselm Strauss. 1967. *Discovery of Grounded Theory. Strategies for Qualitative Research*. New Brunswick, NJ: Aldine Transaction.

Gomm, Roger, Martyn Hammersley, and Peter Foster (eds.). 2000. *Case Study Method. Key Issues, Key Texts*. London: SAGE Publications.

Gumperz, John J. 1982. *Discourse Strategies*. "Studies in Interactional Sociolinguistics I." Cambridge: Cambridge University Press.

Hammersley, Martyn, and Roger Gomm. 2000. "Introduction." In *Case Study Method. Key Issues, Key Texts*, Roger Gomm, Martyn Hammersley, and Peter Foster (eds.), 1–16. London: SAGE Publications.

Hymes, Dell. 1962. "The Ethnography of Speaking." In *Anthropology and Human Behavior* 13(53): 11–74.

Károly, Adrienn. 2014. "Translation in Foreign Language Teaching: A Case Study from a Functional Perspective." *Linguistics and Education* 25: 90–107.

Kuo, Sai-Hua, and Mari Nakamura. 2005. "Translation or Transformation? A Case Study of Language and Ideology in the Taiwanese Press. *Discourse & Society* 16(3): 393–417.

Meyer, Bernd. 1998. "What Transcriptions of Authentic Discourse Can Reveal about Interpreting." *Interpreting* 3(1): 65–83.

Nord, Christiane. 2005. *Text Analysis in Translation: Theory, Methodology, and Didactic Application of a Model for Translation-oriented Text Analysis*. 2nd edition. Amsterdam: Rodopi.

Pöchhacker, Franz, and Mira Kadric. 1999. "The Hospital Cleaner as Healthcare Interpreter: A Case Study." *The Translator* 5(2): 161–78.

Popper, Karl. 1934/1959. *The Logic of Scientific Discovery*. London: Hutchinson.

Stake, Robert E. 2000. "The Case Study Method in Social Inquiry." In *Case Study Method. Key Issues, Key Texts*, Roger Gomm, Martyn Hammersley, and Peter Foster (eds.), 19–26. London: SAGE Publications.

Thomas, Gary. 2010. *How to Do Your Case Study: A Guide for Students and Researchers.* Thousand Oaks, CA: SAGE Publications.

Wadensjö, Cecilia. 1998. *Interpreting as Interaction.* London and New York: Longman.

Yin, Robert K. 1981. "The Case Study as a Serious Research Strategy." *Science Communication* 3: 97–114.

——2012. *Applications of Case Study Research.* Thousand Oaks, CA: SAGE Publications.

15 Conversation analysis

Laura Gavioli

Definition and origins

Conversation Analysis (CA) is a theoretical-methodological approach that was developed in the 1960s–1970s by the US sociologist Harvey Sacks (1964–72/1995) and first conceptualized in a joint work by Sacks et al. (1974). In this seminal paper, the authors postulate that conversation is based on a regulated system that orients participants' contributions to talk. The system is called "turn-taking system" and is organized so that each turn makes relevant a series of actions and reactions, by particular speakers, at a precise moment in talk. The CA approach is based on: (1) a set of orienting theoretical principles; and (2) naturally occurring interactional data.

Theoretical principles

CA is based on the view that talk is an interactional construction and that participants are seen as mutually orienting to and collaborating in the achievement of orderly and meaningful communication (Hutchby and Wooffitt 2008: 1). In contributing to the turn-taking system, interlocutors project next actions and react to previous actions. In so doing, they display their understanding of each other's contributions and their rights to contribute accordingly.

For instance, when asking a question, participants not only accomplish the function of asking, but they also project the next relevant actions, e.g., answering. In replying to a question, then, the next participant not only provides the answer (or evidence that s/he cannot provide it) but also displays understanding (or non-understanding) that what was uttered was in fact a question (and not, for example, a comment or an invitation) and that s/he can (or cannot) provide the answer. Let's take the following short conversation extract as an example:

1. Mother: Do you know who's going to that meeting?
2. Russ: Who?
3. Mother: I don't know!

4. Russ: Ouh: prob'ly: Mr. Murphy an' Dad said prob'ly Mrs. Timpte en some of the teachers.

(Hutchby and Wooffitt 2008: 14)

Here, mother's question in turn 1 projects an answer by Russ. Russ' reaction displays a different understanding of mom's contribution. By asking "Who?" Russ shows that he took mom's turn as a pre-announcement, something like "guess who." The participants' contributions in turns 3 and 4 display the occurring misunderstanding. So by contributing in the system of turns, participants negotiate their contributions as relevant to the meanings and functions that are constructed in talk sequences.

Interaction sequences not only make particular actions relevant in talk, they also construct and display participants' assumptions. Russ' question "Who?" not only accomplishes the function of asking but also displays Russ' assumption that his mother is the "one who knows" and attributes to her the right to display such knowledge. By saying "I don't know," mother not only makes it clear that her question was a real question but also shows that Russ' assumption was wrong. So, sequential contributions display participants' assumptions about each other's rights to display knowledge, a notion that CA analysts call "epistemics" (Heritage 2013). This notion is relevant in accounting for participants' relations (like the mother–son relation in the example above) and has been found to be important in explaining mechanisms of institutional interaction, e.g., in doctor–patient talk (Heritage 2012).

CA data and the transcription method

One of the basic characteristics of the CA method is that it deals with naturally occurring video- or audio-recorded interactions. By looking at recordings of authentic sequences of talk, Sacks et al. (1974) noted that monolingual conversation takes place in coordinated turns, normally with few gaps and overlaps. Interestingly enough, when gaps or overlaps do occur, they have a function. For instance, a gap in taking the next turn may signal hesitation (meaning "I don't know" or "it is difficult to say"). Or a next speaker may intervene before the previous speaker's completion, signaling, for example, that the interlocutor's point is clear enough and that there is no need to add details. CA has thus made clear that there are a number of apparently insignificant small items in conversation, like pauses, overlaps, "mhms" and other backchannel signals, laughter, breath intakes, nodding, gazes, whispers or loud voiced utterances, that are in fact of utmost significance in shaping the meaning of the interlocutors' contributions and in achieving coordination. Pauses may indicate the current speaker's hesitation to speak and may invite the next speaker to take the turn, backchannel may show interest in what the interlocutor is saying, allowing him or her to go on speaking, and "oh" may indicate the receipt of new information (Heritage 1984).

On this basis, CA has developed a particular method of transcription (Jefferson 1978; Psathas and Anderson 1990) that highlights the coordinating features of the turn-taking system. The basic characteristic of this transcription method is that it shows the participants' turn exchange (as in theater or film scripts) with a number of symbols representing sound (pauses, overlaps, sound lengthening, sounds cut short, voice volume or stress, backchannel, intonation) or kinesics (gaze, posture, gestures). In the sequence shown above, for instance, the transcript shows: (1) the utterances produced by Russ and those produced by mother, organized in 4 turns; (2) questioning (?), exclamatory (!) and falling (.) intonation at the end of turns 1–2, 3 and 4, respectively; (3) the "Oh" sound and its lengthening (:) at the beginning of turn 4; and (4) sound ellipsis in the pronunciation of some words ("prob'ly").

Models

Dialogue interpreting, like public-service/community, talk show or business interpreting, involves at least three participants speaking in turns and can thus be analyzed, in CA terms, as a system of turn-taking. The first and most influential study to look at dialogue interpreting as a turn-taking system is Wadensjö (1998). On the basis of recorded and transcribed conversations involving interpreters in Swedish institutional settings, Wadensjö shows that interpreters' renditions are provided as interpretative (re)actions, making the function of the interlocutors' contribution clear in the interaction. She distinguishes between two highly interdependent interpreters' activities: translating and coordinating. While interpreters normally take their turn translating their interlocutors' utterances, such utterances are part of an interactional system that needs to be continually re-established in order for communication to be achieved. Coordination is the activity through which interpreters "interpret" what is going on in talk and make sense of it for their interlocutors. Coordination can be accomplished as part of the rendition work or through explicitly coordinating interpreters' actions. Renditions can be expanded or substituted in order to clarify the meaning of an answer in relation to the question posed or to specify persons, times, objects, and places indicated by words like "it," "then," and "there" (Wadensjö 1998: 146). Interpreters' explicit requests like "what do you mean exactly?" or "did you hear me?" similarly make the function of utterances (including the interpreter's) clear in talk.

In a thorough reflection on models for constructing talk in interpreted discourse, Davidson (2002) highlights two characteristic features of talk through which participants make sense of theirs and their interlocutors' contributions within the system of turn-taking: (1) participants, speaking or listening, are equally engaged in the ongoing process of constructing conversational meaning; and (2) one must be a participant in the discourse itself in order to negotiate and capture the meaning of an utterance produced within an ongoing discourse. Davidson argues that the actual system of conversation is such that, in order for communication to take place, participants need to achieve reciprocity and construct shared ground. He shows that the common difficulty in conversing through an interpreter is based largely on the difficulty of establishing reciprocity of understanding between the primary interlocutors in discourse (2002: 1274–75) and that models need to be developed for interpreted discourse that take the necessity of constructing reciprocity into account.

Sample studies

Recent studies looking at dialogue interpreting "as interaction" have highlighted a number of ways in which reciprocity, in Davidson's terms, is achieved in interpreter-mediated talk. In an analysis of history-taking sequences involving doctors, patients, and interpreters, Bolden (2000) shows that interpreters' actions are primarily structured by their understanding of the ongoing activity and only secondarily by the task of translation. Similarly to Wadensjö, Bolden notes that in order to make sense of what is said, interpreters' contributions (renditional and non-renditional) are oriented toward the particular activity the participants are engaged in. In history-taking sequences of medical interactions, for instance, rendition of a doctor's question rarely receives a straightforward, complete answer by the patient, and interpreters engage in talk with the patients to elicit details relevant to the doctor's diagnosis.

In line with Davidson's suggestion that monolingual talk can be used in interpreter-mediated interaction with the coordinative function of achieving reciprocity in the turn-taking mechanism, a number of studies have investigated dyadic talk sequences of interaction in these triadic conversations. Looking at interpreter-mediated talk in healthcare, for instance, Pasquandrea (2011) has shown that interpreter's engagement in talk with one of the interlocutors is functional, aimed at providing details useful for diagnosis and therapy; Englund Dimitrova (1997) has suggested that interpreters may need to elicit talk from very hesitating or silent patients; Angelelli (2012) has looked at ways in which interpreters can help patients cope with specific medical routines, like expressing the intensity of the pain they feel by using a medical pain scale; Baraldi (2012) has noted that dyadic sequences promote dialogue, encourage and facilitate the patients' participation, and thus empower them; Gavioli (2012) has described ways in which interpreters' minimal responses regulate the shift from dyadic to triadic sequences and back, negotiating the relevance of dyadic or triadic talk in order to achieve particular functions in the interaction.

Disadvantages and risks of engagement in dyadic talk have also been pointed out. Davidson (2000), for instance, has underscored the gatekeeping function interpreters might assume and the filter they exercise in letting information pass through in talk. While some filtering function of the interpreter may facilitate the achievement of reciprocal understanding, it may also impede the sharing of some information. Bolden (2000), for instance, shows that stories of the patients' "lifeworld" are often cut or heavily reduced in rendition since they are considered non-fundamental information in medical interaction.

Similarly, Keselman et al. (2010) suggest that interpreters' gatekeeping may exclude one of the interlocutors from talk, distort their contributions, and even discredit them.

CA studies of interpreter-mediated interaction have shown that, in carrying out their interpreting activity, interpreters systematically orient themselves toward the goals of the interaction. Davitti (2013), for example, focuses on interpreter-mediated parent-teacher meetings in schools. In the increasingly frequent case of immigrant children in European schools, these meetings may be crucial in establishing collaboration between teachers and families. While children's non-appropriate behavior is often a topic in such meetings and sanctions are discussed, teachers' talk seeks to maintain openness and proximity toward the interlocutors. In order to carry out this complex task, interpreters tend to upgrade the teachers' evaluative assessments so as to balance reports of a child's behaviour with recommendations on how to improve it. These sometimes take the form of independently produced evaluations from the interpreter: in this way, interpreters contribute to supporting what seem to be primary functions in these interactions, i.e., reporting, recommending, and also reassuring.

Straniero Sergio (1999, 2012) concentrates on interpreter-mediated conversations in talk shows, where popular guests speak with a host and other guests in TV studios. Straniero Sergio highlights the fact that in this setting participants, including the interpreter, make sense of each other's contributions by shaping them in relation to the necessity of: (1) promoting the interest of the audience in the invited guests, and (2) entertaining the audience. The interpreters' renditions in talk shows are often made into an object of discussion, clarification, and even fun when talk show hosts correct, provide alternatives, or challenge interpreters. Providing opportunities for clarifying particularly complex, possibly culture-specific, items such instances, when translated for the public, can produce humor or general entertainment.

In addition to the works quoted in the section on CA in T&I Studies, Van der Mierhoop et al. (2012) provide an interesting account of interpreter-mediated interaction in a rest home in Belgium, and Zorzi (2012), on the distribution of the right to provide assessments in medical interpreter-mediated talk. The CA method has also been applied to analyses of informal interpreting activity in conversations carried out by "improvised" interpreters to help participants of different languages understand each other. While the focus of this work is on interpreting as a resource for understanding, rather than as a professional activity, some papers may provide useful suggestions for studying the management of translation in bilingual/plurilingual talk, e.g. Bolden (2012); Traverso (2012), and Merlino (2014).

New directions

The studies dealt with above make it clear that interpreter-mediated interaction is a locally organized, socially situated activity. In order to make sense of what is going on in talk, interpreters orient themselves toward the primary functions of the interaction and explicate them to the interlocutors. This implies that the notion of the interpreter as "a conduit" (Roy 1993/2002, after Reddy 1979) or as "invisible" is not tenable in face-to-face interaction (Angelelli 2004; Böser 2013). This has, in its turn, a series of consequences, among which I shall mention three. First, traditional models of dialogue interpreting are challenged. In particular, the idea that interpreters interpret "after each participants' turn" seems to clash with the ability of interpreters "to interpret" what is going on in the interaction. For example, Wadensjö (1998) highlighted the limitations of looking at utterances as "text" since this may cause the contextual chain of actions that gives meaning to single textual utterances to be ignored. Davidson (2002) showed that turn-by-turn renditions that mirror the previous turns may actually impede the construction of reciprocity; similar findings are reported in Metzger (1999). Therefore, more complex models that take into account the necessity of coordinating, in addition to translating, talk are increasingly used in T&I research.

Second, interactional perspectives, such as CA, reinterpret the notion of "interpreting," moving from an essentially cognitive framework toward a more socially constructed, communicative one. Interaction-based studies argue for the need to look at interpreting as a situated, locally organized activity embedded in particular settings since such context gives sense to the participants' actions. As no rendition can be provided without understanding the communication process and interpreting it, interpreters "cannot not participate" in talk (Pöchhacker 2012: 50). It is their participation which allows them to produce meaningful utterances that elicit or provide the intended response from the interlocutors.

Third, the notion of translation "closeness" or equivalence may need to be redefined. In a pragmatic perspective, semantic-structural models may not suffice to account for functional equivalence, and, in some contexts, apparently distant semantic equivalents may be found to be suitable translation pairs. For instance, "yes" can substitute for "no" to confirm a negatively framed question in some languages (see Wadensjö 1998: 23), or the interpreter can capture the meaning of a series of turns summarizing their sense in a single-turn rendition (see Pasquandrea 2011: 459). Functional equivalents may be even more complex and may involve expansion and adaptation to the participants' (contextual) assumptions (see Mason 2006) referring to people, places, or routines. Traditional notions of "formal" translation equivalence are problematized insofar as formal equivalence may not produce equivalence in meaning.

Two applications of the CA method should probably be mentioned here. The first has to do with research, the second with the interpreting profession. As mentioned above, an important feature of CA is that it is based on naturally occurring data, recorded and transcribed. Data analysis is a method that can be applied to a variety of problems in T&I Studies. Transcribed data allow researchers to observe types of renditions used in different settings and for different functions or to compare perceptions about the interlocutors' activities (collected, for example, through interviews) and the actual talk occurrences.

They can inform not only CA-based research but also research on cognitive and social processes in interpreting or research on translation universals.

The second application involves interpreter professionalism, in two respects. The first concerns interpreters' education. Interaction-oriented research has shown that "responding" as participants in talk, interpreters engage in closer collaboration with service providers, co-constructing with them the sense and function of the interaction, and so have suggested that such collaboration can improve services (Turner 2004). Moreover, research based on collections of data in "training" and "real" settings has been used to inform the production of teaching materials and to improve methods for interpreter education and training (Niemants 2013). Studies exploring CA (-derived) methods in interpreter training are rapidly increasing (see Davitti and Pasquandrea 2014), and their impact on interpreter education and training is likely to be felt in the near future.

The second respect concerns the design of codes of ethics. Few studies discuss possible changes to codes of ethics deriving from data-based research (Angelelli 2007; Tebble 2012). Description of what occurs in data does not imply that codes of ethics should take that description as a model of what interpreters *should* do; rather, data can facilitate the design of more informed codes of ethics. Up until now, debates have centered more on whether the recorded interpreters represent reliable models (Martinsen and Dubslaff 2010) than on how to actually translate data-derived descriptions into possible guidelines. Developments along these lines seem worth exploring.

Further reading

Heritage (2008) provides a concise discussion of the main principles and concepts used in CA and their importance in explaining how communication works from an interactional perspective. Heritage and Clayman (2010) offers an account of CA in institutional settings, such as emergency calls, healthcare, court, and news interviews. While analyses concern monolingual interaction in English, they may provide a useful methodological reference. Ten Have (1999), together with Hutchby and Wooffitt (2008) mentioned above, offers a comprehensive manual illustrating basic methods of CA, step by step.

References

Angelelli, Claudia. 2004. *Medical Interpreting and Cross-cultural Communication*. Cambridge: Cambridge University Press.

——2007 "Validating Professional Standards and Codes: Challenges and Opportunities." *Interpreting* 8(2): 175–93.

——2012. "Challenges in Interpreters' Coordination of the Construction of Pain." In *Coordinating Participation in Dialogue Interpreting*, Claudio Baraldi and Laura Gavioli (eds.), 251–68. Amsterdam and Philadelphia: John Benjamins.

Baraldi, Claudio. 2012. "Interpreting as Dialogic Mediation: The Relevance of Expansions." In *Coordinating Participation in Dialogue Interpreting*, Claudio Baraldi and Laura Gavioli (eds.), 297–326. Amsterdam and Philadelphia: John Benjamins.

Bolden, Galina. 2000. "Toward Understanding Practices of Medical Interpreting: Interpreters' Involvement in History Taking." *Discourse Studies* 2(4): 387–419.

——2012. "Across Languages and Cultures: Brokering Problems of Understanding in Conversational Repair." *Language in Society* 41: 97–121.

Böser, Ursula. 2013. "'So Tell Me What happened!' Interpreting the Free Recall Segment of the Investigative Interview." *Translation and Interpreting Studies* 8(1): 112–36.

Davidson, Brad. 2000. "The Interpreter as Institutional Gatekeeper: The Social-linguistic Role of Interpreters in Spanish-English Medical Discourse." *Journal of Sociolinguistics* 4(3): 379–405.

——2002. "A Model for the Construction of Conversational Common Ground in Interpreted Discourse." *Journal of Pragmatics* 34: 1273–300.

Davitti, Elena. 2013. "Dialogue Interpreting as Intercultural Mediation: Interpreter's Use of Upgrading Moves in Parent-teacher Meetings." *Interpreting* 15(2): 168–99.

Davitti, Elena, and Sergio Pasquandrea (eds.). 2014. "Dialogue Interpreting in Practice: Filling the Gap between Empirical Research and Interpreter Training." Special issue. *The Interpreter and Translator Trainer* 8(2).

Englund Dimitrova, Birgitta. 1997. "Degree of Interpreter Responsibility in the Interaction Process in Community Interpreting." In *The Critical Link: Interpreters in the Community*, Silvana Carr, Roda Roberts, Aideen Dufour, and Dini Steyn (eds.), 147–64. Amsterdam: John Benjamins.

Gavioli, Laura. 2012. "Minimal Responses in Interpreter-mediated Medical Talk." In *Coordinating Participation in Dialogue Interpreting*, Claudio Baraldi and Laura Gavioli (eds.), 201–28. Amsterdam and Philadelphia: John Benjamins.

Heritage, John. 1984. "A Change-of-State Token and Aspects of Its Sequential Placement." In *Structures of Social Action*, J. Maxwell Atkinson and John Heritage (eds.), 299–345. Cambridge: Cambridge University Press.

——2008. "Conversation Analysis as Social Theory." In *The New Blackwell Companion to Social Theory*, Bryan Turner (ed.), 300–20. Oxford: Blackwell.

——2012. "Epistemics in Action: Action Formation and Territories of Knowledge." *Research on Language and Social Interaction* 45: 1–29.

——2013. "Action Formation and its Epistemic (and Other) Backgrounds." *Discourse Studies* 15: 547–74.

Heritage, John, and Steven Clayman. 2010. *Talk in Action: Interactions, Identities and Institutions.* Oxford: Blackwell.

Hutchby, Ian, and Robin Wooffitt. 2008. *Conversation Analysis.* Cambridge: Polity Press.

Jefferson, Gail. 1978. "Explanation of Transcript Notation." In *Studies in the Organization of Conversational Interaction*, Jim Schenkein (ed.), xii–xvi. New York: Academic Press.

Keselman, Olga, Ann-Christin Cederborg, and Per Linell. 2010. "'That Is Not Necessary for You to Know!' Negotiation of Participation Status of Unaccompanied Children in Interpreter-mediated Asylum Hearings." *Interpreting* 12(1): 83–104.

Martinsen, Bodil, and Friedel Dubslaff. 2010. "The Cooperative Courtroom: A Case Study of Interpreting Gone Wrong." *Interpreting* 12(1): 21–59.

Mason, Ian. 2006. "On Mutual Accessibility of Contextual Assumptions in Dialogue Interpreting." *Journal of Pragmatics* 38: 359–73.

Merlino, Sara. 2014. "Traduction orale et organisation de la parole: la gestion multimodale des transitions." In *Corps en interaction: participation, spatialité, mobilité*, Lorenza Mondada (ed.), 65–105. Lyon: ENS editions.

Metzger, Melanie. 1999. *Sign Language Interpreting: Deconstructing the Myth of Neutrality*. Washington DC: Gallaudet University Press.

Niemants, Natacha. 2013. "From Role-playing to Role-taking: Interpreter role(s) in Healthcare." In *Interpreting in a Changing Landscape*, Christina Schäffner, Krzysztof Kredens, and Yvonne Fowler (eds.), 305–20. Amsterdam and Philadelphia: John Benjamins.

Pasquandrea, Sergio. 2011. "Managing Multiple Actions through Multimodality: Doctors' Involvement in Interpreter-mediated Interactions." *Language in Society* 40: 455–81.

Pöchhacker, Franz. 2012. "Interpreting Participation: Conceptual Analysis and Illustration of the Interpreter's Role in Interaction." In *Coordinating Participation in Dialogue Interpreting*, Claudio Baraldi and Laura Gavioli (eds.), 45–70. Amsterdam and Philadelphia: John Benjamins.

Psathas, George, and Timothy Anderson. 1990. "The Practices of Transcription in Conversation Analysis." *Semiotica* 78(1/2): 75–99.

Reddy, Michael J. 1979. "The Conduit Metaphor–A Case of Frame Conflict in our Language about Language." In *Metaphor and Thought*, A. Ortony (ed.), 284–97. Cambridge: Cambridge University Press.

Roy, Cynthia. 1993/2002. "The Problem with Definitions, Descriptions and the Role Metaphors of Interpreters." In *The Interpreting Studies Reader*, Franz Pöchhacker and Miriam Shlesinger (eds.), 345–53. London and New York: Routledge.

Sacks, Harvey. 1964–72/1995. *Lectures on Conversation*, G. Jefferson (ed.). Oxford: Blackwell.

Sacks, Harvey, Emanuel Schegloff, and Gail Jefferson. 1974. "A Simplest Systematics for the Organization of Turn-taking for Conversation." *Language* 50: 696–736.

Straniero Sergio, Francesco. 1999. "The Interpreter on the (Talk) Show: Interaction and Participation Frameworks." Special issue. *The Translator* 5(2): 303–26.

——2012. "'You Are Not Too Funny': Challenging the Role of the Interpreter on Italian Talkshows." In *Coordinating Participation in Dialogue Interpreting*, Claudio Baraldi and Laura Gavioli (eds.), 71–98. Amsterdam and Philadelphia: John Benjamins.

Tebble, Helen. 2012. "'Interpreting or Interfering?'" In *Coordinating Participation in Dialogue Interpreting*, Claudio Baraldi and Laura Gavioli (eds.), 23–44. Amsterdam and Philadelphia: John Benjamins.

Ten Have, Paul. 1999. *Doing Conversation Analysis*. London: SAGE Publications.

Traverso, Veronique. 2012. "Ad-hoc Interpreting in Multilingual Work Meetings: Who Translates for Whom?" In *Coordinating Participation in Dialogue Interpreting*, Claudio Baraldi and Laura Gavioli (eds.), 149–76. Amsterdam and Philadelphia: John Benjamins.

Turner, Graham. 2004. "Professionalization of Interpreting *with* the Community: Refining the Model." In *The Critical Link 4*, Cecilia Wadensjö, Birgitta Englund Dimitrova, and Anna-Lena Nilsson (eds.), 181–92. Amsterdam and Philadelphia: John Benjamins.

Van der Mierhoop, Dorien, Giovanni Bevilacqua, and Lotte van Hove. 2012. "Negotiating Discursive Norms: Community Interpreting in a Belgian Rest Home." *Interpreting* 14(1): 23–54.

Wadensjö, Cecilia. 1998. *Interpreting as Interaction*. London: Longman.

Zorzi, Daniela. 2012. "Mediating Assessments in Healthcare Settings." In *Coordinating Participation in Dialogue Interpreting*, Claudio Baraldi and Laura Gavioli (eds.), 229–50. Amsterdam and Philadelphia: John Benjamins.

16 Corpus-based studies

Leonardo Giannossa

Definition

Corpus linguistics studies language use by means of collections of texts selected according to specific criteria and ad hoc tools designed for textual analysis. As pointed out by Bennett (2010: 2), corpus linguistics attempts to identify patterns associated with specific lexico-grammatical features and to understand how said patterns vary within language varieties and registers.

McEnery and Wilson (2001) make a distinction between early and modern corpus linguistics, the former going back to the late 1800s/early 1900s and the latter dating to the 1960s or, generally speaking, the second half of the twentieth century. Harris (1993: 27), with reference to early corpus linguistics, defines the approach used by the structuralist theorists of the time as one that began "with a large collection of recorded utterances from some language, a corpus. The corpus was subjected to a clear, stepwise, bottom-up strategy of analysis." In this context, corpora were used to study (1) language acquisition (Preyer 1889; Stern 1924); (2) spelling conventions (Käding 1897); (3) language pedagogy (Fries and Traver 1940; Bongers 1947); (4) comparative linguistics (Eaton 1940); and (5) syntax and semantics (Lorge 1949; Fries 1952). Modern corpus linguistics, on the other hand, began in the 1960s mainly as a result of advancements in technology and the advent of "first generation" machine-readable corpora.

That being said, the definition of corpus linguistics is still vague, as Taylor (2008) points out in her article "What Is Corpus Linguistics? What the Data Says." The problem is that scholars are split on whether to consider corpus linguistics a discipline or a methodology. Tognini-Bonelli (2001: 1), for example, argues that it has become an independent discipline because it "goes well beyond this purely methodological role," whereas McEnery, Xiao, and Tono (2006) maintain that it is a methodology. Indeed, they point out that, unlike phonetics, semantics, or pragmatics, which are all branches of linguistics describing a particular aspect of language use, corpus linguistics "is not restricted to a particular aspect of language. Rather, it can be employed to explore almost any area of linguistic research" (2006: 7). It is the possibility of using corpus linguistics to investigate disparate aspects and uses of a language that makes it a methodology. Viewed in these terms, it is not difficult to imagine how corpus-linguistics soon found its place in Translation and Interpreting Studies.

According to Biber, Conrad, and Reppen (2000), corpus-based analysis has four fundamental features: (1) it is empirical, in that it is used to investigate actual instances of language use/discourse as they naturally occur in real life; (2) it makes use of large collections of texts, which contributes to the representativeness of the corpus, thus making it possible for findings and results to be generalized; (3) it involves the use of computers and corpus analysis tools, such as WordSmith Tools and ParaConc, which allow linguistic and textual patterns to be isolated; and (4) it is based on both qualitative and quantitative techniques, although the quantitative analysis that is carried out is often confined to a "subjective" interpretation of corpus tool data and does not always take advantage of statistical analysis.

Origins

When it comes to modern corpus linguistics, Father Roberto Busa and Alphonse Juilland may be considered the "founding fathers" of this methodology. Busa was the first to create an electronic corpus of medieval philosophical texts, which he examined through a computer concordancer developed with the help of IBM (McEnery and Wilson 2001: 20). The use of a concordancer enabled him to more easily retrieve all the instances of the preposition *in*, which was the object of his study. Busa started this project in 1949 and ended it in 1967, having collected a corpus of 10,600,000 words in Italian, as well as 5,000,000 words in other languages, such as German, Russian, and Aramaic (2001: 20). Along the same lines was Juilland's ambitious project of building 500,000 word corpora in several languages to perform a contrastive analysis of the languages represented in them (McEnery and Wilson 2001: 21). His project was pioneering in that he made use of sampling and analysis techniques that nowadays form part of corpus linguistics methodology. For example, in gathering the texts for his corpus he sampled several text-types, making sure to select different authors for each text-type (2001: 21). This is an important selection criterion in that it helps avoid idiosyncrasy. He also made use of a more rudimentary form of the annotation that is still often employed in T&I corpus-based studies today in the form of XML tagging, which makes the retrieval of linguistic, discourse, and translation patterns easier. Last but not least, another important feature of Juilland's corpus analysis approach was the investigation of the dispersion of words (meaning the even or uneven distribution of words throughout a text) across both text-types and languages (2001: 21), which, unlike concordances, can tell us whether a certain word is peculiar to a particular text or language variety. In Translation Studies, terminology research has been one area of inquiry that has benefited from this corpus-analysis technique, which allows researchers to extract terms that not only have a high frequency of occurrence in a given domain but also have a consistent and regular use in that domain.

In developing their projects, neither Busa nor Juilland was concerned with the English language; corpus-based studies in the Anglophone world and in the English language go back to the early 1960s when Quirk started the construction of his *Survey of English Usage* and Francis and Kocera began working on the *Brown Corpus*, which took almost two decades to complete (McEnery and Wilson 2001: 23). The largest corpus project in the English language, however, was the one undertaken at Birmingham University in the 1980s by John Sinclair, who built the first learner's corpus and investigated the meanings, collocations, registers, class words, and pragmatic uses of lexical items through the use of concordance lines (Kruger 2002: 72). In his seminal work *Corpus, Concordance, Collocation*, Sinclair (1991) emphasizes the need for a systematic, objective, and evidence-based approach to the study of language. One of the main points made in this book is that sense and structure are intertwined in such a way that the meaning of each word can be associated with a particular structure or collocational pattern. Furthermore, Sinclair put forward some useful, and still used, criteria for corpus gathering, which include text-type, register, subject-field, as well as the age, gender, and nationality of the author (1991: 20).

Sinclair was also the first to carry out computer research on collocations, defined by Firth in 1957 as "actual words in habitual company" (1957: 14) and then further developed by Halliday and Hasan (1976: 284), who refer to collocation as "cohesion that is achieved through the association of lexical items that regularly co-occur." While Firth conceived of collocations as adjacent items co-occurring in a limited stretch of text, Halliday and Hasan's definition takes the macrotextual level into consideration: they defined collocation as referring to lexical items that co-occurred together but not necessarily one next to the other as long as they contributed to the unity of discourse. In language pedagogy, machine-readable corpora were used to carry out research on collocations and other data, both in the construction of language grammars, such as Collins' *Cobuild Basic Grammar*, and to improve foreign language teaching and learning (Kruger 2002: 73). Collocations are today used in Translation Studies for terminology extraction and in translator education.

The above-mentioned corpus selection criteria, along with analysis techniques, such as frequency lists, concordances, collocations, and annotation, have all been used in Translation Studies, providing a methodology and tools for the investigation of research hypotheses in the various areas of research conducted in Descriptive and Applied Translation Studies.

Uses

As far as Descriptive Translation Studies is concerned, corpora have been used to study: (1) translationese (which refers to cases where the target language is affected by the source language); (2) translation universals (features characterizing all translated texts regardless of language directionality and language pair); (3) translation style (linguistic choices that can be easily attributed to a translator across a wide range of his/her translations); (4) translation norms (which like translation universals are not attributable to a singular translator but rather to a specific sociocultural and historical context); and (5) the influence that language and translation mutually have on each other (Zanettin 2013: 21). In addition to these five areas of inquiry, Laviosa (2011) mentions translation ideology, which could be regarded as a sixth area.

As far as Applied Translation Studies (ATS) is concerned, corpora are used in translation classrooms for pedagogical purposes. In this respect, three main areas of inquiry in ATS can be identified: (1) translation training for terminological mining as well as for examining and evaluating equivalents from a stylistic and collocational point of view; (2) subject-field knowledge acquisition; and (3) translation assessment (Laviosa 2011: 24–25).

Though most corpus-based studies in T&I are characterized by the four fundamental features of corpus analysis described in the first section of this chapter, their findings are not always substantiated by statistical significance, which helps corroborate research hypotheses and make data interpretation more objective, thus guaranteeing the replicability of the studies.

Sample studies

In 1995, Stubbs wrote a paper on the investigation of collocation through a corpus-based approach, emphasizing how corpora, unlike dictionaries, can help scholars establish whether a certain node or search word is frequent or typical in a given language, genre, or register. Stubbs (1995) points out that when dealing with instances or patterns retrieved from a corpus analysis tool, the dilemma a researcher often confronts is deciding whether such raw data is meaningful or significant. The author indicates two measures, namely mutual information and t-scores, which have been used to determin whether co-occurrence of words is noteworthy. As far as his study is concerned, Stubbs (1995) sets out to investigate the semantic prosody of certain words by means of a quantitative approach, which, besides looking at raw data, takes into consideration the statistical significance of his results through the computation of I-values and t-scores. The corpus he uses to retrieve this data is the Cobuild Corpus, whose size (120 million words) is big enough to allow him to retrieve as many collocations of a search word as possible. Though there is much emphasis on the use of inferential analysis when interpreting the raw data retrieved from corpora, Stubbs (1995) also argues that even when statistical analysis does not return significant results, the raw data still remains linguistically interesting.

Another interesting study in corpus linguistics that makes use of statistical analysis when interpreting corpus-driven data is Biber, Conrad, Reppen, and Byrd (2002). The premise of their study was that research on academic discourse had until then ignored spoken registers. To help uncover the linguistic features of unexplored academic registers, they designed the TOEFL 2000 Spoken and Written Academic Language Corpus, which encompassed, as they claim, all the written and spoken registers that students may encounter in US university contexts (Biber et al. 2002: 11). In compiling this corpus of 2.7 million words, they first recorded and then transcribed conversations in different university contexts involving students, faculty, and staff and sampled textbooks and lectures from six different academic disciplines. All material was then coded with a header identifying the content area and the register and was grammatically annotated (2002: 22). To investigate the quantitative distribution of linguistic features across texts and text-types, they used multidimensional analysis featuring five dimensions, each consisting of groups of linguistic features that co-occurred with a high frequency. Though no mention of the statistical and corpus analysis tool is made in the article, their methodology is highly meticulous and once again points to the need to use statistical analysis when interpreting corpus-driven data.

Going back to the topic of collocations, McCarthy and Carter (2002/2004) use a corpus-based methodology to study those multiword strings which, though lacking semantic and syntactic integrity, still fulfill pragmatic functions. In this respect, the corpus the authors use to retrieve these multiword strings is the Cambridge and Nottingham Corpus of Discourse in English of 5 million words, containing transcribed conversations. The software they use to retrieve and count the occurrence of multiword units is WordSmith Tools. In particular, this tool is used to compile frequency lists of clusters ranging from two to six words. The analysis of such strings is based on the interpretation of raw data and leads the authors to claim that these syntactically and semantically incomplete strings of words achieve their wholeness when their pragmatic function is taken into consideration, which justifies their study. In this respect, it is clear that in order to study their pragmatic integrity, the bigger picture needs to be taken into account or the research may fail to identify this function. This demonstrates that the macrotextual level is not to be ignored when interpreting corpus-driven data because, as the authors themselves point out, even the frequency and types of multiword strings that one finds in a corpus are not the same across registers and genres. Another important consideration that is worth mentioning here is that, despite not using any type of inferential analysis, the authors still mention it as a further step to be taken in corpus-based studies when interpreting data and drawing conclusions.

When it comes to T&I, there are several studies that are worth mentioning: Puurtinen (2003) provides an interesting study on translationese, focusing on a corpus-based analysis of Finnish translations of children's literature; Laviosa-Braithwaite (1996) focuses on the simplification hypothesis and compares the lexical density of English translations and English originals; Baker (2000) studies the style of two translators, namely Peter Bush and Peter Clark, focusing on the translators' choices as to source text selection as well as translation strategies, including footnotes, glossaries, and prefaces; and last but not least, Baumgarten, House, and Probst (2004) and House (2001) both investigate the impact of translation on language change.

As mentioned above, when it comes to T&I, the list of corpus-based studies that fail to validate their findings through statistical analysis is long. The good news, however, is that scholars in the field have recently begun to acknowledge the importance of statistically validating their results and so are encouraging future researchers to integrate statistical analysis into the process of data interpretation.

Conclusion and potential applications

Corpus-based Translation Studies has come a long way since its first attempts to determine the nature of translated texts in that it has allowed translation scholars to substantiate their findings with analytical and quantitative data, which provide higher quality linguistic evidence. Indeed, computer corpora allow the researcher to identify key words in context through concordance lines and to obtain information about lexical density, typo-token ratio, and average text, sentence, and word length, all of which is important data for investigating differences and similarities between L1 originals and L2 translations, as well as between translated language and non-translated language.

However, quantitative data must in turn be supported by a qualitative analysis that interprets the data in the light of discourse analysis (including genre and ideology studies), ethnographic studies, and pragmatics, to name just a few. Though many studies have used this combined approach in their investigation of translation phenomena, not many have integrated statistical analysis into the process of interpreting the data obtained from corpus query tools. By running the quantitative data in a statistical program such as the Statistical Package for Social Sciences (SPSS), it is possible to obtain information about the significance or insignificance of findings and determine whether they have validity. This kind of analysis prevents scholars from expressing an often personal and subjective interpretation of their findings, thus providing more scientific evidence and a more solid foundation for their research and for Translation/Interpreting Studies as a discipline. Nevertheless, the quantitative data they provide is made up of raw numbers that describe what happens in the sample of data under study. These raw numbers do not tell us anything about the population that the sample of data represents. If we really want to generalize our findings, we need to perform an inferential statistical analysis using such statistical analysis tools as SPSS in order to determine whether our data is representative of the entire population. This is the only step that can guarantee the replicability of a study so that, should a similar study be conducted in the future, similar findings will be obtained. It follows that in order to solve the representative issue that still characterizes most corpus-based studies, it is imperative that T&I scholars make use of inferential statistical analysis.

Moreover, as pointed out above, when using computer corpora, one runs the risk of not taking into account the macrotextual structure of each document making up a corpus, which can produce misleading or inaccurate conclusions about identified patterns. One way to overcome this shortcoming is to tag corpora with extra- or intra-textual information that would allow the study of the macrotextual level features. The importance of the macrotextual level is also evident when dealing with word lists that do not discriminate between words having the same word form but different meanings (homonyms) and words having the same form but belonging to different grammatical categories, i.e., deal (verb) vs deal (noun). This problem can be solved easily by looking at concordances that decontextualize the meanings and grammatical categories of words. It is thus imperative that the translation scholar be aware of the importance of the macrotextual level and that he/she investigate further once the corpus-querying tool returns such results.

Further readings

Laviosa (2002) provides a good analysis of the principles, methods, techniques, and pedagogical applications used in corpus-based studies, which is truly inspiring. Olohan (2004) offers a thorough account of the corpus-driven research in translation along with an overview of its methods and applications. Oakes and Meng (2012) offer an overview of statistical tests that can be used in translation research using corpus linguistics, as well as corpus-based translation case studies adopting quantitative methods.

References

Baker, Mona. 2000. "Towards a Methodology for Investigating the Style of a Literary Translator." *Target* 12(2): 241–66.

Baumgarten, Nicole, Juliane House, and Julia Probst. 2004. "English as Lingua Franca in Covert Translation Processes." *The Translator* 10(1): 83–108.

Bennett, Gena R. 2010. "Part 1: An Introduction to Corpus Linguistics." In *Using Corpora in the Language Learning Classroom: Corpus Linguistics for Teachers*. Ann Arbor: University of Michigan Press.

Biber, Douglas, Susan Conrad, and Randi Reppen. 2000. *Corpus Linguistics: Investigating Language Structure and Use*. Cambridge: Cambridge University Press.

Biber, Douglas, Susan Conrad, Randi Reppen, and Pat Byrd. 2002. "Speaking and Writing in the University: A Multidimensional Comparison." *TESOL Quarterly* 36(1): 9–48.

Bongers, Herman. 1947. *The History and Principles of Vocabulary Control*. Woerden: WOCOPI.

Eaton, Helen. 1940. *Semantic Frequency List for English, French, German and Spanish*. Chicago: University of Chicago Press.

Firth, John Rupert. 1957. "A Synopsis of Linguistic Theory 1930–1955." In *Studies in Linguistic Analysis*. Oxford: Philological Society, 1–32.

Fries, Charles. 1952. *The Structure of English: An Introduction to the Construction of Sentences*. New York: Harcourt-Brace.

Fries, Charles, and Alice A. Traver. 1940. *English Word Lists: A Study of Their Adaptability for Instruction*. Washington DC: American Council on Education.

Halliday, M. A. K., and Ruqaiya Hasan. 1976. *Cohesion in English*. London: Longman.

Harris, Randy Allen. 1993. *The Linguistics Wars*. Oxford: Oxford University Press.

House, Juliane. 2011. "Using Translation and Parallel Text Corpora to Investigate the Influence of Global English on Textual Norms in Other Languages." In *Corpus-Based Translation Studies: Research and Applications*, Alet Kruger, Kim Wallmach, and Jeremy Munday (eds.), 187–208. London and New York: Continuum.

Käding, Friedrich Wilhem. 1897. *Haufigkeitsworterbuch der Deutschen Sprache*. Steglitz: privately published.

Kruger, Alet. 2002. "Corpus-Based Translation Research: Its Developments and Implications for General Literary and Bible Translation." *Acta Theologica Supplementum* 2: 70–106.

Laviosa, Sara. 2002. *Corpus-based Translation Studies. Theory, Findings, Applications*. Amsterdam: Rodopi.

——2011. "Corpus-Based Translation Studies: Where Does It Come From? Where Is It Going?" In *Corpus-Based Translation Studies: Research and Applications*, Alet Kruger, Kim Wallmach, and Jeremy Munday (eds.), 13–32. London and New York: Continuum.

Laviosa-Braithwaite, Sara. 1996. "The English Comparable Corpus (ECC): A Resource and a Methodology for the Empirical Study of Translation." Unpublished Ph.D. dissertation, Center for Translation and Intercultural Studies (CTIS), University of Manchester.

Lorge, Irving. 1949. *Semantic Content of the 570 Commonest English Words*. New York: Columbia University Press.

McCarthy, Michael, and Ronald Carter. 2002/2004. "This That and the Other: Multi-Word Clusters in Spoken English as Visible Patterns of Interaction." *Teanga: The Irish Yearbook of Applied Linguistics* 21: 30–52.

McEnery, Tony, and Andrew Wilson. 2001. *Corpus Linguistics: An Introduction*. Edinburgh: Edinburgh University Press.

McEnery, Tony, Richard Xiao, and Yukio Tono. 2006. *Corpus-Based Language Studies: An Advanced Resource Book*. Abingdon: Routledge.

Oakes, Michael, and Ji Meng. 2012. *Quantitative Methods in Corpus-Based Translation Studies*. Amsterdam and Philadelphia: John Benjamins Publishing.

Olohan, Maeve. 2004. *Introducing Corpora in Translation Studies*. London: Routledge.

Preyer, William. 1889. *The Mind of a Child*. New York: D. Appleton.

Puurtinen, Tiina. 2003. "Genre-Specific Features of Translationese? Linguistic Differences between Translated and Non-Translated Finnish Children's Literature." *Literary and Linguistic Computing* 18(4): 389–406.

Sinclair, John. 1991. *Corpus, Concordance, Collocation*. Oxford: Oxford University Press.

Stern, Wilhelm. 1924. *Psychology of Early Childhood up to Six Years of Age*. London: George Allen & Unwin, Ltd.

Stubbs, Michael. 1995. "Collocations and Semantic Profiles: On the Cause of the Trouble with Quantitative Studies." *Functions of Language* 2(1): 23–55.

Taylor, Charlotte. 2008. "What Is Corpus Linguistics? What the Data Says." *ICAME Journal* 32: 179–200.

Tognini-Bonelli, Elena. 2001. *Corpus Linguistics at Work*. Amsterdam and Philadelphia: John Benjamins.

Zanettin, Federico. 2013. "Corpus Methods for Descriptive Translation Studies." *Procedia – Social and Behavioral Sciences* 95: 20–32.

17 Critical discourse analysis

Ian Mason

Definitions

The term Critical Discourse Analysis (CDA, sometimes known as Critical Linguistics or Critical Discourse Studies) describes a broad approach to the analysis of discourse that employs a variety of methods in order to reveal ways in which discourse practices are closely involved in the exercise of power and control in society. It is a fundamental principle of CDA that discourse practices are both socially constituted and socially constitutive. Discourse, in other words, is seen as an essential part of social practice, at one and the same time being shaped by the latter and also, through repeated use, helping to shape it. CDA is thus both diverse and interdisciplinary; all practitioners would agree that the analysis of texts can assist in providing, but can never on its own provide, a full account of the ways in which language is involved in the exercise of power and control in society and that social theory is an essential component of any CDA study.

Given the multiplicity of senses in which the term "discourse" is employed among specialists, it will be useful to make clear at the outset the senses in which the term is used in this chapter. Following Widdowson (2004), "discourse" (D1) will be understood as the pragmatic process of negotiating meaning in communication, with "text" or "talk" as its product. This process being socially constituted, it gives rise to practices recognizable as giving voice to the attitudes and values of social groups or institutions. These are "discourses" (D2), a sociocultural construct that is closely bound up with those of identity and community.

Origins

Among early studies, Trew (1979) selected a particular social event and, by comparing the headlines and introductory text segments of various UK newspaper articles reporting the event, sought to show that the ideology of any particular newspaper as an institution emerges in the texture of headlines (through the use of passives, agent deletion, and so on). Kress and Hodge (1979) saw language in use as key to an understanding of social and psychological reality. Their goal was to reveal processes of manipulation and the ideologies underlying texts through analysis of such categories as nominalization and transitivity. More recently, Fairclough (e.g., 1993, 2009), whose social theory draws on the work of Foucault and Bourdieu, among others, has analyzed dominant neoliberal discourses of marketization (in education) and globalization (in texts, such as a paper on higher education management and a foreword to a government white paper written by Tony Blair). In the latter case, his linguistic analysis focuses on such categories as personal deixis (use of "we"), modality (unmodalized categorical assertions of truth together with the use of the deontic "must"), and agency (inanimate concepts as agents, such as "change," "new technologies," and "new markets," used with intransitive verbs, such as "emerge" and "open up").

Since much CDA work in T&I Studies cites the major CDA scholars, Norman Fairclough, Ruth Wodak, and/or Teun van Dijk, it makes sense to consider the basic orientations of their approaches and the specific methods they employ. Fairclough's version of CDA has evolved over the years. In his current approach, discourse is seen as one element of the social process, dialectically related to other elements such as social relations, power, institutions, and cultural systems. The methodology can be summarized as follows (Fairclough 2009: 167–71):

Stage 1. Identify a "social wrong" (cf. also van Dijk 2009: 63).

- 1.1 Select a topic.
- 1.2 Set it within transdisciplinary theory and define the object of research.

Stage 2. Identify the obstacles to addressing the social wrong.

- 2.1 Analyze relations between orders of discourse and social practices, between texts and other events.
- 2.2 Select texts and categories for analysis.
- 2.3 Analyze texts.

Stage 3. Consider whether the social wrong is necessary within the social order.

Stage 4. Identify solutions (e.g., how are dominant discourses resisted?).

It will be seen that, for Fairclough, discourse analysis is just one stage within a broader social research project. This point is of obvious relevance to the recent sociological orientation of T&I Studies (cf. Inghilleri 2005; Wolf and Fukari 2007) since disparities of power and their effects are an issue of major concern in T&I research, and CDA offers a means of providing empirical support for the claims such studies might wish to make. CDA scholars generally begin by stating their own political stance and the committed nature of their research goals. At the same time, in contrast to traditional text analysis, they insist on "continuous self-reflection" (Reisigl and Wodak 2009: 87) since no analysis, however principled, can be truly objective: the assumptions and perspective of the analyst have to be made clear. This is likewise a position increasingly adopted in T&I Studies (see, for example, Hermans 2002: 7; Baker 2006: 4; and, as an application of CDA, Bennett 2006).

In the discourse-historical approach of Wodak and colleagues, detailed case studies include quantitative as well as qualitative analysis. Data collection is conducted on ethnographic principles. In all versions of CDA methods, categories for linguistic analysis are eclectic, being selected in function of the particular research question(s). They include, under the discourse-historical approach, the macrostructure and textual progression of topics and arguments, discursive strategies (naming and categorizing, metaphor, evaluative attributions, inclusion/exclusion, perspective, framing, intensification, and mitigation) and, in Fairclough's approach, the categories of time, tense, modality, and transitivity. Van Dijk (e.g., 2009) focuses on textual evidence of mental representations: the presuppositions and implicatures of local meanings, and any pragmatic features that reflect intentions, mood, or perspective.

The practice and methods of CDA have been severely criticized from a range of different perspectives (for a comprehensive account, see Toolan 2002). Stubbs (1997) identifies many shortcomings, one of which is the inescapable "circularity" of CDA studies: the analyst takes an initial theme (say, racism), selects appropriate texts, searches them for evidence of the chosen theme, finds evidence, and then concludes from this that there is indeed a discourse of racism. The objection is a serious one: when Reisigl and Wodak analyze a sample of talk by Czech President Klaus, they describe him at the outset (2009: 100) as having "a strictly (neo-) liberal, anti-communist as well as anti-environmentalist point of view." This is presented as a starting point of the research. Later (2009: 117–18), after conducting a pilot analysis, they conclude that a more detailed study "would help to recognize the underlying ideological positioning in this and other discourse fragments produced by Klaus." Yet if recognition of this positioning was the starting point for the study, then what was the analysis supposed to discover? The argument appears to be circular.

A plausible rationale might be that critical discourse analysts are able to reveal meanings hidden in texts, to demystify them and lay bare the underlying ideologies (or, in the case of T&I, to reveal ideological shifts). From the cognitivist perspective of Chilton (2005: 31), however, scientific evidence suggests that the human mind is equipped not only to mask intentions but also to detect the masking of intentions by others. Humans can therefore detect each other's "Machiavellian use of language." So, he concludes, "what is CDA for if people can do it anyway?" A rejoinder might be that, although every intelligent (and, in the case of T&I, bilingual) adult could do this, few actually expend the time and effort necessary to do so. We thus need the demystifications provided by CDA analysts.

This, in turn, leads to another objection: by what authority can the analyst claim to state unequivocally what texts mean? The claim that an item or structure in a text has a definable meaning is redolent of the conduit model of communication, now universally rejected in T&I Studies. Widdowson (2004) points out that CDA analyses are selective, usually relying on a limited range of linguistic parameters. This being so, he observes, "there is no reason why the partial interpretations that CDA provides should be preferred to any other" (2004: 107). All readers of texts have what he calls "pretext," a previous history and set of assumptions and predispositions to interpret meanings in their own way. Analysts are no exception. So a relevant research question might not be what meanings does the non-participant analyst derive from a text (or translation/interpreted rendition) but rather what meanings do the actual intended receivers pick up as they read/listen to the rendition in real time?

Finally, Schegloff (1997) sees the problems of CDA in different terms. CDA's pre-judgment of textual meanings can actually lead to the analyst overlooking important evidence (e.g., of sexism) to be found in the kind of microanalysis that conversation analysis favors. This detailed analysis, he claims, should take place first so that judgments about discourses are based on textual evidence.

In summary, then, the methodological problems that CDA faces are of various kinds but principally focus on:

- A tendency towards circularity of argument;
- The authority claimed by the analyst;
- Selectivity in the choice of texts and in the evidence found in them ("cherry-picking").

To which we can add, with T&I in mind:

- The general lack of an intercultural perspective in single-language studies that deal with different social groups.

Uses

The perspectives that CDA offers have long been of interest to scholars of translation and interpreting. Issues of ideology, power, and control are central to contemporary concerns in Translation Studies (the "cultural turn," gender and translation, postcolonialism, the translator's agency, translation ethics, and the sociology of translation). With the exception of innumerable doctoral theses, most of the CDA-inspired studies reported in publications have been relatively small-scale: translated journalism (Mason 1994/2010; Munday 2002; Kang 2007), intergovernmental declarations (Schäffner 2003), public service interpreting (Pöllabauer 2004; Angelelli 2011), and academic writing (Bennett 2006). Many of these owe something to descriptive Translation Studies in that their main goal is to show what happens in translation; they mostly avoid claims that they are demystifying text or uncovering hidden agendas. So to what extent can (and do) CDA-influenced studies of translation and interpreting events avoid the pitfalls discussed above?

Sample studies

A review of some key studies will illustrate the potential and limitations of CDA methods in T&I Studies. Munday (2002) analyzes three English-language translations of an essay by Gabriel García Márquez on the topic of a shipwrecked Cuban child refugee adopted by relatives in Miami but claimed by the child's father in Cuba. Such a topic is obviously a prime site for a CDA study of discourse and ideology. Munday's study is, however, firmly situated within descriptive Translation Studies. Thus, it starts with no preconceived notions about discourses in either source or target texts. He states that the goal of the study is to propose a methodology for replicable descriptive studies. The focus is thus on the method and what it can be shown to achieve. Using categories of analysis from Halliday's systemic functional linguistics (such as transitivity, modality, thematic structure, and cohesion), he conducts a qualitative and quantitative analysis of the complete translations as published. To overcome the problem of selective analysis, he employs computer-assisted analysis of the translations, ensuring that all instances of a given phenomenon are taken into consideration. The study reveals important translation shifts that are then related to the sociocultural and political context of the production of source and target texts. The shifts include significant changes in transitivity and agency (e.g., the organizers of the journey are reported in the source text as having "dismantled the engine" of the boat—thus indirectly causing it to capsize—whereas one translation merely reports that the "engine was dismantled"). Still, the analysis remains descriptive and it is only at the end of the study that the author speculates on possible ideological motivations for the translation shifts. In this way the study avoids any accusation of circularity of argument.

Schäffner (2003) examines a joint policy document produced by the German and British governments in a process of negotiation that involved both translation and co-writing (but not professional translators). She focuses on the political background to the production and reception of the text and the origins of and reactions to key terms such as "The Third Way" (English version), "die Neue Mitte" ("new center," German version) and "social justice" ("soziale Gerechtigkeit"). Showing subtle differences between the two language versions, she relates these to political sensitivities on each side and to long-standing traditions and understandings in the political culture of each country. The study thus uses many of the techniques of CDA but positions itself as a "contribution to the study of cultures in contact" (Schäffner 2003: 41) rather than an ideologically committed examination of the Third Way.

Mason (2009) suggests an experimental method for investigating reader response as a way of counterbalancing analysts' assertions about the meanings that are received. In order to test the claim that a discoursal shift was apparent in a translation, respondents were asked to summarize from memory different versions of the text, one with the shifts identified in the translation, the other without. The summaries offered evidence of meanings that had been received and retained.

Among CDA-influenced studies of interpreting are Pöllabauer (2004) and Angelelli (2011). Pöllabauer, whose principal objective was to investigate the interpreter's role, compiled a corpus of 20 asylum-hearing transcripts, amounting to over 20 hours of speech. She finds plentiful evidence of highly visible moves by the interpreter: interrupting asylum seekers' statements, selective omissions, asking supplementary questions, signals of allegiance, face work, and so on. The analysis aims at a "descriptive reconstruction of the motives underlying the speakers' statements" (2004: 153), although it is not entirely clear how the written record of the event can unerringly reveal participants' intentions. Angelelli (2011) investigates power and solidarity in medical consultations at a large US hospital on the basis of the CDA principle that institutions exert power via discourse and that participants' use of discourse may either reinforce or resist power differentials. She triangulates her study through a number of ethnographic methods: monitoring and shadowing of a particular (male) interpreter at work prior to data collection, and post-interviews with the interpreter, including eliciting his feedback when shown parts of her own analysis. Her CDA findings—that the interpreter through his turns at talk exercises his agency and exerts influence on the power differentials between participants—are thus enriched by text-independent evidence gathered from the interpreter and from the institutional framework.

In addition the following studies in T&I are worth mentioning: Hatim (1997: 174–85) provides an important study of the "discourse of alienation" in an Arabic novella translated into English. Baumgarten (2009) is a full-length study investigating the translation of Hitler's *Mein Kampf*, combining discourse as social practice and sociopolitical theory. Kang (2007) investigates the manipulation of news agency reports for ideological purposes. Munday (2008, 2012) offers more CDA-related analyses, including (2012: 42–79) translations of President Obama's inaugural address, using appraisal theory.

While most T&I CDA studies are not as politically committed as those of Fairclough, Wodak, van Dijk, and others, one study that runs counter to this trend is Bennett (2006). She identifies academic English as a hegemonic discourse, which, via globalization, invades and supplants academic styles of writing in other cultures, thus effectively silencing them. Translators are often asked to translate other-language texts into academic English in order to make them publishable in Western academic journals. By acceding to such requests, she claims, translators find themselves collaborating in a form of cultural imperialism (though many translators would consider this as simply a case of localization). Bennett's study, aiming to demonstrate that different assumptions underlie Portuguese and English humanities discourses, is thus closely in tune with mainstream CDA. Her analysis seeks to illustrate what she perceives as a "social wrong" (see discussion of Fairclough 2009 above) and is in some ways a model application of CDA to translation. It is also in line with the intercultural insights offered by Blommaert (2005) concerning "entextualization," the process whereby in today's world texts travel and reappear in alien contexts. In doing so, they often lose "voice," the ability to make themselves heard or be taken seriously. He illustrates the phenomenon with several translation examples.

Conclusion and potential applications

The main challenges posed by CDA's critics were summarized above as the need to (1) avoid circularity, (2) avoid imposing the analyst's interpretation of text and talk as being that of actual participants, and (3) avoid "cherry-picking" from the evidence to suit the argument being made. In the case of the first of these, the review above has shown how most CDA-inspired T&I Studies start with no agenda but rather aim to discover what happens in translation. Where there is a committed stance, it will be necessary to make a clear distinction between initial assumptions, the research question(s), and how the analysis, in answering them, will add to the initial assumptions. The second challenge is to find independent evidence (triangulation) in support of the researcher's own discourse analysis. In this respect, Berk-Seligson's (1990) modified matched guise experiment to test whether rendering politeness features in court interpreting makes a difference to jurors' perceptions is exemplary (cf. also Angelelli 2011, reviewed above). Finally, the "cherry-picking" problem can be avoided by thoroughness and transparency: analysis should include counter-evidence as well as examples that support the case being made; and care must be exercised to ensure that the research claims made are never greater than what the evidence presented actually supports.

Cultural, postcolonial, and activist T&I Studies seek to make far-reaching claims about power and control, the spread of dominant ideologies and the translator's role in either resisting or reinforcing these. Further large-scale critical analyses of discourses in translation could provide important substantiation for (or falsification of) such claims. Indeed, Blommaert's insights about the effects of the (re-)entextualization that translation involves and the suppression of voice in a multicultural but unequal world make this an urgent task (2005). The methodological problems can mainly be avoided; the need for thorough investigation cannot.

Further reading

Saldanha (2009) reviews the uses of CDA in T&I Studies, providing useful examples. Wodak and Chilton (2005) and Wodak and Meyer (2009) are excellent collections of papers discussing the methods and scope of CDA, while Titscher et al. (2000) includes important chapters on method.

References

Angelelli, Claudia. 2011. "Can You Ask Her about Chronic Illnesses, Diabetes and All That?" In *Methods and Strategies of Process Research: Integrative Approaches in Translation Studies*, Cecilia Alvstad, Adelina Hild, and Elisabet Tiselius (eds.), 231–46. Amsterdam and Philadelphia: John Benjamins.

Baker, Mona. 2006. *Translation and Conflict. A Narrative Account*. London and New York: Routledge.
Baumgarten, Stefan. 2009. *Translating Hitler's* Mein Kampf – *A Corpus-Aided Discourse-Analytical Study*. Saarbrücken: VDM Verlag.
Bennett, Karen. 2006. "Critical Language Study and Translation: The Case of Academic Discourse." In *Translation Studies at the Interface of Disciplines*, João Ferreira Duarte, Alexandra Assis Rosa, and Teresa Seruya (eds.), 111–27. Amsterdam and Philadelphia: John Benjamins.
Berk-Seligson, Susan. 1990. *The Bilingual Courtroom. Court Interpreters in the Judicial Process*. Chicago: University of Chicago Press.
Blommaert, Jan. 2005. *Discourse. A Critical Introduction*. Cambridge: Cambridge University Press.
Chilton, Paul. 2005. "Missing Links in Mainstream CDA: Modules, Blends and the Critical Instinct." In *A New Agenda in (Critical) Discourse Analysis. Theory, Methodology and Interdisciplinarity*, Ruth Wodak and Paul Chilton (eds.), 19–51. Amsterdam and Philadelphia: John Benjamins.
Fairclough, Norman. 1993. "Critical Discourse Analysis and the Marketization of Public Discourse." *Discourse and Society* 4(2): 133–68.
——2009. "A Dialectical-Relational Approach to Critical Discourse Analysis in Social Research." In *Methods of Critical Discourse Analysis*, Ruth Wodak and Michael Meyer (eds.), 162–86. London and Thousand Oaks, CA: SAGE Publications.
Hatim, Basil. 1997. *Communication across Cultures. Translation Theory and Contrastive Text Linguistics*. Exeter: University of Exeter Press.
Hermans, Theo. 2002. "Preface." In *Crosscultural Transgressions. Research Models in Translation Studies II, Historical and Ideological Issues*, Theo Hermans (ed.), 1–8. Manchester: St. Jerome.
Inghilleri, Moira. 2005. "The Sociology of Bourdieu and the Construction of the 'Object' in Translation and Interpreting Studies." Special issue. *The Translator* 11(2): 125–45.
Kang, Ji-Hae. 2007. "Recontextualization of News Discourse: A Case Study of Translation of News Discourse on North Korea." *The Translator* 13(2): 219–42.
Kress, Gunther, and Robert Hodge. 1979. *Language as Ideology*. London: Routledge.
Mason, Ian. 1994/2010. "Discourse, Ideology and Translation." In *Language, Discourse and Translation in the West and Middle East*, Robert de Beaugrande, Abdulla Shunnaq, and Mohamed Heliel (eds.), 83–95. Amsterdam and Philadelphia: John Benjamins. Reprinted with a Postface in Mona Baker (ed.) *Critical Readings in Translation Studies*. Abingdon and New York: Routledge.
——2009. "Translator Moves and Reader Response: The Impact of Discoursal Shifts in Translation." In *Translationswissenschaftliches Kolloquium I. Beiträge zür Übersetzungs- und Dolmetschwissenschaft*, Barbara Ahrens, Lothar Černý, Monika Krein-Kühle, and Michael Schreiber (eds.), 55–70. Frankfurt am Main: Peter Lang.
Munday, Jeremy. 2002. "Systems in Translation. A Systemic Model for Descriptive Translation Studies." In *Crosscultural Transgressions. Research Models in Translation Studies II, Historical and Ideological Issues*, Theo Hermans (ed.), 76–92. Manchester and Northampton, MA: St. Jerome.
——2008. *Style and Ideology in Translation. Latin American Writing in English*. London and New York: Routledge.
——2012. *Evaluation in Translation. Critical Points of Translator Decision-Making*. London and New York: Routledge.

Pöllabauer, Sonja. 2004. "Interpreting in Asylum Hearings: Issues of Role, Responsibility and Power." *Interpreting* 6(2): 143–80.

Reisigl, Martin, and Ruth Wodak. 2009. "The Discourse-Historical Approach." In *Methods of Critical Discourse Analysis*, 2nd edition, Ruth Wodak and Michael Meyer (eds.), 87–121. Thousand Oaks, CA and London: SAGE Publications.

Saldanha, Gabriela. 2009. "Linguistic Approaches." In *Routledge Encyclopedia of Translation Studies*, 2nd edition, Mona Baker and Gabriela Saldanha (eds.), 148–52. London and New York: Routledge.

Schäffner, Christina. 2003. "Third Ways and New Centres. Ideological Unity or Difference?" In *Apropos of Ideology. Translation Studies on Ideology – Ideologies in Translation Studies*, María Calzada Pérez (ed.), 23–42. Manchester and Northampton, MA: St. Jerome.

Schegloff, Emmanuel. 1997. "Whose Text? Whose Context?" *Discourse and Society* 8(2): 165–87.

Stubbs, Michael. 1997. "Whorf's Children: Critical Comments on Critical Discourse Analysis (CDA)." In *Evolving Models of Language. Papers from the Annual Meeting of the British Association for Applied Linguistics, September 1996*, Ann Ryan and Alison Wray (eds.), 100–16. Clevedon: Multilingual Matters.

Titscher, Stefan, Michael Meyer, Ruth Wodak, and Eva Vetter. 2000. *Methods of Text and Discourse Analysis*. London and Thousand Oaks, CA: SAGE Publications.

Toolan, Michael (ed.). 2002. *Critical Discourse Analysis: Critical Concepts in Linguistics*. 4 vols. London: Routledge.

Trew, Tony. 1979. "Theory and Ideology at Work." In *Language and Control*, Roger Fowler, Robert Hodge, Gunther Kress, and Tony Trew (eds.), 94–116. London: Routledge and Kegan Paul.

van Dijk, Teun. 2009. "Critical Discourse Studies: A Sociocognitive Approach." In *Methods of Critical Discourse Analysis*, 2nd edition, Ruth Wodak and Michael Meyer (eds.), 62–86. Thousand Oaks, CA and London: SAGE Publications.

Widdowson, Henry G. 2004. *Text, Context, Pretext. Critical Issues in Discourse Analysis*. Oxford and Malden, MA: Blackwell.

Wodak, Ruth, and Paul Chilton (eds.). 2005. *A New Agenda in (Critical) Discourse Analysis*. Amsterdam and Philadelphia: John Benjamins.

Wodak, Ruth, and Michael Meyer (eds.). 2009. *Methods of Critical Discourse Analysis*. 2nd edition. Thousand Oaks, CA and London: SAGE Publications.

Wolf, Michaela, and Alexandra Fukari (eds.). 2007. *Constructing a Sociology of Translation*. Amsterdam and Philadelphia: John Benjamins.

18 Ethnography of communication

Edmund Asare

Definition

The term ethnography of communication was first used by Hymes in a seminal article in linguistics. Hymes argued that linguistic research should be based on the use of language in social contexts, rather than on the linguistic code. He suggested that ethnography must provide the "frame of reference" for studying the use of language in society (Hymes 1964: 3). Half a century later, Hymes' call remains more relevant than ever in many fields, including translation and interpreting (T&I). The term *ethnographies of communication* as used in this article refers broadly to the use of ethnographic methods in T&I.

According to Spradley, ethnography is "the work of describing a culture" (1979: 3). Spradley further defines ethnography as "the study of a social situation," a "stream of behavior (activities) carried out by people (actors) in a particular location (place)" (1980: 86). A social situation is thus a particular convergence of *activities*, *actors*, and *place*, and ethnography is the work of describing this convergence.

Ethnography is concerned with detailed descriptions of people and their activities. Ethnography may focus on a human process, such as communication or the use of technology (Wolcott 1973: xi; Neyland 2008: 30). Atkinson and Delamont have suggested that the study of material artifacts and technology deserves systematic attention in ethnographic contexts (2008: 292). As cross-linguistic and cross-cultural communication activities, T&I lends itself particularly well to ethnographic studies. Ethnography aims at grasping "the native's point of view" (Malinowski 1922: 25). It seeks to obtain the emic or insider's perspective (Fetterman 2010: 2). Willis and Trondman have characterized ethnography not as a single method but as a "family of methods" emphasizing direct sustained contact with actors and descriptions of the encounters (2000: 5). Ethnography, which typically relies on participant observation, is quite flexible and allows the use of multiple data acquisition modes, including interviews, historical and content analysis, questionnaires, and inspection of material artifacts. Participant observation involves spending time with people in the field, typically 12 months or more (Bernard 2006: 349), and making direct observations. Participant observation yields insights that cannot be easily obtained solely through interviews and maximizes a researcher's chances of making valid statements (Bernard 2006: 356).

Moreover, ethnographic research can be conducted at a macro or micro level. Macroethnography is holistic and may investigate a broad social issue, bringing many aspects of the issue into focus. Macroethnography, commonly referred to as "ethnography," is usually based on a year or more of fieldwork. It is also typically the length of a monograph. Wolcott argues that anything less substantial can be "ethnographic not ethnography" (1995: 56).

On the other hand, microethnography is a close-up study of a small social unit. It typically has a narrower focus and a shorter time frame than a macroethnography. Microethnography has also been referred to as constitutive ethnography (Mehan 1979), ethnographic microanalysis (Erickson 1992), microethnography (Mehan 1998; Streeck and Mehus 2005), and microlevel ethnography (Fetterman 2010: 29).

Microethnography is an approach and perspective that employs "fine-grained sequential analysis ... to examine interaction as constitutive of particular settings and activities" (Mehus 2006: 51). Microethnography and conversation analysis are both grounded in sequential analysis, but microethnography focuses on "aspects of bodily communication, such as gaze, gesture, postural configurations, and interactions with artifacts" (Mehus 2006: 73–74). Microethnography has primarily relied on the videotaping of interaction.

A researcher's choice of method may be driven by the research problem and the time available. Ethnography typically focuses on a small number of cases and allows for an in-depth analysis of phenomena. Ethnography involves "a dialogic combination of different viewpoints, those of the observer and those of the observed" (Koskinen 2008: 6). Ethnography is about stepping out in the field, establishing rapport with informants, and conducting direct field-based observations. Ethnography does not aim at testing a pre-existing hypothesis; it begins with a broad research problem, but researchers must strive to remain open-minded and non-judgmental (Fetterman 2010: 1). They must not allow preconceived notions to influence their findings. Ethnographic research is inductive (O'Reilly 2012: 4); theory emerges from data (see Becker et al. 1961: 18). Researchers must have a broad research question before entering the field. Ethnographic research may adjust its initial focus as the study progresses: the focus may become broader or narrower.

In spite of its versatility and other benefits, ethnography has its challenges and limitations. Ethnographic research is subjective (Bernard 2006: 22), and the researcher plays a key role in data interpretation. The researcher must acknowledge personal biases that might affect research findings. Ethnography is also analytical; it focuses on depth rather than scope. Thus, ethnographic research findings may not be easily generalizable (LeCompte and Goetz 1982: 32). Finally, ethnographers must ensure confidentiality (O'Reilly 2012: 70) in their reporting in order to protect their collaborators.

Origins

The term *ethnography* was first used by anthropologists in 1909 to refer to descriptive accounts of non-literate peoples (Radcliffe-Brown 1952: 276). Ethnography initially focused on *foreign* and *exotic* tribes but later turned its attention to advanced societies as well (Cole 1977). While ethnography has its origins in anthropology, participant observation has its origins in sociology (Bernard 2006: 346).

Malinowski, a social anthropologist, used participant observation between 1914 and 1918 to study the people in the Trobriand Islands. He published *Argonauts of the Western Pacific* in 1922. While Malinowski is known for contributing significantly to the development of participant observation, he did not totally invent it (Bernard 2006: 344). Bernard argues that Beatrice Webb was doing participant observation in the 1880s and wrote about the method in 1926 (346). The Chicago School of Sociology also practiced urban ethnography under the direction of Park and Burgess around 1925. In the twentieth century, ethnography emerged as a key research method, shaped and used by both anthropologists and sociologists (Atkinson and Hammersley 1994: 250).

Ethnography has, since its inception, been adapted and used especially in the social sciences, including T&I. In applied settings, ethnography has served a functional purpose. The time for participant observation has been condensed, and researchers conduct focused studies aimed at solving problems. In software design, for example, ethnography serves a very functional purpose, that of describing actual work practices as a basis for providing support. In some cases participant observation is done in a few days or weeks.

Uses of ethnographic methods in T&I

Existing studies in T&I have focused on the roles of translators and interpreters in community and organizational settings, on workflows and the use of tools in organizations. Ethnographic methods can be used to address virtually any research concerns. I will discuss some current potential ethnographic research questions.

I have mentioned that ethnography begins with a big picture question or broad descriptive problem (see Becker et al. 1961: 17). Specific questions emerge as the study progresses. Ethnographic research in translation may begin with a broad question, such as how translators relate to their tools within an organizational context. This question could yield rich descriptions of the work of translators, the socio-organizational setting, the tools used in the setting, and any challenges related to the use of the tools. It could also yield valuable information on how participants cope with challenges (see, for example, Asare 2011).

Ethnographic research in translation or interpreting can focus on descriptions of routine practices, processes, and roles that form part of the culture of the actors in a setting. Given the holistic nature of ethnography, these descriptions would contextualize the study. Broad questions can be narrowed as the research progresses.

A question underlying Koskinen's study of the EU, for example, is "How do translators perceive their role in the EU and what is expected of them?" (2008: 35). This question enables the researcher to seek perspectives from translators in the setting. Previous to that work and related to interpreting, Angelelli had a similar underlying question in her study of California Hope (2004).

Sample studies

Ethnography has been used to investigate police work (Fassin 2013), education (Becker et al. 1961), business (Harper 1998), air traffic control and design (Bentley et al. 1992), and healthcare (McGibbon et al. 2010), among other things. Wacquant (2003) has observed that "Far from being ... extinct or endangered ... ethnography is a proliferating animal that walks on multiplying feet. ... [I]ts two main legs remain anthropology and sociology" (2003: 6). I will briefly discuss two ethnographic studies outside T&I.

Boys in White (Becker et al. 1961) is an ethnography of medical education in the US. The study focuses on the training given to medical students and is based on participant observation and interviews. The researchers participated in the daily life of the students by attending classes and laboratory and ward sessions with them (Becker et al. 1961: 25–26). They entered the field with "no design" and the initial focus of their study changed as the study progressed. For example, their initial research concern was to find out what medical schools did for their students aside from giving them a technical education, but this focus changed to how students at various points in their education perceive and solve the "problems of dealing with their teachers and the tasks they assign" (Becker et al. 1961: 5, 17).

Harper's *Inside the IMF* focuses on documents, technology, and social action in the International Monetary Fund. Harper describes his study as sociological and IT research (1998: 6). The study is based on participant observation and interviews (Harper 1998: 70). Harper's concern was to investigate the document life cycle in the organization. The study is based on the premise that documents are crucial to organizational life (Harper 1998: 13–14). Harper suggests that one way "an ethnographer can get around an organization is by following the career of key information in the organization" (1998: 69). He mentions that an important aspect of ethnography is its ability to serve as a benchmark for the future (1998: 87). As organizations continue to evolve, changes are bound to occur. Such changes can provide an impetus for future ethnographic research.

Of the existing studies in translation, few are based on actual ethnographic fieldwork or any form of participant observation. Koskinen (2008), on the other hand, uses ethnography as a method to study the *actual* work of translators in the EU (2006: 111). Thus, Koskinen's work could serve as a model for the use of ethnographic methods in translation. Koskinen uses multiple data-gathering methods including focus group discussions, questionnaires, field observation, and analysis of source and target texts (2006: 111–13). Her work has provided valuable insight into the work of translators in the EU.

Asare (2011) investigated translation tool usability within the context of a translation agency. The study viewed usability partly as "the relationship between tool users and their tools" (Campbell and Aucion 2003: 172). The study is based on 10 months of participant observation, interviews, user interface walk-throughs, document analysis, and ethnographic microanalysis. The study focused on translation processes and interactions within the agency and investigated disjunctions between tool designers' envisioned use of translation tools and the actual use of the tools.

A review of the literature in interpreting shows a widespread use of discourse analytical methods, surveys, and interviews. Models of ethnography based on sustained immersion or long-term participant observation are rare. Angelelli (2004) stands alone as a full-fledged ethnography of medical interpreting, expanding on the work of researchers, such as Metzger (1999) and Davidson (2000), who used mainly discourse analytical methods to study the interpreter's role. Her work is based on 22 months of participant observation, interviews, artifacts, and surveys. The study includes data from the language service unit of a public hospital in the US. The key informants are ten interpreters and their manager. The study provides insight into the complexities of medical interpreting and draws on theories from social theory, sociological theory, and linguistic anthropology (Angelelli 2004: 26, 132). The research challenges perceptions that the interpreter is and must remain an invisible facilitator of communication. This study allows us to explore the challenges of medical interpreting.

Conclusion and potential applications

Generally, there have been few published ethnographic studies in translation (Koskinen 2006: 111; Asare 2011: 11) and interpreting (Angelelli 2004). The literature reflects the need for a more robust ethnographic research agenda in both fields. The potential benefits of ethnography to T&I have been acknowledged. Koskinen has highlighted its potential to support theory building and to bridge the gap between theory and research (2006: 114); Hubscher-Davidson has argued for its ability to enhance translation process research in an area such as keystroke logging (2011: 3); and Asare has argued that the ethnographic apparatus for detailed descriptions of social and cultural aspects of work can make a significant contribution to translation tool design (2011: 8).

According to Geertz, "theoretical ideas are not created wholly anew in each study." They are adopted from each other, refined, and applied to new interpretive problems (1973: 27). Similarly, T&I can derive immense benefits from *ethnographies of communication.* A shift toward ethnographies of communication is not only timely but vital and would ensure that research keeps pace with changing practices in the field. Ethnographies of communication have the potential to open up new perspectives in translator and interpreter education, translation process research, and translation tool usability, among others. Microethnographies could provide fresh input for translator and interpreter training, while virtual ethnographies could prove useful to the study of translator behavior in virtual spaces. Future ethnographic studies could focus on interpreters' and translators' roles in different organizational settings and on the use of technology. Furthermore, in-depth knowledge of actual practices in both translation and interpreting is essential for designing codes of ethics, as well as appropriate technical support and pedagogical materials.

Further reading

Fetterman (2010) and O'Reilly (2012) are introductory books on ethnographic research. Ellen (1984) is a handbook of ethnography; it includes informative chapters on ethics, fieldwork, and report writing. Spradley (1979) is a valuable guide to the conduct of ethnographic interviews, while Bernard (2006) provides insights into participant observation. Neyland (2008) provides helpful information on organizational ethnography. Atkinson et al. (2001) features an important collection of articles addressing various aspects of ethnography.

References

Angelelli, Claudia. 2004. *Medical Interpreting and Cross-cultural Communication*. Cambridge: Cambridge University Press.

Asare, Edmund. 2011. "An Ethnographic Study of the Use of Translation Tools in a Translation Agency: Implications for Translation Tool Design." Unpublished Ph.D. Dissertation, Kent State University.

Atkinson, Paul, and Sara Delamont. 2008. "Analytic Perspectives." In *Collecting and Interpreting Qualitative Materials*, Norman K. Denzin and Yvonna S. Lincoln (eds.), 285–311. Thousand Oaks, CA: Sage Publications.

Atkinson, Paul, and Martyn Hammersley. 1994. "Ethnography and Participant Observation." In *Handbook of Qualitative Research*, Norman K. Denzin and Yvonna S. Lincoln (eds.), 248–61. Thousand Oaks, CA: Sage Publications.

Atkinson, Paul Anthony, Sara Delamont, Amanda Coffey, John Lofland, and Lyn Lofland (eds.). 2001. *Handbook of Ethnography*. Los Angeles: SAGE Publications.

Becker, Howard S., Blanche Geer, Everett C. Hughes, and Anselm Strauss. 1961. *Boys in White: Student Culture in Medical School*. Chicago: University of Chicago Press.

Bentley, Richard, John A. Hughes, David Randall, Tom Rodden, Pete Swayer, Dan Shapiro, and Ian Sommerville. 1992. *Ethnographically-informed Systems Design for Air Traffic Control*. Lancaster: CSCW Research Center.

Bernard, H. Russell. 2006. *Research Methods in Anthropology*. Lanham, NY: Rowman & Littlefield.

Campbell, Katy, and Robert Aucion. 2003. "Values-based Design of Learning Portals." In *Designing Portals: Opportunities and Challenges*, Ali Jafari and Mark Sheenan (eds.), 162–85. Hershey, PA: Information Science.

Cole, John W. 1977. "Anthropology Comes Part Way Home." *Annual Review of Anthropology* 6: 349–78.
Davidson, Brad. 2000. "The Interpreter as Institutional Gatekeeper: The Social-linguistic Role of Interpreters in Spanish-English Medical Discourse." *Journal of Sociolinguistics* 4(3): 379–405.
Ellen, R. F. 1984. *Ethnographic Research: A Guide to General Conduct*. London: Academic Press.
Erickson, Frederick. 1992. "Ethnographic Microanalysis of Interaction." In *Handbook of Qualitative Research in Education*, Margaret D. Le Compte, Wendy L. Millroy, and Judith Preissle (eds.), 201–26. San Diego: Academic Press.
Fassin, Didier. 2013. *Enforcing Order: An Ethnography of Urban Policing*. Cambridge: Polity.
Fetterman, David M. 2010. *Ethnography Step by Step*. 3rd edition. Thousand Oaks, CA: Sage Publications.
Geertz, Clifford. 1973. *The Interpretation of Cultures*. New York: Basic Books.
Harper, Richard. 1998. *Inside the IMF: An Ethnography of Documents, Technology and Organisational Action*. London: Academic Press.
Hubscher-Davidson, Severine. 2011. "A Discussion of Ethnographic Research Methods and Their Relevance to the Translation Process." *Across Languages and Cultures* 12(1): 1–18.
Hymes, D. 1964. Introduction: Toward Ethnographies of Communication. *American Anthropologist, New Series*, December, 66 Part 2(6): 1–34.
Koskinen, Kaisa. 2006. "Going into the Field: Ethnographic Methods in Translation Studies." In *Ubersetzen – Translating – Traduire*, Michaela Wolf (ed.), 109–17. London: Transaction Publishers.
——2008. *Translating Institutions: An Ethnographic Study of EU Translation*. Manchester: St. Jerome.
LeCompte, Margaret D., and Judith. P. Goetz. 1982. "Problems of Validity and Reliability in Ethnographic Research." *Review of Educational Research* 52(1): 31–60.
Malinowski, Bronislaw. 1922. *Argonauts of the Western Pacific*. New York: Dutton.
McGibbon, Elizabeth, Elizabeth Peter, and Ruth Gallop. 2010. "An Institutional Ethnography of Nurses' Stress." *Qualitative Health Research* 20(10): 1353–78.
Mehan, Hugh. 1979. *Learning Lessons: Social Organization in the Classroom*. Cambridge, MA: Harvard University Press.
——1998. "The Study of Social Interaction in Educational Settings." *Human Development* 41: 245–69.
Mehus, Siri Elizabeth. 2006. *Coordinating Care: A Microethnographic Investigation into Interactional Practices of Childcare*. Austin: University of Texas Press.
Metzger, Melanie. 1999. *Sign Language Interpreting: Deconstructing the Myth of Neutrality*. Washington DC: Gallaudet University Press.
Neyland, Daniel. 2008. *Organizational Ethnography*. Thousand Oaks, CA: Sage Publications.
O'Reilly, Karen. 2012. *Ethnographic Methods*. New York: Routledge.
Radcliffe-Brown, A. R. 1952. "Historical Note on British Social Anthropology: Letters to the Editor." *American Anthropologist* 54(2): 275–77.
Spradley, James P. 1979. *Ethnographic Interview*. New York: Holt, Rinehart and Winston.
——1980. *Participant Observation*. New York: Holt, Rinehart and Winston.

Streeck, Jürgen, and Siri Mehus. 2005. "Microethnography: The Study of Practices." In *Handbook of Language and Social Interaction*, Kristine L. Fitch and Robert E. Sanders (eds.), 381–404. Mahwah, NJ: Lawrence Erlbaum.

Wacquant, Loïc. 2003. "Ethnografeast: A Progress Report on the Practice and Promise of Ethnography." *Ethnography* 4(1): 5–14.

Willis, Paul, and Mat Trondman. 2000. "Manifesto for Ethnography." *Ethnography* 1(1): 5–16.

Wolcott, Harry F. 1973. *The Man in the Principal's Office*. New York: Holt.

——1995. *The Art of Fieldwork*. Walnut Creek, CA: Altamira.

19 Experimental research

Daniel Gile

Definition

Definitions of experiments in scientific literature vary: some are more restrictive, some broader. For reasons explained in this chapter, for translation and interpreting (T&I) research, the following inclusive definition is suggested: Experiments are scientific investigations in which an environment and/or a particular task (beyond simply reporting information, e.g., through questionnaires) are created, controlled, or manipulated for the specific purpose of collecting data in order to improve one's knowledge of the object of study.

The following are two classic examples of experimental studies in T&I research:

- Interpreters were asked to interpret the same speech at different delivery speeds, or with or without preparation, with or without background noise (e.g., Gerver 1976).
- Translators were asked to translate a text which had been manipulated lexically or grammatically or under specific conditions (e.g., with or without time pressure, with or without previous preparation, with or without available documentary sources, from one's native language into a foreign language or vice versa) so as to check whether the differences in what is being manipulated or controlled have an effect on the process or the product (e.g., Jensen 1999, for the effects of time pressure manipulation).

The manipulated variable (time, previous preparation, availability of documentary sources, directionality) is called the "independent variable"; the variable used as an indicator of the effect on the output (speed of the process, language errors, errors and omission, tactics reported) is called the "dependent variable."

Experiments are typically described as quantitative methods designed to test hypotheses. Controlled experiments are those in which some groups, the "experimental groups," receive a "treatment," and another group, the "control group," receives none. Values of the dependent variable in all groups are compared using statistical tests that help decide whether, taking into account individual variability within the groups, it is reasonable to assume that the differences found are due to the treatment (i.e., to the different values of the independent variable) or whether they are not large enough to be attributed to anything but random variation.

Such descriptions do not cover all experimental research in science. Experiments need not be quantitative (see Kleining 1986) and can also be used for exploratory purposes. In fact, Francis Bacon, considered by many to be the father of experimental research, recommended experiments and data collection in a broadly exploratory manner *prior* to theorizing (Bacon 1620/2000: 110). This was also Darwin's approach (2002). For a further discussion of exploratory experimentation and its role in "normal science," see Waters 2007.

Over time, experiments have come to be considered in a more restrictive way as tools devoted to theory and hypothesis testing, but according to Franklin (2005: 888), experimentation not guided by hypothesis or "local" theory "has a broader and more systematic role in scientific inquiry than is commonly recognized."

Four important advantages of experiments over naturalistic studies (in which phenomena and entities are studied in their natural environment) deserve to be mentioned here:

- High observability potential: Experiments are planned and set up. Investigators can therefore prepare the experimental environment to ensure optimal observation and measurement conditions.
- The elimination of (some) confounding effects: Most phenomena investigated by science are caused by more than one factor. In experiments, when exploring the effect of one particular variable, one can try to eliminate or control the effect of other variables (confounding variables, which could interfere by producing noise) through sampling, by changing the physical environment, manipulating materials, or having participants perform specific tasks. In naturalistic studies, filtering out the effect of confounding variables can be done through statistical methods, after the fact, and generally requires much more data (e.g., in epidemiological studies).
- Replicability: Experiments can be replicated under very similar conditions so as to check whether the trends found are constant.
- The possibility of setting up conditions that seldom or never occur in real-life settings, e.g., having many translators or interpreters translate the same text into the same language at the same time and in the same working environment.

The fundamental challenge generally associated with experiments is the issue of ecological validity (see Sabourin 1988: 58; Babbie 1991: 257; Eysenck and Keane 1992: 501). Because of the artificial nature of the setting and controls, it is sometimes difficult to assess the extent to which the same or similar results can be applied to real-life settings.

In order to reach maximum efficiency, experiments need to be planned and implemented rigorously, in such a way as to reduce the effect of confounding variables and bias. Randomization, i.e., random allocation of individual entities to the experimental groups and the control group, is one of the planning and implementation strategies used for this purpose. Experiments that do not meet such rigorous conditions are sometimes referred to as quasi-experiments. Note that this concept is fairly recent, and that it also has different definitions. Some describe "quasi-experiments" as strictly identical to "experiments" except for the randomized allocation element, while others describe them as experiments lacking some controls.

Origins

Experimentation in the broad or "natural" sense of the word, i.e., trying out various actions to achieve improvements, is natural. Experimental research as defined above goes one step further and probably arose from the desire of scientists in early human history to observe and measure natural physical phenomena more accurately and reliably. It first developed in what is now called physics, then in other natural sciences, and was later adopted in behavioral disciplines, such as psychology and sociology, and in some of the human sciences, such as linguistics. It is also prevalent in industrial research.

Technically speaking, T&I Studies are good candidates for experimental research for the following reasons:

1. T&I activities are influenced by many variables—linguistic, textual, personal, work-environmental—and since in the overwhelming majority of cases (except for school translation and literary translation) a text or speech is translated once in a given environment by one team of translators or interpreters, it can be difficult to tease apart the influence of any single variable on the process or the output through naturalistic observation.
2. The input parameters and environment of translation and interpreting (in particular, features of the source text and of the working environment) are generally easy to define and to control, and the output is a well-defined entity, making replications, control, and observation technically convenient. To borrow psychologist Flores d'Arcais' words on conference interpreting (1978: 393): "there are probably very few 'real life' situations which are more similar to a laboratory of psychological experimentation than the situation of the interpreter in a conference booth, both for the control of external variables and for the 'artificiality' of the task in comparison to human linguistic performance."

Very simple experiments in which several participants are asked to translate or interpret the same text or speech make it possible to spot regularities in their performance and assign them on a tentative basis to specific parameters or working conditions. For instance, Seleskovitch (1975) asked 12 professional interpreters to interpret two English speeches consecutively into French in order to study their note-taking output and to target speeches with a view to finding out whether her intuition about an alleged "deverbalization" step between reception and production could be confirmed. There was no special manipulation or control procedure. Gile conducted several experiments in the same mindset, without any particular manipulation, to see, for instance, what happened to proper names in simultaneous interpreting, or how listening was affected by note-taking in beginning student interpreters, or how fidelity was assessed in consecutive interpreting in the classroom, or what happened to accuracy when speeches were interpreted a second time right after a first time, or whether simultaneous or consecutive was more accurate (references to publications describing these experiments can be found in Gile 2009). Simple experiments of the same kind, i.e., with little or no manipulation or complex setups, are numerous in research on interpreting.

In research on written translation, experiments became popular a bit later, starting in the mid-1980s, after Ericsson and Simon (1984) introduced the Think Aloud Protocol paradigm in psychology. This was adopted by translation scholars, starting with Krings (1986) and Lörscher (1991). Many others followed: see, for instance, Tirkkonen-Condit and Jääskeläinen (2000), Alves (2003), and Englund Dimitrova (2005). For the most part, these experiments involved having translators translate texts while verbalizing their thoughts. Investigators used this simple design to identify tactics (commonly referred to as "strategies" in the literature), stages in the translation process, and differences between trainees at various stages of learning. Such simple experiments were soon enhanced with keyboard logging software, which made it possible to trace back all keyboard operations performed by translators and to time them, with retrospection and with and without cues (see Hansen 2006). Gaze analysis through the use of eye-tracking was added later as an additional tool (see Mees et al. 2010).

Challenges and limitations

Most experiments to date have been carried out with trainee translators and interpreters as opposed to professionals. This is unproblematic when experimenters investigate their students' behavior or when they seek to demonstrate something to students in classroom experiments—see, for instance, Gile 2009, Chapter 5, for a simple experiment to show why and how fidelity does not imply word-for-word translation. However, when seeking answers to questions about professional translation and interpreting, extrapolating from students to professionals cannot be taken for granted, precisely because numerous comparisons suggest that their behavior differs significantly in many respects. This is particularly true in research on conference interpreting, where relevant cognitive skills need much time to mature and a sizable proportion of trainees never acquire those skills to a sufficient extent to graduate and qualify as professional interpreters. The reason why so much experimenting is done on students is the small number of professional interpreters who are available and willing to participate in experiments in which their behavior and output will be scrutinized.

Another problem which limits the power of experimental research to detect and/or confirm regularities is high inter-individual variability in the behavior of translators and interpreters, also frequently mentioned in the literature (see Lamberger-Felber 2003 for an example related to conference interpreting). The higher the variability, the larger the required sample sizes, and recruiting participants for experiments is often difficult in T&I Studies. High inter-individual variability also has implications for the usefulness of any statistically significant differences found. Unless they are very large, random variation or variation due to any confounding variable can offset them in any single real instance of translation or interpreting.

Yet another important point is that in T&I Studies (and in many other disciplines where computer simulation is not possible) most experiments are conducted with one, two, or, at most, three different values of one or two independent variables (such as language combination, level of experience, availability of documents, or time pressure). All other factors (hereafter "parameters") with a potentially significant effect on translator and interpreter behavior (training, language proficiency, familiarity with the subject, motivation, working memory capacity, syntactic complexity of the source text, etc.) have only one value in each experiment. In this respect, experiments are far less different from case studies than is generally believed, because they study translator or interpreter behavior in one combination of parameter values—albeit for two or three values of the independent variable(s). Moreover, some of the factors that are not controlled (age, experience, motivation, previous knowledge) can have a potentially strong influence on T&I behavior. Since, as already mentioned, it is often difficult to recruit participants for experimental research, the ideal of controlling all potential confounding variables in an experimental setup through careful selection of a sufficient number of subjects is not within reach of any single experiment.

Variability and/or confounding effects due to lack of control over some relevant factors can be compensated for by replicating studies with different combinations of values for the relevant parameters. But again, this requires recruiting more participants, something more easily said than done. Note that the same need for replication is found in naturalistic studies as in experimental studies—and for the same reasons. The point here is that the limitations explained above reduce considerably two of the advantages of experiments over naturalistic studies, listed in the first section of this chapter, namely replicability and the possibility of overcoming confounding effects.

Ironically, in Interpreting Studies—and even more so in research on written translation—it is rather easy to design experiments with relatively high ecological validity, notwithstanding the protests of some practitioners in the 1970s, mentioned by Flores d'Arcais (1978: 393). Moreover, it is rather easy in such experiments to check the comparability of results with naturalistic studies, especially now that so many conferences are webcast and recorded and that comparisons can be made between "natural" behavior and subsequent behavior in the laboratory when interpreters are asked to interpret the same speeches under experimental conditions.

However, while this holds for experiments with holistic T&I tasks, when subjects are assigned related tasks (reading, or listening without having to interpret, or doing cloze exercises), when the tasks are holistic but conditions are unusual (translating a text from a moving window of several words only, or translating single words or sentences out of context, translation done by "bilinguals" without interpreter or translator training and/or experience), ecological validity is challenged once again. Several early experimental designs by cognitive psychologists and psycholinguists who were interested in simultaneous interpreting had such features. This explains the reservations expressed by pioneer researchers from the ranks of interpreting practitioners as referred to by Flores d'Arcais.

Quasi-experiments or experiments?

The vast majority of experiments conducted on professional T&I to date are exploratory. Investigators tend to design studies with holistic T&I tasks, and ecological validity issues arise mostly from the fact that participants are students rather than full-fledged translators and interpreters, not from the nature of the tasks assigned to them or from environmental conditions that deviate too much from real-life conditions. In research into written translation, doubts have been expressed about the Think Aloud Protocal (TAP) paradigm. Some investigators believe that because thinking aloud is a complex and perhaps taxing cognitive activity, it may have a significant effect not only on the speed of translation but also on some underlying cognitive patterns (see Englund Dimitrova 2005: Chapter 3). Fortunately, there are less invasive techniques and tools that can be used to monitor translation (in particular, keystroke logging, screenshot recording, eye-tracking; see Mees et al. 2010) and interpreting (pupillometry is a promising tool in this respect; see Seeber and Kerzek 2012).

There are actually few hypothesis-testing experiments in T&I with full control, random allocation of participants to experimental and control groups, and inferential statistics, which are standard in the cognitive sciences—with some exceptions, mostly in studies on interpreting cognition. In the eyes of experimental psychologists, the overwhelming majority of experiments in translation and interpreting are therefore "quasi-experiments." Note that the concept and the term are not universally used in science and that some of the conditions used to distinguish quasi-experiments from (canonical) experiments in psychology, including random assignment of individual entities to treatment groups, are not universally relevant in other disciplines. Furthermore, the very use of "quasi-" can be taken as suggesting that the procedure is somewhat inferior, not quite up to scientific standards. This, however, is not the case insofar as scientific standards are based on underlying principles of rigorous investigation, not on technical criteria that apply to some objects of study and research environments and not to others (see Gile 2013).

Future directions

In addition to their didactic use in the classroom, experiments have made important contributions to the exploration of T&I phenomena. Suffice it to mention as illustrations the findings regarding differences between novices and professional translators in terms of foci of attention, decision-making, timing of various actions, and output quality, through TAP experiments and logging experiments with or without retrospection (see Hansen 2006), or findings about quality expectations and perception (see Collados Aís et al. 2007), and about note-taking (see, for example, Dam 2004) in the field of interpreting.

The potential of simple experiments in T&I research remains strong for a number of reasons:

1. On many fundamental issues, such as directionality, training strategies, preparation modes for interpreting, quality expectations and perception, and communication patterns in interpreted mediated communication in specific environments, the volume of empirical research remains insufficient. Hence a need for more exploration and replication work to detect regularities versus environment-specific singularities on a holistic level before going into more fine-grained hypothesis testing.
2. While advanced experimental design and techniques require knowledge and skills that may not always be found among T&I students and their instructors, such students can conduct simple experiments. Every year, hundreds of students must complete graduation theses. This provides a large pool of investigators for relatively simple studies.
3. Over the past decade or so, there has been increasing mutual interest among the various branches of T&I, and new questions arise. Clearly, to compare the behavior of practitioners from such differing environments, setting up experiments where they meet—which does not happen often in natural environments—and perform tasks designed to highlight similarities and differences is an efficient strategy.

Obviously, as our knowledge of the field advances, opportunities also arise for more advanced designs, and advanced experimental research is indispensable to further progress, but it is only one form of research rather than its quintessence.

Further reading

Alvstad, Hild, and Tiselius (2011) is a collected volume on translation and interpreting process research that contains methodological reflections as well as sample studies, including exploratory and hypothesis-testing experiments. Göpferich, Jakobsen, and Mees (2008) is a collection of ten papers describing experiments on translation and reading using eye-tracking techniques. Hinkelmann and Kempthorne (2008) provides a technical introduction to quantitative experiments. Robson (1994) is an introduction to experimental design in psychology which uses simple language and straightforward explanations and advice.

References

Alves, Fabio (ed.). 2003. *Triangulating Translation*. Amsterdam and Philadelphia: John Benjamins.

Alvstad, Cecilia, Adelina Hild, and Elisabet Tiselius (eds.). 2011. *Methods and Strategies of Process Research*. Amsterdam and Philadelphia: John Benjamins.

Babbie, Earl. 1991. *The Practice of Social Research*. Belmont, CA: Wadsworth.

Bacon, Francis. 1620/2000. *The New Organon*. Cambridge: Cambridge University Press.

Collados Aís, Ángela, E. Macarena Prada Macías, Elisabeth Stévaux, and Olalla García Becerra (eds.). 2007. *La evaluación de la calidad en interpretación simultánea: parámetros de incidencia*. Granada: Editorial Comares.

Dam, Helle V. 2004. "Interpreters' Notes. On the Choice of Form and Language." In *Claims, Changes and Challenges in Translation Studies*, Gyde Hansen, Kirsten Malkmjaer, and Daniel Gile (eds.), 251–61. Amsterdam and Philadelphia: John Benjamins.

Darwin, Charles. 2002. *Autobiographies*. London: Penguin Books.

Englund Dimitrova, Birgitta. 2005. *Expertise and Explicitation in the Translation Process*. Amsterdam and Philadelphia: John Benjamins.

Ericsson, Karl Anders, and Herbert A. Simon. 1984. *Protocol Analysis: Verbal Reports as Data*. Cambridge, MA: MIT Press.

Eysenck, Michael W., and Mark T. Keane. 1992. *Cognitive Psychology. A Student's Handbook*. Hove and London, UK and Hillsdale, NJ: Lawrence Erlbaum Associates.

Flores d'Arcais, Giovanni B. 1978. "The Contribution of Cognitive Psychology to the Study of Interpretation." In *Language Interpretation and Communication*, David Gerver and H. Wallace Sinaiko (eds.), 385–402. New York and London: Plenum Press.

Franklin, Laura R. 2005. "Exploratory Experiments." *Philosophy of Science* 72 (December): 888–99.

Gerver, David. 1976. "Empirical Studies of Simultaneous Interpretation: A Review and a Model." In *Translation. Applications and Research*, Richard W. Brislin (ed.), 165–207. New York: Gardner Press.

Gile, Daniel. 2009. *Basic Concepts and Models for Interpreter and Translator Training*. Revised edition. Amsterdam and Philadelphia: John Benjamins.

——2013. "Scientificity and Theory in Translation Studies." In *Handbook of Translation Studies*, vol. 4, Yves Gambier and Luc Van Doorslaer (eds.), 148–55. Amsterdam and Philadelphia: John Benjamins.

Göpferich, Susanne, Arnt Lykke Jakobsen, and Inger M. Mees (eds.). 2008. *Looking at Eyes. Eye-tracking Studies of Reading and Translation Processing*. Copenhagen Studies in Language 36. Copenhagen: Samfundslitteratur.

Hansen, Gyde. 2006. "Retrospection Methods in Translator Training and Translation Research." *Jostrans* 5: 1–41.

Hinkelmann, Klaus, and Oscar Kempthorne. 2008. *Design and Analysis of Experiments, Volume I: Introduction to Experimental Design*. 2nd edition. Hoboken, NJ: Wiley.

Jensen, Astrid. 1999. "Time Pressure in Translation." *Copenhagen Studies in Language* 24: 103–19.

Kleining, Gerhard. 1986. "Das qualitative experiment" [The qualitative experiment]. *Kölner Zeitschrift für Soziologie und Sozialpsychologie* 38(4): 724–50.

Krings, Hans P. 1986. *Was in den Köpfen von Übersetzern vorgeht. Eine empirische Untersuchung der Struktur des Übersetzungsprozesses an fortgeschrittenen Französischlernern*. Tübingen: Narr.

Lamberger-Felber, Heike. 2003. "Performance Variability among Conference Interpreters: Examples from a Case Study." In *La evaluación de la calidad en interpretación: investigación*, Ángela Collados Aís, María Manuela Fernández Sánchez, and Daniel Gile (eds.), 147–68. Granada: Editorial Comares.

Lörscher, Wolfgang. 1991. *Translation Performance, Translation Process, and Translation Strategies. A Psycholinguistic Investigation*. Tübingen: Narr.

Mees, Inger M., Fabio Alves, and Susanne Göpferich (eds.). 2010. *Methodology, Technology and Innovation in Translation Process Research*. Copenhagen: Copenhagen Studies in Language.

Robson, Colin. 1994. *Experiment, Design and Statistics in Psychology. An Introduction*. 3rd edition. London and New York: Penguin Books.

Sabourin, Michel. 1988. "Méthodes d'acquisition des connaissances." In *Fondements et étapes de la recherche scientifique en psychologie*. 3rd edition, Michèle Robert (ed.), 37–58. St-Hyacinthe, Québec and Paris: Edisem et Maloine.

Seleskovitch, Danica. 1975. *Langages, langues et mémoires*. Paris: Minard Lettres modernes.

Seeber, Kilian, and Dirk Kerzek. 2012. "Cognitive Load in Simultaneous Interpreting: Model Meets Data." *The International Journal of Bilingualism* 16(2): 228–42.

Tirkkonen-Condit, Sonja, and Riitta Jääskeläinen (eds.). 2000. *Tapping and Mapping the Processes of Translation and Interpreting*. Amsterdam and Philadelphia: John Benjamins.

Waters, Kenneth C. 2007. "The Nature and Context of Exploratory Experimentation: An Introduction to Three Case Studies of Exploratory Research." *History and Philosophy of the Life Sciences* 29(3): 275–84.

20 *Histoire croisée*

Michaela Wolf

Definition

In the last decade, the history of translation has attracted considerable attention within Translation Studies. Research methods in particular have gained momentum, as signalled by vast and manifold academic activity: a growing number of conferences, books, special issues, and ambitious group projects testify to the importance given today to the topic. Many of the emerging methodologies draw on the field of history, among them, to a lesser extent, the *histoire croisée* approach.

As Michael Werner and Bénédicte Zimmermann, both working at the *Ecole des hautes études en sciences sociales* in Paris, point out, the research method known as *histoire croisée* invites us to reconsider the interactions between different societies and cultures, erudite disciplines of traditions, and, more specifically, social and cultural products: "*Histoire croisée* focuses on empirical intercrossings consubstantial with the object of study, as well as on the operations by which researchers themselves cross scales, categories, and viewpoints" (Werner and Zimmermann 2006: 30).

Histoire croisée is tightly connected with other concepts, such as entangled and shared history, which are also concerned with exploring transnational procedures and enlacements that have for a long time been veiled by national historiographies. The concept of *histoire croisée* goes further inasmuch as it constructs a specific relationship between the observer's position, the perspective, and the historical object. In so doing, the moment of crossing becomes an active occurrence and can be viewed as the result of historical and present processes. What is interlaced is not of primary importance, but rather the mode of enlacement. *Histoire croisée* is not concerned with fixed categories, but with problems and questions that are subject to a certain evolution during the process of analysis; it also analyzes concrete objects like institutions, legal systems, cultural products, or disciplines—and not given models and global constructs, such as nation, society, or culture. It focuses on the level of the agents involved, that is, on the conflicts in which they operate and on the strategies adopted to develop solutions to those conflicts (Werner and Zimmermann 2002: 617). As can be seen, these concerns are also central to the analysis of the translation/interpreting process, including both the actors involved in all its stages and the translation/interpreting product.

The process of "enlacement" or "intercrossing" is conditioned by various dimensions: one is that it is continuously created anew because it takes place between already enlaced objects; this implies that the objects are subject to a permanent transformation during and as a result of the "intercrossing," which generally takes place in asymmetrical constellations. As a result, we have to distinguish among various levels of intercrossing: the one between the objects, the other between the various perspectives that control the view of the enlaced objects, and the third involving the intercrossing of the analytical practices of the researcher (Middell 2005). This, eventually, discloses the self-reflexive nature of this approach.

The objects to be analyzed—in our case "original" and "translation/interpretating" or "translator/interpreter"—are considered to be historically constructed. One of the features of this construction is their interpretation in the specific context of their formation, which distinguishes the object from other comparable objects; this implies a sociological approach to the translation/interpretating phenomena that sheds light on the various stages of the production process and reveals the object's specificity. The conditions of formation are also a product of construction. Also, the (preliminary) ensemble of these objects—in our case, for instance, the translations/interpretations produced at a certain time and in a certain culture—live in a dynamic relationship of exchange with other objects within their social, political, and cultural surroundings (Werner and Zimmermann 2002: 611; Anklam and Schwerendt 2009); consider the various cultural reference systems and the personal experience of the "oberserver" that deliver the context of the translation/interpreting production.

For Werner and Zimmermann, the constituents of the "intercrossing" process are manifold. Typological factors include observations and viewpoints, which for the translational context could mean various perspectives on translation/interpreting and their reflection in time and space; abstract objects, such as economic systems, educational systems, or traditions of ideas, which in translation/interpreting can be related to the consideration of political and aesthetic traditions of thought; concrete objects, such as books (in Translation Studies, these are the very object of the discipline); and human beings, the last and perhaps most important group of constituents, especially migrants who create a tissue of multifold relationships (Werner and Zimmermann 2002: 618). In the context of translation/interpreting, these refer to translators, interpreters, and other agents or institutions involved in the translation process.

Origin

Histoire croisée has been developed in historical sciences in the course of debates over various established theoretical methods, such as the comparative history (Kocka 1996) or cultural transfer approaches (Wolf 2003). The most salient arguments in this debate refer to the position of the observer, traditionally assumed to be external to the objects that are compared; to the choice of the scale of the comparison (levels of region, nation-state, etc. are not generalizable); to the definition of the object of the comparison, which is always marked in advance by a particular representation; and to conflicts between synchronic and diachronic logics, as the comparative approach privileges a synchronic cross-section over a diachronic view (Kocka 2003: 41–42; Werner and Zimmermann 2006: 34–35). On the other hand, the inquiry into cultural transfers is clearly located in a diachronic perspective. What makes this approach problematic, however, is its concept of culture. Based on national categories, it is clearly unsuited to the study of the complex game of identity constructions and hybridizations characteristic for both historical (see, e.g., the Habsburg or Ottoman Empire) and contemporary contexts (Celestini and Mitterbauer 2003: 11). Consequently, "transfer" can no longer be seen as a linear connection between two units to be analyzed, but as a procedure based on multiple and dynamic exchanges of symbols, informative discourses, and practices subject to continuous transformation (12). As a response to these critical points and in view of the accelerated processes of internationalization and renewed debates on globalization, we can witness a new stress on transnational approaches to history, among them *histoire croisée* (Kocka 2003: 42).

Uses

So far, the approach of *histoire croisée* has scarcely been applied in Translation and Interpreting Studies research. On a conceptual level, D'hulst (2012: 143, 152) has referred to various principles discussed in the *histoire croisée* approach. He particularly draws on "pragmatic induction," which might serve as one of the steps to be taken in the design of a practical methodology for "transfer histories," with transfer understood here as a dynamic category. While the author clearly points to the methodological potential of *histoire croisée*, the concept as such is not further developed or applied on an analytical level.

So far, Reiter's work (2013) on eighteenth-century interpreters at the Vienna Habsburg Court is the only one to have thoroughly adopted the *histoire croisée* approach to historically oriented questions in Translation and Interpreting Studies. The author conceives of the court's organization as a social system and explores the makeup of the interpreters' activity and status in various cultural mediation processes. The conceptual tools of *histoire croisée* help her to shed light on the research object from various perspectives, fostering interdisciplinary perceptions, and to unfold the Habsburg interpreting field from both the interpreter's (archival research) and the researcher's (study of secondary sources) viewpoint.

Drawing on *histoire croisée*, Reiter is able to approach her topic from two perspectives: first, on a historiographical level, by exploring the office of the court interpreter and the internal organization of the Vienna court; second, from an Interpreting Studies perspective, which allows her to consider the interpreters and their functions and tasks, their participation in social networks, the impact of power on their activities, and their labor as mediators between the various "clients" involved. Both perspectives are tinged by the researcher's self-reflexive choices and observations and connected with (selected) results from pertinent secondary sources. On the other hand, both perspectives are more closely determined by the ideas circulating both in research literature and in collective memory on the functioning of imperial courts, ceremonial roles, and conventions of diplomacy. These constituents need contextualization in order to reconstruct the institutional frame within which the interpreters' office is situated and which had a decisive impact on the interpreters' professional life. Reiter then emphasizes the time factor. On a micro level, she illustrates the integration of the Polish and Russian court interpreters' office into the court's administrative body at the beginning of the eighteenth century, while from a macro perspective she shows the rather longitudinal development of the court interpreters' office for Oriental languages, again with a special focus on the eighteenth century. In so doing, the perspectives are continuously changed and tied together in order to facilitate sketching a comprehensive image of the situation under research. Shifting between the timescales enables her to test whether the researcher can apply the arguments from the particular case under investigation to more general developments and whether this particular case can reveal characteristic tendencies which might be true for a larger number of court interpreters. In the final stage, the interpreter is discussed as a figure positioned at the points where the various perspectives intersect, which also gives the readers a clue into the way the interpreting "profession" was depicted in the period and space investigated.

In summary, the adoption of *histoire croisée* in Reiter's analysis illuminates the multiple codings of the court interpreter's activity and his involvement in a rigorous ceremonial at the imperial court, both on a timescale that charts the different rhythms in the development of the interpreter's office of Polish, Russian, and Oriental languages (the latter designed for working at the Sublime Porte of Constantinople or for ministering to diplomatic visitors from the Ottoman Empire) and at the intersections of interdisciplinary perspectives involving the researcher's self-reflexivity.

Another example, which is presented here for the first time, should elucidate the strong potential offered by *histoire croisée.* It draws on a historical account by Lars Westerlund from 2008, called *Saksan vankileirit Suomessa ja raja-alueilla 1941–1944* [German prisoners of war camps in Finland and in border areas 1941–44] (see Kujamäki 2012: 96). In Westerlund's report, the Ukrainian prisoner Mihail escapes from a German prisoner of war (POW) camp. After being recaptured by Finnish headhunters, Mihail is shot in front of other camp inmates as a warning. As his last words he shouts: "Kahi [*sic*] žive Radjanska Ukraina" (Long live Soviet Ukraine). The officer in charge asks the interpreter to interpret the message into German. The interpreter obviously does not want to talk openly about Mihail's patriotic thoughts and so says that the executed prisoner bade farewell to the other prisoners of war. In so doing, the interpreter positions himself on the side of the executed man's fellow captives, perhaps in order to protect them. As we do not know which army the interpreter served, we might assume the existence of a widespread practice according to which the role of mediator was forced upon bilingual prisoners of war. Therefore, it might also be true that in the execution scene other reasons came into play, such as loyalty to the interpreter's own nationality or political sympathy with the executed prisoner's political stance.

Adopting a *histoire croisée* approach to the analysis of this situation in the POW camp, we might identify various perspectives. First, the objects to be analyzed in the present context involve both the "interpreting situation" and the various participating agents and institutions: Mihail, the camp inmates, the German officer, the interpreter, and the Finnish headhunters, as well as the camp and the army as institutions. This perspective thus presents an ensemble of objects who or which converge in the interpreting situation after the execution and whose dynamics are primarily conditioned by the atmosphere of violence dominating the scene. Their interlacement is particularly revealed in the crossing of the different levels where the participating agents are being staged: Mihail at the moment of his execution, his fellow inmates being forced to watch the scene, the German officer struggling to linguistically understand what is going on, and the interpreter who shifts between different levels, that of the Ukrainian ideological stance and that of military obedience. Another perspective results from the dynamic exchange modes with other objects of the social, political, and cultural environment; in the present case this might apply to the ideological constraints placed upon the camp interpreter. The motivation behind Westerlund's perspective might be reconstructed from the usage of his sources: did he get his relevant information from archival material, or through oral history, or private letters, or memoirs? And what were his selection criteria? On the other hand, the researcher's perspective is that of controlling—willingly or not—the emphasis placed on the various elements of information that nourish the scene: where is his or her focus? On the agents and their potential motivation to act as observable units in the scene, or on the terrifying moments of the execution? What is the researcher's bias: the "value" of military loyalty or the absurdity of war?

What seems particularly relevant is the interlacement of the various participating objects. The method proposed involves several elements which mold our understanding of this interpreting scene. The instants of terror, arbitrariness, and panic which seem quite characteristic for this scene can be brought to the fore particularly through an emphasis on the moment of intercrossing: the presence at and passive or active participation in the scene on behalf of the agents, institutions, the author, and the researcher allow for a dynamics which are simultaneously nourished (involving imagination) and blocked (through lack of information) by the fact that we lack the information as to why the interpreter misinterpreted Mihail's crucial message. What counts is the permanent move between the various perspectives and its inherent potential to create or better construct new views on the research object.

Sample studies

D'hulst (2012) and Reiter (2013) are the only works which so far have applied *histoire croisée* in Translation Studies. While D'hulst refers to some central principles of the method without applying it analytically, Reiter fully exploits the conceptual tools in her study of court interpreters in the Habsburg monarchy.

Conclusion and potential applications of this method

The *histoire croisée* approach helps to disclose a series of features that in many traditional approaches in translation/interpreting history might have been overlooked or at least not given the attention they deserve. One of the central features to be highlighted when adopting the analytical tools of *histoire croisée* is the transnational orientation given to the translation and interpreting activity under various perspectives. This specifically multi-dimensional orientation contributes allows us to better identify the spaces between identifiable historical processes and to go beyond dichotomies of "past" and "present." In addition, "the entities and objects of research under investigation are not merely considered in relation to one another, but also *through* one another, in terms of relationships, interactions, and circulation" (Werner and Zimmermann 2006: 38, original emphasis). Such a view prompts a methodological claim: the contemporary "observer"—the researcher—crosses with the agents of the research being done and thus helps to transcend the classical divide of researcher and object of study. This procedure brings about the idea of a "doubling" (Werner and Zimmermann 2002: 624) of—at least—two levels of reflection and puts the focus on their interdependency and on the numerous interactions taking place between these levels.

The *histoire croisée*—and this has been stressed by Werner and Zimmermann—can be seen neither as an accomplished program to be readily adopted nor as a theory to be continuously refined and reshaped. Rather, it is a collection of heuristic instruments (Middell 2005) that help sensitize the experiences drawn from the intertwinement and interrelatedness of communication processes in general and mediation processes qua interpreting and translating in particular. The widely applicable approach will be successfully introduced in Translation and Interpreting Studies as an intricate and epistemically relevant theoretical approach only when it is based on an array of multifaceted case studies.

Further reading

Middell (2005) delivers a valuable review of Werner and Zimmermann's book (2004), providing useful arguments on the pros and cons of the *historire croisée* approach. Werner and Zimmermann (2002, 2004, and 2006) present the basic features of *histoire croisée*, thoroughly discussing its innovative potential against more traditional approaches, such as comparative history and cultural transfer.

References

Anklam, Ewa, and Matthias Schwerendt. 2009. "Histoire croisée." In Educational Media Research. Available online at www.edumeres.net/informationen/glossar/histoire-croisee.html (last accessed April 27, 2014).

Celestini, Federico, and Helga Mitterbauer. 2003. "Einleitung." In *Ver-rückte Kulturen. Zur Dynamik kultureller Transfers*, Federico Celestini and Helga Mitterbauer (eds.), 11–17. Tübingen: Stauffenburg.

D'hulst, Lieven. 2012. "(Re)locating Translation History: From Assumed Translation to Assumed Transfer." *Translation Studies* 5(2): 139–55.

Kocka, Jürgen. 1996. "The Uses of Comparative History." In *Societies Made Up of History. Essays in Historiography, Intellectual History, Professionalism, Historical Social Theory and Proto-industrialisation*, Ragnar Björk and Karl Molin (eds.), 197–209. Edsbruk: Akademitryck AB.

——2003. "Comparison and beyond." *History and Theory* 42(1): 39–45.

Kujamäki, Pekka. 2012. "Mediating for the Third Reich: On Military Translation Cultures in World War II in Northern Finland." In *Languages and the Military. Alliances, Occupation and Peace Building*, Hilary Footitt and Michael Kelly (eds.), 86–99. Basingstoke: Palgrave Macmillan.

Middell, Matthias. 2005. "Review: *De la comparaison à l'histoire croisée*, Michael Werner and Bénédicte Zimmermann, eds. 2004. Paris: Seuil." H-Soz-u-Kult, April. Available at: http://hsozkult.geschichte.hu-berlin.de/rezensionen/2005-2-075 (last accessed April 27, 2014).

Reiter, Clara. 2013. "Vermittler zwischen West und Ost: Hofdolmetscher am Habsburger Hof (1650–1800)" [Mediators between Occident and Orient: Court interpreters at the Habsburg Court (1650–1800)]. In *Politische Kommunikation zwischen Imperien* [Political communication between empires], Gunda Barth-Scalmani, Harriet Rudolph, and Christian Steppan (eds.), 257–73. Innsbruck: StudienVerlag.

Werner, Michael, and Bénédicte Zimmermann. 2002. "Vergleich, Transfer, Verflechtung. Der Ansatz der *Histoire croisée* und die Herausforderung des Transnationalen." *Geschichte und Gesellschaft* 28: 607–36.

——(eds.). 2004. *De la comparaison à l'histoire croisée*. Paris: Seuil.

——2006. "Beyond Comparison: *Histoire croisée* and the Challenge of Reflexivity." *History and Theory* 45(1): 30–50.

Wolf, Michaela. 2003. "'Cultures Do Not Hold Still for their Portraits'. Kultureller Transfer als 'Übersetzen zwischen Kulturen." In *Ver-rückte Kulturen. Zur Dynamik kultureller Transfers*, Federico Celestini and Helga Mitterbauer (eds.), 85–98. Tübingen: Stauffenburg.

21 Interviews and focus groups

Ursula Böser

Definitions

Interviews and focus groups provide contextualization of human behavior that allows researchers to understand the meaning of that behavior (Silverman 2006). The central purpose of both methods is the generation of data on lived experiences and on the meaning which individuals or groups under investigation derive from them. The two methods draw on common procedures and assumptions, which will be discussed below. However, as facilitated interactions on a given topic that involve multiple participants, focus groups are distinctive in a number of respects.

The particular format of an interview or focus group will reflect its function within a given research design. The structured interview uses a standardized sequence of closed questions and is generally conducted within a pre-set time frame to elicit factual or quantitative information. Here, standardization, neutrality, and optimization of the reliability and validity of findings are paramount. Semi-structured interviews feature a core of common questions around which interaction in response to the interviewee's framing of central interview issues is allowed to emerge. The focus here is on the elicitation of perceptions, beliefs, or motives. The unstructured interview maintains the focus on the central research question but will develop conversationally, allowing for interviewee-led contributions. Sometimes data from semi-structured and unstructured interviews provides the basis for further focus group investigations. While recruiting participants and organizing interviews and focus groups require considerable planning, these data-gathering methods can generate rich data (albeit limited in terms of the generalization of results) within a relatively short period of time.

Numerous guides have shaped the formalization of interviews (see Gillhalm 2000; Seidman 2006; Roulston 2010; Kvale and Brinkman 2014) and focus groups (Morgan 1993), the central features of which are highlighted below. Research using interviews and focus groups for data collection may require prior ethical approval, and participants should be asked to provide informed consent. If participants are associated with institutions (e.g., universities, hospitals, governmental agencies, or companies), they may be subject to that institution's particular approval requirements. The setting of the interview or focus group should safeguard participants' privacy and facilitate rapport with the interviewer or the group facilitator. The nature of data collection and analysis requires recording of the interaction. The use of audio or video equipment may affect interactions in various ways and should be acknowledged. Thus, a reflection about the potential impact of recording on participants' behavior in the specific context of any study should form part of the analysis. The means to conduct audiovisual recording in order to access verbal and non-verbal communication are readily available. In choosing a setup for the recording equipment, in particular, in the case of focus groups, researchers should make sure that significant features are captured without the arrangements being overly intrusive.

Interview and focus group questions and prompts should operationalize and translate research questions into terms that are understood and shared by the participants. Kvale (1996: 131) provides a helpful inventory of generic interview prompts, which is applicable to both methods:

Introductory questions (How did you get interested in X?)
Follow-up questions (What does X mean?)
Probing questions (Could you say more about X?)
Specifying questions (What did they reply to X?)
Direct question (Are you happy with X?)
Indirect questions (How do you feel about X?)
Interpreting questions (Would it be right to say that you are happy here?)
Structuring prompts (I now would like to change the topic.)
Silent prompt (Signals time for reflection.)

While the prompt/response format will play some part in the running of a focus group, Robson (2011) notes that this should not be maintained at the cost of the interaction among group members, which constitutes a particular strength of this method.

Purposive sampling, in which participants are matched to central research criteria, is frequently adopted in interviews and focus group research. On the issue of sample size for interviews, Seidman (2006) proposes two guiding principles. First, it must reflect the range of participants that make up the population, and therefore display sufficiency. Second, saturation is achieved when interviews cease to yield new information. Both principles can be applied to studies using single or multiple focus groups; however, a further consideration is optimum group size to engender group interaction. Morgan suggests a group size in the range of six to ten participants (1993). Advantages and disadvantages associated with different types of group composition, and the characteristics of data generated through them, should be considered when setting up focus groups. Homogeneous groups, for example, might present a more monolithic and consensual view of a given issue, whereas groups whose participants represent different backgrounds and perspectives may provide a less consistent or more multifaceted outlook.

When planning is completed, a trial run of the plan with a small representative sample or group can assist in finalizing procedures. With regard to the interviewing itself, Kvale (1996: 147) identifies the following qualities of a good interviewer:

Knowledgeable—is familiar with the focus of the interaction
Structuring—states the purpose of the interaction, checks whether participants have questions, brings discussion to a conclusion
Clear—asks simple, short questions, avoiding jargon
Gentle—allows thinking, pausing, finishing
Sensitive—is an attentive, empathetic listener
Open—is flexible in response to what is important
Steering—is clear about what is to be found out
Critical—is prepared to challenge, points out inconsistencies
Remembering—relates statements to what was said previously
Interpreting—clarifies meaning without imposing it

In addition to the above, good focus group moderators should be able to create a balance between ensuring the effective participation of group members while permitting interactive dynamics to emerge among them.

Initial engagement with the data will often involve the transcription and coding of the recordings; however, the chosen method of analysis will depend on the research question. In light of the interpersonal nature of interviews and focus groups, a reflective engagement with issues, such as the potential impact of researcher bias or expectancy effect, perceptions of social desirability, or the rapport between the interviewer or facilitator and interviewees or participants, must be factored into the analysis. In addition, when the data generated requires translation, the translation processes should form part of this methodological reflection.

Digital tools and online platforms now make it possible to hold interviews and focus groups with participants who previously might have been difficult to reach. The impact of these new technologies on forms of interactivity between interviewer or facilitator and respondent(s), as well as on the dynamics within a focus group, requires researchers' attention and further investigation (see Paulus et al. 2014).

Origins

The research interview has long been a staple of research in the social sciences. Charles Booth first developed and used interviews for an 1886 ethnographic survey of the socioeconomic conditions of life in London. Psychological and sociological studies on social attitudes in the 1920s adopted qualitative interviewing, and, following the rise of opinion polling and market research in the mid-1930s, survey interviews became a prominent feature of sociological research.

The recognition that consumers' decisions are made in a social context underlies the initial use of interviewing in a group setting. The use of this method can be traced back to market research in the 1920s. From the 1960s onward, focus groups became the method of choice for testing the market acceptance of and marketing strategy for new products. Lazarsfield and Merton used focus groups in the context of applied sociological research to explore how the media influenced attitudes toward US involvement in World War II. The method did not find wider academic application during the 1950s, and it was only in the 1980s that the use of focus groups re-emerged in the health and social sciences.

Uses

An increasing emphasis on experience, belief, and perception testifies to a "turn" that positions translation and interpreting as social practice (see, for example, special issues of *TIS* Angelelli 2012). The increasing use of interview studies (e.g., Torikai 2011) and their more frequent integration within a mixed methods design (e.g., Napier 2002; Koskinen 2008) for the purposes of contextualization or triangulation reflect this "turn" at the level of methodology. This trend is most evident in public service interpreting research.

The relevant focus in Translation Studies has been on translators' working contexts (e.g., Koskinen 2008), professional status and identity (Sela-Sheffy 2010), professional skills (Shih 2006), and training (Károly 2011). Populations studied include literary (Flynn 2004) and non-literary translators (Sela-Sheffy 2010), in institutions (Koskinen 2008), agencies, or freelancing contexts (Abdallah and Koskinen 2007), recruiters of translators (Chan 2011), as well as translation students (Mirlohi et al. 2011).

In Interpreting Studies, research using interviews and focus groups focuses on interpreters' roles and role perceptions in institutional contexts. Legal (e.g., Berk-Seligson 2002), healthcare (Angelelli 2007b), and also social work settings (Tipton 2010) are predominant. Users' voices, such as those of medical staff (Leanza 2005), judicial staff (Lipkin 2008), social workers (Tipton 2010), and non-institutional users of interpretation (Edwards et al. 2005), also feature in a number of studies, as do the voices of other stakeholders such as managers or educators of interpreting and interpreters (e.g., Witter-Merrithew and Johnson 2005).

Interview- and focus group-based studies of simultaneous interpreting explore the impact of specific parameters on interpreting strategies (e.g., Chang and Schallert 2007) and the perception and self-perception of interpreters (e.g., Angelelli 2004; Napier 2011), or they explore simultaneous interpreting (SI) as situated activity (e.g., Diriker 2004). The training of interpreters (e.g., Shaw et al. 2004) for public service interpreting (PSI) and simultaneous interpreting has also been explored through interviews and focus group studies.

Sample studies

This section provides a selective overview of studies using interviews and focus groups. It is subdivided into works relating to translation and to interpreting. Koskinen (2008) explores the role and professional identity of members of the Finnish translation unit of the EU Commission. Her "study of both texts and people" (2008: 6) draws on a mixed method design including observation, textual analysis, questionnaires, and focus groups. Koskinen's ethnographic approach seeks to capture and synthesize the microlevel of individuals' behaviors and statements, and the institutional macrostructures. Three tape-recorded focus groups with members of the Finnish translation unit contribute to this microlevel data and allow the author to "probe shifting feelings of belonging which constitute identity" (82) and to explore the meanings and attitudes represented in the groups. Limitations of the focus groups are reflected upon, such as the fact that the focus groups comprised half of the translation unit and that participants expressed reservations about speaking openly in the group. Koskinen discusses the (dis)advantages of her multiple role as researcher, focus group moderator, and prior member of the unit under investigation and how this affected the data she derived. Her analysis of the focus group interaction is based on the Finnish transcript, of which a structurally close translation is provided. Koskinen identifies a pervasive ambiguity in the perception of her participants as an "integral part of the Commission, but separate from it" who see their "task as serving the European citizens, but claim that they cannot take their readers into consideration" (118).

The interview-based exploration of translators' working environments also extends into other contexts such as the complex production environment which characterizes the modern language industry (Abdallah and Koskinen 2007). Aspects of the perception and reality of translators' professional status are explored with the use of interviews from a variety of angles, such as the impact of certification on recruitment prospects or translators' status-seeking strategies (Sela-Sheffy 2010; Chan 2011).

Revision practices as a subset of translation skill are the focus of studies using focus groups (Schjoldager et al. 2008) and interviews (Rasmussen and Schjoldager 2011). In Shih's (2006) interview study, the aim of investigating a specialized form of human behavior within a professional group provides the rationale for the choice of methodology. Revision checklists designed by translator trainers inform the core questions of the interviews. These interviews, conducted in Mandarin with 26 non-literary Taiwanese translators, were summary-translated into English and intra-rated and inter-rated for reliability. Study participants are translators with varying degrees of experience and different working contexts. This diversity is seen to be representative of the industry. The author notes "the constraints of time and resources available to the translator" (Shih 2006: 296) and acknowledges differences in revision practices associated with text types in her findings. However, while the study aims to derive rich contextualization of a professional practice from interviews, the isolation of findings about revision practices from external factors which shape them somewhat weakens findings about the behavior of a professional group.

In the field of translator training, the translation skills and competencies of student translators (Károly 2011) and the conditions under which they are best acquired (Mirlohi et al. 2011) have been explored using interviews. In addition, an inventory of the training needs of professional interpreters as well as trainee translators was compiled through interviews (Li 2000) and focus groups (Li 2002). Peter Flynn's interview-based study stands apart from the work discussed above. His objective in interviewing a group of translators of poetry is to provide an empirical basis for skopos theory (2004).

Post-encounter interviews are a methodological component in Wadensjö's (1998) ground-breaking study on dialogue interpreting. The inadequacy of the conduit model, demonstrated by her work, is further explored in many subsequent interview-based studies (e.g., Clifford 2004; Dysart-Gale 2005) and most notably in Angelelli's (2004) ethnography of medical interpreting in a US hospital. Her large-scale study (392 interpreted encounters over 22 months) employs social and sociological theory and linguistic anthropology to investigate the interplay of the interpersonal, institutional, and societal factors in which hospital interpreting is embedded. Her data includes audio-recorded interpreted encounters and interviews with the hospital service manager and ten interpreters, field notes from observation and informal interviews, artefacts, and a survey instrument designed to capture the interpreter's perception of role across a larger data set. Interviews focus on the recipients of interpreting, the role of the interpreters and the challenges they encounter. They show that interpreters perceive and enact their own visibility and inform "emerging metaphors" (Angelelli 2004: 129) through which the author captures a range of role descriptions. Angelelli triangules interpreters' reflection on their role with her observation and survey data.

Other aspects of the interpreter's role in medical settings have been subjected to a series of interview- (e.g., Leanza 2005; Hsieh 2006, 2007) and focus group-based (e.g., Gerrish et al. 2004; Hsieh 2010) studies. Highly controversial findings were derived from the interview-based exploration by Green et al. (2005: 2109) of the experience of bilingual child interpreters in healthcare settings. The authors describe this work as beneficial to the children and "the informal health care economy."

The use of technology in medical interpreting, user preferences relating to telephone and remote interpreting (Jones et al. 2003), and the use of hospital-trained, ad hoc, or telephone interpreters (Garcia et al. 2004) have been investigated using interviews with patients and parents of child patients.

Professional codes for medical interpreters are central to Angelelli's focus group study (2007a) in which she analyses reactions of medical interpreters to the California Standards for Healthcare Interpreting. Also using focus groups, the same author explores the design of an assessment instrument for medical interpreters with healthcare providers, interpreters, and community members (Angelelli 2007b).

Susan Berk-Seligson's study on court interpreting (2002), the most extensive contribution to research on legal interpreting to date, combines observation, the analysis of audio-recording, and extensive interviews with attorneys and interpreters. The author highlights these interviews as important sources of information on the modification of court procedure when an interpreter is present, and the findings inform experimental research on how interpreting may affect jurors' evaluation of witness testimony. The author does not elaborate on how the interview data was elicited or subsequently analysed. Further interview-based research in the field of legal interpreting includes studies which focus on issues such as norms and ethical rules that inform the work of untrained legal interpreters (Lipkin 2008) and the role of interpreters in providing access to the legal system (Brennan and Brown 1997).

The attitude of users and interpreters toward sign-language interpreting is explored by Napier (2011). Using focus groups to generate data which is subjected to linguistic analysis she investigates participants' perceptions and how these are expressed. Two focus groups are held with each stakeholder sector (deaf consumers, hearing consumers, and interpreters), resulting in eight hours of data. Findings point to diverging priorities between hearing, non-interpreting participants and deaf participants and users. Sanz's (1930) observation and interview-based study on the working conditions of conference interpreters in Geneva is credited with being the first academic publication in Interpreting Studies and as such should not go unmentioned in this overview. Diriker's work on conference interpreting (2004) distinguishes itself as an investigation of simultaneous interpreting from a sociocultural perspective. The analyses of recorded interpretations are contextualized by and contrasted with examples of public and metadiscourses on interpreting as well as semi-structured interviews with the conference organizer, conference speakers, interpreters, and users of interpreting. This juxtaposition highlights the tensions between the actuality of interpreting and metadiscourses about "ideal interpreters," which support the construction of a commercially viable image of the profession.

Focus group-based research on interpreter training and its perception include studies on trainee students' difficulties in applying their spoken or sign language skills when learning to interpret (Shaw et al. 2004) and users' perception of the learning outcomes of interpreter training programs (Witter-Merrithew and Johnson 2005). The role of self-regulatory processes in developing interpreting expertise (Hild 2014) draws on interviews, as does the investigation of the impact of cultural background knowledge on students' sight translation performance (2014).

Conclusions and further applications

The use of interviews and focus groups has advanced our understanding of translation and interpreting as a form of social behavior and our perceptions of this behavior. It has also provided insights into the experiential aspects of the acquisition and application of interpreting and translation skills.

The ubiquity of interviews in modern society has tended to desensitize researchers to their methodological implications (Talmy 2011). Viewed as "commonsensical, product-oriented" instruments (25), interviews seem to offer an unproblematic "epistemological conduit" into respondents' worlds (27), which necessitates greater reflection on the dialogic construction of meaning within the immediate and wider social context of interviews (Mishler 1986). This call for methodological engagement with the process and context of data generation in relation to focus groups is echoed by other researchers (e.g., Robson 2011), and, while group interaction is central to focus groups, it is frequently ignored in the analysis. TIS can draw on its linguistic toolbox to help build an analytical approach in which verbal and non-verbal interaction and the co-construction of meaning in interviews and focus groups can become subjects of study in their own right.

Similarly, interview- and focus group-based research can provide useful contextualization for findings derived from linguistic analysis. With a view to research into face-to-face interpreting, Mason states the need to add "explanation to description" by demonstrating "regularities of motivated behaviour" (1990: 230). Here, as with other modes of interpreting, linguistic analysis can derive useful contextualization from interviews and focus groups.

The disaggregation of categories of users, recipients, and other stakeholders along institutional or person-based categories is another avenue for further interview- and focus group-based research in TIS. In this way, our understanding of PSI practices may be further refined by inquiry into the impact of different categories of interlocutors on interactional dynamics. How, for example, do untrained interpreters, who still undertake the majority of work in PSI settings, understand and enact their role? What can we learn from the difference between how trained and untrained interpreters represent their role? What are the expectations of non-institutional users of interpreters in different institutional contexts? How are special communication needs, such as those of children, perceived and accommodated in interpreted interactions?

The increasing significance of audiovisual translation for more established formats of film and television, as well as for new interactive audiovisual formats, such as computer games, calls for empirical audience research to explore the needs of different categories of viewers in different media contexts. Finally, the use of digital platforms and human–computer interaction in the translation process stands to benefit from factoring in human perceptions and attitudes that relate to this interaction.

Further reading

David L. Morgan's *Successful Focus Groups: Advancing the State of the Art* (1993) traces the development of focus groups and provides an overview of the basic principles to be borne in mind when using focus groups as self-contained research or in conjunction with other methods. Steinar Kvale and Svend Brinkman's *InterViews: Learning the Craft of Qualitative Research Interviewing* (2014) is a useful resource for students who set out to learn the craft of interviewing in a variety of disciplines. Student assignments support the book's dual focus on reflection and application. Jaber F. Gubrium, James A. Holstein, Amir B. Marvasti, and Karyn McKinney's *Interview Research. The Complexity of the Craft* (2012) provides a comprehensive reflection on the history and epistemological foundations of interviewing. In-depth discussions of interviewing techniques are also included.

References

Abdallah, Kristiina, and Kaisa Koskinen. 2007. "Managing Trust: Translating and the Network Economy." *Meta* 52(4): 673–87.

Angelelli, Claudia V. 2004. *Medical Interpreting and Cross-cultural Communication*. Cambridge: Cambridge University Press.

——2007a. "Validating Professional Standards and Codes: Challenges and Opportunities." *Interpreting* 8(2): 175–93.

——2007b. "Assessing Medical Interpreters: The Language and Interpreting Testing Project." *The Translator* 13(1): 63–82.

——2012. "The Sociological Turn in Translation and Interpreting Studies." Special issue. *Translation and Interpreting Studies* 7(2): 125–28.

Berk-Seligson, Susan. 2002. *The Bilingual Courtroom: Court Interpreters in the Judicial Process*. Chicago: University of Chicago Press.

Brennan, Mary, and Richard Brown. 1997. *Equality before the Law: Deaf People's Access to Justice*. Durham: Deaf Studies Research Unit, University of Durham.

Chan, Andy Lung Jan. 2011. "Effectiveness of Translator Certification as a Signaling Device: Views from the Translator Recruiters." In *Identity and Status in the Translational Professions*, Rakefet Sela-Sheffy and Miriam Shlesinger (eds.), 31–48. Amsterdam: John Benjamins.

Chang, Cha-Chien, and Diane L. Schallert. 2007. "The Impact of Directionality on Chinese/English Simultaneous Interpreting." *Interpreting* 9(2): 137–76.

Clifford, Andrew. 2004. "Is Fidelity Ethical? The Social Role of the Healthcare Interpreter." In *Traduction, éthique et société / Translation, Ethics and Society* 17(2): 89–114.

Diriker, Ebru. 2004. *De-/Re-contextualizing Conference Interpreting*. Amsterdam: John Benjamins.

Dysart-Gale, Deborah. 2005. "Communication Models, Professionalization, and the Work of Medical Interpreters." *Health Communication* 17: 91–103.

Edwards, Rosalind, Bogusia Temple, and Claire Alexander. 2005. "Users' Experience of Interpreters: The Critical Role of Trust." *Interpreting* 7(1): 77–96.

Flynn, Peter. 2004. "Skopos Theory: An Ethnographic Enquiry." *Perspectives: Studies in Translatology* 12(4): 270–85.

Garcia, Estevan A., Lonnie C. Roy, Pamela J. Okada, Sebrina C. Perkins, and Robert A. Wiebe. 2004. "A Comparison of the Influence of Hospital-trained, Ad Hoc, and Telephone Interpreters on Perceived Satisfaction of Limited English-proficient Parents Presenting to a Pediatric Emergency Department." *Pediatric Emergency Care* 20(6): 373–78.

Gerrish, Kate, Ruby Chau, Abi Sobowale, and Elizabeth Birks. 2004. "Bridging the Language Barrier: The Use of Interpreters in Primary Care Nursing." *Health and Social Care in the Community* 12(5): 407–13.

Gillhalm, Bill. 2000. *The Research Interview.* London: Continuum.

Green, Judith, Caroline Free, Vanita Bhavnani, and Tony Newman. 2005. "Translators and Mediators: Bilingual Young People's Accounts of their Interpreting Work in Health Care." *Social Science and Medicine* 60: 2097–110.

Gubrium, Jaber F., James A. Holstein, Amir B. Marvasti, and Karyn McKinney. 2012. *Interview Research. The Complexity of the Craft.* London: SAGE Publications.

Hild, Adelina. 2014. "The Role of Self-regulatory Processes in the Development of Interpreting Expertise." *Translation and Interpreting Studies* 9(1): 128–49.

Hsieh, Elaine. 2006. "Conflicts in How Interpreters Manage their Roles in Provider–Patient Interactions." *Social Science & Medicine* 62(3): 721–30.

——2007. "Interpreters as Co-diagnosticians: Overlapping Roles and Services between Providers and Interpreters." *Social Science and Medicine* 64(4): 924–37.

——2010. "Provider–Interpreter Collaboration in Bilingual Health Care: Competitions of Control over Interpreter-mediated Interactions." *Patient Education and Counseling* 78(2): 154–59.

Jones, David et al. 2003. "An Exploratory Study of Language Interpretation Services Provided by Videoconferencing." *Journal of Telemedicine and Telecare* 9: 51–56.

Károly, Adrien. 2011. "Translation Competence and Translation Performance – Lexical, Syntactic and Textual Patterns in Student Translations of a Specialised EU Genre." *English for Specific Purposes* 31(1): 36–46.

Koskinen, Kaisa. 2008. *Translating Institutions: An Ethnographic Study of EU Translation.* Manchester: St. Jerome.

Kvale, Steinar. 1996. *InterViews: An Introduction to Qualitative Research Interviewing.* London: Sage.

Kvale, Steinar, and Svend Brinkman. 2014. *InterViews: Learning the Craft of Qualitative Research Interviewing.* 3rd edition. London: Sage.

Leanza, Yvan. 2005. "Roles of Community Interpreters in Pediatrics as Seen by Interpreters, Physicians and Researchers." *Interpreting* 7(2): 67–192.

Li, Defeng. 2000. "Tailoring Translation Programmes to Social Needs: A Survey of Professional Translators." *Target* 12(1): 127–49.

——2002. "Translator Training: What Translation Students Have to Say." *Meta* 47(4): 513–31.

Lipkin, Shira L. 2008. "Norms, Ethics and Roles among Military Court Interpreters: The Unique Case of the Yehuda Court." *Interpreting* 10(1): 84–98.

Mason, Ian. 1990. "Models and Methods in Dialogue Interpreting Research." In *Intercultural Faultlines. Research Methods on Translation Studies I. Textual and Cognitive Aspects*, Maeve Olohan (ed.), 215–32. Manchester: St. Jerome.

Mirlohi, Mehdi, Joy Egbert, and Behzad Ghonsooly. 2011. "Flow in Translation: Exploring Optimal Experience for Translation Trainees." *Target* 23(2): 251–71.

Mishler, Elliot G. 1986. *Research Interviewing: Context and Narrative.* Cambridge, MA: Harvard University Press.

Morgan, David L. (ed.).1993. *Successful Focus Groups: Advancing the State of the Art.* London: SAGE Publications.
Napier, Jemina. 2002. *Sign Language Interpreting. Linguistic Coping Strategies.* Coleford: Douglas McLean.
——2011. "'It's Not What They Say but the Way They Say it'. A Content Analysis of Interpreter and Consumer Perceptions of Signed Language Interpreting in Australia." Special issue. *International Journal of the Sociology of Language* 207: 59–87.
Paulus, Trena M., Jessica N. Lester, and Paul G. Dempster. 2014. *Digital Tools for Qualitative Research.* London: SAGE Publications.
Rasmussen, Kirsten W., and Anne Schjoldager. 2011. "Revising Translations. A Survey of Revision Policies in Danish Translation Companies." *The Journal of Specialised Translation* 15: 87–120.
Robson, Colin. 2011. "Interviews and Focus Groups." In *Real World Research*, Colin Robson (ed.), 278–310. Chichester: Wiley.
Roulston, Kathryn J. 2010. *Reflective Interviewing: A Guide to Theory and Practice.* London: SAGE Publications.
Sanz, Jesús. 1930. "Le travail et les aptitudes des interprètes parlamentaires." *Anals d'Orientació Professional* 4: 303–18.
Schjoldager, Anne, Kirsten W. Rasmussen, and Christa Thomsen. 2008. "Précis-writing, Revision and Editing: Piloting the European Master in Translation." *Meta* 53(4): 798–813.
Seidman, Irving. 2006. *Interviewing as Qualitative Research: A Guide for Researchers in Education and Social Sciences.* New York: Teachers College Press.
Sela-Sheffy, Rakefet. 2010. "'Stars' or 'Professionals': The Imagined Vocation and Exclusive Knowledge of Translators in Israel." *MonTI* 2: 131–52.
Shaw, Sherry, Nadja Grbić, and Kathy Franklin. 2004. "Applying Language Skills to Interpretation. Student Perspectives from Signed and Spoken Language Programs." *Interpreting* 6(1): 69–100.
Shih, Claire Yi-Yi. 2006. "Revision from Translators' Point of View – an Interview Study." *Target* 18(2): 295–312.
Silverman, David. 2006. *Interpreting Qualitative Data: Methods for Analysing Talk, Text and Interaction.* 3rd edition. London: SAGE Publications.
Talmy, Steven. 2011. "The Interview as a Collaborative Achievement: Interaction, Identity and Ideology in a Speech Event." *Applied Linguistics* 23(1): 25–42.
Tipton, Rebecca. 2010. "On Trust: Relationships of Trust in Interpreter-mediated Social Work Encounters." In *Text and Context: Essays on Translation and Interpreting in Honour of Ian Mason*, Mona Baker et al. (eds.), 188–208. Manchester: St. Jerome.
Torikai, Kumiko. 2011. "Conference Interpreters and their Perception of Culture: From the Narratives of Japanese Pioneers." *Translation and Interpreting Studies* 5(1): 75–93.
Wadensjö, Cecilia. 1998. *Interpreting as Interaction.* London and New York: Longman.
Witter-Merrithew, Anna, and Leilani J. Johnson. 2005. *Toward Competent Practice: Conversations with Stakeholders.* Alexandria, VA: Registry for Interpreters for the Deaf.

22 Narrative analysis

Mona Baker

Definition and origin

It is difficult to determine the origins of narrative analysis as a methodology, given that the key concept it draws on has pervaded practically all areas of scholarly endeavour, to the point of being considered "a meeting ground of disciplines" (Baker 2008: 21).

"Narrative" is understood as a story that unfolds in time, with a (perceived) beginning and a (projected) end. A narrative is constructed and emplotted; it is populated by participants, real or imaginary, human or non-human, in a configured relationship to each other and to the unfolding story. This much is shared by practically all definitions of "narrative." Where definitions vary is with respect to the ontological status of narrativity: whether narrative is a mode of discourse, to be contrasted with other modes, such as exposition and argumentation; one of two modes of constructing the world, the other being "logical-scientific reality construction" (Bruner 1991: 4); or, as assumed in this chapter and now increasingly accepted in studies of translation and interpreting that draw on narrative analysis, the only means by which we experience the world and hence "the shape of knowledge as we first apprehend it" (Fisher 1987/1989: 193). What the latter definition assumes is not that everything we know about the world comes to us already constructed in narrative form, but rather that in order to make sense of experience, the human mind ultimately has to emplot whatever comes its way within the format of a narrative.

Given the ubiquity of the concept across the humanities, and indeed the natural sciences, there are naturally numerous models of narrative analysis being applied to different types of data. For example, models applied in literary narratology tend to focus on the formal structure of fictional narratives and draw on a set of conceptual tools that include plot, characters, point of view, focalization, and setting. Labovian narrative analysis, which originated in linguistics, focuses on naturally occurring, mostly elicited oral speech, which is then transcribed and analyzed to extract the narrative and parse it into numbered clauses, with each clause assigned to one of six elements: Abstract; Orientation; Complicating Action; Evaluation; Result; and Coda (Patterson 2008/2012: 24).[1]

In T&I Studies, the model of analysis that has so far been applied derives from the work of Baker (2005, 2006a, 2007/2010, 2010a, 2010b, 2014), who pieced together a set of conceptual tools drawn from social theorists Somers and Gibson (1994) and cognitive psychologist Jerome Bruner (1991) and explored their potential for analyzing translation and interpreting data. The model, which has been extended and combined with elements from literary and cultural theory in a number of doctoral theses and case studies in recent years,[2] consists of two main parts: a typology of narratives, and a set of features that explain how narratives are realized in concrete terms. Baker (2006a, 2006b, 2010c) applies a different model of narrative analysis, Fisher's (1984) narrative paradigm, to explore the values that inform our decision to subscribe to one narrative rather than another and to assess the veracity and integrity of narratives elaborated by different types of volunteer and activist T&I communities.

Narrative typology

The model of textual analysis applied assumes that there are four types of narrative that construct our world and guide our understanding of the events in which we are embedded. **Personal narratives** are narratives of the self; they are the stories we tell ourselves and others about our place in the world and our own personal history. **Public narratives** are stories that emerge within any social grouping, from the family to the classroom, workplace, and the media. McDonough Dolmaya (2010) offers a detailed analysis of the various ways in which the official public narrative of Canada as a multicultural society is realized on 25 global brand websites localized for Canadian users. **Disciplinary narratives** are the theoretical and historical accounts that circulate in any field of knowledge. Examples include theories of climate change, Bourdieu's field theory, Even-Zohar's polysystem theory, and Reiss and Vermeer's skopos theory.[3] They also include accounts of the historical development of a discipline such as T&I Studies or a subset of it (see, for example, Gile 2000; Snell-Hornby 2006). And finally, **metanarratives** are the exceptionally powerful and resilient narratives "in which we are embedded as contemporary actors in history … Progress, Decadence, Industrialization, Enlightment, etc." (Somers and Gibson 1994: 61). Boéri (2009: 246–52) offers an extended critique of the metanarratives of rationality and expertise that dominate the discourse on engagement and objectivity in the field of interpreting.

The relevance of this typology to the analysis of various types of T&I data has been explored from a number of perspectives, one of which concerns the implications of the interdependence between personal and public narratives. As Baker explains, personal narratives "are dependent on and informed by the collective narratives in which they are situated. But they are also crucial for the elaboration and maintenance of these same narratives" (2006a: 29). A phenomenon such as **non-translation**, which has received very little attention in the literature, may thus be partly explained by the need to suppress certain personal narratives that threaten a dominant public account of events. Baker (2014) offers the example of Mark Edelman, one of the commanders of the Warsaw uprising, whose first-hand narrative of this event was published as *The Ghetto Fighting* in 1945 but was not translated into Hebrew until 2001. Edelman was an anti-Zionist whose personal account would have seriously undermined the official, Israeli public narrative of this important historical moment. Another phenomenon whose analysis has been shown to benefit from attention to the interplay between personal and public narratives is **retranslation.** Retranslations of canonical texts provide an opportunity for elaborating new roles and values at a point in time when an emerging ideology requires individual members of a society to adjust their personal narratives in its direction. Examples include the retranslation of the Bible in apartheid South Africa in 1983, just three years before the Dutch Reformed Church retracted the biblical justification of apartheid in 1986 (Baker 2006a: 34–35). They also include retranslations of children's stories: Enid Blyton's books, for instance, were revised and retranslated to tone down or eliminate what are now considered unsavory models of behavior that draw on negative stereotypes of gender, race, and class. A personal narrative may further be appropriated to bolster a social or historical public narrative, as Summers (2012) demonstrates with respect to the East German writer Christa Wolf, whose works and biographical details have simultaneously been appropriated into public narratives of intellectual dissidence in the Anglophone world and complicity with the Stasi regime in Germany. Al-Sharif (2009) and Baker (2010a) demonstrate how personal narratives are appropriated to perpetuate a public narrative of Palestinians and Muslims as irrational extremists in translations by the Middle East Media Research Institute. Among other strategies, as Al-Sharif points out (2009: 197–99), such appropriation is accomplished through patterns of selection and foregrounding of certain episodes in the life of a symbol of Palestinian resistance such as Um Nidal, and de-selection of other episodes and excerpts from interviews that would serve to humanize her and hence the community she represents.

Narrative features

The model outlined here draws on four main features of narrativity as tools of analysis: temporality, relationality, selective appropriation, and causal emplotment (Somers and Gibson 1994; Baker 2006a). Temporality refers to the embeddedness of narrative in time and space. Rather than being restricted to the linear progression of time on a past/present/future trajectory, the concept accommodates complex types of embeddedness in time and space. For example, Boéri (2008: 34) demonstrates how Peter Naumann's critique of Babels, the activist community that provides volunteer interpreting in Social Fora, is temporally emplotted to align him, Naumann, with a "positively narrated group of professionals who are temporally constructed as belonging to the 'superior' past of the profession." Relationality concerns the interconnectedness of all elements within a narrative, as well as among narratives. Baker (2014) offers the example of the biblical term "Kingdom of God," which is typically rendered as *malakuut* in Arabic, and shows how the two terms are embedded in very different narrative environments that frustrate any attempt to map them fully onto each other. Selective appropriation means that in order to elaborate a coherent narrative, the human mind must de-select some aspects of what it perceives and foreground others, whether consciously or unconsciously. Causal emplotment allows us to turn a set of propositions into an intelligible sequence about which we can form an opinion and charges the events depicted with moral significance.

In addition to these four core features, Baker (2006a) discusses and exemplifies another four, drawn mostly from Bruner (1991). Narrative accrual means that our experience of the world is shaped by our repeated exposure to sets of related narratives that accrue over time, ultimately defining what we understand by a culture, tradition, or history. Morales-Moreno (2011) offers a detailed analysis of some of the ways in which slum narratives emerge and are consolidated over time, and argues that "the narrative imagination accrues totalitarian meaning" through processes of "repetition and continuous exposure" (2011: 10). Genericness acknowledges that individual narratives have to be elaborated within established frameworks of narration, such as a novel or editorial, in order to be intelligible and effective, and that every genre comes imbued with its own meanings. As Morales-Moreno points out, "the laws of genre limit or expand horizons of expectations in readers, modes of writing for writers, and translating choices for translators" (2011: 10). Particularity means that a given narrative will refer to specific events and people but will also invitably cast these elements within a familiar storyline that gives the specific happenings their meaning and import. Finally, normativeness/canonicity and breach are part of the dynamic of all narratives. A breach presupposes a norm or canon, and normativeness is a feature of all narratives, whether dominant or marginalized.

For the above features to become operative, and for a set of events to be constituted as a narrative with a specific pattern of causal emplotment, a considerable amount of discursive and/or visual work has to be undertaken by the narrator. Narrative analysis can draw on any verbal or non-verbal element to capture this process and explain how the above features are configured in the elaboration of a given narrative. For example, Karunanayake (in progress) demonstrates how the replacement of a reference to the Cold War in Dario Fo's *Trumpets and Raspberries* with a reference to Operation Desert Storm in *Diwthwa*, the Sinhala translation performed in Sri Lanka during a particularly violent period in the country's history, relocates the events in time and space and effects a challenge to state-sanctioned narratives of the conflict. The translator's/dramatist's "allusions to narrative elements associated with Operation Desert Storm," she argues:

> bring the action in the play forward temporally to 1991. The reference also works at a more symbolic level, for … Operation Desert Storm …

was an open war and is therefore more reflective of the two conflicts in Sri Lanka which were characterised by open warfare and guerrilla style combat techniques. The allusion to Desert Storm could also be an insinuation to the unequal powers in the two Sri Lankan conflicts.

In her analysis of the translation project of the Middle East Media Research Institute, Baker (2010a) includes disparate features, such as the choice and strict separation of source and target languages, selective appropriation of the material to be translated, the section headings under which the translations are grouped on the site, the titles MEMRI uses to frame each translation, and the addition of images and links to videos that establish a connection between the narrative elaborated in a text and other narratives and steer the reader's interpretation in the direction of a specific pattern of causal emplotment. The ability of narrative analysis to draw on practically any form of signifier (from layout to color, and from lexical and grammatical patterns to costume and lighting) distinguishes it clearly from other methods of analysis deployed in T&I Studies.

Narrative paradigm

Fisher's influential narrative paradigm (1984, 1987/1989, 1997) argues that human beings are essentially storytellers who make decisions on the basis of "good reasons," rather than mere rationality, with what we consider good reasons being determined by our history, culture, experience of the world, and, ultimately, the stories we come to believe about the world in which we live. His model, which has been applied in Baker (2006a, 2006b, 2010c) to study narrative communities such as Babels and Translators without Borders, attempts to reveal the values implicitly or explicitly promoted by a narrative, and the effect that adhering to it might have on the world and a particular individual's ability to maintain a sense of self-respect and relate to others. It is this ability to judge narratives on the basis of their moral implications and the values they promote, Fisher argues, that ultimately guides human behavior.

Fisher's model tests a narrative in relation to coherence and fidelity. He discusses three types of coherence: structural or argumentative (i.e., internal consistency); material (how a narrative relates to other narratives that engage with the same issues, including what "facts" and counter-arguments it downplays or foregrounds); and characterological (i.e., the credibility or trustworthiness of characters and narrators). Testing a narrative for fidelity involves assessing its reasons and the values it promotes. Fisher stresses that the concept of good reasons "does not imply that every element of rhetorical transaction that warrants a belief, attitude, or action – that any 'good reason' – is as good as any other. It only signifies that whatever is taken as a basis for adopting a rhetorical message is inextricably bound to a value – to a conception of the good" (1987/1989: 197).

This model is particularly suited to the study of communities of different types—whether professional (such as AIIC or a given translation agency) or activist (such as Babels, Tlaxcala, and Translator Brigades). As Fisher points out, "[all] communities are co-constituted through communication transactions in which participants co-author a story that has coherence and fidelity for the life that one would lead" (1997: 323). In her application of the model, Baker (2006a, 2006b, 2010c) gives priority to fidelity over coherence, arguing that structural incoherence in the way Translators without Borders narrates itself to the world is less worrying than the pattern of commodification of humanitarian work revealed by an assessment of its "fidelity." She further concludes that TWB "ultimately sustains and justifies an ethics of consumerism through the commodification of human grief" (2010c: 38–39). Although this model of analysis has not been applied yet in studies other than Baker's, Robinson (2011) devotes an entire chapter to fleshing out and critiquing Fisher's paradigm and Baker's application of it in T&I Studies. He does not, however, offer analyses of new data.

Sample studies

Harding (2012a) offers an overview of extended studies that have drawn on narrative analysis since the publication of Baker's *Translation and Conflict* in 2006. These mostly consist of a flurry of doctoral studies, the first group of which was completed in 2009: Harding's own study of translation in the context of the Chechen conflict, later published as *Beslan: Six Stories of the Siege* (Harding 2012b); Al-Herthani's investigation of the ways in which Edward Said was renarrated in the Arab World, focusing in particular on translations and (re)translations of *Orientalism*, *Culture and Imperialism*, and *Covering Islam*; Al-Sharif's examination of the Middle East Media Research Institute's renarration of the Palestine–Israel conflict; and Boéri's investigation of Babels' narrative construction of its activist project of volunteer (mainly simultaneous) interpreting in the context of the Social Forum and the wider Alter-Globalization Movement. Other doctoral studies that have since been completed include Ayoub (2010, children's literature) and Summers (2013, East German author Christa Wolf). Studies currently in progress include Pasmatzi (Anglophone novels about the Greek Civil War translated into Greek), Xiao Di (English translations of Chinese novels), Karunanayake (Sinhala theater translation), Sadler (Twitter reporting of the events of July 3, 2013 in Egypt), and Johnson (post 9/11 hip hop music videos and films that challenge narrative hegemonies relating to Islam).

Apart from the work of Baker, Harding, and Boéri cited above, published case studies that have drawn on narrative theory include Pérez-González (2010, ad hoc Spanish narrative community of untrained translators), Jones (2010, poetry translation during the Yugoslav wars); van Rooyen (2011, radio news), Kontos and Sidiropoulou (2012, news headlines in English and Greek), Boéri and Manuel Jerez (2011, innovative teaching in conference interpreting), and Morales-Morino (2011, narratives of slums).

Conclusion and potential applications

Potential applications of narrative analysis, including the narrative paradigm, in T&I Studies are diverse and only limited by the researcher's imagination. The model lends itself to the study of almost any kind of data, from novels to plays, children's literature, media reporting, religious translation, interpreting of EU debates, political speeches, life writing, audiovisual material, and the stories professional and activist communities tell about themselves. Building on the relatively small range of existing case studies, questions that might be addressed in a more sustained manner in the future include how individuals and groups are positioned or position themselves in relation to specific personal, public, disciplinary or metanarratives (Boéri 2008, 2009; Baker 2009); what strategies translators and interpreters draw on to renegotiate/reframe a narrative in a new setting, for instance the narrative of an asylum seeker that is unlikely to resonate or be considered credible in the host narrative environment; and how personal narratives, elaborated in the form of eyewitness reports, testimonies of survivors, or memoirs, may be mobilized to generate empathy or undermine/bolster dominant narratives of a given conflict (Said 1984). Ongoing research, including Karunanayake (in progress), Sadler (in progress), and Johnson (in progress), promises to refine the model further by elaborating more robust definitions of some of its categories (such as "metanarrative" or "particularity") and demonstrating how it can be operationalized at the microlevel of verbal and non-verbal analyses, thus making it easier to apply in a sustained manner in future studies.

Further reading

Baker (2006a) is the first and most detailed exposition of narrative analysis. Baker (2010a) offers an extended narrative analysis of the use of translation by the Middle East Media Research Institute. Baker (2010c) is an extended application of Fisher's narrative paradigm, focusing in particular on Translators without Borders, an offshoot of a translation agency based in France. Boéri (2008) draws on narrative theory to challenge professional discourses that attempt to undermine the work of activist groups such as Babels. Harding (2012a) is an excellent overview and extension of the application of narrative theory in Translation Studies. Morales-Morino (2011) analyzes public narratives of slums, focusing in particular on the feature of narrative accrual. Pérez-González (2010) draws on narrative theory to demonstrate how translation is increasingly being appropriated by activists to contest the socioeconomic structures that sustain global capitalism.

Notes

1 Of particular interest to scholars of T&I is Reissman's remark that narrative analyses of transcripts of translated interviews rarely acknowledge the politics of translation and "typically erase translation problems, assuming questions about equivalence of meaning are irrelevant" (2008: 42).

2 See, in particular, Al-Herthani (2009), Baldo (2009), Harding (2012a, 2012b), and Summers (2013).
3 See Baker (2008: 21–22) for a discussion of skopos theory as a disciplinary narrative.

References

Al-Herthani, Mahmoud. 2009. "Edward Said in Arabic: Narrativity and Paratextual Framing." Unpublished Ph.D. dissertation. Centre for Translation and Interpreting Studies, University of Manchester.

Al-Sharif, Souhad. 2009. "Translation in the Service of Advocacy: Narrating Palestine and Palestinian Women in Translations by the Middle East Media Research Institute (MEMRI)." Unpublished Ph.D. dissertation. Centre for Translation and Interpreting Studies, University of Manchester.

Ayoub, Amal. 2010. *Framing Translated and Adapted Children's Literature in the Kilani Project: A Narrative Perspective.* Cairo: Helwan University.

Baker, Mona. 2005. "Narratives *in* and *of* Translation." *SASE Journal of Translation and Interpretation.* Available online at www.skase.sk.

——2006a. *Translation and Conflict: A Narrative Account.* London and New York: Routledge.

——2006b. "Translation and Activism: Emerging Patterns of Narrative Community." *The Massachusetts Review* 47(3): 462–84.

——2007/2010. "Reframing Conflict in Translation." *Social Semiotics* 17(2): 151–69; reprinted in *Critical Readings in Translation Studies,* Mona Baker (ed.), 113–29. London and New York: Routledge.

——2008. "Ethics of Renarration: Mona Baker Is Interviewed by Andrew Chesterman." *Cultus* 1(1): 10–33. Available online at www.escholar.manchester.ac.uk/uk-ac-man-scw:1b7072.

——2009. "Resisting State Terror: Theorizing Communities of Activist Translators and Interpreters." In *Globalization, Political Violence and Translation,* Esperanza Bielsa and Christopher W. Hughes (eds.), 222–42. Basingstoke: Palgrave Macmillan.

——2010a. "Narratives of Terrorism and Security: 'Accurate' Translations, Suspicious Frames." *Critical Studies on Terrorism* 3(3): 347–64.

——2010b. "Interpreters and Translators in the War Zone: Narrated and Narrators." In special issue, "Translation and Violent Conflict," Moira Inghilleri and Sue-Ann Harding (eds.). *The Translator* 16(2): 197–222.

——2010c. "Translation and Activism." In *Translation, Resistance, Activism,* Maria Tymoczko (ed.), 23–41. Amherst and Boston: University of Massachusetts Press.

——2014. "Translation as Renarration." In *Translation: A Multidisciplinary Approach,* Juliane House (ed.), 158–77. Basingstoke: Palgrave Macmillan.

Baldo, Michela. 2009. "Translation as Renarration in Italian Canadian Writing: Codeswitching, Focalisation, Voice and Plot in Nino Ricci's Trilogy and Its Italian Translation." Unpublished Ph.D. dissertation. Centre for Translation and Intercultural Studies, University of Manchester.

Boéri, Julie. 2008. "A Narrative Account of the Babels vs. Naumann Controversy: Competing Perspectives on Activism in Conference Interpreting." *The Translator* 14(1): 21–50.

——2009. "Babels, the Social Forum and the Conference Interpreting Community: Overlapping and Competing Narratives on Activism and Interpreting in the Era of

Globalisation." Unpublished Ph.D. dissertation. Centre for Translation and Intercultural Studies, University of Manchester.
Boéri, Julie, and Jesús de Manuel Jerez. 2011. "From Training Skilled Conference Interpreters to Educating Reflective Citizens: A Case Study of the Marius Action Research Project." *The Interpreter and Translator Trainer* 5(1): 41–64.
Bruner, Jerome. 1991. "The Narrative Construction of Reality." *Critical Inquiry* 18(1): 1–21.
Fisher, Walter. 1984. "Narration as a Human Communication Paradigm: The Case of Public Moral Agreement." *Communication Monographs* 51: 1–22.
——1987/1989. *Human Communication as Narration: Toward a Philosophy of Reason, Value, and Action.* Columbia: University of South Carolina Press.
——1997. "Narration, Reason, and Community." In *Memory, Identity, Community: The Idea of Narrative in the Human Sciences,* Lewis P. Hinchman and Sandra K. Hinchman (eds.), 307–27. Albany: State University of New York Press.
Gile, Daniel. 2000. "The History of Research into Conference Interpreting: A Scientometric Approach." *Target* 12(2): 297–321.
Harding, Sue-Ann. 2012a. "How Do I Apply Narrative Theory: Socio-Narrative Theory in Translation Studies." *Target* 24(2): 286–309.
——2012b. *Beslan: Six Stories of the Siege.* Manchester and New York: Manchester University Press.
Johnson, Rebecca. (in progress). "The Clash of Articulations: A Narrative Account of Creative Subversion, Intersectional Identity and Islam in Post-9/11 Britain and France." Unpublished Ph.D. dissertation. Centre for Translation and Intercultural Studies, University of Manchester.
Jones, Francis. 2010. "Poetry Translation, Nationalism and the Wars of the Yugoslav Transition." *The Translator* 16(2): 223–53.
Karunanayake, Dinithi. (in progress). "Theatre Translation, Communities of Practice and the Sri Lankan Conflicts: (Re)narration as Political Critique." Unpublished Ph.D. dissertation. Centre for Translation and Intercultural Studies, University of Manchester.
Kontos, Petros, and Sidiropoulou, Maria. 2012. "Socio-political Narratives in Translated English-Greek News Headlines." *Intercultural Pragmatics* 9(2): 195–224.
McDonough Dolmaya, Julie. 2010. "(Re)imagining Canada: Projecting Canada to Canadians through Localized Websites." *Translation Studies* 3(3): 302–17.
Morales-Moreno, Mónica. 2011. "Displacing the 'Slum-line': A Narrative Approach." *Social Semiotics* 21(1): 1–13.
Pasmatzi, Kalliopi. (in progress). "Theorising Translation as Cultural Repatriation: The Greek Civil War Narrative Translated into Greek." Unpublished Ph.D. dissertation. Centre for Translation and Intercultural Studies, University of Manchester.
Patterson, Wendy. 2008/2012. "Narratives of Events: Labovian Narrative Analysis and Its Limitations." In *Doing Narrative Research,* Molly Andrews, Corinne Squire, and Maria Tamboukou (eds.), 22–40. London: SAGE Publications.
Pérez-González, Luis. 2010. "Ad-hocracies of Translation Activism in the Blogosphere: A Genealogical Case Study." In *Text and Context: Essays on Translation & Interpreting in Honour of Ian Mason,* Mona Baker, Maeve Olohan, and María Calzada Pérez (eds.), 259–87. Manchester: St. Jerome.
Reissman, Catherine Kohler. 2008. *Narrative Methods for the Human Sciences.* Thousand Oaks, CA: Sage.

Robinson, Douglas. 2011. *Translation and the Problem of Sway.* Amsterdam and Philadelphia: John Benjamins.

Sadler, Neil. (in progress). "Analysing Fragmented Narratives: Twitter Reporting of the 3 July 2013 Events in Egypt." Unpublished Ph.D. dissertation. Centre for Translation and Intercultural Studies, University of Manchester.

Said, Edward. 1984. "Permission to Narrate." *Journal of Palestine Studies* 13(3): 27–48.

Snell-Hornby, Mary. 2006. *The Turns of Translation Studies.* Amsterdam: John Benjamins.

Somers, Margaret R., and Gloria D. Gibson. 1994. "Reclaiming the Epistemological 'Other': Narrative and the Social Constitution of Identity." In *Social Theory and the Politics of Identity,* Craig Calhoun (ed.), 37–99. Oxford and Cambridge, MA: Blackwell.

Summers, Caroline. 2012. "Translating the Author-Function: The (Re)narration of Christa Wolf." *New Voices in Translation Studies* 8: 170–87.

——2013. "Narratives of Dissidence and Complicity: Translating Christa Wolf before and after the Fall of the Wall." Unpublished Ph.D. dissertation. Centre for Translation and Intercultural Studies, University of Manchester.

van Rooyen, Marlie. 2011. "A Mediation Model for the Translation of Radio News Texts in a Multicultural Newsroom." *Southern African Linguistics and Applied Language Studies* 29(1): 17–29.

Xiao Di. (in progress). "Renarrating China: The Construction of Chinese Cultural Identity in English Translations of Chinese Novels in the UK and US, 1980–2010." Unpublished Ph.D. dissertation. Centre for Translation and Intercultural Studies, University of Manchester.

23 Observations

Claudio Baraldi and Christopher D. Mellinger

Definition

In broad terms, observations may be considered a fundamental data collection method used to gain an understanding of participants, behaviors, processes, or artifacts (Angrosino 2004, 2007; Bottorff 2004). Observational research takes a variety of forms depending on the object of analysis, and the approach adopted is often discipline specific. In the social sciences, scholars may opt to conduct naturalistic observation, whereby researchers observe participants in their natural setting (Mehl and Robbins 2012). This type of observation situates the researcher as a neutral outside party to a given activity or interaction, though achieving absolute neutrality can be difficult. Creswell (2013) refers to this role as a non-participant observer, and suggests that the researcher need not be physically present. In contrast, Kawulich (2005) describes participant observation in which the researcher adopts the dual role of observer and active participant in activities. Here, the researcher operates from within the social interaction or context, which, as DeWalt and DeWalt note, aims to "develop a holistic understanding of the phenomena under study" (2011: 110). Brief mention should also be made of the notion of self-observation, in which participants observe their own behavior and act as informants (Rodriguez and Ryave 2002).

Likewise, observational studies in statistics and medicine attempt to determine causal relationships of specific treatments or policies under non-experimental conditions (e.g., Cochran 1965; Rosenbaum 2002; Patterson and Morin 2012). This more unobtrusive approach is contrasted with experimental studies, in which researchers actively manipulate at least one, if not several, independent variables or treatments while controlling the experimental environment to rule out other causes (see Chapter 19, "Experimental research" in this volume).

Scholars have also focused on observations themselves as an object of analysis, and epistemological reflections on first and second order observations can be made (Luhmann 1990). Such inquiry contrasts first order observations, which posit activities as facts, with second order observations, which acknowledge the researcher's influence on the observation process. As such, second order observations suggest a *constructivist* epistemology (von Glasersfeld 1995). This position is in line with post-positivist recognition of the potential biases in research design.

Origins

Observational research finds its roots in anthropology, sociology, psychology, and statistics. Field or participant observation, for example, has long served as a methodological foundation for ethnography (see Chapter 16, "Corpus-Based Studies" in this volume) and qualitative sociology (e.g., Anderson 1923; Thrasher 1927; Whyte 1943/1993). Participatory observation has long been employed as a research method to investigate a wide range of behaviors in schools, hospitals, court rooms, and agencies.

Another type of observational research developed in health sciences and statistics is Cochran's (1965) seminal study. In contrast to participatory observation, Cochran characterizes the observational study as an empirical study that investigates the potential effects a specific treatment or condition may have on a population. In contrast to experimental studies, Cochran discusses issues in planning observational studies that do not manipulate any of the variables due to feasibility or ethical considerations. The research design tenets established by Cochran have since influenced countless observational studies of this nature.

Self-observation has a strong tradition in psychology, and draws heavily on the work of Ericsson and Simon (1980, 1984). Verbal reports, as argued by Ericsson and Simon, are data that can be used to observe cognitive behavior and processes. Data may either be obtained as the participant performs a task, in which participants concurrently verbalize their thoughts, or retrospectively, with participants describing their behavior after the fact. These studies have seen numerous applications in the social sciences.

Uses

Many of the previously mentioned approaches to observational research have been used in both Interpreting and Translation Studies. Since the late 1990s, interpreter-mediated interactions have been studied as complex social processes (Berk-Seligson 1990; Wadensjö 1998), in which interpreters' utterances are interposed with those of the interlocutors. These studies use participatory observation to investigate interpreting as an instantiation of social interaction. The observations include both the content and form of the interpreters' utterances as well as the interrelations between the various participants' utterances. Community and public service interpreting in particular can be observed as social interaction, given the triadic nature of the communicative events in question.

Field observations of interpreter-mediated interactions allow for the description and categorization of the functions of interpreters' actions in interpreter-mediated interactions and the cultural contexts displayed through these actions. Categorizations of types of renditions and non-renditions permit the function of interpreting to be described as coordination (Wadensjö 1998) or orchestration (Angelelli 2004) of interactions, promotion of interlocutors' active participation (Baraldi 2012; Gavioli 2012), production of cultural assumptions (Mason 2006), and mediation between different speech and cultural communities (Angelelli 2004, 2012).

Categorizations of field observations can also highlight problems in interpreters' ways of taking ownership of the text in interactions, for instance, problems of either zero or reduced renditions (e.g., Davidson 2000) or expanded renditions and non-renditions (e.g., Bolden 2000; Hsieh 2007). In these cases, analytical observations have led researchers to describe interpreters' actions in terms of limiting or preventing the interlocutors' participation (Baraldi and Gavioli 2008).

Translation scholars rely on the collection of observational data; however, the way in which researchers use observations differs from that of Interpreting Studies, insofar as direct observation of participants has not yet provided as fruitful a data set. Instead, scholars interested in the translation process employ a number of data collection methodologies, such as keystroke logging, eye-tracking, and screen recording, to observe the translation process as it unfolds. When this approach is contextualized with research in cognitive psychology and psycholinguistics, cognitive behavior and processes can be indirectly observed (e.g., Shreve and Angelone 2010; Alvstad, Hild, and Tiselius 2011; Muñoz Martín 2014). Many of these studies employ an experimental approach to manipulate the conditions under which participants work; however, several exploratory studies have employed keystroke logging, screen recording, and eye-tracking to generate hypotheses for future research projects. Similarly, Läubli et al. (2013) have used observational methodologies to elicit data in the workplace, lending greater ecological validity to their study.

Observations may also focus on individual activities, for example, teaching and other performances in educational settings, or translators and interpreters at work. For example, Ehrensberger-Dow (2014) outlines the challenges of observational studies of situated translation in a language agency, and suggests potential solutions. Jääskeläinen (2002) provides an extensive review of studies employing a form of self-observation—namely, think-aloud protocols (TAPs). First used by translation scholars in the 1980s, TAPs attempted to elicit observations from participants about their cognitive behavior. This type of data collection, however, is now often criticized as participants may be unable to articulate their actual cognitive processes and the act of articulation itself may alter the behavior observed. Nevertheless, TAPs still serve as an important observational tool, particularly within the realm of metacognition and expertise studies. Retrospective verbalizations have also been used to mitigate the problems associated with TAPs and provide a self-observed verbal report for further analysis. The observation of teacher–student interactions during interpreter training (e.g., Davitti and Pasquandrea 2014) has also been identified as an important locus of investigation.

In order for researchers to adequately capture participatory observational data, field observations have long relied on note-taking about ongoing or recently concluded activities. For Creswell (2013), observation involves taking field notes about activities on the basis of an observational protocol, which guides the writing by defining the types of events, situations, and actions that need to be observed. By providing an immediate record of what happens in prolonged (and sometimes complex and delicate) social situations and informal interviews (e.g., Angelelli 2004), note-taking is a valuable data collection tool. In the case of interpreter-mediated interactions, however, mere note-taking proves inadequate as a method of observation. Field observations of interpreter-mediated interactions have significantly improved in light of recent developments of audio and video recording technology, making it possible to store and retrieve information for later analysis (Bottorff 2007).

Many researchers prefer video recording when observing interpreter-mediated interactions, as it enables simultaneous and synchronous storage of verbal utterances, non-verbal actions (such as gaze, gestures, facial expressions, physical contact, and activities of various kinds, including writing and consulting data on the computer), and details about the physical environment (spatial arrangement and participants' positions). However, it can be more difficult to obtain permission for video recording than for audio recording. Both audio and video recording require written consent, but the risk of interference by the researcher in the ongoing activity is much higher with video recording. Moreover, anonymity cannot necessarily be guaranteed to participants, despite the possibility of manipulating the video recording so as to make visual identification impossible. Similar concerns related to confidentiality and anonymity are often raised in translation process research and must be addressed during the initial design of the study. Audio recording presents fewer challenges, as it mitigates interference and makes participants' identities less recognizable than in video recording. Audio recording, however, does not capture as many details as video recording does. Moreover, in particular situations, such as sign language interpreting, video recording is essential for field observations.

Researchers, then, must weigh the relevance of the details that inevitably go uncaptured using audio recording. It should be noted, however, that not all non-verbal or contextual aspects can be retrieved through video recording; the physical position of the recording equipment depends on the interactants' positions in space, and they cannot be adapted to video recording, as they do not depend on the researcher's will. Moreover, observation of all the situational details through video recording is not possible; in general, completeness of observations can never be achieved as the observer always needs to select what s/he can and wants to observe, while attempts to achieve completeness can be unnecessarily intrusive. One could also argue that the visual aspects of an interpreted communicative event are subordinate to the verbal aspects (if we exclude the case of sign language interpreting), as interpreting is primarily a *verbal* activity; therefore, audio recording remains the basic component of observations, even in video recordings. The ultimate recording method should be based on reflection concerning the relationship between the verbal and non-verbal aspects of communication. When audio recording is the only option for observing interpreter-mediated interactions, then non-verbal and contextual aspects can be recorded by taking notes or interviewing participants, or both. In such cases, field notes can complement the audio recording when video recording is not an option (see Angelelli 2004).

Observational research on translation faces similar data collection challenges. Keystroke logging, for example, is a widely used method for collecting translation process data, in which a record is made of every time a key is pressed. These key presses, or events, which can be replayed and analyzed, are used to reconstruct the translator's progress during a translation (see Jakobsen 1999). These programs generally require translators to work within a specific program, which can alter the way in which a translator works. In this case, translators may not be able to access external resources, thereby eliminating an important source of information about the translator's behavior. Consequently, the researcher must either limit the participant to translating without resources or sacrifice this information to allow for a more naturalistic process. To overcome this limitation, researchers may employ screen recording as another data collection method. Screen recording captures in real time what appears on the translator's screen, granting the researcher access to information unavailable through keystroke logging. Nevertheless, screen recording may not provide this level of detail about specific text production processes that keystroke logging allows, and therefore may not allow for a sufficiently detailed analysis of the text production itself.

As a result, methodological triangulation is paramount. Several scholars have highlighted the importance of triangulation in translation process research and suggest its use as a best practice in observational research (e.g., Alves, Pagano, and da Silva 2009; O'Brien 2010; Shreve and Angelone 2010). In fact, technological advancements continuously provide researchers of both translation and interpreting with tools that facilitate mixed-method research designs (see Alvstad, Hild, and Tiselius 2011).

Interpreting Studies have also benefited from technological developments with regard to data collection, which have altered how researchers may participate in observations. As mentioned previously, naturalistic observation is difficult to achieve, yet recording equipment may help in this regard. Audio or video recording allows interpreters themselves to participate in the research, functioning as either participant-observers or as non-participant observers. In the former case, interpreters can describe contextual elements related to dates contained in field notes or recordings. In the latter, they can use recording equipment on behalf of the researcher or provide their own recordings. Each of these approaches, however, has disadvantages. On the one hand, participant observation of interpreting activities may be considered intrusive, and participant-researchers may be requested not to report on parts of the observation. On the other hand, non-participant observation may prevent researchers from taking relevant field notes, particularly in the case of audio recording, and may also impede building relationships with their interlocutors.

Regardless of the data collection method, field observations inevitably influence the manner in which interpreter-mediated interactions are accomplished. It is difficult, if not impossible, to determine exactly what influence is produced, but its mere existence raises concerns. Nevertheless, a post-positivist, second order observational perspective leads to the awareness that (1) observers' influence must always be assumed, but (2) the contributions of field observations to research should not necessarily be discredited, provided that the observers' presence does not unduly influence the interaction.

Field notes on their own, however, must be organized and stored to truly be effective as a data collection method. The organization of audio or video recorded field observations, in particular, is based on a simple observational protocol. These protocols describe the way the recording equipment is used, and also require accurate transcriptions. Although time-consuming, transcriptions are necessary in the process of field observation. For example, Conversation Analysis (see Chapter 15) puts forward a very detailed transcription of artificially stored field observations. The methodological requirement of Conversation Analysis is that transcriptions should be sufficiently detailed to allow for the observation of interpreter-mediated interactions. Other, perhaps less detailed, forms of transcription may be used for analyzing either the linguistic content of translation or the cultural foundations of translation (as done by discourse analysis; see Chapter 17,"Critical discourse analysis" in this volume), rather than the dynamics of interpreter-mediated interaction. Transcriptions of field notes, pictures, or diagrams may also be used to organize additional written or oral information, in particular when recording equipment is limited or not allowed. In sum, field observation of interpreting activities is a complex task that poses several challenges. While imperfect, field observations have improved in light of developments in storage and retrieval methodologies, and are increasingly appreciated for their usefulness in research.

After observational data has been collected, researchers must then analyze the data in light of their specific research questions. The method of data analysis should be determined prior to data collection, although exploratory studies may allow for subsequent revisions of the data analysis method. In the case of field observations, the initial recordings and organization subsequently require "coding" and analysis (Creswell 2013). Coding involves categorizing observations to allow for general descriptions to be made that can subsequently be analyzed in detail. Therefore, the construction of meaning in field observations, and specifically in the categories that organize the collected data, requires a combination of coding and analysis. Both qualitative and quantitative analysis is possible, and may take into account repetitions and turn-taking sequences (e.g., Angermeyer 2009; Major and Napier 2012). In the case of keystroke logging data, eye-tracking data, or any other translation process data, both qualitative and quantitative data must be interpreted based on the specific conventions of the data collection method. Statistical analyses or descriptions of the data are insufficient, but rather must be contextualized within the larger analytical framework used to justify the study. Analytical observations must be coherent with the epistemological orientation and the theoretical presuppositions of research (see the chapters in Part II of this volume).

Sample studies

Studies based on field observations have produced categorizations of the functions of interpreters' actions in interpreter-mediated interactions. Two noteworthy examples of these categorizations are in Angelelli (2004) and Wadensjö (1998). Angelelli (2004) proposes a categorization of the interpreters' communicative strategies, whereby interpreters take "ownership of the text" (2004: 86), exercising agency (see Chapter 1) and orchestrating the interaction. According to her analysis of field observations, interpreters' strategies include replacing interlocutors (e.g., providing information, explaining, suggesting, commenting), brokering cultural issues, expressing solidarity and affect, exercising forms of power, expanding on or summarizing interlocutors' utterances, exploring interlocutors' answers, altering the interlocutors' register (i.e., using a different level of linguistic complexity in translation), and controlling the flow of information.

Wadensjö (1998) proposes a categorization of the ways in which interpreters coordinate the interaction by providing (or not providing) renditions of what has been proffered by other participants. First, interpreters' renditions can summarize, reduce, or expand the original utterances; moreover, expanded renditions may be provided in a single turn or in a series of turns (two-part or multipart renditions). Second, interpreters' "non-renditions" produce talk that has not been produced by any of the other participants. Coding of different types of renditions is described as implicit coordination of the interaction (by translating); coding of non-renditions is described as explicit coordination of the interaction (without translating). Finally, interpreters' "zero renditions," that is, when interpreters do not translate what has been proffered by other participants, correspond to untranslated originals.

Many studies on translation also use observations, and the scope of inquiry is quite broad. For example, Hubscher-Davidson (2013) uses verbalization data to investigate intuition during decision-making tasks. O'Brien (2006, 2007) and Carl et al. (2011) use mixed-model research designs to elicit observational data to explore cognitive effort during post-editing of machine translation output. The impact of technology on the translation process (e.g., Dragsted 2005), as well as the uses of self-observation data in the classroom, have also been explored (Massey and Ehrensberger-Dow 2011). Balling (2008), in an effort to analyze word recognition and, by extension, translation in a more naturalistic setting, suggests multiple regression models as a statistical technique to analyze observational data.

Sight translation, arguably a hybrid of translation and interpreting, has been investigated by Shreve, Lacruz, and Angelone (2010), who employ observational data collection methods, namely eye-tracking, audio recording, and keystroke logging. Their findings suggest that the translator's behavior in the sight translation task is affected by visual interference on the part of the written text. This finding, however, contrasts with those obtained by Lambert (2004), who observed potential benefits in participants having visual access to the text. Discrepancies in observational studies highlight the importance of continued research in these areas and should spur further methodological innovation to investigate these phenomena.

Other studies based on field observations have developed categorizations of the function of renditions and non-renditions in interpreter-mediated interactions. For the most part, these developments concern expanded (and multipart) renditions. Drawing on audio-recorded observations of interpreter-mediated interactions involving Moroccan interpreters and patients in Italian healthcare services, Baraldi (2012) identifies three categories of interpreters' expanded renditions: (1) promotional questions, which clarify the content of utterances; (2) multipart renditions, which provide additional information for interlocutors; and (3) formulations of the gist of what has been proffered by participants, which enhance affect and solidarity.

Mason (2006) proposes a categorization of expanded renditions as contextual assumptions. A contextual assumption is produced by the interpreter when one interlocutor's utterance is "underdetermined," meaning that important contextual information is not explicitly provided. The interpreter in such instances can add or explain this context to the interlocutor in order to promote her or his understanding. Thus, the interpreter makes one interlocutor's utterance more explicit to the other interlocutor(s) by rendering not only what is said in the utterance but also the contextual assumption(s) implicit in it.

Angelelli (2004, 2012) proposes a categorization that analyzes expanded (and multipart) renditions as a way of mediating cultural differences between participants. Angelelli analyzes a dyadic interaction between an interpreter and a Mexican patient, which is based on the assumption that the patient is not used to applying the 1–10 pain scale that is typically used in the US. Thus, the interpreter becomes the patient's partner in the task of applying the pain scale, explaining its use in determining intensity of pain.

Developments of categorizations of interpreters' non-renditions have also looked at the ways in which interpreters act as responders for their interlocutors. Non-renditions in such cases have been categorized as minimal responses (Gavioli 2012), requests for clarification (Baraldi 2012), assessments (Zorzi 2012), and independent provisions of information (Baraldi 2012; Hsieh 2007). Video recording also allows the categorization of interpreters' non-renditions as non-verbal actions. The interpreters' gaze, in particular, has been categorized as a way of signaling attention, coordinating talk, or regulating participation (Mason 2012; Davitti 2013).

Conclusion and potential applications

Research using observations requires an attention to the epistemological foundations that shape the ways in which observations of activities can be made. Moreover, the analysis of observations involves reflection on the observational process itself, which may include coding and analysis for field observations, qualitative and quantitative research design, acknowledgement of study limitations, and methodological triangulation to contextualize findings.

Observation of the interaction resulting from interpreters' active participation in a communicative event and of the translators' behavior and process not only deepens our understanding of these complex activities but also stimulates participants' reflections on actions which support the interlocutors' interaction. This incentive may have unique consequences for translator and interpreter pedagogy.

Further reading

Foerster (1981) and Luhmann (1990) explain the difference between first order and second order observations. Angrosino (2007) presents an updated, synthetic description of techniques of field observations regarding activities, conversations, and interactions, including the use of technological equipment. Mason (1999) and Baraldi and Gavioli (2012) provide collections of papers based on field observations, highlighting a variety of ways for analyzing interpreter-mediated interactions. Hale (2004) analyzes and discusses field observations of court interpreting.

References

Alves, Fabio, Adriana Pagano, and Igor da Silva. 2009. "A New Window on Translators' Cognitive Activity: Methodological Issues in the Combined Use of Eye Tracking, Key Logging, and Retrospective Protocols." In *Methodology, Technology and Innovation in Translation Process Research*, Inger Mees, Fabio Alves, and Susanne Göpferich (eds.), 267–91. Copenhagen: Samfundslitteratur.

Alvstad, Cecilia, Adelina Hild, and Elisabet Tiselius (eds.). 2011. *Methods and Strategies of Process Research: Integrative Approaches in Translation Studies*. Amsterdam and Philadelphia: John Benjamins.

Anderson, Nels. 1923. *The Hobo: The Sociology of the Homeless Man*. Chicago: University of Chicago Press.

Angelelli, Claudia. 2004. *Medical Interpreting and Cross-cultural Communication*. Cambridge: Cambridge University Press.

——2012. "Challenges in Interpreters' Coordination of the Construction of Pain." In *Coordinating Participation in Dialogue Interpreting*, Claudio Baraldi and Laura Gavioli (eds.), 251–68. Amsterdam and Philadelphia: John Benjamins.

Angermeyer, Philip Sebastian. 2009. "Translation Style and Participant Roles in Court Interpreting." *Journal of Sociolinguistics* 13(1): 3–28.

Angrosino, Michael V. 2004. "Observational Research." In *The SAGE Encyclopedia of Social Science Research Methods*, Michael S. Lewis-Beck, Alan Bryman, and Tim Futing Liao (eds.), 754–57. Thousand Oaks, CA: SAGE Publications.

——2007. *Doing Ethnographic and Observational Research*. Thousand Oaks, CA: SAGE Publications.

Balling, Laura Winther. 2008. "A Brief Introduction to Regression Designs and Mixed-Effects Modelling by a Recent Convert." *Copenhagen Studies in Language* 36: 175–92.

Baraldi, Claudio. 2012. "Interpreting as Dialogic Mediation: The Relevance of Interpreters' Expansions." In *Coordinating Participation in Dialogue Interpreting*, Claudio Baraldi and Laura Gavioli (eds.), 297–326. Amsterdam and Philadelphia: John Benjamins.

Baraldi, Claudio, and Laura Gavioli. 2008. "Cultural Presuppositions and Re-contextualisation of Medical Systems in Interpreter-Mediated Interactions." *Curare. Journal of Medical Anthropology* 31(2/3): 193–203.

——2012. "Understanding Coordination in Dialogue Interpreting." In *Coordinating Participation in Dialogue Interpreting*, Claudio Baraldi and Laura Gavioli (eds.), 1–21. Amsterdam and Philadelphia: John Benjamins.

Berk-Seligson, Susan. 1990. *The Bilingual Courtroom: Court Interpreters in the Judicial Process*. Chicago: University of Chicago Press.

Bolden, Galina B. 2000. "Toward Understanding Practices of Medical Interpreting: Interpreters' Involvement in History Taking." *Discourse Studies* 2(4): 387–418.

Bottorff, Joan L. 2004. "Types of Observation." In *The SAGE Encyclopedia of Social Science Research Methods*, Michael S. Lewis-Beck, Alan Bryman, and Tim Futing Liao (eds.), 753–54. Thousand Oaks, CA: SAGE Publications.

——2007. "Types of Observation." In *Encyclopedia of Social Science Research Methods*, Michael S. Lewis-Beck, Alan Bryman, and Tim Futing Liao (eds.). Beverly Hills, CA, London, and Delhi: SAGE Publications. Available online at http://dx.doi.org/10.4135/9781412950589 (last accessed October 15, 2014).

Carl, Michael, Barbara Dragsted, Jakob Elming, Daniel Hardt, and Arnt Lyyke Jakobsen. 2011. "The Process of Post-Editing: A Case Study." In *Proceedings of the 8th International NLPSC Workshop*, Bernadette Sharp, Michael Zock, Michael Carl, and Arnt Lykke Jakobsen (eds.), 131–42. Frederiksberg: Samfundslitteratur.

Cochran, W. G. 1965. "The Planning of Observational Studies of Human Populations." *Journal of the Royal Statistical Society. Series A* 128(2): 234–66.

Creswell, John W. 2013. *Qualitative Inquiry and Research Design*. London: SAGE Publications.

Davidson, Brad. 2000. "The Interpreter as Institutional Gatekeeper: The Social-linguistic Role of Interpreters in Spanish-English Medical Discourse." *Journal of Sociolinguistics* 4(3): 379–405.

Davitti, Elena. 2013. "Dialogue Interpreting as Intercultural Mediation: Interpreters' Use of Upgrading Moves in Parent-Teacher Meetings." *Interpreting* 15(2): 168–99.

Davitti, Elena and Sergio Pasquandrea. 2014. "Enhancing research-led interpreter education: an exploratory study in Applied Conversation Analysis." *The Interpreter and Translator Trainer* 8(3): 374–398.

DeWalt, Kathleen M., and Billie R. DeWalt. 2011. *Participant Observation: A Guide for Fieldworkers*. Lanham, MD: AltaMira Press.

Dragsted, Barbara. 2005. "Segmentation in Translation: Differences across Levels of Expertise and Difficulty." *Target* 17(1): 49–70.

Ehrensberger-Dow, Maureen. 2014. "Challenges of Translation Process Research at the Workplace." *MonTI* 1(1): 355–83.

Ericsson, K. Anders, and Herbert A. Simon. 1980. "Verbal Reports as Data." *Psychological Review* 87(3): 215–51.

——1984. *Protocol Analysis: Verbal Reports as Data*. Revised edition. Cambridge, MA: MIT Press.

Foerster, Heinz von. 1981. *Observing Systems*. Seaside, CA: Intersystems Publications.

Gavioli, Laura. 2012. "Minimal Responses in Interpreter-mediated Medical Talk." In *Coordinating Participation in Dialogue Interpreting*, Claudio Baraldi and Laura Gavioli (eds.), 201–28. Amsterdam and Philadelphia: John Benjamins.

Hale, Sandra Beatriz. 2004. *The Discourse of Court Interpreting*. Amsterdam and Philadelphia: John Benjamins.

Hsieh, Elaine. 2007. "Interpreters as Co-diagnosticians: Overlapping Roles and Services between Providers and Interpreters." *Social Science & Medicine* 64: 924–37.

Hubscher-Davidson, Séverine. 2013. "The Role of Intuition in the Translation Process." *Translation and Interpreting Studies* 8(2): 211–32.

Jääskeläinen, Riitta. 2002. "Think-aloud Protocol Studies into Translation: An Annotated Bibliography." *Target* 14(1): 107–36.

Jakobsen, Arnt Lykke. 1999. "Logging Target Text Production with Translog." In *Probing the Process in Translation: Methods and Results*, Gyde Hansen (ed.), 9–20. Copenhagen: Samfundslitteratur.

Kawulich, Barbara B. 2005. "Participant Observation as a Data Collection Method." *Forum: Qualitative Social Research* 6(2). Available online at http://nbn-resolving.de/urn:nbn:de:0114-fqs0502430 (last accessed October 16, 2014).

Lambert, Sylvie. 2004. "Shared Attention during Sight Translation, Sight Interpretation and Simultaneous Interpretation." *Meta* 49(2): 294–306.

Läubli, Samuel et al. 2013. "Assessing Post-editing Efficiency in a Realistic Translation Environment."*Proceedings of MT Summit XIV Workshop on Post-editing Technology and Practice (WPTP-2), Nice, France, September 2, 2013*, 83–91. Allschwil, Switzerland: European Association for Machine Translation.

Luhmann, Niklas. 1990. *Die Wissenschaft der Gesellschaft*. Frankfurt: Suhrkamp.

Major, George, and Jemina Napier. 2012. "Interpreting and Knowledge Mediation in the Healthcare Setting: What Do We Really Mean by 'Accuracy'?" In *Linguistica Antverpiensia: Translation and Knowledge Mediation in Medical and Health Settings*, Vincent Montalt and Michael Shuttleworth (eds.), 207–26. Antwerp: Artesius University College.

Mason, Ian. 1999. *Dialogue Interpreting*. Manchester: St. Jerome.

——2006. "On Mutual Accessibility of Contextual Assumptions in Dialogue Interpreting." *Journal of Pragmatics* 38: 359–73.

——2012. "Gaze, Positioning and Identity in Interpreter-mediated Dialogues." In *Coordinating Participation in Dialogue Interpreting*, Claudio Baraldi and Laura Gavioli (eds.), 177–99. Amsterdam and Philadelphia: John Benjamins.

Massey, Gary, and Maureen Ehrensberger-Dow. 2011. "Commenting on Translation: Implications for Translator Training." *The Journal of Specialised Translation* 16: 26–41.

Mehl, Matthias R., and Megan L. Robbins. 2012. "Naturalistic Observation Sampling: The Electronically Activated Recorder (EAR)." In *Handbook of Research Methods for Studying Daily Life*, Matthias R. Mehl and Tamlin S. Conner (eds.), 176–92. New York: Guilford Press.

Muñoz Martín, Ricardo (ed.). 2014. "Minding Translation/Con la traducción en mente." Special issue. *MonTI* 1(1).

O'Brien, Sharon. 2006. "Eye-Tracking and Translation Memory Matches." *Perspectives: Studies in Translatology* 14(3): 185–205.

——2007. "An Empirical Investigation of Temporal and Technical Post-Editing Effort." *Translation and Interpreting Studies* 2(1): 83–136.

——2010. "Eye Tracking in Translation Process Research: Methodological Challenges and Solutions." *Copenhagen Studies in Language* 38: 251–66.

Patterson, Barbara, and Karen Morin. 2012. "Methodological Considerations for Studying Social Processes." *Nurse Researcher* 20(1): 33–38.

Rodriguez, Noelie, and Alan Ryave. 2002. *Systematic Self-Observation*. London: SAGE Publications.

Rosenbaum, Paul R. 2002. *Observational Studies: Second Edition*. New York: Springer.

Shreve, Gregory M., and Erik Angelone (eds.). 2010. *Translation and Cognition*. Amsterdam and Philadelphia: John Benjamins.

Shreve, Gregory M., Isabel Lacruz, and Erik Angelone. 2010. "Cognitive Effort, Syntactic Disruption, and Visual Interference in a Sight Translation Task." In *Translation and Cognition*, Gregory M. Shreve and Erik Angelone (eds.), 63–84. Philadelphia: John Benjamins.

Thrasher, Frederic Milton. 1927. *The Gang: A Study of 1,313 Gangs in Chicago*. Chicago: University of Chicago Press.

von Glasersfeld, E. 1995. *Radical Constructivism: A Way of Knowing and Learning*. London: The Falmer Press.

Wadensjö, Cecilia. 1998. *Interpreting as Interaction*. London: Longman.

Whyte, Foote William. 1943/1993. *Street Corner Society. The Social Structure of an Italian Slum*, 4th edition. Chicago: University of Chicago Press.

Zorzi, Daniela. 2012. "Mediating Assessments in Healthcare Settings." In *Coordinating Participation in Dialogue Interpreting*, Claudio Baraldi and Laura Gavioli (eds.), 229–49. Amsterdam and Philadelphia: John Benjamins.

24 Survey-based studies

Sanjun Sun

Definition

The survey is probably the most common empirical research method in the social sciences and the humanities. It is a method designed to gather data about a human population (commonly referred to as a sample) through a sequence of focused questions. One distinguishing characteristic of the survey, according to Marsh (1982) and De Vaus (2011), concerns the form of its data: a structured set of data that forms a rectangle (or variable-by-case grid), in which rows usually represent cases (e.g., respondents, countries), columns represent variables (i.e., questions), and the cells contain information about a case's attributes (e.g., respondents' answers). Experiments and tests also use data in this form. The experimental method is different from the survey method in that with the former, "the variation between the attributes of people is created by intervention from an experimenter wanting to see if the intervention creates a difference" (De Vaus 2014: 5).

There are two data collection mechanisms used in surveys: standardized interviews and self-administered questionnaires. Standardized interviews are often conducted in person or over the phone, while self-administered questionnaires are used in group settings (e.g., in a classroom) or in individual settings (e.g., postal survey) (De Leeuw 2008). Each of these forms has a computer-assisted equivalent, such as Internet surveys, which are now more common than postal ones.

Surveys are often used to collect different types of data by asking questions, including (1) factual questions, regarding the demographic characteristics (e.g., age, gender, mother tongue, level of education) of the respondents, to help interpret the findings of the survey; (2) behavioral questions, regarding such things as personal history and language learning strategies; (3) and attitudinal questions, concerning the respondents' attitudes, opinions, beliefs, interests, and values (Dörnyei and Taguchi 2010: 8–9).

Based on the format of the responses, there are two broad types of questions in a survey: open-ended and closed-ended questions. Open-ended questions do not provide specific answer alternatives and ask the respondent to provide his or her own answers. They can elicit rich information, but they are not easy to code or quantify. As a result, survey researchers often use open-ended questions to help design closed questions or pilot studies and pretests. They also use open-ended questions sparingly in formal questionnaires (e.g., Holyk 2008). Closed-ended questions contain a predetermined set of answer alternatives for the respondent to select, and can be grouped into two classes: structured answer (dichotomous and multiple choice) and scales (McNabb 2010: 118). Scales are collections of items that measure the level of an underlying variable (DeVellis 2012: 15), which is placed along a quantitative continuum (e.g., from being very favorable to being very unfavorable in attitude or opinion).

Scales are usually used in the measurement of attitudes. There are many types of measurement scales, which fall into two broad categories: comparative and non-comparative. Comparative scales allow the respondent to compare two or more items, while a non-comparative scale allows the respondent to evaluate only a single item. The former category includes paired comparison, rank order, and others; the latter includes, among others, the Likert scale (Likert 1932), which is the most widely used rating scale (see Reddy and Acharyulu 2008: 101). The Likert scale consists of multiple items that typically are summed or averaged to yield an overall score (Brill 2008), and usually includes five to seven response categories, e.g., Strongly Agree, Agree, Neither Agree Nor Disagree, Disagree, and Strongly Disagree. An important consideration for the response categories is whether or not to include a middle position (e.g., "Neither Agree Nor Disagree") or a "No opinion" option. There have been studies supporting both possibilities (e.g., Maitland 2008).

The steps in conducting survey research include: (1) determining the survey purpose and objectives; (2) defining and operationalizing key concepts; (3) developing specific research questions (and hypotheses); (4) determining the sampling procedure; (5) creating and pretesting the instrument; and (6) collecting, reducing, and analyzing data (e.g., Newman and McNeil 1998; Bartlett 2005). Questions/items need to be reliable and valid (Fowler 2014). Reliability is the extent to which an instrument yields consistent results upon testing and retesting. There are four common types of reliability estimates: test-retest, parallel forms, internal consistency, and inter-rater or inter-observer. In order to increase the reliability of a scale, one can include the number of items in the scale and eliminate items that have lower-than-average correlation with the other items, or have low inter-item consistency. These facets plus item difficulty are tested through item analysis (Angelelli 2004b). Validity refers to the extent to which an instrument measures what it has been designed to measure. Major measures of validity are face, content, construct, and criterion-related validity (see Brown 2001). Determination of face and content validity evidence is often made by expert judgment; a typical method includes several judges who rate each item in terms of its relevance to the content (Angelelli 2004b: 47–63; Kaplan and Saccuzzo 2013: 137). To think about the likely construct validity of a measure, the best way is "to see the full wording, formatting, and the location within the questionnaire of the question or questions that were used to gather data on the construct" (Lavrakas 2008: 135).

In terms of research purpose, surveys are mainly used for descriptive or explanatory purposes (e.g., De Vaus, 2006). Marsh (1982: 6) claims that "[s]urveys and experiments are the only two methods known to me to test a hypothesis about how the world works." This, however, is debatable. Dumont (2008: 25) argues that "the survey method does not provide empirical evidence that proves the existence of a causal relationship (only the experimental design can do this)" although it "can provide empirical evidence that a causal relationship between two (or more) variables does not exist." In TIS, many kinds of research questions exist, including descriptive and explanatory ones. This makes survey research one of the most frequently used methods in TIS (e.g., Toury 2012: 263).

Origin

The roots of survey research can be traced back to population count (census) in ancient times for raising taxes or conscripting soldiers. The first surveys that resemble the modern social survey are believed to be Charles Booth's surveys of the lives and occupations of the working classes in London, conducted in the early 1890s and reported in a multivolume book entitled *Life and Labour of the People in London* (e.g., Converse 1987/2009; Bulmer, Bales, and Sklar 1991)

Four basic developments in survey research method set early surveys apart from modern surveys (Wright and Marsden 2010: 3–4): (1) the development of sampling methods for drawing representative samples from human populations; (2) the theory of statistical inference for estimating population parameters from sample statistics; (3) the development of question design strategies for eliciting valid and reliable answers; and (4) the development of data analysis techniques for estimating complex statistical relationships among many variables. Major advances in such aspects as the idea of probability sampling, the use of structured questionnaires, and the basic tools of statistical analysis were already made before the First World War, but they did not spread overnight or were not applied to survey research (Marsh 1982; Alastalo 2008).

According to Groves (2011), the history of social survey research can be divided into three stages: (1) the first era (1930–60), during which the basic components of survey research and related tools were developed, and surveys were conducted in the private, academic, and government sectors; (2) the second era (1960–90), which witnessed significant growth in the use of surveys and quantitative information; and (3) the third era (1990–today), which witnessed the growth of alternative modes of data collection and of continuously produced process data from digital systems in all sectors and the Internet.

Early surveys did not involve sampling; investigators simply questioned everyone in a certain area. The idea of sampling was introduced in 1895, when Anders Kiaer presented a report on "Representative Method" at a meeting of the International Statistical Institute (see Adèr and Mellenbergh 1999: 112). However, according to Biemer and Lyberg (2003: 10), "[i]n the 1930s and 1940s most of the basic survey sampling methods used today were developed." In 1934, Jerzy Neyman delivered a paper entitled "On the Two Different Aspects of the Representative Method: The Method of Stratified Sampling and the Method of Purposive Selection," which established the foundations for modern sampling theory. Based on Neyman's inference theory, survey sampling pioneers developed optimal methods for sample design and other statistical theories (see Heeringa, West, and Berglund 2010: 4). In 1936, George Gallup's polling company, based on a small quota sample of 50,000 people (versus over 2 million returned questionnaires in the poll by *Literary Digest* magazine), correctly predicted that Roosevelt would win the presidential election, which proved that a small but representative sample yields better inferences than a large but unrepresentative sample with a low response rate.

Question wording did not get much attention from investigators in early surveys, as their focus was often on factual information, such as age and education. Things changed when researchers started to investigate people's opinions, attitudes, and feelings. They found that minor changes in question wording, format, or the context could have a major impact on respondents' answers (e.g., Cantril 1944). The first book devoted to question design was *The Art of Asking Questions* (1951) by Payne, which gave a concise checklist of 100 considerations in question formulation. Today, nobody would deny that questionnaire design is an art. Most researchers, however, would also say that it is a science. Since the early 1980s, survey researchers, cognitive scientists, and statisticians have started to investigate questionnaire design from a psychological perspective (e.g., Jabine et al. 1984; Tourangeau, Rips, and Rasinski 2000). They have developed tools for improving questionnaire design, such as cognitive interviewing for questionnaire pretesting (see Willis 2005).

Among data collection methods in social surveys, the face-to-face interview was the most common method until the end of the 1970s (Corbetta 2003: 142). Due to concerns over the escalating cost, telephone surveys became a standard survey practice by the 1980s. Mailed paper questionnaires have been used since the early twentieth century for measuring literate populations. Compared with the face-to-face interview, it is cheaper, but the turnaround time may last months. Since the world wide web became widely available around 1995, e-mail and web surveys have become increasingly common, enabling the expanded use of visual and audiovisual instruments, as well as innovations in sampling (Wright and Marsden 2010: 22). Computerization has also increased the availability of survey data and made secondary analyses attainable (Alastalo 2008: 34). Face-to-face interviews, despite the decline in volume, are still the mainstream method for complex academic surveys (Fu and Chu 2008: 290).

Uses

Surveys can be used for studying most, if not all, of the topics in TIS, such as quality evaluation (e.g., Kurz 2001), training (Chmiel 2010), roles of translators and interpreters (Angelelli 2004b), their social status (Dam and Zethsen 2008), and translation/interpreting strategies (PACTE 2008). To date, there have been hundreds of survey-based studies in the field of TIS published in English and many more in other languages.

Many survey-based studies have focused on the translation profession. For example, the special issue of *Translation and Interpreting Studies*, "Profession, Identity and Status: Translators and Interpreters as an Occupational Group" (4.2 [2009]) contains reports from survey studies. The survey has been one of the most productive methods in quality assessment research. Kurz (2001), for instance, offers an overview of 17 questionnaire-based studies on quality in conference interpreting, which focused on user expectations and/or user responses. Many research questions in translator and interpreter training can be addressed using surveys. For example, "How Effective Is Teaching Note-Taking to Trainee Interpreters?" (Chmiel 2010). Surveys are often used to investigate audience reception, e.g., Widler's "A Survey among Audiences of Subtitled Films in Viennese Cinemas" (2004).

The most notable surveyor in TIS is probably Common Sense Advisory, an independent Massachusetts-based market research company with a research team that focuses on localization, translation, and interpreting practices. Since 2002, they have published on commonsenseadvisory.com over 500 reports, and their typical methods are questionnaire and interview. Their surveys of buyers and suppliers of translation services and technology vendors from the language industry perspective have covered various topics, such as translation quality, language services market (e.g., "Wages of Translation," "Trends in Translation Pricing"), and best practices ("How to Buy Translation"). There are over a dozen reports on translation quality, including "The Buyer-Supplier Quality Gap: How Customer and Language Supplier Views of Translation Quality Differ," and "Selling Different Levels of Quality." Proz.com, a translation portal, frequently conducts quick polls, in which often over 1,000 translators and interpreters throughout the world participate. All kinds of questions are asked in these polls, such as "Do you have professional indemnity insurance?" and "Do you find translation theories useful for your professional practice?"

Sample studies

Surveys have become part of our life. Throughout the world, thousands of surveys are being undertaken every day (De Leeuw, Hox, and Dillman 2008). While some surveys are complex and may require years of development, some are simple and easy to conduct. A common type of survey is the public opinion poll (e.g., the Gallup Poll), which seeks opinions regarding social and political issues. Official statistics (e.g., censuses) are another common type, produced by government agencies to facilitate decision making. Also, in the business world, surveys (e.g., the Job Attitude Scale) have been frequently used. According to Biemer and Lyberg (2003: 7), the survey industry employs more than 130,000 people in the United States alone. There are many professional organizations and societies (e.g., the International Association of Survey Statisticians) and academic journals (e.g., *Survey Research Methods*, *Journal of Survey Statistics and Methodology*) dedicated to improving survey work. Many universities have survey research centers or institutes, which are housed in the departments of statistics, sociology, psychology, education, communication, or business (Biemer and Lyberg 2003).

For examples of survey-based studies, one can refer to compendiums of questionnaires, scales, and tests. In the field of second language research, for instance, Dörnyei and Taguchi (2010) present a list of published L2 questionnaires on language anxiety, attitudes, language course evaluation, language learner beliefs, language learning motivation, language learning strategies, language learning styles, needs analysis, self-evaluation, teacher evaluation, etc. Of these questionnaires, a notable example is the Strategy Inventory for Language Learning (SILL) (Oxford 1990), which is the most widely employed second language learning strategy questionnaire. It has several versions. SILL Version 5.1 is for native English speakers and contains 80 items assessing the frequency of strategy use, while Version 7.0 is geared to students of English as a second or foreign language and contains 50 items. SILL uses a 5-point Likert scale (for all versions) ranging from "Never or Almost Never" to "Always or Almost Always." It has been extensively field tested from a psychometric viewpoint. For example, the internal consistency reliability of a slightly earlier, 121-item version of the SILL using Cronbach's alpha is .96 for a 1,200-person university sample; content validity is .95, based on classificatory agreement between two independent raters, who "blindly" matched each of the SILL items with the strategies in the comprehensive list; concurrent validity of the 121-item form is found in strong, statistically significant relationships between SILL results and self-ratings of target language proficiency and motivation in the 1,200-person university sample; no evidence of social desirability response bias appeared in three samples (Oxford 1990: 255). SILL Versions 5.1 and 7.0 have also been evaluated and are high in reliability and validity (Oxford 1996). They have been translated into various languages and tested (e.g., Demirel 2009). In the field of business training, Cook (2007) provides nearly 100 assessment questionnaires and checklists regarding communication, performance management, personal effectiveness, teamwork, training and development, and others.

Many research topics in translator and interpreter training can be studied through a survey. Li (2000), for example, conducted a questionnaire survey of practicing translators in Hong Kong in an attempt to study ways of tailoring translation programs to social needs. Ulrych (2005) investigated translation teaching practices and curricula in 41 academic institutions in Europe and North America. With an online questionnaire, Katan (2009) investigated

890 respondents on how translation should be taught, on the role and status of the profession (ideally and in practice), and on personal satisfaction. As admitted by the author, however, issues of validity and reliability were not given adequate attention. Another issue pertains to the Likert scale. Katan (2009: 189) mentioned that for many questions "a 5-point Likert rating scale was used." One of the items in his questionnaire, for example, was "How satisfied are you with your present job in comparison with your initial expectations regarding the field of translating/interpreting" followed by five response options: Extremely, Pretty, Fairly, Not Very, and Not at All. However, this is not a Likert item. First, in a Likert scale, it is usually a specific statement (e.g., "As an interpreter, I should adhere to the conversational conventions established by the speakers") expressing an attitude or opinion that is followed by the response points (Strongly Agree, Agree, Neither Agree Nor Disagree, Disagree, Strongly Disagree); it is not a question. Second, a Likert scale contains multiple items to measure the same latent variable, which need to be summed or averaged to produce a more reliable measure. According to Brill (2008: 427), the previous example item from Katan (2009) is just "an ordered-category rating item with the Likert-like properties of a bipolar and balanced response set."

Angelelli (2004b) provides an outstanding example of measurement instrument development in the field of TIS. The book-length report details how she developed the Interpreter's Interpersonal Role Inventory, and describes ways to improve and test the reliability and validity of the measurement scale. For example, she took advantage of surveys, feedback from peers at a seminar for measurement instrument design, literature reviews, and interviews with interpreters in composing the 80 initial items; expert opinion and focus groups were then used to establish the content validity of the scale. In that study, Angelelli recognized five sub-components of the construct of visibility: alignment, trust/respect, affect, cultural gaps, and communication rules.

PACTE Group (2008) presents a typical study using mixed methods. In this study, the researchers designed an experiment for the validation of their translation competence model. Their data collection instruments included: (1) texts and translations, (2) translation protocols, which were recorded using software programs, (3) direct observation, (4) questionnaires, and (5) retrospective interviews. Three questionnaires were used: (1) an initial questionnaire to ensure that the participants selected for inclusion in the experimental groups fulfilled selection criteria; (2) a questionnaire eliciting information on translation problems encountered during the translation process; and (3) a questionnaire designed to obtain information on the participant's knowledge of translation, which was conceptualized in terms of seven dimensions.

Conclusion and potential applications

Investigating the attitudes, opinions, beliefs, interests, and behavior of stakeholders in the field of translation and interpreting through a survey can bring new perspectives to existing research questions in TIS, raise awareness of new concerns, help researchers better understand the profession, and reach beyond the ivory tower.

Yet, in using the survey method, many existing studies have methodological inadequacies. Kurz (2001), in her review of 17 questionnaire-based studies on quality in conference interpreting, found that there was little comparability among the individual surveys. Similarly, Pöchhacker (2009), after reviewing 40 survey studies on the profession of conference interpreting, observes that most of the findings are not solid enough in terms of sampling and there is a lack of thoroughly tested instruments (cf. Angelelli 2004b). This has several implications. First, researchers need to pay more attention to reporting guidelines or best practices. For example, survey-based studies should provide access to the questionnaire items, describe participant characteristics and sampling procedures in detail, and provide information on the validity and reliability of the instrument (see Kelley et al. 2003; Angelelli 2004b; Bennett et al. 2011). A detailed description of the methods used enables the reader to evaluate the methods and results, and facilitates research replication. Second, TIS researchers need to develop standard questionnaires (e.g., Angelelli's Interpreter's Interpersonal Role Inventory) and replicate previous studies to determine whether there are any significant differences between cultures or socioeconomic conditions.

It should be noted that the survey method can be used alone or with other methods in a study. In TIS, especially in translation process research, the idea of triangulation has been adopted. For example, process researchers have typically used questionnaires, verbal protocols, keystroke logging, and/or eye-tracking in an experimental setting (see Alvstad, Hild, and Tiselius 2011), while interpreting researchers have used a combination of surveys, observations, and interviews (see Angelelli 2001 and 2004a).

Further reading

Fowler (2014) is probably the most widely read and quoted book on survey research methods; it provides a comprehensive introduction. Dörnyei and Taguchi (2010) detail how to produce and use questionnaires in second language research, and include a list of published L2 questionnaires. Fishman and Galguera (2003) introduce in an accessible way how to construct tests for research purposes. Angelelli (2004b) provides an excellent example of measurement instrument development in the field of TIS.

References

Adèr, Herman J., and Gideon J. Mellenbergh. 1999. *Research Methodology in the Social, Behavioural and Life Sciences*. London: SAGE Publications.

Alastalo, Marja. 2008. "The History of Social Research Methods." In *The SAGE Handbook of Social Research Methods*, Pertti Alasuutari, Leonard Bickman, and Julia Brannen (eds.), 26–41. Los Angeles: SAGE Publications.

Alvstad, Cecilia, Adelina Hild, and Elisabet Tiselius (eds.). 2011. *Methods and Strategies of Process Research: Integrative Approaches in Translation Studies.* Amsterdam: John Benjamins.

Angelelli, Claudia V. 2001. *Deconstructing the Invisible Interpreter: A Study of the Interpersonal Role of the Interpreter in a Cross-linguistic/Cultural Communicative Event.* Stanford, CA: Stanford University Press.

——2004a. *Medical Interpreting and Cross-cultural Communication.* New York: Cambridge University Press.

——2004b. *Revisiting the Interpreter's Role: A Study of Conference, Court, and Medical Interpreters in Canada, Mexico, and the United States.* Amsterdam and Philadelphia: John Benjamins.

Bartlett, Kenneth R. 2005. "Survey Research in Organizations." In *Research in Organizations: Foundations and Methods of Inquiry*, Richard A. Swanson and Elwood F. Holton (eds.), 97–113. San Francisco: Berrett-Koehler.

Bennett, Carol, Sara Khangura, Jamie C. Brehaut, Ian D. Graham, David Moher, Beth K. Potter, and Jeremy M. Grimshaw. 2011. "Reporting Guidelines for Survey Research: An Analysis of Published Guidance and Reporting Practices." *PLoS Medicine* 8(8): 1–11.

Biemer, Paul P., and Lars Lyberg. 2003. *Introduction to Survey Quality.* Hoboken, NJ.: Wiley.

Brill, Jonathan E. 2008. "Likert Scale." In *Encyclopedia of Survey Research Methods*, Paul J. Lavrakas (ed.), 427–29. Thousand Oaks, CA: SAGE Publications.

Brown, James Dean. 2001. *Using Surveys in Language Programs.* Cambridge: Cambridge University Press.

Bulmer, Martin, Kevin Bales, and Kathryn Kish Sklar. 1991. *The Social Survey in Historical Perspective, 1880–1940.* Cambridge: Cambridge University Press.

Cantril, Hadley. 1944. *Gauging Public Opinion.* Princeton, NJ: Princeton University Press.

Chmiel, Agnieszka. 2010. "How Effective Is Teaching Note-Taking to Trainee Interpreters?" *The Interpreter and Translator Trainer* 4(2): 233–50.

Converse, Jean M. 1987/2009. *Survey Research in the United States: Roots and Emergence 1890–1960.* New Brunswick, NJ: Transaction Publishers.

Cook, Sarah. 2007. *Compendium of Questionnaires and Inventories.* 2 vols. Amherst: HRD Press.

Corbetta, Piergiorgio. 2003. *Social Research: Theory, Methods and Techniques.* London: SAGE Publications.

Dam, Helle V., and Karen Korning Zethsen. 2008. "Translator Status: A Study of Danish Company Translators." *The Translator* 14(1): 71–96.

De Leeuw, Edith. 2008. "Self-Administered Questionnaires and Standardized Interviews." In *The SAGE Handbook of Social Research Methods*, Pertti Alasuutari, Leonard Bickman, and Julia Brannen (eds.), 313–27. Los Angeles: SAGE Publications.

De Leeuw, Edith D., Joop J. Hox, and Don A. Dillman. 2008. "The Cornerstones of Survey Research." In *International Handbook of Survey Methodology*, Edith D. De Leeuw, Joop J. Hox, and Don A. Dillman (eds.), 1–17. New York: Lawrence Erlbaum.

De Vaus, David. 2006. "Social Survey." In *The Sage Dictionary of Social Research Methods*, Victor Jupp (ed.), 284–85. London: SAGE Publications.

——2011. "Survey Design." In *The Sage Dictionary of Quantitative Management Research*, Luiz Moutinho and Graeme Hutcheson (eds.), 318–20. London: SAGE Publications.

——2014. *Surveys in Social Research.* 6th edition. London: Routledge.

Demirel, Melek. 2009. "The Validity and Reliability Study of Turkish Version of Strategy Inventory for Language Learners." *World Applied Sciences Journal* 7(6): 708–14.

DeVellis, Robert F. 2012. *Scale Development: Theory and Applications*. 3rd edition. Applied Social Research Methods Series. Thousand Oaks, CA: SAGE Publications.

Dörnyei, Zoltán, and Tatsuya Taguchi. 2010. *Questionnaires in Second Language Research: Construction, Administration, and Processing*. 2nd edition. New York: Routledge.

Dumont, K. 2008. "Research Methods and Statistics." In *Introduction to Psychology*, Lionel Nicholas (ed.), 9–48. Claremont: University of Cape Town Press.

Fishman, Joshua A., and Tomás Galguera. 2003. *Introduction to Test Construction in the Social and Behavioral Sciences: A Practical Guide*. Oxford: Rowman & Littlefield Publishers.

Fowler, Floyd J. 2014. *Survey Research Methods*. 5th edition. Thousand Oaks, CA: SAGE Publications.

Fu, Yang-chih, and Yun-han Chu. 2008. "Different Survey Modes and International Comparisons." In *The SAGE Handbook of Public Opinion Research*, Wolfgang Donsbach and Michael W. Traugott (eds.), 284–93. Los Angeles: SAGE Publications.

Groves, Robert M. 2011. "Three Eras of Survey Research." *Public Opinion Quarterly* 75(5): 861–71.

Heeringa, Steven, Brady T. West, and Patricia A. Berglund. 2010. *Applied Survey Data Analysis*. Boca Raton, FL: CRC Press.

Holyk, Gregory G. 2008. "Questionnaire Design." In *Encyclopedia of Survey Research Methods*, Paul J. Lavrakas (ed.), 656–59. Thousand Oaks, CA: SAGE Publications.

Jabine, Thomas B., Miron L. Straf, Judith M. Tanur, and Roger Tourangeau (eds.). 1984. *Cognitive Aspects of Survey Methodology: Building a Bridge between Disciplines*. Washington DC: National Academy Press.

Kaplan, Robert M., and Dennis P. Saccuzzo. 2013. *Psychological Testing: Principles, Applications, and Issues*. 8th edition. Belmont, CA: Wadsworth Cengage Learning.

Katan, David. 2009. "Occupation or Profession: A Survey of the Translators' World." *Translation and Interpreting Studies* 4(2): 187–209.

Kelley, Kate, Belinda Clark, Vivienne Brown, and John Sitzia. 2003. "Good Practice in the Conduct and Reporting of Survey Research." *International Journal for Quality in Health Care* 15(3): 261–66.

Kurz, Ingrid. 2001. "Conference Interpreting: Quality in the Ears of the User." *Meta* 46(2): 394–409.

Lavrakas, Paul J. 2008. "Construct Validity." In *Encyclopedia of Survey Research Methods*, Paul J. Lavrakas (ed.), 134–35. Thousand Oaks, CA: SAGE Publications.

Li, Defeng. 2000. "Tailoring Translation Programs to Social Needs: A Survey of Professional Translators." *Target* 12(1): 127–49.

Likert, Rensis. 1932. "A Technique for the Measurement of Attitudes." *Archives of Psychology* 22(140): 1–55.

Maitland, Aaron. 2008. "Attitude Measurement." In *Encyclopedia of Survey Research Methods*, Paul J. Lavrakas (ed.), 37–39. Thousand Oaks, CA: SAGE Publications.

Marsh, Catherine. 1982. *The Survey Method: The Contribution of Surveys to Sociological Explanation, Contemporary Social Research Series*. London and Boston: Allen & Unwin.

McNabb, David E. 2010. *Research Methods for Political Science: Quantitative and Qualitative Approaches*. 2nd edition. Armonk, NY: M. E. Sharpe.

Newman, Isadore, and Keith A. McNeil. 1998. *Conducting Survey Research in the Social Sciences*. Lanham, MD: University Press of America.

Oxford, Rebecca L. 1990. *Language Learning Strategies: What Every Teacher Should Know*. New York: Newbury House Publisher.

——1996. "Employing a Questionnaire to Assess the Use of Language Learning Strategies." *Applied Language Learning* 7(1/2): 25–45.

PACTE Group. 2008. "First Results of a Translation Competence Experiment: 'Knowledge of Translation' and 'Efficacy of the Translation Process'." In *Translator and Interpreter Training: Issues, Methods and Debates*, John Kearns (ed.), 104–26. London: Continuum.

Payne, Stanley Le Baron. 1951. *The Art of Asking Questions*. Princeton, NJ: Princeton University Press.

Pöchhacker, Franz. 2009. "Conference Interpreting: Surveying the Profession." *Translation and Interpreting Studies* 4(2): 172–86.

Reddy, Narayana, and G. V. R. K. Acharyulu. 2008. *Marketing Research*. New Delhi: Excel Books.

Tourangeau, Roger, Lance J. Rips, and Kenneth A. Rasinski. 2000. *The Psychology of Survey Response*. Cambridge: Cambridge University Press.

Toury, Gideon. 2012. *Descriptive Translation Studies – and Beyond*. 2nd expanded edition. Amsterdam: John Benjamins.

Ulrych, Margherita. 2005. "Training Translators: Programmes, Curricula, Practices." In *Training for the New Millennium: Pedagogies for Translation and Interpreting*, Martha Tennent (ed.), 3–33. Amsterdam: John Benjamins.

Widler, Brigitte. 2004. "A Survey among Audiences of Subtitled Films in Viennese Cinemas." *Meta* 49(1): 98–101.

Willis, Gordon B. 2005. *Cognitive Interviewing: A Tool for Improving Questionnaire Design*. Thousand Oaks, CA: SAGE Publications.

Wright, James D., and Peter V. Marsden. 2010. "Survey Research and Social Science: History, Current Practice, and Future Prospects." In *Handbook of Survey Research*, Peter V. Marsden and James D. Wright (eds.), 3–25. Bingley: Emerald.

Index

Lightning Source UK Ltd.
Milton Keynes UK
UKOW01f0931130218
317795UK00003B/53/P

9 780415 732543